MEDITERRANEAN LIGHT

Also by Martha Rose Shulman

Light Basics Cookbook
Provençal Light
Mexican Light
Entertaining Light
Fast Vegetarian Feasts
The Vegetarian Feast
Little Vegetarian Feasts
Feasts and Fêtes
The Classic Party Fare Cookbook
Great Breads
Gourmet Vegetarian Feasts
The Spice of Vegetarian Cooking

MEDITERRANEAN
LIGHT

DELICIOUS RECIPES FROM
THE WORLD'S HEALTHIEST CUISINE

MARTHA ROSE SHULMAN

William Morrow
An Imprint of HarperCollins*Publishers*

HarperCollins books may be purchased for educational, business, or sales
promotional use. For information please write: Special Markets Department,
HarperCollins Publishers Inc., 10 East 53rd Street, New York, NY 10022.

A hardcover edition of this book was published in 1989 by Bantam Books, a
division of Bantam Doubleday Dell Publishing Group, Inc.

FIRST WILLIAM MORROW EDITION PUBLISHED 2000

Designed by Barbara N. Cohen

Library of Congress Cataloging-in-Publication Data

Shulman, Martha Rose.
    Mediterranean light: delicious recipes from the world's healthiest
  cuisine / Martha Rose Shulman.
        p. cm.
      Previously published: New York: Bantam Books, 1989.
      Includes bibliographical references and index.
      ISBN 0-688-17467-1
        1. Low-calorie diet–Recipes. 2. Low-fat diet–Recipes.
    3. Cookery, Mediterranean. I. Title.
  RM222.2.S528 2000
  641.5'635'091822–dc21   99-053830

00 01 02 03 04 QW 10 9 8 7 6 5 4 3

For Bill, with love

CONTENTS

FOREWORD

In 1980, while finishing medical school, I began planning a cardiovascular research study to determine whether a life-style program that includes a low-fat vegetarian diet can begin to reverse coronary heart disease. I needed to find a cook who understood that food could be tasty and attractive as well as being healthful, to help me create a new way of eating, not just a diet.

So I went to a large bookstore and looked at all of the vegetarian cookbooks. Unfortunately, the diets were either too rich (one can eat more fat on some vegetarian diets than by eating meat) or too unappetizing. Finally, I came across *The Vegetarian Feast*, Martha's first cookbook. When I saw the recipes and the photograph of her—smiling, healthy, and holding up bushels of fresh produce—I thought, "I hope she's interested in this project."

Fortunately, she was. And she designed recipes for the patients in our study that were less than 10 percent fat, virtually devoid of cholesterol, and yet delicious, satisfying, and beautiful.

The improvements were striking: after only 24 days, patients in the experimental group demonstrated a 55 percent average increase in their ability to exercise, a 20.5 percent overall decrease in cholesterol levels, a 91 percent average reduction in frequency of chest pain, and improvements in the heart's ability to pump blood. In contrast, these improvements were not seen in a control group of similar patients eating a traditional high-fat American diet.

We reported these findings in the *Journal of the American Medical Association* in 1983, and they formed the basis of my first book, *Stress, Diet, & Your Heart*, which included more than 100 of Martha's recipes.

Of course, the point of eating this way is not simply to reverse or prevent illness. I began following this diet when I was 19, not because I was worried about heart disease but because it made me feel so much better. Eating this way will likely help us to live longer—but who wants to live longer if we're not enjoying life?

Enter Martha. During the past decade, she has further developed and refined her cooking abilities, culminating in her newest work, *Mediterranean Light*. By shifting to foods that are lower in fat—as in *Mediterranean Light*—most people find they consume fewer calories even if they eat the same amount of food. It's more fun—and more effective—than a daily battle of deprivation and self-denial. By reducing the fat content of most recipes while increasing the joys of eating, Martha makes it easy for almost anyone to make dietary changes that can last a lifetime—a lifetime that may last even longer.

Dean Ornish, M.D.
President and Director,
Preventive Medicine Research Institute

INTRODUCTION

"It is not really an exaggeration to say

that peace and happiness begin, geographically,

where garlic is used in cooking."

Marcel Boulestin, quoted by
Elizabeth David in *Mediterranean Food*

People are always asking me what kind of cooking I do, and my answer over the years, especially since I moved to France, has become "It's healthful, elegant food that draws primarily on the cuisines of the Mediterranean." Here, for example, are a few menus I recently served to guests:

MIXED PROVENÇAL HORS D'OEUVRES
SOUPE AU PISTOU
FRENCH COUNTRY BREAD
FIG TART

RAVIOLI AND BROCCOLI SALAD
CRUSTY COUNTRY BREAD
DEEP-DISH EGGPLANT TORTE
ROASTED RED AND YELLOW PEPPERS
FRUIT GRATIN

PASTA PRIMAVERA
POACHED FISH WITH EGG LEMON SAUCE
STEAMED ZUCCHINI
FRUIT SALAD

It's obvious where my tastes in food lie.

I've always felt that garlic and olive oil were in my blood. When I began cooking, one of the first dishes I learned to make was *ratatouille*, the *Provençal* vegetable stew, and I made it all the time. When I discovered *hummus*, the Middle Eastern chick-pea puree, and Middle Eastern salads like *tabouli* and *cacik*, eating them gave me such pleasure and the dishes seemed so familiar somehow, that I decided I must have a deep, subconscious memory of these foods, a passion and understanding inherited from my Jewish forebears.

Given the choice of traveling north or south, to visit the regions of France renowned for rich, buttery food or the lands of sunshine, tomatoes, garlic, and olive oil, I won't hesitate: I head for the sun and the lively cuisines of the south.

Anyone who has traveled in southern Europe, North Africa, or the Middle East might question whether these cuisines can really be drawn upon effectively by those who want to lose weight, since olive oil has traditionally been used with such a free hand. I say they are a natural for dieters, because the heavier meat dishes—made with lamb, pork, and sometimes beef—can be eliminated without cutting very far into the Mediterranean repertoire, and virtually everything else that is delicious—with the exception of a few rich dishes like *aïoli*, *bourride*, *brandade*, and olive paste—can be made with less oil than the authentic recipes call for.

Nutritionists have been studying the Mediterranean diet for the last 20 years or so and have found that Mediterranean dwellers have a very low incidence of heart disease. With the recent discovery of "good" cholesterol (called *high-density lipoprotein*, or *HDL*), scientists have begun to understand why people from, say, Spain have a very healthy cholesterol balance, as healthy as that of people who have a very low-fat diet, despite their high consumption of olive oil. This is because olive oil, a monounsaturated oil, helps to stimulate the body's production of HDL, and HDL helps the body limit the buildup of substances that block arteries, causing heart disease.

So some olive oil is nutritious and even necessary for a balanced diet, especially if animal fats have been reduced. Since we are concerned with calories as well as fats, I still feel that it's important to keep olive oil to a minimum, which is why some typically Mediterranean recipes won't be found in this collection—sauces like the traditional Genoese *pesto*, which has quite a bit of oil and Parmesan, as well as high-fat nuts, or *aïoli*, the garlic mayonnaise from Provence. Other recipes will be lower in oil than their traditional counterparts. And after you reduce the oil, what do you have? Vibrant, luxurious vegetables—juicy red tomatoes, succulent eggplant, sweet and hot peppers, potatoes, zucchini, cucumbers, beans, artichokes, sweet peas, and more; high-protein fish and lean meats like rabbit and chicken; sturdy, filling grains, legumes, and pastas; wholesome breads and pizzas; and sweet, ripe, juicy fruit—figs, melons, peaches, apricots. Then there is garlic—braids and braids of pink and white heads, some with fat cloves and some with small cloves, and lemon, lime, spices, and herbs—basil, parsley, rosemary, thyme, sage, coriander, and mint, to name just a few. It's these innocent ingredients that give the ingenious cuisines of the Mediterranean their heady aromas and characteristic flavors.

And *flavor* is what we are talking about here. The Mediterranean condiments are so tasty that a little goes a long way. A tablespoon of Parmesan cheese contains only 23 calories and 1.5 grams of saturated fat and is quite sufficient to season a serving of pasta. A sprinkling of olive oil will perfume a dish as efficiently as a shower. A piece of bread dipped into a pungent pasta sauce or fish broth is as rich-tasting and satisfying as a piece of bread slathered with butter. Or how about the typical Italian *crostini*, toasted bread brushed with a little olive oil and rubbed with garlic? Butter is not the only food that will melt in your mouth. As for desserts, perfectly ripe fruit sweetened and enhanced with a touch of honey and lemon juice is much more pleasing to my palate than a dessert loaded with sugar.

I could spend the rest of my life going to markets in Mediterranean countries, just to see the beautiful displays of produce and fish. In the central market in Athens, baskets bursting with an array of vegetables that you never see in restaurants—okra, greens, various kinds of chili peppers, long green beans—adorn the stalls and tell you that at home people are cooking many marvelously healthful dishes. In Palermo the bustling street market stretches for blocks and blocks through the middle of this old city. It's one of the most impressive markets I've ever seen and made me long for a kitchen; I would have loved to cook some of that bounty of glistening fish and fresh vegetables. In Egypt I lost myself in the labyrinth of spice stalls in the souks and marveled at all the beautiful grains and legumes—orange lentils, tawny wheat berries, chick-peas, huge white fava beans, and the ubiquitous brown beans, or *ful*. When I go to Provence, my favorite region of France, my weekly schedule revolves around the colorful markets: Saturday, Apt; Sunday, Ile sur Sorgue; Monday, Cavaillon; Tuesday, Aix. I never tire of them; for me, a perfect summer vacation consists of mornings in the markets after an early swim, late afternoons in the kitchen, and evenings around a congenial table.

Mediterranean countries tend to be poor countries, and their cuisines take advantage of everything nature has to offer. In Palermo I saw a cook take one piece of tuna fish and stretch it into the most delicious tuna and tomato sauce for pasta to serve four people (page 176). Leftover bread in Italy becomes a pungent salad (page 59) or soup (page 139); stale pita in Egypt becomes the bottom layer of a delicious casserole called a *fattet* (pages 264–268) or the basis for a *fattoush* salad (page 88). Nothing is wasted—and everything is tasty.

This is the kind of food made for losing weight painlessly and sensibly if you are too heavy, for maintaining it if you are just right. You can eat the dishes, as I have revised them, and never feel like you are on a diet. A friend with whom I shared a house in Provence for a few weeks told me she lost ten pounds during that time and never gained it back. She wasn't consciously dieting, either. A very important friend—my husband—*was* dieting when we met; I was working on this book, and he reaped the benefits—he lost 50 pounds in six months, and he never went hungry. He also never gained it back, because these recipes and menus illustrate the way we eat all the time. Also, his tastes changed, as yours will once you've made this cuisine a way of life. He began to dislike the rich food he had been eating for so many years; a *croissant* made him feel like he was eating a lump of butter, and a lump of butter was no longer appetizing. He began to crave *Niçoise* salads for dinner instead of steak. And when he would take an occasional bite of a heavy meat, it felt and tasted too rich for him. Even cheese, which he truly loved and still loves, has become a food he prefers to eat in moderation, certainly not every day, and in small portions.

I've been collecting these recipes for years. Ever since I moved to France seven years ago I have sought out great cooks in Provence and learned their recipes, women like Lulu Peyraud, proprietress of a Bandol winery called Domaine Tempier, and my friend Christine Picasso, who has a farm in the Vaucluse, another department in Provence. I have spent a harvest at Domaine Tempier, helping Lulu cook hearty lunches for the grape pickers every day for three weeks, and I've visited the Peyrauds just to learn a specific recipe. I visit Christine's farm several times a year and always come back with new recipes as well as sacks of basil and vegetables from her marvelous garden.

But I wanted to include flavors from all around the Mediterranean Basin. For Mediterranean food doesn't mean just pasta, pizza, and heady *Niçoise* vegetable dishes and fish. It means *tapas*, soups, and *paellas* from Spain; marvelous garlicky beans and salads from Greece; pungent, spicy salads and *couscous* from North Africa; refreshing salads, yogurt, and hearty grain and legume dishes from the Middle East. Everywhere, salads and fish. Each country puts its culinary mark on its dishes. North Africans like fiery-hot chili peppers, caraway, cilantro, and cinnamon; Egyptians like allspice and cilantro; the Lebanese like cumin; Italians and the French love tomatoes and basil. Everyone likes garlic and saffron and fresh herbs and heavenly, grainy breads.

And so I traveled, ate, studied, and cooked. I took a cruise up the Nile and talked to the chef every night. In Cairo I took notes on the dishes that filled the buffets at the El Gezirah Sheraton. I met a cook in Palermo who gave me all of his recipes; I was so inspired by the food at Villa Cheta, a gorgeous hotel in a little coastal village in southern Italy called Acquafredda, that I went home and made a great dinner party based on all of the dishes I'd eaten there. Wherever I went I would take notes on the food, then come home to study cookbooks and work out my own low-calorie versions. I drew from my own repertoire, dishes I've been cooking and perfecting over the years, and from those of many other wonderful cooks.

What I have come up with is this sampling of Mediterranean cuisines, guaranteed to bring you healthful, low-fat pleasure. I have altered authentic recipes to make them into lighter, less caloric versions without sacrificing the characteristics of each dish. When frying was necessary, I used nonstick and heavy-bottomed pans to sauté in a fraction of the amount of olive oil called for in most recipes (another advantage of using olive oil for cooking is that it stands up to heat more effectively than other oils, which burn more easily, breaking down their chemical structure and forming possibly unhealthy compounds). I baked some dishes with no oil added at all in tightly sealed baking dishes or a clay *römertopf*. In some recipes I found I could eliminate oil altogether or substitute plain low-fat yogurt for some of it. Often I took away fatty meats and replaced them with "meaty" vegetables like wild mushrooms. I always used low-fat yogurt, draining it to thicken it when necessary. With calories kept to a minimum in this way, a little Parmesan or an egg or two every once in a while can't hurt (unless you have a cholesterol problem), and you will find a few omelets and pastas garnished with Parmesan in these pages. Deprivation just isn't necessary here. Desserts were easy, because of all of the delicious fruit the Mediterranean has to offer. Tarts can be made in yeasted crusts with no butter, and I can't think of a more delicious cookie than *biscotti*, the hard, nutty Italian cookies made with no butter at all.

One of the most significant things I learned as I cooked side by side with my Mediterranean friends and acquaintances, and studied their cuisines, is that most of the recipes are simple. The complexity is in the flavors of the ingredients, not the techniques you'll be using to work with them. You don't need to be a highly skilled cook for the recipes to work. But all of the basic pleasures of cooking are here: working with fresh, colorful, fragrant ingredients, transforming them into delicious dishes and filling your kitchen with wonderful aromas as you do so. And just because this is a diet, you don't have to worry about being deprived of the joy of making bread. You'll have many wholesome varieties to choose from in Chapter One.

I had only one problem in writing this book, and that was knowing when to stop. There are so many countries and culinary traditions to explore, I could have written volumes of recipes revised to meet our caloric parameters. So many good cookbooks are available that my research could have taken years. Italian or *Provençal* cooking alone would have provided me with enough material for a book. One day, I just had to say *"Basta!"* and put the recipes and menus together so that you can use them. You will find a mixture of dishes that are simple enough for everyday, family enjoyment and elegant enough for entertaining, whether it be a small dinner party or a lavish buffet. The recipes are designed for slow, steady weight loss; this is not a crash diet. But it will be the most enjoyable low-calorie eating you've ever indulged in—and you won't gain the weight back.

HOW TO USE THIS BOOK

This diet is based on common sense and pleasure, not on deprivation. And common sense says: don't overeat; eat low-fat foods and foods that are low in sugar. That covers all the recipes in this book. If you are using these recipes for weight loss, you'll find that you will never feel hungry, because the dishes are filling without being rich.

The menus in the back of the book (pages 373–383) are dinner menus, because that's usually the big meal of the day in America. But the recipes in the book are great for lunches and in some cases even for breakfast. Here are some guidelines for using this book for all of your meals. It's easy to make this diet into a life-style.

BREAKFAST

In Middle Eastern countries breakfast is a big meal that includes grains, beans, and vegetables, dishes most of us wouldn't think of eating in the morning, such as *hummus* (page 92) and *ful* (page 245), *falafels*, other Middle Eastern salads, and vegetables like tomatoes, cucumbers, sweet peppers, and onions. These hearty breakfasts stick to the ribs all day, and often one does not eat again until the evening meal.

I must admit I don't have the appetite for eating like that in the morning, but for those of you who do, a hearty breakfast consisting of a choice of salads and starters from Chapter Two, or *belila* (page 244), a nourishing cereal dish consisting of cooked whole wheat berries and sweetened milk (low-fat here), will sustain you for hours, and you will require a light lunch at most and an even lighter dinner. This is really the most effective way to lose weight: you burn off the calories you consume in the morning throughout the day; at night you just sleep on them.

But most of us are too busy getting to work and getting children off to school in the morning to devote a lot of time to an elaborate breakfast, at least during the week. The breakfast suggestions below might be more realistic:

- 2 slices of any of the breads in this book (or 1 pita bread, or 2 slices any whole-grain bread), with ¼ to ⅓ cup low-fat cottage cheese or yogurt; 1 piece of fruit (such as a banana, apple, half grapefruit or melon) or 6 ounces orange or grapefruit juice

- ½ cup whole-grain cereal sweetened with no more than ½ teaspoon honey (cinnamon, nutmeg, and vanilla make a delicious alternative to honey or sugar), dry or cooked, with ⅓ cup skimmed milk; 1 piece of fruit or 6 ounces orange or grapefruit juice

- Once a week: 1 egg, cooked with no additional butter or oil, plus 2 pieces whole-grain bread; 1 piece of fruit or 6 ounces orange or grapefruit juice

INSTEAD OF SPREADING BUTTER ON TOAST, try low-fat yogurt or cottage cheese, or a mixture of the two, mashed together—or part-skim ricotta. INSTEAD OF SUGARY JAMS AND PRESERVES, try the unsweetened fruit spreads now widely available in natural-food stores and supermarkets, or applesauce, or mashed banana.

LUNCH

Lunch is the elaborate meal of the day in many southern European countries, like France and Spain, where one can spend hours around a table at midday and follow that with a *siesta*, a few hours of work, and a light supper. Again, these festive long lunches don't jibe with most of our life-styles. If they did, we might not get as much work done, but we'd probably wake up every morning feeling much lighter and better rested than we do after going to bed on a full stomach.

Our lunches tend to be light. The salads and starters, soups, and fish in this book will provide you with a wide range of choices. When my husband was losing 50 pounds he ate *Niçoise* salads (page 74) almost daily (though he usually pushed the hard-cooked egg to the side); that is also my most frequent choice when I eat lunch at a French café (and even though that's a good choice, I feel a little heavy afterward, because restaurants tend to use tuna canned in oil, and I'm used to tuna packed in brine). At a more elaborate restaurant I'll order very simply grilled or steamed fish and a salad. I usually eat lunch at home and eat whole-grain bread, a light salad, and/or low-fat yogurt or cottage cheese. If I have a soup on hand, perhaps left over from last night's dinner, I might heat up a bowl, and I'll be sustained for hours (soup is always good for dieters because all the liquid fills you up). Choose dishes from Salads and Starters (Chapter Two) and Soups (Chapter Three) for light lunches and recipes from Pasta and Pizza (Chapter Four), Grains, Beans, Stuffed Vegetables, and *Fatta* (Chapter Five), or Fish, Chicken, and Rabbit (Chapter Six) for more substantial midday meals.

Other lunch suggestions: tuna sandwich or salad (moisten water-packed tuna with yogurt, lemon juice, and mustard); plain low-fat yogurt or cottage cheese and *crudités* (as much as you want of the raw vegetables) with whole-grain bread; *hummus* (page 92) on whole-grain bread, with *crudités*.

What you eat for lunch, and how much, depends to a great extent on taste and life-style (if you are physically active in the mornings, you'll be hungry for lunch, especially if you don't eat much breakfast). The main thing to remember is to eat a light dinner if you eat a big lunch.

DINNER

For most of us, this is the main meal of the day, the meal we really plan. It's the one time of day when families sit down together, and it's the meal we choose for entertaining. The menus at the back of this book (pages 380–383) are designed with this meal in mind.

I have a few formulas I use for my everyday dinners. Dinner is most often very light, either a selection of salads or a substantial salad containing protein of some kind, such as the Egyptian black-eyed pea salad on page 98, the Middle Eastern fish salad on page 89, or *Salade Niçoise* (page 74), which we eat with whole-grain bread and might follow with a piece of fruit; or soup and a green salad (always with the bread, sometimes with fruit afterward). A fish dinner would include any of the fish recipes in Chapter Six, a vegetable side dish and sometimes a grain, potatoes or a side of whole-grain pasta (whole-grain bread will often suffice). I may or may not include a green salad with this; usually I do, because I like eating salads at every meal. A pasta or pizza dinner, frequent in our house, will include pasta or pizza as the main dish and a mixed green salad, or sometimes a *Niçoise* salad (often without the eggs, or with just 1 egg between the two of us). If my main dish is a grain or grain and legume dish—I try to combine the two for complete protein—I usually accompany this with a green salad and often a vegetable side dish. Dessert, if either of us is hungry for it, is never more than a piece of fruit.

WHAT TO DRINK WITH MEALS

If you are trying to lose a lot of weight, you should cut way down on alcohol consumption. With this diet, because it's so low-fat, you needn't cut out wine altogether, but don't drink more than two glasses a day (one, of course, is better, and none even better); you will still lose weight. Drink lots of mineral water, flat or bubbly, both with and between meals. Another beverage that goes nicely with these recipes is iced peppermint or spearmint tea. Make it by the pitcher and keep it on hand in the refrigerator.

EATING IN RESTAURANTS

You can't go wrong if you order salads and broiled, grilled, steamed, poached, or baked fish or chicken breasts. Order fish or chicken with the sauce on the side and moisten your fish or chicken ever so slightly with it or, better still, take no sauce at all (except tomato-based sauces). Season with fresh lemon juice and pepper. Always ask that the side vegetables not be tossed in butter, or they will come with hundreds of extra unwanted calories.

In Italian restaurants, order pasta with tomato-based sauces, pizzas with little or no cheese, fish or chicken breasts prepared as above. I often eat at an excellent Italian restaurant in London called Eleven Park Walk, where one of my favorite dishes is *tonno e fagioli*, a delicious tuna and bean salad (page 60) that provides all the nourishment I need to get me through the day. I might begin my meal with a plate of asparagus vinaigrette or a spinach salad and have the tuna and beans as my main course, or I'll order the tuna and beans to start and follow with a light Italian egg drop soup (*stracciatella*, page 151).

At Greek and Middle Eastern restaurants a selection of *mezze*, salads, and spreads like *tzatziki* (page 85), *tabouli* (pages 90–91), *baba ghanouj* (page 94), and *hummus* (page 92) can make a marvelous, filling meal. Drink a glass or two of *retsina* or Lebanese wine, and you'll be transported to the shores of the Mediterranean.

Remember that, no matter where you eat, in all restaurants cooks use more oil than you will be using here (even if you order a *Niçoise* salad or tuna and bean salad, the tuna will be packed in oil, which means an added 339 fat calories per can of tuna), so compensate for the extra calories by eating lighter meals during the rest of the day.

SNACKING

If you feel like eating between meals, try sticking to raw vegetables, the same vegetables that make up the backbone of Mediterranean cuisines (you'll have them on hand anyway). Dip them into a little Dijon mustard, yogurt seasoned with Dijon mustard or herbs, or a little *hummus* (page 92). I find that noshing on a carrot or two, or strips of red or green pepper pepped up with mustard, really does the trick. Raw vegetables are so low in calories that it's difficult to eat too much. Also, they're quite filling.

If snacking to you means chips, and you've really got an urge, keep on hand a supply of *carta di musica*, the crisp Sardinian flat bread, as well as *salsa cruda* for a garnish. You'll get the same satisfaction of the crunch, without the fat and the salt.

If you crave sweets, eat a piece of fruit—an apple or an orange, for instance—or one or two *biscotti*, the crunchy Italian cookies on page 366. These are filling and very low in sugar and fat.

SPLURGING

Sometimes you want to eat a really rich dish or serve one for a dinner party. There are several recipes in this book that *seem* rich, that make you feel like you're splurging, but that really aren't. They are filling, elegant dishes, great for entertaining or for a special dinner. Dishes like the *lasagne* on page 194 and some of the *risottos* (pages 226–232) seem rich because they're "creamy," even though they contain no cream. The *paella* on page 236 has such a wealth of seafood and such brilliant colors that it satisfies those cravings for something really special. The *couscous* dishes on pages 217–225 are elaborate, pungent dishes with complex flavors that are served in a ritualistic way; they are dishes for festive occasions that will fill you up without weighing you down.

As you work your way through this book you'll see that many of your cravings can be satisfied without fats and useless calories. Soon you'll begin to lose your taste for high-fat dishes altogether, even to be turned off by them, and you'll wonder how you ever managed to eat any other way than in this sensible Mediterranean fashion.

THE NUTRITIONAL DATA

The figures in the nutritional data (prepared by Hill Nutrition Associates) for each recipe have been rounded off to the nearest whole number. Optional ingredients have not been included, nor have variations on a dish. Oil for the baking pan, where not listed in the ingredients, has not been factored in; however, the additional fat will be negligible, since you won't need more than a teaspoon in most cases and some of it stays in the pan. Because I have left the amount of salt up to your taste in most recipes, sodium counts in the data are low. Garnishes have not been included except when they contain significant nutrients. In recipes where the number of servings varies, the estimates are for the larger number of servings—i.e., if a dish serves 2 to 4, the data was prepared for 4 servings.

The analyses are included as a general guideline to the nutrient content of this diet. They should help you understand *approximately* how much fat, protein, carbohydrate, sodium, cholesterol, and overall calories you will be getting from each dish.

CHAPTER ONE

BREADS

I've spent much more time seeking out bread in Mediterranean countries than I have going to museums and churches. Along with wine, olives, and garlic, bread is historically one of the four essential components of the Mediterranean diet. Each country has something good and healthy to offer, from the simple, nutty sesame rings of Greece and Egypt to the vast array of loaves that you find in Italian and French bakeries. When I visit friends in Bologna, they make lists of the best bakeries for me, and I spend my days traversing the city and coming home with shopping bags filled with different kinds of rustic breadsticks, or *grissini*—thyme, spinach, cheese, sesame, and more (page 42—country breads and rolls made from various grains, and flat, dimpled *focacce* (page 37).

I love the Middle Eastern *pita*, puffed flat bread that can be stuffed, dipped into *hummus* or an eggplant puree and used to scoop it up, or just eaten plain. In Egypt the pita bread is most often dense and heavy, made with whole-wheat flour. But at one Cairo restaurant, the Kebabky, right next to the El Gezirah Sheraton, a woman makes light, puffy white pitas, fragrant with wood smoke, that are as large as hats. She sits right outside the tent/dining room at a beehive-shaped wood oven making the pitas throughout the evening meal.

One of the most ingenious aspects of Mediterranean peasant cuisines is the way day-old bread can be transformed into other dishes. A typical Spanish lunch consists of slightly stale bread rubbed with garlic, soaked with olive oil, and rubbed with tomato. I make the same dish but toast the bread and just brush it with a little olive oil, then rub in enough tomato to moisten the bread sufficiently. The Italian version of this recipe is the *bruschette* or *crostini* (pages 52 and 53), and a more elaborate French version is the *pain bagnat* (page 75). Italians also make a fine salad with dry bread (page 59), as well as a delicious soup (page 139). The Middle Eastern version of the bread salad is *fattoush*, made with crisp pita and vegetables (page 88), and pita is a key component of *fatta*, delicious casseroles of toasted pita, vegetables or meat, and yogurt. Another bread transformation is toasted croutons, rubbed with garlic and floated on savory soups or tossed into salads.

But it's the fresh, homemade bread we're concerned with here. The variety throughout the Mediterranean is astounding; what a treat it was to have these breads around the house when I was testing recipes. And you might not believe this, but you can continue to eat bread while you lose weight. The whole-grain flours in these breads are complex carbohydrates; their calories are energy calories, much easier to burn off than fat and protein. The key to losing weight while continuing to eat bread is to do without the butter, which is rarely spread on breads in Mediterranean countries. Dipping the bread into a soup or sauce is the light, Mediterranean way of moistening. The breads are very low in fat; indeed, some have no oil added at all.

I can imagine a meal without meat or a meal without cheese, but it's impossible for me to conceive of eating a meal without bread.

INGREDIENTS

This list describes the properties and uses of most of the ingredients—flours, grains, yeast—that you'll find in the recipes in this chapter.

Unbleached white flour: This is flour that has not been bleached by chemicals, but by a natural aging process. I use it wherever white flour is required.

Whole-wheat flour: Dark whole-grain flour that has not had the bran and germ milled out of it. The best is stone-ground and has a nutty, wholesome flavor. I try to work some whole-wheat flour into most of my breads. Some whole-wheat flours are coarser than others. If the flour is too coarse, it will have a somewhat sandy texture and will result in a very heavy bread. If this is all you can find, a better bread will result if you replace a third to a quarter of the whole-wheat flour called for with whole-wheat pastry flour or unbleached white flour.

Whole-wheat pastry flour: This is made from softer wheat and is more finely milled than whole-wheat flour. Makes a lighter bread and is better for pastry.

Durum flour: Durum flour is ground from durum wheat, the hardest kind of wheat. The golden-hued flour is very fine and has a very high gluten content.

Semolina: These are tiny, coarse grains milled from the hearts of durum wheat berries. Good for dusting baking sheets, but should not be substituted for semolina flour when the flour is called for in bread recipes.

Semolina flour: Golden flour ground from the semolina grain. The best industrial pasta is made with semolina flour; it absorbs much less water than other flours. One of my favorite breads, from Sicily, is made with this lovely yellow flour (page 27). If you can't find it, use durum flour or grind up semolina in a blender with some unbleached white flour.

Cornmeal: Buy the yellow stone-ground cornmeal for the breads in this chapter. It has a grainy texture, sweet taste, and lovely golden color. Use for dusting baking stones and sheets. Store in the refrigerator to prevent oils from turning rancid.

Chick-pea flour: Flour made by grinding dried chick-peas. It has a marvelous, earthy flavor and is the main ingredient in *socca*, a polenta-like *Niçoise* specialty (page 44). Store in the refrigerator to prevent oils from turning rancid.

Bran: Bran comes from the high-fiber shell of the wheat berry. When wheat is stone-ground, you lose very little bran. The addition of bran to any bread dough will make a very high-fiber loaf (page 26).

Sesame seeds: Tiny, nutty-tasting seeds that are used in Italian, Middle Eastern, and Greek breads (pages 27, 29, and 42). They should be stored in the refrigerator to prevent the oils from turning rancid.

Malt syrup: Malt syrup, or malt extract, is a syrup, usually made from malted barley, that is added to some bread doughs in very small amounts to aid the yeast and give the bread a golden crust.

Honey: I use honey in small amounts in some breads to aid the yeast and in slightly larger amounts in sweeter breads. It's important to use mild-flavored honey; the light-colored ones like acacia and clover are the best.

Yeast: The recipes in this chapter call for active dry yeast, small granules that are activated when the yeast is dissolved in warm water. It comes in envelopes— about 2½ teaspoons per envelope—and in bulk. It's much cheaper to buy in bulk; large packages are available in most whole-foods stores. Store in the refrigerator or freezer. It should keep for a year, depending on how long it's been on the grocery shelf.

Starters: Some of the breads in this chapter combine starters with yeast, resulting in slightly sour, crusty, hearty loaves. The starters are made by dissolving flour in water and allowing the mixture to sit for one to three days, depending on the recipe (the Italian *biga*, which also contains a very small amount of yeast, sits for 24 hours, whereas the stronger French *chef* "works" for three days before it is ready).

EQUIPMENT

Bowls: These can be stainless steel, earthenware, glass, plastic, or ceramic. You should have a large one that holds at least 3 quarts, preferably more. Having more than one large bowl helps, as some breads require you to mix liquid ingredients and dry ingredients separately. You should also have a smaller one, because some recipes call for dissolving the yeast first in a small bowl.

Measuring cups and spoons: Have two sets of each, one for dry ingredients and one for liquid.

Kitchen scale

Large whisk: For beating in flours.

Wooden spoon: For folding in ingredients.

Pastry scraper or dough scraper: This is essential for turning and kneading many of these breads, as many of the doughs are very sticky. A traditional dough scraper is a stainless steel rectangle with a wooden handle; a plastic pastry scraper has a curved edge, useful for scraping dough out of a bowl, and works just as well for kneading, although it's not as effective for cutting the dough.

Banneton: A *banneton* is a bowl or basket lined with muslin or tea towels, where dough rises and keeps its shape at the same time, before being transferred to baking stones or sheets. All you have to do to devise your own is to line a bowl with dish towels and dust the towels on the inside with flour. Place the dough in this bowl and just before baking reverse onto a hot baking stone or baking sheet.

Baking stone or tiles: Porous clay baking stones or clay tiles that are fired at high heat and distribute the heat evenly in your oven. They absorb the moisture of the dough and assure a thick, hard crust. I keep my round baking stone in the oven even when I'm baking loaves in pans or on baking sheets. I prefer the large stones to the tiles, because the tiles don't always stay close together when you turn the dough onto them. Preheat in the oven for 30 minutes at 400 to 450 degrees before baking and sprinkle with cornmeal or semolina if baking the loaves directly on the stones. Baking stones can be obtained in cookware shops and some hardware stores.

Shallow pan or water spray-bottle: A little steam in the hot oven helps to assure a hard crust. There are two ways to obtain the steam. I usually put an empty baking pan on a rack near the bottom of the oven while the oven is preheating, and just before baking I pour 2 cups of water into it and immediately close the door. If you use this method, be sure that your pan isn't too close to the baking tiles or stone, because the sudden rush of steam could cause the stone to crack. The other method is to spray the loaf or loaves immediately after putting them into the oven and repeat the spraying two or three times during the first 10 minutes of baking.

Nonstick baking sheets: I use these for some breads and *focacce,* pizzas, and the *biscotti* on page 366.

Nonstick bread pans: These require either no oil or very little, and eliminate the problem of finding your beautiful baked loaves adhered to the pans.

Heavy-duty electric mixer with dough hook: This is optional, and expensive, but it really makes a difference with some of the stickier doughs. I have a KitchenAid and use the paddle to mix up the dough and the dough hook for kneading.

NOTES ON MAKING YEAST BREADS

The steps for making the yeast breads in this chapter are fairly uniform. You begin by dissolving the yeast in lukewarm water. Make sure the water isn't hotter than lukewarm or you'll kill the yeast. Once the yeast is dissolved you can wait about 10 minutes, until the yeast "proofs," or bubbles, or you can begin stirring in the ingredients for the dough—the starter, if a starter is called for, salt, oil, herbs or spices, and finally the flour. If you are going to knead the dough by hand, you whisk in half the flour, then fold in the rest with a wooden spoon, a cup at a time. Using an electric mixer, you can add all the flour at once, mix it in with the paddle, then change to the dough hook to knead for 8 to 10 minutes. If kneading by hand, flour your hands and work surface generously and scrape out the dough using a pastry scraper. If the dough is very soft, you'll have to use the pastry scraper to help fold it over when you knead, or else it will be a sticky mess. Work briskly, folding the dough over toward you, pressing or leaning into it with the palms of your well-floured hands and turning the dough a quarter turn. Fold, lean, turn; fold, lean, turn. Keep flouring the board and your hands to prevent sticking and manipulate the dough with a pastry scraper if sticking is unavoidable. After about 10 minutes the dough will be stiff and elastic (though not necessarily "smooth," as most recipes tell you it should be). Form the dough into a ball and place it in a bowl, which in most cases should be oiled lightly, seam side facing up first, then seam side down. Cover loosely with plastic wrap and/or a damp towel and place in a warm place to rise for the stated time. A warm place could be on top of a heater or next to a radiator, over a pilot light (it's a good idea to put a pan or something between the bowl and the pilot light so the dough won't get too hot), or in an oven that has been turned on for a minute and then turned off. If none of these choices is available, just make sure the bowl is out of the draft. The dough will rise slightly more slowly.

At the end of the first rise you will punch down the dough (lightly flour your fist and stick it into the dough a few times), and in most cases you'll scrape or turn out the dough and shape it for its final rise. If the dough spreads out too much during the final rise, gently reshape and wait another 15 to 20 minutes before baking. Then you'll bake it in the preheated oven for the designated amount of time. Bread is done when the crust is golden brown and it responds to tapping with a hollow sound. Remove from the oven and cool on a wire rack away from the heat.

If I am eating a freshly baked crusty bread immediately, like the Crusty Country Bread on page 35), I don't wrap it at all, because wrapping these hard-crusted breads softens the crust. Once I cut it I cover the cut end with foil. Other breads can be wrapped in foil or kept in plastic bags. After a couple of days, refrigerate the bread in plastic bags. Almost all the breads here can be frozen. Wrap in heavy foil, then seal in a plastic bag and place in the freezer for up to six months.

If you are in the middle of bread making and have to go out, don't feel like a prisoner of your bread dough. You can always put the dough in the refrigerator to retard rising, or you can freeze it. It takes a few hours to thaw and then must come to room temperature before it begins to behave like fresh bread dough, but it is possible. This is especially useful for the *focaccia* (page 37) and pizza recipes on pages 200–213, because sometimes you don't want to make as many *focacce* or pizzas as a dough recipe yields. In this case, just freeze left-over dough and use it on another occasion. It will keep in the freezer for several weeks.

ROSEMARY AND THYME BREAD

MAKES 2 SMALL ROUND LOAVES OR 1 LARGE LOAF, ABOUT 30 SERVINGS

This bread could be Italian or *Provençal*, because the hills of Tuscany, Liguria, and Provence are full of both herbs, growing into big bushes all over the countryside. The dough smells enticing while rising and even better while baking.

This bread should really be made with fresh herbs. But if that simply isn't possible, use dried herbs and halve the quantities.

    1 tablespoon plus ¾ teaspoon (1½ envelopes) active
        dry yeast
    2 cups lukewarm water
    2 tablespoons plus 1 teaspoon olive oil
    1 tablespoon salt
    4 tablespoons finely chopped fresh rosemary
    2 tablespoons fresh thyme leaves
    2 large garlic cloves, minced or put through a press
    3 cups whole-wheat flour
    2 cups unbleached white flour, plus additional flour for
        kneading

Dissolve the yeast in water and let sit 10 minutes. Whisk in the olive oil and salt, then stir in the rosemary, thyme, and garlic. Whisk in 2 cups of the whole-wheat flour, a cup at a time, then fold in the remaining cup of whole-wheat flour plus the white flour, a cup at a time.

Scrape the dough out onto a generously floured kneading surface, flour your hands, and knead for 10 minutes. Use a pastry scraper to help you turn the dough if it is very sticky and keep flouring your hands.

(You can also knead the dough in an electric mixer. Mix together as instructed above, combining the ingredients with the paddle, then change to the dough hook to knead for 5 minutes and finish kneading—just for a minute or so—by hand.)

Shape the dough into a ball, oil your bowl, and place the dough in it seam side up, then turn the oiled side up. Cover with plastic wrap and let rise in a warm, draft-free place for 1½ hours or until doubled.

For the second rising you can either use a *banneton* (page 19) or let the loaves rise right on a lightly oiled baking sheet.

Punch the dough down, turn out onto a floured surface, and divide in half. Shape each half into a ball and place in the floured *bannetons* or on lightly oiled baking sheets. Cover with a towel and let rise 45 minutes to an hour. Reshape if necessary.

Thirty minutes before baking, preheat the oven to 450 degrees, with a baking stone or tiles in it if you are using them. Just before baking, sprinkle the stone with cornmeal and transfer the dough in *bannetons* to the stone. Slash the tops of the loaves with a razor or sharp knife and place in the hot oven. If you aren't using *bannetons* or a baking stone, simply slash with a razor or sharp knife and place in the hot oven on the baking sheet. Set the timer for 10 minutes and spray the inside of the oven with water three times during the first 10 minutes (page 19). Reduce the heat to 400 degrees and bake 30 to 35 minutes longer, until the loaves are brown and respond with a hollow sound when tapped. Remove from the oven and cool on racks.

Storing and Freezing: Do *not* wrap in plastic or foil. Once you cut the bread, just cover the cut end with foil. Otherwise the crust will soften. To freeze, wrap tightly in heavy-duty aluminum foil, then seal in a plastic bag. Thaw in the wrapping, then unwrap.

PER PORTION:

Calories	89	Protein	3 G
Fat	1 G	Carbohydrate	17 G
Sodium	220 MG	Cholesterol	0

FOUGASSE

MAKES 1 LOAF, ABOUT 20 SERVINGS

A *fougasse* is a lattice-shaped bread that is usually made with baguette dough in southern France, where it is a specialty. Bakers in France often add anchovies, olives, nuts, or herbs to their *fougasse* dough. This one is my own recipe; it has a nutty, whole-wheat taste and a hard crust.

2½ teaspoons (1 envelope) active dry yeast
  2 cups lukewarm water
2½ teaspoons salt
  2 cups unbleached white flour
2½ cups whole-wheat flour
  ½ cup bran

Dissolve the yeast in the water and let sit 10 minutes. Add the salt and fold in the flour, a cup at a time, and the bran. Turn out and knead on a lightly floured surface, using a paddle to help you turn the dough, as it will be quite sticky (this can all be done in an electric mixer using a dough hook). Knead the dough for about 10 minutes, dusting with flour as necessary.

Place the dough in an oiled bowl, seam side up first, then seam side down, cover with plastic wrap and a towel, and allow to rise for 1½ hours, until doubled in bulk.

Scrape the dough out onto a dusted work surface, knead for a couple of minutes, and press or roll out the dough to a rectangle, about 12 inches long by 6 to 8 inches wide. In the middle of the rectangle, cut three crosswise incisions at equal intervals along the length of the dough to within 2 inches of the edges of the dough. Pull the dough apart at these incisions so that the dough looks like a ladder with rungs across the top and bottom and two in the middle. Place on an oiled baking sheet dusted with cornmeal and cover with a damp towel. Let rise 1½ hours. Reshape if necessary.

Preheat the oven to 400 degrees. Bake the bread in the preheated oven for 45 minutes, until it is golden and crusty and responds with a hollow sound when tapped. Remove from the oven and cool on a rack.

Storing and Freezing: Do not wrap the bread. Cover the cut ends with foil. This bread goes stale after about two days. Wrap in foil and seal in a plastic bag to freeze. Thaw in the wrapping, then unwrap.

PER PORTION:

Calories	101	Protein	4 G
Fat	.46 G	Carbohydrate	21 G
Sodium	276 MG	Cholesterol	0

WHOLE-WHEAT TUSCAN BREAD

MAKES 1 LARGE LOAF
ALLOW 2 DAYS' PREPARATION TIME

Tuscan bread is dense, rustic country bread made with no salt. If you've never tasted saltless bread, you might find it bland, but the texture of the bread, with its hard crust and chewy grain, and the sweet taste of the wheat are quite satisfying. Dip it into a soup or use it to mop up a pasta sauce or salad dressing, and you won't miss the salt at all. If you find that it just doesn't have enough flavor, try adding herbs such as rosemary and thyme to the dough. The bread becomes stale quickly, but don't throw out the leftovers. Use the stale bread for *pappa ai Pomodori* (page 139) or Italian Bread Salad (page 59). The dough is quite stiff, and kneading requires a lot of elbow grease (or an electric mixer with a dough hook).

FOR THE STARTER:

1 teaspoon active dry yeast
⅔ cup lukewarm water
⅔ cup unbleached white flour
⅔ cup whole-wheat flour

FOR THE DOUGH:

2 teaspoons active dry yeast
1⅓ cups lukewarm water
the starter (recipe above)
4 cups whole-wheat flour
unbleached white flour for kneading

FIRST DAY: MAKE THE STARTER

Dissolve the yeast in the water. Whisk in the white flour, then stir in the whole-wheat flour and beat with a wooden spoon for about 5 minutes. The mixture will be like sticky dough. Cover loosely with plastic wrap and let rise until tripled in size, 12 to 24 hours.

SECOND DAY: MAKE THE BREAD

Dissolve the yeast in the water and let stand 10 minutes. Add the starter and stir until dissolved. Stir in the whole-wheat flour, a cup at a time. If kneading by hand, turn out onto a floured work surface and knead for 10 minutes, flouring your hands and dusting the surface often. If using a mixer, mix the flour into the water, yeast, and starter with the paddle, then change to the dough hook and knead 5 to 10 minutes.

Shape the dough into a ball and place in a lightly oiled bowl, seam side up, then turn oiled side up. Cover loosely with plastic wrap and a damp towel; let rise until doubled, 1 to 1½ hours.

Punch down the dough and turn onto a floured work surface. Shape into a ball. Place in a *banneton* (page 19) or on a lightly oiled baking sheet. Sprinkle the top lightly with flour and allow to rise, lightly covered, for another hour. Reshape if necessary.

Thirty minutes before baking, preheat the oven to 450 degrees, with a baking stone in it if using one. Place an empty pan in the lower part of the oven, and fill with water just before putting the bread in.

If using a *banneton* and baking stone or heavy baking sheet, sprinkle the stone or baking sheet with cornmeal and reverse the loaf onto it. Slash with a razor or a sharp knife and place in the oven. If the dough rose on the baking sheet, just slash the tops and place in the oven. Set the timer for 15 minutes, and if you haven't put the empty pan in the preheating oven and filled with water, then spray the oven three times during the first 10 minutes of baking. Reduce the heat to 400 degrees and bake another 25 to 30 minutes, until the crust is brown and hard and responds with a hollow sound when tapped. Remove from the oven and cool on a rack.

TUSCAN ROSEMARY BREAD

Add 3 to 4 tablespoons chopped fresh rosemary just before you begin to add the flours. Substitute 2 cups unbleached white flour for 2 cups of the whole-wheat flour in the dough. Proceed as above.

Storing and Freezing: Do not wrap the bread. Cover the cut end with foil. This bread does not freeze well.

PER ½-INCH SLICE:

Calories	81	Protein	3 G
Fat	.41 G	Carbohydrate	17 G
Sodium	1 MG	Cholesterol	0

BRAN BREAD

MAKES 1 ROUND LOAF, ABOUT 30 SERVINGS

This is my version of a delicious bran bread made by an excellent baker in Apt, a *Provençal* town in the valley of the Luberon mountains. When I visit my friend Christine at her nearby farm, we eat it morning, noon, and night, and I never tire of it.

This is a very wet dough, best kneaded in an electric mixer; if you don't have a mixer, knead it right in the bowl, use a pastry scraper, and keep flouring your hands generously.

- 2½ teaspoons (1 envelope) active dry yeast
- 2 cups lukewarm water
- 2 teaspoons salt
- 2 cups whole-wheat pastry flour
- 2 cups unbleached white flour
- ⅔ cup bran

Dissolve the yeast in the water and let sit for 10 minutes. Add the salt, then stir in the whole-wheat pastry flour, a cup at a time. Add the white flour, a cup at a time, and the bran. If using an electric mixer, do this part with the paddle, then change to the dough hook. Knead for 10 minutes. If kneading by hand, use a pastry scraper and knead right in the bowl. Keep flouring your hands and scraping off the dough. It will be sticky and wet.

Lightly oil a large bowl and scrape or pour the dough into it. Turn the dough over. Cover tightly with plastic wrap and/or a damp towel; let rise at room temperature until tripled, from 3 to 5 hours.

Flour your work surface and your hands well and scrape out the dough. Knead for a minute or so, flouring your hands and work surface as necessary, and shape the dough into a ball. Place in a *banneton* (page 19) or on an oiled baking sheet dusted with cornmeal. Cover with a towel dusted with flour and let rise another 1½ to 2 hours, until doubled. Reshape if necessary.

Thirty minutes before baking, preheat the oven to 425 degrees, with a baking stone in it if you have one. Reverse the dough onto the baking stone or place the baking sheet on top of the stone and bake 40 to 45 minutes, until the crust is hard and brown and responds with a hollow sound when tapped. Remove from the oven and cool on a rack.

Storing and Freezing: Do not wrap. Cover cut end with foil. To freeze, wrap in heavy-duty foil, then seal in plastic bags. Thaw in wrapping, then unwrap.

PER SLICE:

Calories	71	Protein	2 G
Fat	.19 G	Carbohydrate	15 G
Sodium	147 MG	Cholesterol	0

SICILIAN BREAD

MAKES 1 LARGE LOAF OR 2 BAGUETTES, ABOUT 40 SERVINGS

This is my loose version of the bread I ate every day when I was in Sicily. Perhaps it shouldn't be called "Sicilian bread," but I call it that because it's encrusted with sesame seeds, like the marvelous bread I ate there. In Sicily the bread is a pale yellowish-white color, and the hard crust is covered with sesame seeds. In her book *The Italian Baker*, Carol Field has a recipe for the bread that uses either hard durum flour, which is easier to find than the authentic semolina flour, or finely ground semolina for pasta. When I was playing with the recipe in Paris, I had trouble finding durum flour but did find finely ground semolina, and that's what I use for this bread. The recipe is very close to Carol Field's.

In Sicily the bread is shaped a number of ways. It can be rolled into a long cylinder and curled back and forth over itself; or it can be shaped like a small ladder; it can also be shaped like a coiled S or as a crown; or it can simply be left as a baguette, which is the easiest.

This is one of my favorite breads in this chapter. It is especially nice toasted.

2½ teaspoons (1 envelope) active dry yeast
1¼ cups lukewarm water
1 teaspoon malt syrup or mild-flavored honey
1 tablespoon olive oil
2 teaspoons salt
2½ cups finely ground semolina for making pasta
¾ to 1 cup whole-wheat pastry flour
¼ cup sesame seeds

Dissolve the yeast in the water and let sit 10 minutes. Stir in the malt syrup or honey, the olive oil, and the salt. Stir in the semolina, a cup at a time. Place the whole-wheat pastry flour on your kneading surface, turn out the dough, and knead until smooth and firm, about 10 minutes (this can also be done in an electric mixer with a dough hook).

Form into a ball and place the dough in a lightly oiled bowl, seam side up first, then turn the seam side face down. Cover loosely with plastic wrap and/or a damp towel and allow to rise in a warm place until doubled, about 1½ hours.

Punch down the dough, knead a few times on a floured surface, then shape into either a large round loaf, two baguettes, or a crown shape. For the crown shape, flatten the dough into a rectangle and, starting from the edge on one of the long sides, make three crosswise cuts, cutting only about one third of the way across, using a pastry scraper or a knife. Pull the resulting fingerlike pieces slightly apart.

Place the loaves on a lightly oiled baking sheet and brush thoroughly with water. Sprinkle with the sesame seeds and gently pat the seeds into the dough. Brush again with water. Cover lightly with plastic wrap and a towel and let rise for 1 to 1½ hours, until doubled. Reshape if necessary.

Thirty minutes before baking, preheat the oven to 425 degrees. Place the bread in the oven, set the timer for 10 minutes, and spray three times with water during the first 10 minutes. Reduce the heat to 400 degrees and bake 25 to 30 minutes longer, until golden brown and the bread responds with a hollow sound when tapped. Remove from the heat and cool on racks.

Storing and Freezing: Do not wrap in plastic or foil. Cover the cut end with foil. The bread freezes well. Wrap tightly in foil and seal in a plastic bag. Thaw in the wrapping, then unwrap.

Calories	50	Protein	1 G
Fat	.88 G	Carbohydrate	9 G
Sodium	110 MG	Cholesterol	0

SESAME BREAD RINGS

MAKES 12 RINGS

Vendors in Cairo and Athens string these hard, nutty bracelets of bread on thin ropes and sell them from morning to night. I have a weakness for sesame seeds, and the breads are encrusted with them. My recipe isn't quite authentic, as I have replaced some of the white flour in the traditional recipe with whole-wheat flour and added a bit of finely ground semolina for texture. These changes give the bread rings a richer flavor and of course make them more nutritious.

    1 teaspoon active dry yeast
  ¼ cup lukewarm water
       pinch sugar
  ⅓ cup lukewarm skimmed milk
  ½ teaspoon salt
    1 tablespoon olive or safflower oil
  ½ cup whole-wheat flour
  ½ cup unbleached white flour, plus additional for
           kneading
  ¼ cup finely ground semolina for making pasta
    1 egg, beaten
    4 tablespoons sesame seeds

   Dissolve the yeast in the water and add sugar. Let sit 10 minutes. Stir in the milk, salt, and oil. Add the whole-wheat flour, the unbleached white flour, and the semolina. Knead for a few minutes in the bowl, adding a little water if the dough is too stiff. Let the dough rest for 15 minutes. Now turn out onto a lightly floured board and knead vigorously for 10 minutes, adding flour if necessary. Shape into a ball and place in an oiled bowl, seam side up, then turn the oiled side up. Cover loosely with plastic wrap and/or a damp towel; set in a warm place to rise for about 2 hours, until doubled in size.

Punch down the dough and turn out onto your kneading surface. Cut into 12 pieces and roll out each piece into a thin sausage shape.

Place the sesame seeds on a baking sheet. Brush the sausagelike pieces of dough with beaten egg and roll in the sesame seeds. Then join at the ends so that they form a braceletlike circle. Place on oiled baking sheets, leaving space for rising, and cover lightly with parchment paper or a towel. Set in a warm spot to rise for 30 minutes.

Meanwhile, preheat the oven to 425 degrees. Use a baking stone if you like—it's not necessary. Bake the rings for 10 minutes, then reduce the heat to 325 degrees and bake another 10 to 20 minutes, until the bread is golden brown and responds with a hollow sound when tapped. Remove from the heat and cool on racks.

Storing and Freezing: These keep well in a cookie tin. You can keep them in plastic bags, but the crust will soften. Freeze in sealed plastic bags.

PER PORTION:

Calories	93	Protein	3 G
Fat	3 G	Carbohydrate	13 G
Sodium	101 MG	Cholesterol	23 MG

SOURDOUGH STARTERS

Sourdough starters are added to breads to give more strength to the flour and a special porous texture and flavor to the breads. My whole-wheat versions of sourdough breads have a slightly less porous texture than breads made with white flour, but they also have a marvelous grainy quality. Sourdough country breads are sometimes made with no addition of yeast, but I find that without the yeast my whole-grain breads are too sour and heavy.

The following starters, one from Italy and one from France, will keep in the refrigerator for about a week and can also be frozen for several months and refrozen every time you have to be away from bread making for a while. It takes about three hours for the starters to come to room temperature after you remove them from the refrigerator. Then they'll be ready to use. If you've frozen the starter, thaw it at room temperature for a day before using it.

When you make bread with sourdough starter, remove a cup of the dough before you shape the loaves and refrigerate in a covered bowl or container in order to have some starter for your next batch of bread.

ITALIAN SOURDOUGH STARTER (Biga)

MAKES 2 CUPS

This starter is adapted from Carol Field's recipe in her wonderful book *The Italian Baker*. It is a wetter, lighter mixture than the French *chef*, and sourdough breads made with the *biga* are consequently a bit lighter than those made with the French starter.

¼ teaspoon active dry yeast
¼ cup plus ¾ cup lukewarm water
1⅓ cups whole-wheat flour
1 cup unbleached white flour

Dissolve the yeast in the ¼ cup lukewarm water in a bowl. Stir in the remaining water and add the flour, a cup at a time. Mix with a wooden spoon or the paddle of an electric mixer for about 3 to 5 minutes, until you have a sticky dough.

Transfer the dough to a lightly oiled bowl, cover with plastic wrap, and let rise at room temperature for 24 hours. The starter will be sticky, wet, and tripled in volume. Use all of this starter the first time you make sourdough bread and remove a cup from the dough before you form your loaf for subsequent loaves.

PER 1-CUP STARTER:

Calories	495	Protein	17 G
Fat	2 G	Carbohydrate	104 G
Sodium	4 MG	Cholesterol	0

FRENCH SOURDOUGH STARTER (Chef)

MAKES 2 CUPS

I make thick-crusted country bread with this starter at least once a week. It's a strong, powerful one with great staying power. Over the last four years I've traveled with my *chef* all over Europe, through France and Italy, on to a Yugoslavian island and back, making bread with it all along the way with whatever flours and grains I could find. I've taken it with me to the United States and back to Paris and continue to use the same starter after all this time.

The *chef* is based on Patricia Wells's recipe in *The Food Lover's Guide to Paris* (Workman, revised edition 1988), which in turn is based on that of the famous Paris baker Lionel Poilane.

THE FIRST DAY:
- ⅓ cup water
- 1 cup whole-wheat or unbleached white flour

Mix together the water and flour and knead into a smooth ball on a lightly floured work surface. The dough should be soft and sticky. Flour your hands so you can work with it. Return to the bowl, cover with a damp towel, and let sit at room temperature for 72 hours. The dough will form a crust on the top and turn a grayish color, which is normal. Occasionally wetting the towel will reduce the drying. The dough will rise slightly and take on an acidic aroma.

AFTER 72 HOURS:
- ½ cup lukewarm water
- 1 ½ cups whole-wheat or unbleached white flour

Turn the crusty starter over and add the water to the bowl. Let the starter sit in the water for about 10 minutes so that the crusty top softens. If after soaking the crust is still like cardboard or wood, you will have to peel it off and discard. Try blending it before you resort to this. Blend together the mixture, add the flour, and stir to blend. Transfer to a floured work surface and knead into a smooth ball.

Return to the bowl, cover with a damp towel, and let sit in a warm place for 24 to 48 hours. Again, a crust may form on the top. If it is like cardboard or wood, peel off and discard before proceeding with a bread recipe. Use all of the starter the first time you make a sourdough bread (recipes here call for a cup of the starter, but the initial recipe will yield more than that). Remove a cup of it before forming the loaf and refrigerate in a covered container until you make your next loaf.

SOURDOUGH COUNTRY BREAD
WITH BRAN

MAKES 1 LARGE LOAF, ABOUT 30 SERVINGS

Like the bran bread on page 26, this is a wet dough. It has a nice sour taste and a coarse texture.

- 2 teaspoons active dry yeast
- 2 cups lukewarm water
- 1 cup *chef* (page 32) or *biga* (page 31)
- 2 teaspoons salt
- 3 cups whole-wheat flour
- 1 cup unbleached white flour
- 1 cup bran

Dissolve the yeast in the water and let sit for 10 minutes. Add the *chef* or *biga* and stir to break it up. Add the salt, then stir in the whole-wheat flour, a cup at a time. Add the white flour and the bran. If using an electric mixer, do this part with the paddle, then change to the dough hook. Knead for 10 minutes. If kneading by hand, use a pastry scraper and knead right in the bowl. Keep flouring your hands and scraping off the dough. It will be sticky and wet.

Lightly oil a large bowl and scrape or pour the dough into it. Turn the dough over. Cover loosely with a plastic wrap and/or a damp towel; let rise at room temperature until doubled, 1½ to 2 hours.

Flour your work surface and your hands well and scrape out the dough. Knead for a minute or so, flouring your hands and work surface as necessary, and shape the dough into a ball. Place in a *banneton* or on an oiled baking sheet dusted with cornmeal. Cover with a kitchen towel dusted with flour and let rise another 1½ to 2 hours, until doubled.

Thirty minutes before baking, preheat the oven to 425 degrees, with a baking stone in it if you have one. Place an empty pan in the lower part of the oven (not too close to the baking stone) and fill with water just before putting the bread in to bake. Sprinkle the baking stone with cornmeal and reverse the dough onto the baking stone or place the baking sheet on top of the stone and bake 40 to 45 minutes, until the crust is hard and brown and responds with a hollow sound when tapped. Remove from the oven and cool on a rack.

Storing and Freezing: Do not wrap. Cover the cut end with foil. To freeze, wrap in heavy-duty foil, then seal in a plastic bag. Thaw in wrapping, then unwrap.

PER SLICE:

Calories	78	Protein	3 G
Fat	.43 G	Carbohydrate	16 G
Sodium	148 MG	Cholesterol	0

MOROCCAN BREAD

MAKES 2 SMALL LOAVES, ABOUT 28 SERVINGS

This recipe is based on one of Paula Wolfert's, although I've changed the proportions of whole-wheat flour and spices. I also decided not to bother with the traditional Moroccan shape, which is cone-shaped with a flattened top. The breads are sweet and fragrant with anise; they're marvelous for breakfast.

      2½ teaspoons (1 envelope) active dry yeast
       ¼ cup lukewarm water
       1 teaspoon sugar
       ½ cup lukewarm skimmed milk
       2 cups whole-wheat flour
      1½ cups unbleached white flour
       2 teaspoons salt
       2 tablespoons sesame seed
       4 teaspoons aniseed or fennel seed
          about ½ cup warm water (or more as needed)
          cornmeal

Dissolve the yeast in the water. Add the sugar and let stand in a warm place for 20 minutes. Stir in the milk.

Combine the flour, salt, sesame seeds, and aniseed in a large bowl. Make a well in the center and pour in the yeast mixture. Stir together with the flour. Add warm water as necessary to form a stiff dough. Turn out onto a floured surface and knead for 10 to 15 minutes, until smooth and elastic (this can also be done in an electric mixer in 8 minutes at low speed).

Divide the dough in half and shape into 2 balls. Let stand 5 minutes. Brush with a little oil and place on an oiled baking sheet that has been sprinkled lightly with cornmeal. Cover the dough with a damp towel and let rise for 2 hours in a warm place.

Preheat the oven to 400 degrees. Prick the dough in several places with a fork and place in the oven. Bake 12 minutes, then reduce the heat to 300 degrees and bake another 30 to 40 minutes, until the loaves are brown and respond with a hollow sound when tapped. Remove from the heat and cool on racks. Slice in wedges to serve.

Storing and Freezing: This can be stored in plastic bags or wrapped in foil, or you can just cover the cut end with foil. Wrapping it will keep it moist. Either way, it will keep about 5 days. To freeze, wrap in foil and seal in plastic bags. Thaw in the wrapping.

PER SLICE:

Calories	63	Protein	2 G
Fat	.59 G	Carbohydrate	12 G
Sodium	160 MG	Cholesterol	0

CRUSTY COUNTRY BREAD

MAKES 1 LARGE LOAF, ABOUT 30 SERVINGS

Both in France and in Italy (and I imagine in Spain and Portugal as well), this hearty, slightly sour crusty bread, made in wood-fueled stone ovens, is a joy to eat at any time of day. This recipe is a loose adaptation, combining elements from the French country bread that I make every week and Carol Field's version of Italian whole-wheat bread. The starter, whether you use the French *chef* (page 32) or the Italian *biga* (page 31), gives it its sour flavor and contributes to the hard crust and texture. *Biga* is wetter and less sour than the French *chef*.

The dough is very wet and sticky, so you should use a plastic pastry scraper to help you work with it; it's much easier to knead in an electric mixer than by hand. I have introduced the French method of letting the dough rise in a *banneton* (page 19) for the second rise so that it has a rounded shape when you invert it onto your baking sheet or stone. When you transfer the dough to the baking sheet or stone, it will deflate, but if your oven is hot enough it will puff up as soon as you put it in to bake.

- 1 teaspoon active dry yeast
- 2 cups water
- 1 cup *biga* (page 31) or *chef* (page 32)*
- 2 teaspoons salt
- 3 cups whole-wheat flour
- 1 cup unbleached white flour, plus up to ½ cup (or more) for kneading and flouring your hands

Dissolve the yeast in the water in a large mixing bowl and let stand for 10 minutes. Add the *biga* or *chef* and stir together well until the starter is broken up. Stir in the salt and the whole-wheat flour, a cup at a time. Fold in the unbleached white flour.

When all the flour has been added, knead either using the dough hook of your electric mixer or by hand, using a pastry scraper to help you turn the dough and flouring your kneading surface and hands often, for about 10 minutes. If you use an electric mixer, after 10 minutes scrape the dough out onto a floured surface, flour your hands, and knead for a minute or two by hand.

Transfer the dough to a lightly oiled large bowl, turn over, cover lightly with plastic wrap, and/or a damp towel. Let rise for 2 to 3 hours, until tripled in size.

Turn out the dough onto a floured work surface and shape into a ball. If you want to save some starter for another loaf, remove a cupful of dough and reshape the remaining dough into a ball. Refrigerate the reserved starter in a covered container or bowl.

Place the dough in a *banneton*, seam side up, and cover with another towel. Let rise in a draft-free place for 1 to 1½ hours.

Thirty minutes before baking, preheat the oven to 450 degrees, with baking stones if you have them. If you don't have baking stones, use a heavy baking sheet and heat that in the oven for about 10 minutes. Place an empty pan on a lower rack, not too close to the baking stone, and just before you put the loaves in, fill with water. This creates steam that will contribute to a hard crust.

Sprinkle the stone or baking sheet with cornmeal and invert the dough

---

*If this is the first time you are using the *biga* or *chef*, you will have approximately 2 cups. Use the full amount and add up to ½ cup flour as necessary for kneading.

onto it. Slash the loaf about ¼ to ½ inch deep with a sharp knife and immediately place in the upper part of the hot oven. Bake 45 minutes, until dark brown and the hard crust responds with a hollow sound when tapped. Remove from the heat and cool on a rack.

Storing and Freezing: Do not wrap the bread. Cover the cut end with foil. To freeze, wrap in heavy-duty aluminum foil and seal in a plastic bag. Thaw in the wrapping, then unwrap.

PER ½-INCH SLICE:

Calories	80	Protein	3 G
Fat	.37 G	Carbohydrate	17 G
Sodium	147 MG	Cholesterol	0

WHOLE-WHEAT FOCACCIA WITH HERBS

MAKES 3 9- OR 10 INCH ROUND *FOCACCE* OR 2 10½- BY 15½-INCH RECTANGULAR *FOCACCE,* ABOUT 30 SERVINGS

Focacce are found all over Italy, under one name or another (*sardinaira* or *sardenara* in western Liguria, *schiacciata* in Florence, *pinze* in southern Italy). They are rustic, round or rectangular leavened breads, only about a half inch to an inch thick, with dimpled tops and a variety of seasonings. Sometimes they are merely sprinkled with coarse salt and olive oil, or they can be flavored with herbs like sage or rosemary or studded with olives, anchovies, or garlic. They are fragrant with olive oil even though there really isn't too much in the breads, and they are very easy to make. I often serve them, cut into small squares, with cocktails. These require a long rising time, so begin early in the day.

    2½ teaspoons (1 envelope) active dry yeast
    2½ cups lukewarm water
     2 tablespoons olive oil
     1 scant tablespoon salt
     3 tablespoons chopped fresh sage or rosemary
     4 cups whole-wheat flour
    2½ to 3½ cups unbleached white flour
        olive oil for brushing the surface

Dissolve the yeast in the water in a large bowl and let sit 10 minutes. Stir in the olive oil, salt, and sage or rosemary. Whisk in the whole-wheat flour, a cup at a time. Stir in the white flour, a cup at a time. As soon as the dough comes together, turn out onto a lightly floured surface and knead, adding flour as necessary, for 10 minutes, until the dough is smooth and elastic.

Oil your bowl, shape the dough into a ball, and place in the bowl, seam side up, then turn the dough so the oiled side is up. Cover loosely with plastic wrap and/or a damp towel and let rise in a draft-free spot for 1½ hours, until doubled.

Turn the dough out onto a lightly floured surface, knead for a minute, and cut into 3 pieces for round *focacce*, 2 pieces for rectangular. Oil pie plates or jelly roll pans and roll out the dough to fit the pans. Place in the pans, cover with damp towels, and let rise for 30 minutes.

Using your fingertips, dimple the surface of the dough all over. Cover again and let rise 2 hours.

Thirty minutes before baking, preheat the oven to 400 degrees, preferably with a baking stone or tiles, which will improve the texture of the bread. Brush the dough lightly with olive oil and place in the oven, on the baking stone or tiles. Bake 25 minutes, until the tops are golden brown. Spray with water three times during the first 10 minutes of baking. Remove from the heat and invert the *focacce* onto a rack so that the bottoms don't get soggy.

Eat warm or at room temperature, preferably the same day you bake them. Do not refrigerate. The *focacce* can be frozen but will dry out somewhat.

PER PORTION:

Calories	112	Protein	4 G
Fat	2 G	Carbohydrate	21 G
Sodium	199 MG	Cholesterol	0

FOCACCIA WITH SWEET RED PEPPERS

MAKES 2 RECTANGULAR *FOCACCE*, ABOUT 30 SERVINGS

These sweet-tasting *focacce*, studded with bright red peppers, are as pleasing to the eye as they are to the palate.

      2 large red peppers
    2½ teaspoons (1 envelope) active dry yeast
    2½ cups lukewarm water

2 tablespoons olive oil
1 scant tablespoon salt
1 teaspoon dried thyme
4 cups whole-wheat flour
2 to 3 cups unbleached white flour
   olive oil for brushing the surface

Roast the peppers over a gas burner or under the broiler until blackened on all sides. Remove from the heat and place in a plastic or paper bag until cool enough to handle. Remove the charred skins, cut in half, remove seeds and membranes, rinse, and pat dry. Chop the peppers into small dice and set aside.

Dissolve the yeast in the water in a large bowl and let sit 10 minutes. Stir in the olive oil, salt, and thyme. Whisk in the whole-wheat flour, a cup at a time. Stir in the white flour, a cup at a time. As soon as the dough comes together, turn out onto a floured surface. Sprinkle the diced roasted pepper over the dough and knead, adding flour as necessary, for 10 minutes, until the dough is smooth and elastic. Flour your hands and add flour to the board as necessary.

Oil your bowl, shape the dough into a ball, and place in the bowl, seam side up, then turn the dough so the oiled side is up. Cover loosely with plastic wrap and/or a damp towel and let rise in a draft-free spot for 1½ hours, until doubled.

Turn the dough out onto a lightly floured surface, knead for a minute, and cut into 3 pieces for round *focacce*, 2 pieces for rectangular. Oil pie plates or jelly roll pans and roll out the dough to fit the pans. Place in the pans, cover with damp towels, and let rise for 30 minutes.

Using your fingertips, dimple the surface of the dough all over. Cover again and let rise 2 hours.

Thirty minutes before baking, preheat the oven to 400 degrees, preferably with a baking stone or tiles, which will improve the bread's texture. Brush the dough lightly with olive oil and place in the oven directly on the stone or tiles. Bake 25 minutes, until the tops are golden brown. Spray with water three times during the first 10 minutes of baking. Remove from the heat and invert the *focacce* onto a rack so that the bottoms don't get soggy.

Eat warm or at room temperature, preferably the same day you bake them. Do not refrigerate. These can be frozen but will dry out somewhat in the process.

PER PORTION:

Calories	106	Protein	3 G
Fat	2 G	Carbohydrate	20 G
Sodium	199 MG	Cholesterol	0

WHOLE-WHEAT PITA BREAD

MAKES ABOUT 12 LOAVES

The number of loaves this recipe makes depends on the size you want the loaves to be. In one restaurant I went to in Cairo the breads, all very large, were baked in an outdoor woodburning oven, then placed over the hot dishes on their way to the table—like lids to keep the food warm. This was not only lovely to look at, but the arrangement had a clever purpose.

The pita breads in Egypt are dark and grainy for the most part, although at some restaurants they're made with white flour. They also contain quite a bit of olive oil, which makes them heavy; after a while I found them difficult to digest. The pitas I make aren't as heavy or tough as the traditional Egyptian pita.

There are two tricks to making pita. First, the oven must be very hot so that the bread puffs up. Second, the bread should not be left in the oven too long, or it will begin to get crisp and won't be flexible. There is, however, another Egyptian bread—*lavash*—that *is* crisp, and it's delicious. If you want to make *lavash*, just leave the pita in until it crisps, and once it's cool, break it into pieces.

> 2 tablespoons (2 envelopes plus 1 teaspoon) active dry yeast
> ¼ teaspoon mild-flavored honey (such as clovers or acacia)
> ½ cup plus 1½ cups lukewarm water
> 2 tablespoons safflower oil
> 1 scant tablespoon salt
> 3 cups whole-wheat flour
> 2 to 2½ cups unbleached white flour
> cornmeal for the baking sheet

Dissolve the yeast and honey in ½ cup of the lukewarm water in a large bowl and let sit for 10 minutes, until the mixture begins to bubble. Add the remaining water and mix well, then whisk in the oil and salt. Stir in the whole-wheat flour, a cup at a time. Fold in 1 cup of the white flour. Place the remaining cup on your board and turn out the dough. Knead for 10 to 15 minutes, adding flour as necessary to prevent sticking, until the dough is smooth and elastic, then shape into a ball and place in an oiled bowl, seam side up first, then turn seam side down. Cover with a damp towel or loosely with plastic wrap and allow to rise in a warm place for 1½ to 2 hours or until doubled in bulk.

Punch down the dough and turn it onto your board. Knead for a couple of minutes and allow to rest for 10 minutes. Then divide into 8 to 12 equal pieces and shape each piece into a ball. Place the balls on a floured surface, cover with a towel, and let rise for 30 minutes.

Using a well-floured rolling pin, flatten each ball and roll it out into a circle approximately ⅛ inch thick and 8 inches in diameter. Dust 2 unoiled baking sheets with cornmeal and place 2 circles on each sheet. (Leave the remaining ones on your lightly floured board.) Cover all the breads with a towel and let rise again for 30 minutes. Meanwhile, preheat the oven to 500 degrees.

Place one of the baking sheets on the rack in the middle of your oven and bake for 5 minutes without opening the oven door. Check the loaves, and if they are beginning to brown, remove from the oven. If they still smell yeasty and not like baking bread, leave for another 2 to 5 minutes. Bake the remaining pitas this way and cool on racks.

Storing and Freezing: Store or freeze in sealed plastic bags.

PER PORTION:

Calories	218	Protein	7 G
Fat	3 G	Carbohydrate	41 G
Sodium	497 MG	Cholesterol	0

CARTA DI MUSICA
(Sardinian Flat Bread)

MAKES 10 LARGE BREADS

I never dreamed it would be so easy to make *carta di musica*, the crunchy, paper-thin Sardinian flat bread that is such a treat that I always imagined one would need to be highly skilled to make it. Thanks to cook and writer Carlo Middione, I now know that I was wrong. This recipe, with slightly less salt, is from his book *The Food of Southern Italy*.

    2 cups unbleached white flour
    1 cup fine semolina (use 3 cups unbleached white flour
           in all if semolina isn't available)
    ¾ teaspoon salt
    1 to 1¼ cups lukewarm water

Mix together the flour, semolina, and salt in a bowl. Gradually add 1 cup water and stir into the flour with a wooden spoon. Add more water if necessary to form a smooth, easy-to-handle dough that isn't sticky or elastic. Gather the dough into a ball (dust with flour if it is sticky) and divide into 10 equal-sized pieces. Form small balls and set aside on a lightly dusted board or baking sheet, covered with plastic wrap and a towel, for 20 minutes.

Meanwhile, 20 minutes before baking, preheat the oven to 400 degrees, with baking sheets or baking stones in the oven.

Roll out each piece of dough on a lightly dusted work surface, dusting the top of the dough and the work surface as necessary to prevent sticking, to a very thin disk, less than 1/16 inch thick. Transfer to the hot baking sheet or stone and bake on the lowest rack of the oven for 2½ to 3 minutes, until beginning to blister. Turn the bread over and bake approximately 2½ minutes more. Watch carefully, as once the dough begins to burn it will burn very quickly. The flat breads should be paper-thin and crisp with brown bubbles. Cool on a rack and proceed in this way with all the breads.

Store in sealed plastic bags in a cool, dry place. They will keep for a couple of weeks. Serve topped with *salsa cruda* (page 57) or other dips.

PER ½-BREAD PORTION:

Calories	71	Protein	2 G
Fat	.19 G	Carbohydrate	15 G
Sodium	83 MG	Cholesterol	0

WHOLE-WHEAT SESAME BREADSTICKS

MAKES ABOUT 24 BREADSTICKS

I'm always coming home from Italy with bags of different kinds of breadsticks. In one bakery in Bologna I found whole-wheat *grissini*, sesame *grissini*, *grissini* with Parmesan, with spinach, with herbs, with dried mushrooms, with little bits of sausage, with anchovies, with spinach and basil, even with tomato. Don't worry, I won't be giving you all those recipes. Simple whole-wheat breadsticks studded with sesame seeds are special enough homemade items to have around, and how different they are from those characterless commercial breadsticks. It's amazing how easy it is to make these; they require only one rise, and shaping them takes no time at all.

2 teaspoons active dry yeast

1 ¼ cups lukewarm water

1 tablespoon malt syrup *or* 1 teaspoon honey

2 tablespoons olive oil, plus additional for brushing the
dough

1 ½ teaspoons salt

4 tablespoons sesame seed for the dough

1 cup unbleached white flour

2 ½ cups whole-wheat flour, as necessary (you may need a
few tablespoons more for kneading)

1 egg white, lightly beaten, for glaze

4 heaped tablespoons sesame seed for topping

Dissolve the yeast in the water in a large bowl, stir in the malt syrup or honey, and allow to sit 10 minutes, until the water is cloudy and the yeast is beginning to bubble.

Stir in the olive oil, salt, and sesame seeds. Stir in the white flour, then fold in the whole-wheat flour, a cup at a time. After the second cup you should be able to scrape the dough out onto a lightly floured kneading surface. Knead, adding additional whole-wheat flour as necessary, for about 10 minutes, until the dough is stiff and elastic.

Lightly flour a large cutting board. Using your hands or a rolling pin, press the dough into a rectangle on the board, about 14 inches long by 4 inches wide. Lightly oil the top and cover with plastic wrap and a kitchen towel. Place in a warm place to rise for 1 hour.

Preheat the oven to 400 degrees. Oil 3 baking sheets. Cut the dough crosswise into 4 equal-sized pieces. Brush each piece with beaten egg white and sprinkle each with 1 heaped tablespoon sesame seeds. Now cut these pieces crosswise into 6 short strips (they'll be like fat fingers).

There are two ways to shape the breadsticks. You can roll them between your hands and the board until they are as long as the width of your baking sheet, then twist them to get a pretty shape. Or you can take each strip and stretch it out, squeezing gently, to the width of your baking sheet. I wrap both hands around the pieces of dough and squeeze and pull from the center out, which goes very quickly. Lay the breadsticks about an inch apart on the baking sheets.

Bake 25 minutes, switching racks top to bottom and turning the breadsticks over halfway through the baking. When golden brown (they will probably be darker on one side), turn off the oven and leave the breadsticks in another 15 minutes. Remove from the oven and cool on racks. These will keep for several days in a breadbox and can be frozen for up to three months, sealed in plastic bags.

PARMESAN BREADSTICKS

Omit the sesame seeds for the dough. Add 2 ounces (½ cup) Parmesan, grated, toward the end of the kneading and work into the dough. Bake at 450 degrees for 12 to 15 minutes.

THYME BREADSTICKS

Omit all the sesame seeds. Add 1 tablespoon dried thyme, along with the salt and flour.

SPINACH AND GARLIC BREADSTICKS

Omit all the sesame seeds. Use 2 cups unbleached white flour and 1½ cups whole-wheat flour. Add 1 garlic clove, minced or put through a press, to the yeast/water mixture when you add the salt. Proceed as in master recipe, but at the end of kneading, knead in 2 ounces fresh spinach, washed, dried thoroughly, and very finely chopped (1 cup).

PER PORTION:

Calories	103	Protein	3 G
Fat	4 G	Carbohydrate	15 G
Sodium	140 MG	Cholesterol	0

SOCCA (Chick-pea Flour Pancake)

MAKES 6 SERVINGS

Socca is a *Niçoise* specialty, and I have a great weakness for it. It is a thick chick-pea flour pancake, almost like polenta in texture but finer. Whenever I go to Nice or Monte Carlo I make a point of going to the market expressly to eat *socca*, which is made on huge griddles over a wood fire or in a woodburning oven; greasy portions are scraped off the griddle and served in pieces of waxed paper. Once when I was in Nice and had spent most of the day eating specialties from the region, I went into a shop to buy some chick-pea flour so I could make my own *socca*, less greasy than the *Niçoise* version but very tasty. You can find chick-pea flour in natural food stores and Indian import stores.

⅔ cup chick-pea flour
¼ to ½ teaspoon salt (to taste)
1 cup cold water
2 tablespoons olive oil
freshly ground pepper

Thirty minutes before baking, preheat the oven, lined with a baking stone or tiles if possible, to 475 degrees. Brush a 14-inch nonstick cake pan, pizza pan, tart pan, or heavy baking dish all over with 1 tablespoon of the olive oil. (A heavy iron or copper tart pan is best. I usually use a Le Creuset enameled cast-iron *gratin* dish.)

Beat together the flour, salt, and water until there are no lumps; this can be done in a blender at high speed. Add freshly ground pepper to taste. Let sit 30 minutes.

Heat the oiled baking pan in the preheated oven for about 10 to 15 minutes, until good and hot, then pour in the batter. It should be about ¼ inch thick. Drizzle the remaining oil over the top of the batter. Set in the upper third of the oven and bake for about 5 minutes, until set. Then place the pan under the broiler and brown for 3 to 4 minutes, turning the pan several times. Remove from the heat and scrape out servings with a spatula. Don't worry if it sticks to the pan; it does in Nice too.

SOCCA WITH GARLIC

Add 1 or 2 garlic cloves, minced or put through a press, to the batter.

SOCCA WITH HERBS

Add 1 or 2 teaspoons chopped fresh thyme, sage, or rosemary (or ½ to 1 teaspoon dried) to the batter, along with 1 or 2 garlic cloves, minced or put through a press, if desired.

PER PORTION:

Calories	89	Protein	3 G
Fat	5 G	Carbohydrate	8 G
Sodium	142 MG	Cholesterol	0

BASQUE CORN MUFFINS

MAKES 8 LARGE OR 12 TO 16 SMALLER MUFFINS

These simple grainy breads are somewhat like English muffins and make a marvelous breakfast bread or accompaniment to soups. They will dry out after a day or two, but they freeze well—anyway, they're so good you probably won't have them on your hands too long.

2½ teaspoons (1 envelope) active dry yeast
1½ cups lukewarm water
   1 tablespoon mild-flavored honey (such as clover or acacia)
1½ teaspoons salt
   1 cup whole-wheat flour
   1 cup unbleached white flour, plus additional for kneading
   2 cups yellow stone-ground cornmeal

Dissolve the yeast in the water and add the honey. Let sit 10 minutes. Stir in the salt and the flour. Fold in the cornmeal and scrape out onto a floured work surface. Knead for about 10 minutes, adding only enough flour as necessary to prevent sticking.

Shape the dough into a ball and place in an oiled bowl, seam side up, then turn the dough so the oiled side is up. Cover with plastic wrap and set in a warm spot to rise until doubled in volume, about 1 hour.

Turn the dough out onto a lightly floured surface, knead for a few minutes, and divide into 8, 12, or 16 pieces. Press out each piece with the palm of your hand and roll out ½ inch thick. Place on a baking sheet that has been dusted with cornmeal. Cover with a kitchen towel or parchment paper and allow to rise in a warm spot for 50 minutes.

Thirty minutes before baking, preheat the oven to 450 degrees. Bake in the middle (or, if you're using 2 baking sheets, middle and bottom shelves) of the oven for 20 minutes, switching the baking sheets halfway through the baking. Remove from the heat and cool on a rack.

Storing and Freezing: Store in sealed plastic bags. Freeze in sealed plastic bags for up to 3 months.

PER SMALL MUFFIN:

Calories	133	Protein	4 G
Fat	.54 G	Carbohydrate	29 G
Sodium	207 MG	Cholesterol	0

BASQUE PUMPKIN AND CORN BREAD

MAKES 10 SERVINGS

Pumpkin found its way back to the Basque country and into this bread from the New World just as it found its way into many French, Italian, and Spanish dishes. I have modified the authentic recipe so that it's not quite as dense and heavy. It's reminiscent of American corn bread, slightly sweet, with the addition of the tasty pumpkin.

- 1 cup pureed pumpkin
- 1 cup skimmed milk *or* ½ cup skimmed milk and ½ cup plain low-fat yogurt
- 1 tablespoon safflower oil
- 1½ tablespoons mild-flavored honey (such as clover or acacia)
- 2 eggs
- 1½ cups yellow stone-ground cornmeal
- ½ cup whole-wheat pastry flour
- 1 tablespoon baking powder
- ½ teaspoon baking soda
- ½ teaspoon salt

Preheat the oven to 400 degrees.

Blend together the pumpkin, milk, safflower oil, and honey. Beat in the eggs.

Sift together the cornmeal, pastry flour, baking powder, baking soda, and salt. Mix into the liquid ingredients and blend well but don't overwork.

Oil or butter a 1-quart baking dish (square, oval, or rectangular) and heat for 5 minutes in the oven. Scrape in the batter and place in the oven. Bake for 35 to 40 minutes or until a tester comes out clean. Remove from the oven and allow to cool for at least 20 minutes in the pan before serving.

Storing: Cover the baking dish with foil, or store cut pieces in plastic bags. This bread does not freeze well.

PER PORTION:

Calories	155	Protein	5 G
Fat	3 G	Carbohydrate	28 G
Sodium	306 MG	Cholesterol	55 MG

TURKISH CORN BREAD

MAKES 12 SERVINGS

This is slightly heavier than our American corn bread, with the distinct flavor of olive oil. It's very nice as an accompaniment to soups and bean dishes.

- ½ cup whole-wheat flour
- 2 teaspoons baking powder
- 1 teaspoon sugar
- ½ teaspoon salt
- 1 cup stone-ground yellow cornmeal
- 1½ cups plain low-fat yogurt
- 2 eggs
- 2 tablespoons olive oil

Preheat the oven to 425 degrees. Oil an 8″ × 4″ loaf bread pan or an 8″ × 8″ round cake pan.

Sift together the flour, baking powder, sugar, salt, and cornmeal.

Beat together the yogurt, eggs, and olive oil. Stir in the dry ingredients and mix well but don't overwork.

Pour into the oiled pan and bake for 30 minutes, until the top is golden and the bread firm. Cool in the pan for 5 minutes, then transfer to a wire rack to cool another 15 minutes or more before slicing (for a loaf) or cutting into squares or wedges if baked in a cake pan.

Storing: Cover the pan with foil, or keep leftover pieces in plastic bags. This bread does not freeze well.

PER PORTION:

Calories	111	Protein	4 G
Fat	4 G	Carbohydrate	15 G
Sodium	194 MG	Cholesterol	47 MG

CHAPTER TWO

SALADS
AND
STARTERS

Italy

France

Spain

Greece

The Middle East

North Africa

When I told people I was going to Egypt to explore the cuisine for this book, they looked puzzled and insisted that I was going to the wrong place. When friends come home from their vacations in Greece and tell me that the cuisine there is a big bore, I look just as puzzled. I could have spent weeks in both of these countries and lived happily on their wonderful salads and starters. My palate would never have tired.

What I saw and ate in Egypt was representative of many of the other Middle Eastern countries. One night, when I was cruising up the Nile, I counted—and tasted—15 vegetable salads that were part of a beautiful ship-board buffet. They were cooked vegetable salads like the black-eyed peas salad on page 98 or the cauliflower and potato salad on page 113, raw vegetable salads like the spicy tomato salad on page 100 and the *fattoush* on page 88, cucumber salads, yogurt salads, hummus and eggplant purees to be eaten with pita bread. These are some of my favorite *mezze*, the colorful hors d'oeuvres that are eaten with drinks and are part of every meal in the Middle East, and I was often happy to make an entire meal of them.

Likewise in Greece, my dinners usually consisted of an assortment of salads. I never tired of *tzatziki*, the garlicky mixture of cucumbers and yogurt, or the Greek eggplant salads. When I was hungry for something more substantial, the purees and salads made with beans were always satisfying. After two weeks of eating this kind of food on a tiny island called Simi, not far from Turkey, I came home and went right to work in my kitchen, duplicating the dishes I'd left behind. I had felt terrific the entire time I was on Simi, and I wanted to continue to eat light, garlicky food.

It's not surprising that this chapter contains more recipes than any of the other chapters in the book. Every country around the Mediterranean has its own style of salads and hors d'oeuvres, and they are the perfect choice for the dieter, with hardly any calories in the vegetables and a minimum of oil in the dressings. Minimal oil doesn't mean minimal flavor, however; Mediterranean dressings are distinctive and zesty and offer a wide choice of tastes. The French vinaigrette, for example, is mustardy, with vinegar and lemon juice as well as fruity olive oil, whereas Italians dress their salads with nothing more than oil and vinegar. The Moroccans like sweet, subtle spices and orange flower water, and Tunisians like to fire up their zesty, lemony vegetable salads and unique purees (called *ajloukes*) with hot red pepper sauce (*harissa*) and to season them with pungent spices like caraway, coriander, and cumin.

The Spanish version of the *mezze* is the *tapa*. Tasty morsels served in bars to tide people over until the late Spanish dinners, tapas sit in puddles of oil in Spain, but not here. The mushrooms on pages 80 and 81, the *tortilla Española* on page 79, and the marinated eggplant on page 61 are all *tapas*, perfect as hors d'oeuvres or a first course.

And the Italians? My favorite Italian *antipasti* are *bruschette* (page 52) and *crostini* (page 53), grilled or toasted bread rubbed with garlic and covered with any number of savory toppings—sautéed peppers or *porcini* mushrooms, tomato sauce, or simply a rub of garlic and tomato.

Whether served as hors d'oeuvres with drinks or as first courses, these salads and starters can be enjoyed alone or in combination. I love to make colorful combination plates for my dinner parties. Try some of the combinations on pages 373–379 in the menu section of this book. In this section, recipes are organized by country of origin, which is the key to combining them.

RECIPES FROM ITALY

BRUSCHETTE

MAKES 12 BRUSCHETTE

Bruschette are the original garlic bread, grilled slices of crusty bread rubbed with garlic and usually drenched in good virgin olive oil. They are one of Italy's simplest feasts. I was at the home of friends in Florence the first time I tasted real *bruschette*. My host said, "Do you know that one of the best dishes Italy has to offer is grilled bread?" And with that he cut thick slices of hearty Tuscan bread, toasted them under the broiler until they were just beginning to brown, rubbed them with garlic, and drizzled on thick green olive oil. I agreed with him instantly.

Here, of course, the oil is just brushed on lightly, but I still call this *bruschette*. The tomato provides enough moisture to saturate the bread.

All of the suggested toppings and variations for *crostini* on the following pages can be used for *bruschette* too.

> **several slices coarse bread, such as Crusty Country Bread**
> **on page 35, cut into 1-inch slices**
> 2 **garlic cloves, cut into 1-inch slices**
> 2 **tablespoons olive oil (optional)**
> 1 **or 2 tomatoes (to taste), cut in half**

Grill the bread over a fire or under a broiler just until beginning to brown around the edges. It should remain soft inside.

Remove from the heat and rub while still hot with a cut clove of garlic. Brush with olive oil and rub with the cut side of the tomato, squeezing a little juice of the tomato onto the bread.

PER 1-INCH PORTION:

Calories	204	Protein	6 G
Fat	5 G	Carbohydrate	35 G
Sodium	297 MG	Cholesterol	0

CROSTINI

MAKES 12 CROSTINI

Crostini differ from *bruschette* in that they are thinner and thus a little more delicate, and they're toasted in a 350-degree oven and can be cooled and held for several hours. This makes them very convenient for entertaining. They can be served with any number of toppings. Omit tomato if using as toasted croutons for soups.

The ingredients are the same as for *bruschette*, but cut the bread only ½ inch thick.

Preheat the oven to 350 degrees. Toast the bread until it begins to color, 10 to 20 minutes. Like *bruschette*, it shouldn't be crisp all the way through. Remove from the heat, rub with garlic, and brush with olive oil. If you're serving them later, cover lightly with foil or transfer to a paper bag. Do not rub with the tomato until just before you top and serve. Some topping suggestions are listed below; also see the variations that follow.

TOPPINGS FOR CROSTINI OR BRUSCHETTE

> *Caponata* (page 58)
> *Salsa Cruda* (page 57)
> Tomato Topping for *Bruschette* (page 56)
> *Hummus* (page 92)
> Eggplant Puree (page 93)

PER ½-INCH PORTION:

Calories	102	Protein	3 G
Fat	3 G	Carbohydrate	17 G
Sodium	148 MG	Cholesterol	0

CROSTINI OR BRUSCHETTE WITH SWEET RED PEPPERS

MAKES 6 SERVINGS

This is a less oily version of a marvelous dish I had at the Villa Cheta in Acquafredda. In Italy the *crostini*, made with delicious country bread, were piled high with red and yellow peppers, sautéed in olive oil with garlic. I sauté the peppers in a small amount of oil in a nonstick skillet, and just when they begin to stick I add a tablespoonful of red wine vinegar. This addition brings out their sweetness all the more. The peppers are exquisite; they retain their texture, and the longer they sit, the sweeter they taste.

Both the pepper topping and the *crostini* can be made several hours before serving. Reheat the peppers gently before topping the *crostini*.

    3 large red peppers or a combination of red and yellow
          peppers, cut in half lengthwise, seeded, and
          sliced into thin lengthwise strips
    1 tablespoon olive oil
    2 large garlic cloves
       salt and freshly ground pepper
    1 tablespoon red wine vinegar
   12 to 18 *crostini* (page 53) or *bruschette* (page 52)

Heat the olive oil in a nonstick skillet over medium-high heat and add the peppers. Sauté, stirring, for a few minutes and add the garlic and salt and pepper to taste. Continue to sauté over medium-high heat, stirring, for about 10 minutes, until the peppers are softened and quite aromatic but not yet beginning to brown. Add the vinegar and sauté another 5 minutes. Remove from the heat, adjust seasonings, and set aside.

Just before serving, rub the *crostini* with the cut tomato and top with the peppers. Serve 2 to 3 per person as an hors d'oeuvre.

PER PORTION:

Calories	239	Protein	6 G
Fat	8 G	Carbohydrate	38 G
Sodium	298 MG	Cholesterol	0

CROSTINI OR BRUSCHETTE WITH PORCINI MUSHROOMS

MAKES 6 SERVINGS

A classic *crostini* topping is an intense minced chicken liver spread. This "meaty" topping for *crostini* looks similar; the savory mushroom topping is earthy and substantial. Both the mushroom topping and the *crostini* can be made hours ahead of serving time. Reheat the topping gently before topping the *crostini*.

   2 ounces dried *porcini* mushrooms or *cèpes*
   1 quart warm water
   1 tablespoon olive oil
   4 garlic cloves, minced or put through a press
   4 tablespoons white wine
  ¼ teaspoon dried thyme (more to taste)
  ¼ teaspoon crumbled dried rosemary (more to taste) *or*
        ½ teaspoon chopped fresh
     salt and freshly ground pepper
   4 tablespoons chopped fresh parsley
   4 tablespoons fresh lemon juice (more to taste)
 12 to 18 *crostini* (page 53) or *bruschette*
     (page 52)

Soak the mushrooms in the warm water for 30 minutes. Lift the mushrooms from the soaking water and gently squeeze over the soaking liquid. Place in a bowl and rinse thoroughly in several changes of water. Squeeze dry again and chop coarsely. Strain the soaking water through a strainer lined with kitchen towels and reserve.

Heat the olive oil over medium heat in a large heavy-bottomed skillet and add the garlic. Sauté, stirring, until it begins to turn golden, in a couple of minutes, and add the mushrooms. Sauté, stirring, for another minute or two and add the white wine. Sauté, stirring, until the wine has just about evaporated, and add the soaking liquid from the mushrooms, the thyme, rosemary, and salt and freshly ground pepper to taste. Increase the heat to high and continue to cook, stirring, until most of the liquid has evaporated and the mushrooms are glazed. Stir in 3 tablespoons of the parsley and the lemon juice and remove from the heat. Top the *crostini* with the mushrooms, sprinkle with the remaining parsley, and serve.

PER PORTION:

Calories	258	Protein	7 G
Fat	8 G	Carbohydrate	43 G
Sodium	302 MG	Cholesterol	0

BRUSCHETTE OR CROSTINI
WITH TOMATO TOPPING

MAKES 4 SERVINGS

I ate this luscious dish in a restaurant in Palermo. The savory, garlicky tomatoes seep into the toasted garlic bread, and as simple as the *bruschette* are, they taste very rich. The dish makes a marvelous first course.

> 2 teaspoons olive oil
> 3 garlic cloves, minced or put through a press
> 1 ½ pounds very ripe tomatoes, peeled and coarsely chopped
> salt and freshly ground pepper
> 2 tablespoons chopped fresh basil
> 8 to 12 *bruschette* (page 52) or *crostini* (page 53)

First make the tomato topping. Heat the oil over low heat and sauté the garlic in it for 1 minute. Add the tomatoes, increase the heat to medium-high, and cook for 15 minutes, stirring and crushing the tomatoes with the back of a wooden spoon. Add salt and pepper to taste and the basil, cook another minute, and remove from the heat. Adjust seasonings.

Top the *bruschette* with the tomatoes and serve.

PER PORTION:

Calories	668	Protein	20 G
Fat	18 G	Carbohydrate	112 G
Sodium	903 MG	Cholesterol	0

CARTA DI MUSICA WITH SALSA CRUDA

MAKES 6 SERVINGS

Carta di musica is crisp, thin bread made in Sardinia. It is kind of like a crisp Indian *pappadum* in texture. You can get *carta di musica* in imported-food stores or make it at home (see recipe, page 41). You can also substitute *pappadums*. This is a simple, satisfying first course that was served to me in a Sardinian restaurant in Rome.

8 rounds homemade *carta di musica* (page 41) *or* 1 or 2
      whole large sheets of imported *carta di musica*
      or about 10 plain *pappadums,* crisped in a dry
      skillet or in the oven
1 recipe *salsa cruda* (recipe follows)

Break the *carta di musica* into large pieces. Top the crisp bread with the tomato sauce and serve.

PER PORTION:

Calories	179	Protein	8 G
Fat	2 G	Carbohydrate	41 G
Sodium	69 MG	Cholesterol	0

SALSA CRUDA

This light, vibrant uncooked tomato sauce makes a lively and refreshing topping for *crostini* as well as the Sardinian flat bread called *carta di musica* (see following recipe), both of which make wonderful starters. It can also be used as a topping for an entree of steamed or poached fish. Make it in the spring and summer, when tomatoes are sweet and ripe and fresh basil is plentiful.

2 pounds firm, ripe red tomatoes, peeled, seeded, and
      chopped
2 to 3 garlic cloves (to taste), minced or put through a
      press
4 tablespoons chopped fresh basil
1 to 2 teaspoons balsamic vinegar (to taste; optional)
      salt and freshly ground pepper
1 or 2 small hot chili peppers (to taste), minced (optional)

Mix together all the ingredients. Let stand at room temperature or refrigerate. It will hold for several hours.

PER RECIPE:

Calories	81	Protein	2 G
Fat	.19 G	Carbohydrate	17 G
Sodium	.89 MG	Cholesterol	0

CAPONATA

MAKES 6 SERVINGS

This is a kind of *ratatouille*, with eggplant, onions, peppers, garlic, tomatoes, and capers. Unlike *ratatouille*, though, it is seasoned with vinegar and is sweetened slightly (not enough to add significant calories). It's very easy; all you have to do is throw everything in a baking dish and put the baking dish in the oven. It keeps well, and it's great to have on hand all through the summer.

2 medium-sized eggplants, peeled and diced into 1-inch
  cubes
salt
4 ripe fresh tomatoes *or* 8 canned Italian plum tomatoes,
  peeled, seeded, and chopped
pinch of salt
2 large red peppers, seeded and cut into 1-inch pieces
2 medium-sized zucchini, washed and sliced ¼ inch thick
2 medium-sized onions, very thinly sliced
4 garlic cloves, peeled and coarsely chopped
2 heaped tablespoons capers, rinsed
1 bay leaf
½ teaspoon fresh thyme leaves
salt and freshly ground black pepper
¼ cup white wine, sherry, or cider vinegar
1½ teaspoons sugar
1 tablespoon olive oil
chopped fresh parsley or basil (or both) for garnish

Place the eggplant in a colander and sprinkle generously with salt. Put a plate on top of the eggplant and a weight (such as a pan of water) over the plate. Let sit for 1 hour while you prepare the other ingredients.

Heat the tomatoes with a pinch of salt in a heavy-bottomed skillet or saucepan. Simmer over low heat for 15 minutes. Mash with the back of a wooden spoon.

Preheat the oven to 350 degrees. Oil a large roasting pan or ceramic oven casserole, large enough to accommodate all the vegetables.

Rinse the eggplant thoroughly and pat dry with kitchen towels. Toss together in the casserole with all the other vegetables, the garlic, capers, bay leaf, and thyme. Sprinkle with salt and pepper to taste.

Heat the vinegar and sugar together in a saucepan just until the sugar melts. Toss with the vegetables. Add the olive oil and toss again.

Cover the baking dish tightly with foil and place in the oven. Bake 1½ to 2 hours, turning the vegetables every 30 minutes. When they are cooked through and fragrant, the *caponata* is done. Remove from the heat and allow to cool. Transfer to an attractive serving dish, cover, and refrigerate over-night. Serve at room temperature, garnished with parsley or basil (or both).

Note: This could also be prepared in a *römertopf,* using the same instructions as for *ratatouille* (page 66).

PER PORTION:

Calories	118	Protein	4 G
Fat	3 G	Carbohydrate	23 G
Sodium	274 MG	Cholesterol	0

ITALIAN BREAD SALAD

MAKES 6 SERVINGS

This is one of the most delicious ways to use up stale bread. It is just one of several Mediterranean bread salads (see *fattoush,* page 88).

1 pound stale whole-wheat or French bread
1 small red onion
1 pound (4 or 5 medium) tomatoes, chopped
2 tablespoons chopped fresh basil
2 tablespoons chopped fresh parsley
4 to 5 tablespoons red wine vinegar (to taste)
1 large garlic clove, minced or put through a press
  salt and freshly ground pepper
3 tablespoons olive oil
2 tablespoons plain low-fat yogurt

Place the bread in a bowl and cover with cold water. Peel the onion, cut in half, and place over the bread. Soak 20 minutes. Drain and squeeze all the water out of the bread. Don't worry if the bread crumbles (whole-wheat bread usually does).

Slice the onion very thin and toss with the bread, tomatoes, basil, and parsley.

Mix together the vinegar, garlic, and salt and pepper to taste and whisk in the oil and yogurt. Toss with the bread, cover, and refrigerate at least 2 hours before serving.

Note: If you are using bread that isn't really stale and hard, only moisten with water and squeeze; omit the soaking step.

PER PORTION:

Calories	267	Protein	9 G
Fat	9 G	Carbohydrate	41 G
Sodium	409 MG	Cholesterol	3 MG

ITALIAN BEAN AND TUNA SALAD

MAKES 4 SERVINGS

This is a great salad for those nights when you come home from work and there's hardly any food in the house. That was exactly the case the first time I ate the combination, when I was visiting a friend in Bologna. He pulled out a can of beans, a can of tuna, an onion, some garlic and basil, sprinkled it all with vinegar, lemon, and olive oil, and we had a feast. You can use canned beans for this salad or cook them yourself. I have also used Italian *borlotti* beans, which are the same as our cranberry beans, and had great results. Use whatever fresh herbs you have on hand—parsley, sage, basil, or a combination.

- 1 red onion, very thinly sliced
- 3 to 4 tablespoons red wine vinegar (to taste)
- 2 cups cooked white beans or cranberry beans
- 1 6½-ounce can water-packed tuna, drained
- 2 tomatoes, diced
- 1 garlic clove, minced or put through a press
  juice of 1 lemon
- 3 to 4 tablespoons chopped fresh basil or parsley
- 1 teaspoon chopped fresh sage
- 2 tablespoons olive oil
- 1 tablespoon plain low-fat yogurt
- 1 tablespoon capers, rinsed
  salt and freshly ground pepper
- 2 tomatoes, cut into wedges, for garnish
  romaine lettuce (optional)

Toss the onion with 2 tablespoons of the vinegar and add water to cover. Let soak 30 minutes and drain.

Toss together the remaining ingredients (including the remaining vinegar) except the tomato wedges and the romaine. Line a bowl or platter with the lettuce leaves, top with the salad, and garnish with the tomatoes. Serve immediately or chill.

WINTER ITALIAN BEAN AND TUNA SALAD

My husband loves this salad so much that I once gave him a Christmas stocking full of cans of tuna and beans, garlic, and onions so he could make it himself. For the simpler winter version, omit the tomatoes, fresh herbs, and capers and proceed with the master recipe.

PER PORTION:

Calories	266	Protein	22 G
Fat	8 G	Carbohydrate	29 G
Sodium	215 MG	Cholesterol	17 MG

MARINATED EGGPLANT

MAKES 6 SERVINGS

Steaming eggplant makes it tender and very absorbent, a perfect consistency for this pungent marinade. In a traditional Italian recipe the eggplant would probably be fried. This tangy version is very light in comparison.

    2 pounds (about 3 medium) eggplant, preferably the
        long thin Japanese ones
      salt
    3 to 4 garlic cloves (to taste)
    5 tablespoons red wine vinegar
    1 tablespoon olive oil
    ½ cup coarsely chopped fresh basil
      salt and freshly ground pepper

Slice the eggplant about ¼ inch thick and place in a colander. Sprinkle with salt and let sit 30 minutes. Rinse and pat dry.

Steam the eggplant in a steaming apparatus for 20 minutes or until tender. It will not necessarily be translucent, as it is when sautéed. Remove from the heat.

Mix together the garlic, vinegar, and olive oil. Toss the eggplant slices with the garlic mixture and layer in a serving dish, topping each layer with basil, salt if necessary, and freshly ground pepper to taste. Refrigerate until shortly before serving.

This will keep for several days in the refrigerator. Serve as a first course over lettuce leaves, with tomatoes on the side, or add to salads.

PER PORTION:

Calories	60	Protein	2 G
Fat	2 G	Carbohydrate	10 G
Sodium	96 MG	Cholesterol	0

BROILED ZUCCHINI WITH LEMON, BASIL, AND HOT PEPPER

MAKES 6 SERVINGS

I had this delightful dish at a terrific Sardinian restaurant in Rome called Il Drappo, where all the appetizers were astonishing. Simple and imaginative, they had flavors that surprised my palate but were easy to understand. The zucchini was probably fried, but grilling it under a broiler is even easier and requires much less oil.

    1 pound (4 medium or 3 large) zucchini
      salt
    1 tablespoon olive oil
    ½ teaspoon hot pepper flakes
      salt and freshly ground pepper
      juice of 1 large lemon
    1 tablespoon slivered fresh basil leaves (about 12 large
        leaves)

Slice the zucchini on the diagonal so that you have longish oval slices about ¼ inch thick. Salt and place in a colander and let sit 30 minutes. Rinse and pat dry.

Preheat the broiler and place the zucchini on an oiled baking sheet. Brush with the olive oil. Grill about 10 inches from the heat source for 7 to 12 minutes, until still bright green around the edges and just barely beginning to brown on top.

Remove from the heat and transfer to a serving dish. Sprinkle with the hot pepper flakes and salt and pepper to taste. Chill until shortly before serving. Just before serving, toss with the lemon juice and sprinkle on the basil.

PER PORTION:

Calories	33	Protein	1 G
Fat	2 G	Carbohydrate	3 G
Sodium	2 MG	Cholesterol	0

TOMATOES STUFFED WITH TUNA

MAKES 4 SERVINGS

The idea for these tomatoes comes from Tunisian and Italian recipes, which usually combine tuna with rice, lentils, or white beans. I decided to make a cold dish, with tuna alone.

- 8 firm but ripe medium-sized tomatoes
- 1 9-ounce can water-packed tuna, drained
- 1 small shallot, minced
- ¼ cup plain low-fat yogurt
- 1 teaspoon Dijon mustard
  juice of ½ to 1 lemon (to taste)
- 1 garlic clove, minced or put through a press
- 1 small bunch parsley, finely chopped
- 8 fresh mint leaves, finely chopped
- ¼ to ½ teaspoon ground cumin (to taste)
  salt and freshly ground pepper
  fresh mint leaves for garnish

Cut the tops off the tomatoes about ½ inch down from the stem. Carefully scoop out the pulp. Discard the seeds and chop the pulp.

Break up the tuna in a bowl and mix it with the tomato pulp, shallot, yogurt, mustard, lemon juice, garlic, parsley, mint, cumin, and salt and pepper to taste.

Fill the tomato halves with the tuna mixture and arrange on a platter. Garnish with fresh mint leaves and serve.

PER PORTION:

Calories	155	Protein	22 G
Fat	1 G	Carbohydrate	15 G
Sodium	304 MG	Cholesterol	27 MG

ZUCCHINI MARINATA

MAKES 4 SERVINGS

In this recipe the zucchini is uncooked but acquires an *al dente*, almost cooked texture as it marinates throughout the day in lemon juice. A simple and delightful dish.

1 pound (4 medium or 3 large) zucchini, sliced
    paper-thin or grated
  juice of 1 large lemon (more to taste)
2 garlic cloves, crushed and cut in half
1 tablespoon olive oil
  salt and freshly ground pepper
2 to 3 tablespoons chopped fresh parsley or basil

Toss the zucchini with the lemon juice, garlic, olive oil, and salt and pepper to taste. Cover and refrigerate for 4 to 8 hours, stirring occasionally. Toss with the herbs just before serving. Remove the garlic, and if you wish, squeeze half of one of the cloves into the mixture and toss. Correct seasonings and serve. Once tossed with the herbs, the zucchini should be served. It will keep for a couple of days if necessary, but loses its vibrant color and fresh lemony taste.

PER PORTION:

Calories	52	Protein	1 G
Fat	4 G	Carbohydrate	5 G
Sodium	5 MG	Cholesterol	0

GRILLED SARDINES WITH LEMON

MAKES 4 SERVINGS AS A STARTER

This dish is very simple and can be prepared hours ahead of time. The sardines can be either grilled or broiled. It helps to have a hinged grilling rack so that you can turn the fish all at once by flipping the rack (but make sure you squeeze the handle tightly when you do this so none of the sardines slide out).

Fresh sardines are not very easy to come by in the United States, but other small, oily-fleshed fish such as herring, shad, and smelts can be substituted.

12 to 16 fresh sardines (about 1½ pounds) or fresh
        herring, shad, or smelts
    salt and freshly ground pepper
 1 tablespoon olive oil
 2 garlic cloves, finely chopped
    juice of 2 lemons
12 fresh mint leaves, cut into thin slivers

Clean the sardines by cutting a small incision along the belly and scooping out the insides with your finger. Rinse the fish thoroughly under cold water and drain. Pat dry with paper towels and lay on a plate or baking dish.

Sprinkle the fish with salt and pepper to taste and toss with the olive oil. Let sit for 15 minutes, turning the fish once.

Preheat the broiler or prepare a grill. Place the sardines in one layer on a grill or broiler rack above a pan. Grill or broil the sardines, placing them no more than 3 inches from the heat source, for 2 minutes. Turn and continue to grill for 2 more minutes. They should flake easily when done.

Remove the sardines from the heat and allow to cool. When cool enough to handle, gently remove the skins. Lay on a serving dish and add a little more salt and pepper. Sprinkle with the garlic and juice of 1 lemon and let marinate for 1 hour or longer (covered in the refrigerator if not serving within an hour). If you have refrigerated the sardines, allow them to come to room temperature before serving. Just before serving, sprinkle with the remaining lemon juice and the mint. Divide the sardines equally among plates and serve.

PER PORTION:

Calories	153	Protein	11 G
Fat	11 G	Carbohydrate	2 G
Sodium	51 MG	Cholesterol	40 MG

RECIPES FROM FRANCE

RATATOUILLE

MAKES 6 SERVINGS

Even though I've included recipes for this heady *Provençal* vegetable stew in other books, a Mediterranean cookbook, diet or otherwise, would not be complete without it. *Ratatouille* is great served hot or cold and should be made the day before you serve it to allow flavors to ripen.

 Ratatouille is best made in spring, summer, and early fall, when fresh basil, ripe tomatoes, and tender zucchini are in season. I must admit, however, that I often make tasty *ratatouille* out of season using canned tomatoes and substituting 1 to 2 teaspoons dried basil for the fresh. I add the dried basil along with the other dried herbs in the recipe.

> 1 pound (1 large or 2 small) eggplant, cut in half lengthwise
> 2 tablespoons olive oil
> 1 pound (3) medium-sized onions, sliced
> 6 garlic cloves, peeled and chopped
> ½ pound (1½) red peppers, seeded, cut in half
>   crosswise, then cut into wide strips
> ½ pound (1½) green peppers, seeded, cut in half
>   crosswise, then cut into wide strips
> 1 pound (4 to 5) ripe tomatoes, peeled, seeded, and cut
>   into wedges, or drained canned tomatoes
> salt and freshly ground pepper
> 1 bay leaf
> 1 teaspoon dried oregano or a mixture of dried thyme
>   and dried oregano
> 1 pound zucchini, thickly sliced
> 2 additional tomatoes, peeled and coarsely chopped
> 3 tablespoons chopped fresh basil *or* 1 to 2 teaspoons
>   dried (to taste)
> pinch cayenne pepper (optional)
> chopped fresh parsley for garnish

 Preheat the oven to 450 degrees. Oil a baking sheet. Score the eggplant down the center of the cut sides, being careful not to cut through the skin.

Place cut side down on the baking sheet. Bake in the oven 15 minutes, until the skin begins to shrivel. Remove from the heat, allow to cool, and dice.

Heat half the oil in a very large heavy-bottomed casserole and sauté the onion with half the garlic over medium-low heat until the onions are softened and translucent. Add the remaining oil, the peppers, and the eggplant, and continue to cook over medium-low heat for about 10 minutes, stirring with a wooden spoon. Add 1 pound tomatoes, the remaining garlic, salt and pepper to taste, bay leaf, and dried herbs. Continue to cook over low heat, stirring the vegetables gently, until they are almost submerged in their own liquid. Raise the heat to high and bring these juices to a boil, stirring, then immediately lower the heat, cover partially, and simmer 1 hour over a low flame, stirring occasionally. Add zucchini, 2 tomatoes, and basil and continue to simmer 20 to 30 minutes or until the zucchini is tender but still bright green.

Place a colander over a bowl and drain the *ratatouille*. Allow to drain 10 minutes, then return to the casserole. Place the liquid in a saucepan and reduce over high heat, stirring often, until syrupy. Pour back over the vegetables, stir, and simmer together for a few minutes. Taste and adjust salt, pepper, and garlic. If you wish, add a small pinch of cayenne. If serving cold, transfer to a nonmetallic bowl and allow to cool. Cover and refrigerate overnight. If serving the *ratatouille* hot, bring back to a simmer over low heat. Serve, topping each helping with chopped fresh parsley.

RATATOUILLE BAKED IN A RÖMERTOPF

This technique is much simpler, and the resulting *ratatouille* is incredibly fragrant. First, put the *römertopf* (a covered clay pot) to soak in water to cover for at least 15 minutes. Use the same ingredients as in the master recipe. Bake the eggplant at 450 degrees, as directed, until shriveled and softened. Allow to cool, remove and discard the skins, and dice the flesh.

Sauté the onions and half the garlic in 1 tablespoon of olive oil over medium heat for about 10 minutes, stirring, and transfer to the *römertopf*.

Sauté the peppers for about 5 to 10 minutes, until wilted, and transfer to the *römertopf*.

Heat the second tablespoon of oil and sauté the zucchini for about 5 minutes, just until it begins to color. Transfer to the *römertopf*.

Now add the eggplant and all the remaining ingredients except the last 2 tomatoes and the fresh basil to the *römertopf*. Stir together, add salt and freshly ground pepper to taste, cover, and place in the oven. Turn on the heat gradually, first to 250 degrees and after 10 minutes to 300 degrees for 5 minutes, then to 325 degrees for 5 minutes, then to 350 degrees for 5 minutes, and finally to 375 degrees. Bake for 45 minutes, stirring from time to time, or until the vegetables are cooked through and fragrant. Add the remaining garlic, tomatoes, and basil, cover, and return to the oven for 10 minutes.

Remove from the heat and proceed as in the master recipe, reducing the liquid, adding the final seasoning, and serving.

PER PORTION:

Calories	135	Protein	4 G
Fat	5 G	Carbohydrate	21 G
Sodium	18 MG	Cholesterol	0

ARTICHOKES À LA BARIGOULE

MAKES 4 SERVINGS

This is my friend Christine's version of a traditional *Provençal* dish. Every *Provençal* cookbook has a different recipe, each claimed to be the authentic one. In the end I opt for the one that tastes the best, and I am sure it is Christine's, with all the garlic and the sweet green pepper.

    8 small young purple artichokes *or* 4 globe artichokes
    1 lemon, cut in half
    1 tablespoon olive oil
    3 medium-sized white onions, chopped
    1 small head garlic, cloves separated, crushed slightly,
           and peeled
    1 large green pepper *or* 2 small, diced
 1½ pounds (6 medium) tomatoes
    1 tablespoon tomato paste (optional)
    2 sprigs fresh thyme *or* ¼ teaspoon dried
    1 bay leaf
       salt and freshly ground pepper
    2 cups simmering water

Trim the stems off the artichokes, cut off the very tops, trim off the spiny tips of the outer leaves with scissors, and rub thoroughly with the cut lemon. Cut large artichokes in halves or quarters and rub with lemon juice.

Heat the olive oil over medium heat in a large heavy-bottomed casserole and sauté the onion and the garlic cloves until the onion begins to turn golden. Add the green pepper and continue to sauté until it softens, about 5 minutes. Add the tomatoes and sauté about 10 minutes, until they have begun to release their juice and cook down.

Stir in the tomato paste, then add the artichokes, thyme, bay leaf, salt and pepper to taste, and about ½ cup of simmering water. Cover and simmer 45 minutes to an hour, stirring occasionally and adding water from time to time if the liquid evaporates. When the artichokes are tender, taste and adjust seasonings before serving. This dish is also good at room temperature or chilled. Cover and keep at room temperature or chill for up to a day.

PER PORTION:

Calories	174	Protein	7 G
Fat	4 G	Carbohydrate	33 G
Sodium	120 MG	Cholesterol	0

ROASTED SWEET RED PEPPERS

MAKES 4 TO 6 SERVINGS

I don't know anybody who doesn't love this dish, although people do vary as to how garlicky they like it. My Yugoslavian friend Zoran is used to lots of garlic and a fair amount of vinegar, whereas Christine Picasso uses no vinegar or garlic at all, just olive oil and salt. My version is a toned-down Yugoslavian style, with a hint of Provence if I have fresh basil on hand.

    4 to 6 medium-sized red peppers (to taste)
    2 large garlic cloves, minced or put through a press
    2 tablespoons red wine vinegar (more to taste)
    1 tablespoon olive oil
       salt
    1 to 2 tablespoons chopped fresh basil (to taste;
          optional)

There are several ways to roast the peppers. You can place them directly in a gas flame or below a broiler. Or you can place them in a dry skillet over an electric or gas burner or in a baking dish in a hot oven. You want all the skin to blister and blacken. Keep turning the peppers until they are uniformly charred, then place in a plastic bag or wrap in a kitchen towel until cool enough to handle.

Peel off the blackened skin, split in half, and remove the seeds and inner membranes. Rinse quickly under cool water and pat dry. Cut the halved peppers in half lengthwise or into wide strips. Place in a bowl or serving dish and toss with the garlic, vinegar, olive oil, and salt to taste. Cover and refrigerate until ready to serve. Toss with the basil, if available, shortly before serving. This will keep up to a week in the refrigerator, without the basil.

PER PORTION:

Calories	39	Protein	1 G
Fat	3 G	Carbohydrate	4 G
Sodium	2 MG	Cholesterol	0

ARTICHOKES À LA GRECQUE

MAKES 6 SERVINGS

Funnily enough, I've never come across artichokes, or any other vegetable, *à la Grecque* in Greece. They are a typical French hors d'oeuvre. The dish must have acquired its name because of the currants (called *raisins de Corinthe* in France) and the Middle Eastern flavor of the spices.

FOR THE BOUILLON/MARINADE:

  2 cups water
  1 cup dry white wine
    juice of 2 large lemons
  3 tablespoons cider or wine vinegar
  2 tablespoons olive oil
  2 garlic cloves
 12 black peppercorns
  1 tablespoon coriander seed
  1 bay leaf
  4 sprigs parsley
 ½ teaspoon mustard seed
  1 teaspoon fennel seed
 ½ teaspoon salt
  1 large shallot, chopped
 ¼ cup raisins or currants

FOR THE ARTICHOKES:

> 4 to 6 large globe artichokes
>
> 1 lemon, cut in half, plus juice of 1 lemon for the bowl of water
>
> 10 to 12 sprigs chervil *or* 1 tablespoon chopped fresh parsley or dill

PREPARE THE BOUILLON/MARINADE:

Combine all the ingredients for the bouillon in a large flameproof casserole or stockpot and bring to a simmer. Simmer, covered, while you prepare the artichokes (10 to 15 minutes).

PREPARE THE ARTICHOKES:

Cut the stems off the artichoke bottoms and rub with the cut lemon. Starting at the base of the artichoke, break off all the leaves by bending them backward, until you reach the part of the artichoke where it begins to curve inward. Cut off the tops (the remaining leaves) with a sharp knife. Rub the fresh cuts with the cut lemon so the artichokes won't discolor.

Cut away all the tough green skin from the bottoms of the artichokes so that the white fleshy part underneath the leaves is exposed. Rub the cut surfaces with the cut lemon and drop into a bowl of water acidulated with the juice of 1 lemon.

When all the artichoke bottoms are prepared, drop into the simmering bouillon. Simmer, covered, for 30 to 40 minutes or until tender. Remove from the heat and allow to cool in the marinade.

Now remove the chokes from the artichoke bottoms:* Remove the artichoke bottoms from the marinade, carefully pull apart at the center, and scoop out the little hairs with a spoon. Return to the marinade and refrigerate for at least 2 hours.

Again remove the artichokes from the marinade and heat the marinade to boiling. Reduce to ¾ cup, taste, and adjust seasonings.

Place the artichoke bottoms on a platter or on individual serving plates and pour on the reduced bouillon. Allow to cool or serve with the warm marinade. Garnish with chervil, parsley, or dill and serve. The artichokes will hold for several hours in the refrigerator.

PER PORTION:

Calories	157	Protein	5 G
Fat	5 G	Carbohydrate	28 G
Sodium	316 MG	Cholesterol	0

*You can also remove the chokes from the artichoke bottoms before you cook them, by cutting them out with a knife. I find it's easier to do after they are cooked.

WARM CHICK-PEA SALAD

MAKES 6 SERVINGS

One of my favorite ways to prepare chick-peas, this makes a very satisfying lunch or dinner, especially during winter. You can substitute canned chick-peas for the dried beans.

FOR THE SALAD:

- 2 cups dried chick-peas, washed and picked over, *or*
    - 3 19-ounce cans chick-peas, drained and rinsed
- 6 cups water
- salt
- 4 scallions, chopped, *or* 1 small red onion, chopped
- 4 radishes, sliced
- 1 green or red pepper, chopped
- ½ cup chopped fresh parsley
- 2 tablespoons freshly grated Parmesan or Cheddar cheese

FOR THE YOGURT VINAIGRETTE:

- juice of 1 large lemon
- 3 tablespoons red wine vinegar
- 1 small garlic clove, minced or put through a press
- 2 teaspoons Dijon mustard
- ¾ cup plain low-fat yogurt
- salt

- freshly ground pepper
- leaf lettuce, washed and dried

PREPARE THE SALAD:

Pick over the beans, wash, and soak for several hours or overnight in 6 cups water. Drain and place in a large pot with 6 cups fresh water. Bring to a boil, cover, and reduce heat. Cook 1 to 2 hours, until soft, adding salt to taste halfway through the cooking.

If you're using canned beans: drain, rinse, and heat through.

Drain the cooked beans and toss with the scallions, radishes, red or green pepper, parsley, and grated cheese.

PREPARE THE YOGURT VINAIGRETTE:

Mix all ingredients well and use immediately or set aside at room temperature.

Toss the chick-pea mixture with the yogurt vinaigrette and season with freshly ground pepper to taste. Serve warm on individual plates or from a bowl lined with lettuce leaves.

PER PORTION:

Calories	283	Protein	16 G
Fat	5 G	Carbohydrate	45 G
Sodium	127 MG	Cholesterol	3 MG

VEGETABLES À LA GRECQUE

MAKES 6 SERVINGS

These vegetables are cooked and marinated in the same heady bouillon used for the artichokes *à la Grecque* (page 70). You can use the assortment I've suggested here or just choose one or two vegetables. This keeps several days in the refrigerator and is great to have on hand.

- 1 recipe bouillon/marinade used in artichokes *à la Grecque* (page 70)
- 12 pearl onions, trimmed and peeled
- 8 whole garlic cloves, peeled
- 2 medium-sized fennel bulbs, cut into eighths
- 6 medium or small carrots, cut into 3-inch sticks
- ½ pound mushrooms, cleaned and trimmed
- 4 medium zucchini, trimmed and cut into 3-inch sticks
- 3 tablespoons chopped fresh parsley
- 2 tablespoons snipped fresh chervil, tarragon, or dill
  radishes for garnish

Combine the bouillon ingredients and simmer for 10 to 15 minutes while you prepare the vegetables.

Add the onions, garlic, and fennel to the bouillon and simmer for 10 minutes. Add the carrots and simmer for 10 minutes. Add the mushrooms, simmer for 10 minutes, and add the zucchini. Simmer all the vegetables for another 15 minutes.

Remove from the heat and cool in the cooking liquid. Refrigerate several hours or overnight or keep at room temperature.

Drain the vegetables, retaining the bouillon, and return the bouillon to the stockpot. Discard the bay leaf and parsley sprigs, bring to a boil, and reduce to ¾ cup over high heat.

Place the vegetables on a serving platter or on individual plates, pour on the marinade, and sprinkle on the parsley and the chervil, tarragon, or dill. Garnish with radishes and serve. Or refrigerate for several hours and serve chilled.

PER PORTION:

Calories	146	Protein	4 G
Fat	5 G	Carbohydrate	24 G
Sodium	270 MG	Cholesterol	0

SALADE NIÇOISE

MAKES 4 TO 6 SERVINGS

I serve this for dinner more frequently than any other dish. I use the term *salade Niçoise* loosely, and so, apparently, does every café owner in France. Some of these salads contain green peppers, and some do not; some include green beans, and others do not. The mayor of Nice claims that a true *Niçoise* salad contains nothing cooked; therefore, potatoes and green beans, two ingredients I consider essential, would be out. In France there are four ingredients a *Niçoise* salad always includes: lettuce, tomatoes, tuna, and anchovies. In my low-fat version I rinse the oil from the canned anchovies, use water-packed tuna, and substitute plain low-fat yogurt for some of the olive oil in a traditional vinaigrette. I like to toss all of the salad ingredients together in a big bowl, but others like to arrange them neatly on a platter and pour on the dressing.

FOR THE VINAIGRETTE:
    2 tablespoons fresh lemon juice
    2 to 3 tablespoons red wine vinegar (to taste)
    1 garlic clove, minced or put through a press
    1 teaspoon Dijon mustard (more to taste)
    2 tablespoons chopped fresh herbs, such as basil,
          parsley, sage, tarragon, thyme, chervil—alone or
          in combination, such as basil with thyme, sage
          with parsley, tarragon with thyme
    salt and freshly ground pepper
    3 tablespoons olive oil
    5 tablespoons plain low-fat yogurt

FOR THE SALAD:

    4 medium-sized new potatoes, scrubbed and diced
    1 small head Boston lettuce, leaves separated, washed,
        and broken into medium to large pieces
    ½ pound (2 or 3) carrots, peeled and grated
    1 pound (4 or 5) tomatoes, sliced
    ½ pound green beans, steamed until crisp-tender
    1 small cucumber, peeled, seeded, and thinly sliced
    1 green or red pepper, thinly sliced
    2 eggs, hard-cooked, peeled, and sliced
    1 6½-ounce can water-packed tuna, drained
    2 anchovy fillets (canned but not pickled), rinsed and
        chopped

PREPARE THE VINAIGRETTE:

Combine the lemon juice, vinegar, garlic, mustard, herbs, and salt and pepper to taste. Whisk in the olive oil and yogurt.

PREPARE THE SALAD:

Steam or boil the potatoes until tender and toss with the vinaigrette in a large salad bowl. Add the remaining vegetables and the eggs to the bowl, crumble in the tuna, add the anchovies, and toss together. Adjust seasonings and serve. If you're not serving right away, do not toss with the dressing. Cover with plastic wrap and refrigerate for up to 2 hours.

PER PORTION:

Calories	249	Protein	15 G
Fat	10 G	Carbohydrate	28 G
Sodium	233 MG	Cholesterol	104 MG

PAIN BAGNAT

MAKES 6 SERVINGS

A *pain bagnat* is like a *Niçoise* salad on a bun. In Cannes they're sold all along the waterfront from little stands, and when I'm there that is what I eat for lunch every day. The filling always consists of lettuce, tomato, tuna, peppers, and anchovies, but it can be more elaborate. Whether the *pain bagnat* is memorable or banal really depends on the quality of the bread, vinegar, and olive oil, so try to find the best baguette or country bread you can.

FOR THE SANDWICH:

    3 baguettes *or* 6 roll-size *pains de campagne*, such as
        Crusty Country Bread, page 35, or similar
        hard-crusted rolls
    1 garlic clove, cut in half lengthwise
    1 tablespoon red wine vinegar
    1 tablespoon plain low-fat yogurt
    1 small head Boston lettuce, leaves separated, washed,
        and broken into small pieces
    ½ pound (2 to 3) carrots, peeled and grated
    1 pound (4 to 5) tomatoes, sliced
    1 small cucumber, peeled, seeded, and thinly sliced
    1 green pepper, sliced thin
    3 eggs, hard-cooked, peeled, and sliced
    1 6½-ounce can water-packed tuna, drained
    2 anchovy fillets (canned but not pickled), rinsed and
        chopped

FOR THE VINAIGRETTE:

    3 tablespoons red wine vinegar
    1 garlic clove, minced or put through a press
    1 teaspoon Dijon mustard (more to taste)
      salt and freshly ground pepper
    2 tablespoons chopped fresh herbs, such as basil,
        parsley, tarragon, thyme—alone or in combination,
        such as basil with parsley, parsley with tarragon,
        thyme with parsley
    1 tablespoon olive oil
    5 tablespoons plain low-fat yogurt

PREPARE THE SANDWICH:

Cut the baguettes or rolls in half and scoop out some of the bread; set aside the crumbs. Rub the inside of the bread halves with a cut clove of garlic. Mix together the vinegar and yogurt and drizzle on a small amount. Toss the bread crumbs together with the vegetables, eggs, tuna, and anchovies.

PREPARE THE SALAD DRESSING:

Combine the vinegar, garlic, mustard, salt and pepper to taste, and herbs. Whisk in the oil and yogurt. Toss with the salad. Mound the salad onto the bread and top with the other half. Cut each baguette into 3 equal pieces. Squeeze together well and wrap tightly in plastic or foil. Refrigerate for an hour before eating. It will hold for up to 2 hours in the refrigerator, but will become very soggy after that.

PER PORTION:

Calories	317	Protein	19 G
Fat	8 G	Carbohydrate	43 G
Sodium	568 MG	Cholesterol	152 MG

FENNEL AND RED PEPPER SALAD

MAKES 4 SERVINGS

The sweet-tasting, juicy red peppers and the crunchy, clean, anisy fennel combine here to make the liveliest of salads. The ingredients keep well, so it's one of those dishes that you can shop for several days before you get around to making it.

FOR THE SALAD:

- 1 pound (2 small or 1 large) fennel bulbs, cut into thin crosswise slices
- 2 red peppers, seeds and membranes removed, sliced lengthwise (cut in half if very long)
- 8 mushrooms, cleaned and thinly sliced

FOR THE DRESSING:

- juice of 1 lemon
- 2 tablespoons wine vinegar
- 1 garlic clove, minced or put through a press
- ¼ teaspoon minced fresh thyme
- 1 tablespoon minced fresh parsley
- 1 tablespoon minced fresh chives
- salt and freshly ground pepper
- 6 tablespoons olive oil

Toss together the vegetables. Mix together the lemon juice, vinegar, garlic, herbs, and salt and pepper to taste and combine well. Whisk in the olive oil. Toss with the salad and serve.

PER PORTION:

Calories	216	Protein	2 G
Fat	21 G	Carbohydrate	7 G
Sodium	106 MG	Cholesterol	0

LEEKS À LA NIÇOISE

MAKES 4 TO 6 SERVINGS

This pungent *Niçoise* dish, slightly spicy with its hint of cayenne, should be made with very ripe tomatoes. The tomatoes are cooked along with the leeks, just until the leeks are tender. This is a much peppier dish than some of the tired leeks vinaigrette salads I have seen in Paris *brasseries*.

    2   pounds leeks, white part only, thoroughly cleaned
    1   tablespoon olive oil
        salt and freshly ground pepper
    2   tablespoons red wine vinegar (or to taste)
    2   garlic cloves, minced or put through a press
    1   pound tomatoes, peeled and chopped
    ¼   to ½ teaspoon dried thyme (to taste)
        pinch cayenne pepper
    2   tablespoons chopped fresh parsley or basil

Clean the leeks by trimming off the root end and the green stalk, then cutting in half lengthwise and running under cold water until all the sand and grit are washed away.

Heat the oil in a large nonstick skillet and sauté the leeks for about 5 minutes over medium-low heat. Add salt and pepper to taste, 1 tablespoon of water, the vinegar, garlic, tomatoes, and thyme. Cover the pan and cook 15 minutes or until leeks are tender, stirring occasionally and adding water to prevent sticking. Add cayenne, taste for salt and pepper, and transfer to a serving dish. Serve hot or at room temperature.

PER PORTION:

Calories	76	Protein	2 G
Fat	3 G	Carbohydrate	13 G
Sodium	20 MG	Cholesterol	0

RECIPES FROM SPAIN

TORTILLA ESPAÑOLA

MAKES 4 MAIN DISH SERVINGS OR 8 TO 10 *TAPA* SERVINGS

The bars in Spain are filled with platters and bowls of *tapas*, hors d'oeuvres to be eaten while you sip sherry or aperitifs. Dinner is not usually eaten before 10:00 P.M., so the *tapas* are essential. The most beautiful, to my eye, are the Spanish omelets, called *tortillas españolas*. The classic one here is made with just egg, onion, and potato, but when you begin to add other vegetables (see the following pages), the sliced *tortillas* look like mosaics.

- 1 **large russet potato (5 or 6 ounces), scrubbed and diced**
- 1 **tablespoon olive oil**
- ½ **medium-sized onion (2 ounces), chopped**
  salt and freshly ground pepper
- 5 **eggs**

Steam the potato until crisp-tender, 5 to 10 minutes. Set aside.

Heat the olive oil over medium heat in a 10- or 12-inch skillet, well-seasoned omelet pan, or ovenproof nonstick pan (you'll need a lid) and sauté the onion until tender and beginning to color. Stir in the potatoes.

Beat the eggs in a bowl until thoroughly amalgamated and add a little salt and freshly ground pepper to taste. Pour the eggs into the skillet and stir once, then tilt the pan to spread evenly over the surface. Turn the heat to low, cover, and cook 10 to 15 minutes, until the eggs are just about set. Meanwhile, preheat the broiler.

Uncover the pan and finish for 2 to 3 minutes under the broiler. Remove from the heat, allow to cool to room temperature, and serve, cut into wedges or squares. Or serve at once, cut into wedges, as a main dish.

PER MAIN-DISH PORTION:

Calories	178	Protein	9 G
Fat	10 G	Carbohydrate	12 G
Sodium	91 MG	Cholesterol	343 MG

TORTILLA ESPAÑOLA WITH RED PEPPER AND GARLIC

To the ingredients in the master recipe add 1 or 2 red peppers, seeded and diced, and 1 to 2 garlic cloves, peeled and sliced. Sauté these ingredients along with the onion until tender. You can also omit the onion in this *tortilla* if you wish. Proceed as in master recipe.

TORTILLA ESPAÑOLA WITH ZUCCHINI AND/OR CARROT

To the ingredients in the master recipe add 1 medium-sized zucchini and/or 1 medium-sized peeled carrot, both diced. Steam for about 5 minutes, until crisp-tender, and add to the onion along with the potato (you can also add some garlic). Proceed as in master recipe.

TORTILLA ESPAÑOLA WITH STEAMED PEAS AND/OR ASPARAGUS

To the ingredients in the master recipe add ¾ cup fresh peas and/or ½ cup chopped fresh asparagus. Steam until tender but bright green and add to the onion when the onion is tender. Proceed as in master recipe.

TORTILLA ESPAÑOLA WITH MUSHROOMS AND PARSLEY

To the ingredients in the master recipe add 1 cup sliced mushrooms, 1 garlic clove, minced or put through a press, and 2 tablespoons chopped fresh parsley. Add the mushrooms and garlic to the onion when the onion is tender and continue to sauté, stirring, until the mushrooms are tender and aromatic. Add salt and pepper to taste, the parsley and potatoes, and a pinch of dried or fresh thyme and rosemary. Proceed as in master recipe.

A TAPA OF MUSHROOMS SIMMERED IN WINE

MAKES 6 SERVINGS

You see this dish in almost every *tapa* bar in Spain, and it's one of my favorites. It's a little oilier in Spain, of course. In addition to being a perfect *tapa*, this makes a lovely first course or vegetable side dish; you can also toss the mushrooms with pasta.

    2 pounds fresh mushrooms, cleaned and trimmed
    1 tablespoon olive oil
    1 or 2 shallots (to taste), minced
    4 to 6 garlic cloves (to taste), minced or put through a
           press
    1 cup dry white wine
    ½ teaspoon dried thyme
    ½ teaspoon dried rosemary
       salt and freshly ground pepper
    ½ cup chopped fresh parsley

Cut the mushrooms in half or quarters if very large.

Heat the oil over medium-low heat in a large heavy-bottomed frying pan and add the shallots and half the garlic. Sauté, stirring, until the shallots are tender, and add the mushrooms and remaining garlic. Sauté over medium-high heat until the mushrooms begin to release some of their liquid. Add the wine, thyme, rosemary, salt and pepper to taste, and half the parsley. Cook, stirring often, over medium heat, until the mushrooms are tender, about 20 minutes. Some of the wine should still be in the pan. Add the remaining parsley, correct seasoning, and transfer to a serving dish. Serve warm, with toothpicks stuck in the mushrooms if serving as an hors d'oeuvre. This dish can also be cooled and refrigerated, then reheated just before serving.

PER PORTION:

Calories	66	Protein	3 G
Fat	3 G	Carbohydrate	9 G
Sodium	11 MG	Cholesterol	0

A TAPA OF EGGPLANT AND PEPPERS

MAKES 4 TO 6 APPETIZER SERVINGS OR 8 TO 10 *TAPA* SERVINGS

Many Spanish dishes could be served as *tapas,* nibbled at a bar before dinner. When I went to Andalusia, *tapas* more often than not *were* dinner. They were often oily; I've adjusted the recipes for some of my favorite ones so they can be included in this book.

    1   pound (2 small) eggplant
    2   large green peppers (about ⅔ pound)
    2   large red peppers (about ⅔ pound)
    1   tablespoon olive oil
    2   tablespoons fresh lemon juice
    1   tablespoon red wine vinegar
    1   garlic clove, minced or put through a press
        salt and freshly ground pepper

Roast the eggplants and peppers in a very hot oven or under a broiler, turning often, until they are tender and uniformly charred. Remove from the heat and place the peppers in a plastic bag. When they and the eggplants are cool enough to handle, remove the skins. Cut the eggplants into chunks or narrow strips and slice the peppers. Toss with the remaining ingredients and marinate for a couple of hours in or out of the refrigerator. The dish will keep for a day or two in the refrigerator.

PER APPETIZER PORTION:

Calories	55	Protein	1 G
Fat	3 G	Carbohydrate	8 G
Sodium	5 MG	Cholesterol	0

RECIPES FROM GREECE

GIANT WHITE BEAN SALAD

MAKES 4 SIDE-DISH SERVINGS

This is a simple and delicious Greek salad. All you need is good vinegar and good olive oil (and not much of it) to dress the beans.

- ½ pound dried giant white beans, available in Greek and Italian import stores
- 1 quart water
- 1 bay leaf
  salt
- 1 garlic clove, minced or put through a press (optional)
- 3 tablespoons fresh lemon juice
- 4 tablespoons good-quality red wine vinegar
- 3 tablespoons good-quality olive oil
- ½ teaspoon dried oregano
  freshly ground pepper

Pick over the beans and soak overnight in 3 times their volume of water. Use bottled water if your tap water is hard. Drain.

Combine the beans and add 1 quart water in a large pot and bring to a boil. Add the bay leaf, cover, and cook 45 minutes. Add salt to taste and cook another 15 to 30 minutes, until the beans are cooked through but not mushy. Remove from the heat and drain.

Toss the beans with the garlic, lemon juice, vinegar, olive oil, and oregano. Add more salt, if desired, and freshly ground pepper to taste. Chill for an hour or more. This salad will keep for a few days in the refrigerator.

PER PORTION:

Calories	286	Protein	13 G
Fat	11 G	Carbohydrate	36 G
Sodium	9 MG	Cholesterol	0

PUREED YELLOW SPLIT PEAS

MAKES 4 SERVINGS

I used to eat this at a taverna in Kifisiá, a suburb just north of Athens, at one end of the metro line. It was called *fev*, and I saw it only at this one *taverna*, which was too bad because I loved it. But it's easy enough to make it at home. In Greece, of course, they add a lot of olive oil to this dish, but it isn't really necessary. You can moisten the puree with the cooking liquid from the split peas and with plain low-fat yogurt.

You can find yellow split peas wherever ingredients for Indian food are sold.

- 1 cup dried yellow split peas, washed and picked over
- 2 garlic cloves, peeled and mashed
- 1 quart water
- ½ teaspoon salt (or to taste)
- 1 bay leaf
- 1 tablespoon olive oil
- 2 to 3 tablespoons plain low-fat yogurt (to taste)
- 3 tablespoons cooking liquid from the split peas (more to taste)
- additional salt
- juice of ½ lemon
- ½ onion, chopped (optional)

Combine the split peas, garlic, water, salt, and bay leaf in a large saucepan and bring to a boil. Reduce heat, cover, and simmer 45 minutes, until the split peas are tender. Drain and retain the cooking liquid. Remove the bay leaf.

Puree the split peas in a food processor or blender or mash in a mortar and pestle. Blend in the olive oil, yogurt, and 3 tablespoons of the cooking liquid. If the mixture seems very dry, thin out with a few more tablespoons of the cooking liquid. Taste and adjust salt. Transfer to a bowl and top with lemon juice and chopped onion if desired. This dish can be stored for two or three days in the refrigerator. Do not add the lemon juice or onion, though. Reheat gently, transfer to a bowl and add the lemon juice and onion.

PER PORTION:

Calories	207	Protein	13 G
Fat	4 G	Carbohydrate	31 G
Sodium	287 MG	Cholesterol	1 MG

TZATZIKI

MAKES 4 SERVINGS

This is my favorite Greek dish. In Greece the yogurt is very rich and thick, and there is so much garlic in the *tzatziki* that the dish is almost *picante*. You can achieve a thick, creamy low-fat or nonfat yogurt if you drain the yogurt in a sieve lined with cheesecloth or a linen napkin for several hours. I think it's worth the price of the extra yogurt (you lose about half the volume) to get the richness without the calories. As for the garlic, I leave the amount up to your taste; I like it the Greek way, but I love garlic.

    4 cups plain low-fat yogurt
    1 long European cucumber *or* 2 small cucumbers
       salt
    2 to 4 large garlic cloves (more to taste)
       juice of ½ lemon
       freshly ground pepper

Line a sieve with a double thickness of cheesecloth or a linen napkin or towel. Pour in the yogurt and place the sieve over a bowl. Refrigerate for 2 to 3 hours.

Meanwhile, peel the cucumber and slice paper-thin. Place in a colander in the sink or over a bowl and toss with a generous amount of salt. Let sit for an hour. Rinse and pat dry with a clean dish towel or paper towels. Cut the slices in thin julienne strips. You don't have to be very neat about this. I place the slices on a chopping board and cut them with a large chopping knife, as if I were really going to mince the cucumbers, but I cut them in only one direction. If you prefer, you can leave the cucumbers in thin slices, but in Greece I saw them only in thin julienne.

Place the thickened yogurt in a bowl and beat with a whisk until creamy. Mash the garlic with a little salt in a mortar and pestle until you have a smooth puree or put the garlic through a press. Stir into the yogurt.

Stir the cucumbers into the yogurt and add the lemon juice and salt to taste. Serve chilled and add pepper to taste. This dish will keep for a day or two in the refrigerator.

PER PORTION:

Calories	136	Protein	12 G
Fat	4 G	Carbohydrate	15 G
Sodium	113 MG	Cholesterol	14 MG

MELITZANNA SALATA
(Greek Eggplant Salad)

MAKES 4 SERVINGS

I ate this simple dish on the Greek island of Simi. Unlike the Middle Eastern eggplant purees, the eggplant in the salads I ate on Simi didn't have a smoky taste. I love both. The flavor of this one is particularly refreshing.

2 pounds (about 2 medium) eggplant
2 to 3 garlic cloves (to taste), mashed to a paste in a
        mortar and pestle or put through a press
    juice of 2 lemons
    salt and freshly ground pepper
1 tablespoon plain low-fat yogurt
1 tablespoon olive oil

Preheat the broiler. Cut the eggplants in half and place cut side down on an oiled baking sheet. Place under the broiler 2 to 4 inches from the flame for 10 to 15 minutes (depending on the size of the eggplants), until the skin is charred and the eggplants soft. Remove from the heat and allow to cool.

Scoop the eggplant flesh out of the skin and discard the shells. Puree in a food processor, blender, or mortar and pestle. Combine with the garlic, lemon juice, salt and pepper to taste, yogurt, and olive oil. Chill several hours. This dish will keep for about 3 days in the refrigerator.

PER PORTION:

Calories	86	Protein	2 G
Fat	4 G	Carbohydrate	14 G
Sodium	10 MG	Cholesterol	0

ELLENIKI SALATA (Greek Salad)

MAKES 4 SERVINGS

This is the ubiquitous Greek salad, the one everybody except me tires of after being in Greece for a while. Since I never tire of sweet ripe tomatoes and good feta cheese, I can eat this day after day. I'm not much of an onion eater, but the lasting effects of onions can be diminished if you let them steep in a vinegar-water solution for an hour or so. In Greece the salads are usually served on individual plates, each one with a large slab of feta. This recipe calls for tossing everything together, crumbling the feta. Although it's less authentic this way, I've left out the fattening olives and reduced the olive oil.

    2 medium-sized red or yellow onions, thinly sliced
    4 large ripe tomatoes, sliced
    2 green peppers, thinly sliced
  ½ European cucumber, peeled and thinly sliced, *or* 2
           American cucumbers, peeled if bitter and thinly
           sliced
  ¼ pound feta cheese, crumbled
    3 tablespoons red wine vinegar
    2 tablespoons olive oil
  ½ teaspoon dried oregano
       salt and freshly ground pepper

If you have time and want to reduce the sharpness of the onions, steep for an hour or more in ⅓ cup vinegar mixed with ½ cup water, then drain.

Toss together the onions, tomatoes, peppers, cucumber, and feta. Add the vinegar and olive oil and toss again, then add the oregano and salt and pepper to taste. Give a final toss and chill until ready to serve.

TURKISH VERSION

Cut the vegetables into smaller pieces and add the following:

    6 large radishes, grated
    1 small hot green pepper, minced
    1 cup minced fresh parsley
       juice of 2 large lemons

Proceed as in master recipe.

PER PORTION:

Calories	199	Protein	7 G
Fat	13 G	Carbohydrate	16 G
Sodium	335 MG	Cholesterol	25 MG

RECIPES FROM THE MIDDLE EAST

FATTOUSH

MAKES 6 SERVINGS

Every Mediterranean country has an ingenious way to use old bread, and this Syrian vegetable salad does so with crisp pieces of pita bread. I have replaced the olive oil used in the traditional dish with plain low-fat yogurt.

    2 whole-wheat pita breads (stale loaves are fine)
          store-bought or use recipe on page 40
       juice of 2 lemons
    2 garlic cloves, minced or put through a press
       salt and freshly ground pepper
  ½ cup plain low-fat yogurt
    1 large or 2 small cucumbers, chopped, *or* 1 small head
          romaine lettuce, leaves washed and cut into
          1-inch pieces
    1 bunch scallions, both white and green parts, chopped,
          or 1 medium-sized red onion, chopped
    1 pound (4 to 5) firm, ripe tomatoes, chopped
    1 green pepper, chopped (optional)
    1 bunch parsley, finely chopped
    2 tablespoons chopped fresh mint
    3 tablespoons chopped cilantro

Open up the pitas and toast until crisp and brown. Break into small pieces and place in a salad bowl.

Mix together the lemon juice, garlic, salt and pepper to taste, and yogurt and toss with the broken-up bread. Then add the vegetables and herbs and toss together again. Adjust seasonings and serve.

PER PORTION:

Calories	124	Protein	5 G
Fat	2 G	Carbohydrate	24 G
Sodium	198 MG	Cholesterol	1 MG

FISH SALAD WITH CILANTRO AND MINT

MAKES 6 SERVINGS

The idea for this salad comes from a fish filling for filo pastries (*tiropetes*). When I made the filling for the pastries I was delighted with the flavor, but when I baked the *tiropetes* the herbs lost their fresh green color and much of their fragrance. I decided to turn this mixture into a salad, seasoned with lots of lemon juice, cilantro, and mint and tossed with bright, crisp diced red peppers. The fish flakes when you mix up the salad; it's not supposed to remain in neat chunks. This dish makes a fabulous starter and a beautiful addition to a party buffet.

2¼ pounds cod fillets
1 bunch cilantro, cleaned and chopped
2 to 4 tablespoons chopped fresh mint (to taste)
2 tablespoons chopped chives
1 large red pepper, seeded and chopped into small dice
2 garlic cloves, minced or put through a press (more to taste)
   salt and freshly ground pepper
¼ teaspoon ground cumin (optional)
   juice of 2 large lemons (more to taste)
2 tablespoons olive oil
1 head leaf or Boston lettuce, leaves separated and washed

Rinse the fillets and steam until they are opaque and flake easily with a fork, about 7 minutes (5 minutes per ½-inch thickness). Remove from the heat and let drain in a colander.

Transfer the fish to a large bowl and toss with half the herbs and the remaining ingredients except lettuce. Season again to taste with salt and freshly ground pepper, cover, and chill until ready to serve.

Shortly before serving, remove from the refrigerator and add the remaining herbs. Toss and correct seasoning, adding more lemon juice and salt if you wish. Line a bowl or platter with lettuce leaves, top with the salad, and serve. This salad will keep for several hours in the refrigerator.

PER PORTION:

Calories	202	Protein	32 G
Fat	6 G	Carbohydrate	5 G
Sodium	104 MG	Cholesterol	73 MG

TABOULI I

MAKES 6 SERVINGS

I get cravings for the *tabouli* served in Middle Eastern restaurants in Paris. Theirs is more like a parsley salad than a cracked wheat salad, with lots of lemon juice and a small sprinkling of bulgur. I have two versions of the salad. The one here, more authentic than my other version (except that I've omitted the olive oil), is like a garden of herbs, tart with lemon juice and brimming with vitamins.

2 ounces (⅓ cup) fine bulgur wheat
1 garlic clove, minced or put through a press
  juice of 3 large lemons (more to taste)
  salt and freshly ground pepper
8 large bunches flat-leaf parsley (enough to make 8 cups chopped)
1 large bunch fresh mint
4 scallions, both white and green parts, thinly sliced or finely chopped
3 ripe tomatoes, diced
  small romaine lettuce leaves to use as scoops

Pour water over the bulgur and soak in a large bowl for 20 minutes, until slightly softened. Drain and squeeze out excess water. Toss with the garlic, lemon juice, and salt and pepper to taste. Let sit for 30 minutes, until the bulgur is soft.

Meanwhile, wash the parsley and mint, dry thoroughly, and chop in a food processor or with a knife, being careful not to turn the herbs into a puree. Transfer to a bowl.

Toss the bulgur with the herbs, scallions, and tomatoes. Taste, and if it doesn't taste extremely lemony, add more lemon juice. Adjust salt and pepper, garnish with romaine lettuce leaves, and serve. The tabouli will keep in the refrigerator, without the romaine lettuce leaves, for 2 to 3 hours.

PER PORTION:

Calories	94	Protein	4 G
Fat	.86 G	Carbohydrate	21 G
Sodium	37 MG	Cholesterol	0

TABOULI II

MAKES 6 SERVINGS

This is a less authentic but more substantial *tabouli*. It calls for more bulgur than the previous recipe and also contains chick-peas and cucumbers. The lemony dressing is seasoned with a small amount of cumin.

4½ ounces (¾ cup) medium-grain bulgur
    juice of 3 lemons (more to taste)
¼ to ½ teaspoon ground cumin
    salt and freshly ground pepper
1 garlic clove, minced or put through a press
4 bunches flat-leaf parsley (enough to make 4 cups chopped)
1 large bunch fresh mint
4 to 5 scallions (to taste), both white and green parts,
    thinly sliced or chopped
1 small cucumber, peeled and diced
1 cup cooked chick-peas (if using canned chick-peas,
    drain and rinse)
3 tomatoes, chopped
1 tablespoon olive oil (optional)
    small romaine lettuce leaves to use as scoops

Place the bulgur in a bowl and pour on water to cover. Let sit 20 minutes, until slightly soft. Squeeze out excess water.

Toss with the lemon juice, cumin, salt and pepper to taste, and the garlic. Let sit 30 minutes, or until softened. If the bulgur seems too hard, add more lemon juice.

Meanwhile, wash the parsley and mint, dry thoroughly, and finely chop in a food processor or with a knife, being careful not to puree.

Toss the bulgur with the herbs and remaining ingredients except the romaine lettuce. Taste and adjust seasoning, adding more salt, lemon juice, cumin, or garlic if you wish. Refrigerate until ready to serve.

To serve, transfer to a bowl or platter and garnish with the romaine lettuce leaves. The salad will keep in the refrigerator, without the lettuce leaves, for two or three hours.

PER PORTION:

Calories	170	Protein	7 G
Fat	2 G	Carbohydrate	35 G
Sodium	26 MG	Cholesterol	0

HUMMUS

MAKES 12 SERVINGS

I never tire of *hummus*, and I always make it when I'm a little hungry, because I can never resist tasting. This version is much less oily than traditional *hummus*. It doesn't contain nearly as much tahini, and I thin it out with low-fat yogurt instead of olive oil. The secret ingredient here is ground cumin.

½ pound dried chick-peas, washed and picked over, *or* 2
    cups canned chick-peas
1 quart water
1 teaspoon salt
2 large garlic cloves
4 to 6 tablespoons fresh lemon juice (to taste)
2 tablespoons olive oil
3 tablespoons tahini (more or less to taste)
½ teaspoon ground cumin
½ to 1 teaspoon salt (to taste)
½ cup plain low-fat yogurt

Soak the chick-peas overnight in a quart of water (use bottled water if your tap water is hard).

The next day, drain the beans and combine in a large pot with a fresh quart of water. Bring to a boil, reduce heat, cover, and simmer 2 hours, until the beans are tender. Add 1 teaspoon salt.

Drain the beans and puree along with the garlic in a food processor or blender or through a food mill. Add the lemon juice, olive oil, tahini, cumin, salt to taste, and yogurt and blend until thoroughly smooth. Taste and adjust seasonings, adding more salt, garlic, or lemon juice as needed. Transfer to a serving bowl and cover. Refrigerate until ready to serve. This dish will keep for up to 5 days in the refrigerator.

PER PORTION:

Calories	120	Protein	5 G
Fat	6 G	Carbohydrate	14 G
Sodium	16 MG	Cholesterol	1 MG

SMOKY EGGPLANT PUREE

MAKES ABOUT 2 CUPS

This has become one of my favorite hors d'oeuvres. The smoky flavor of the charred eggplant is what gives this dish its unique taste. I use a food processor to make this puree as airy as I can get it. It is best if left to mellow for a day in the refrigerator.

2½ pounds (3 medium) eggplant
1½ teaspoons olive oil
  3 tablespoons plain low-fat yogurt
  4 tablespoons fresh lemon juice (more to taste)
  1 to 2 garlic cloves (to taste), minced or put through a
        press
     salt and freshly ground pepper
 ¼ teaspoon ground cumin
  2 tablespoons finely chopped fresh parsley
     crudités and/or bread, pita, or crackers for serving

Preheat the broiler. Place the eggplants on an oiled baking sheet and place about 4 inches under the broiler. Broil, turning every 5 minutes or so, until the eggplants are charred and soft. Remove from the heat and allow to cool.

Remove all the charred skin from the eggplant and carefully squeeze out the liquid from the flesh. Puree the flesh with the olive oil, yogurt, lemon juice, garlic, salt and pepper to taste, and cumin until smooth, using a food processor, blender, or mortar and pestle. I like to whip it in the food processor until very smooth. Taste and adjust seasonings and transfer to an attractive serving bowl. Cover and refrigerate, preferably overnight or for several hours.

Shortly before serving, remove from the refrigerator and sprinkle on the parsley. Garnish with *crudités*, such as thickly sliced red and green peppers, fennel, carrot, and cucumber sticks, and crackers, pita, or thinly sliced bread, and serve. The puree will keep for 3 or 4 days in the refrigerator.

PER 1-TABLESPOON PORTION:

Calories	11	Protein	0
Fat	.25 G	Carbohydrate	2 G
Sodium	3 MG	Cholesterol	0

BABA GHANOUJ

MAKES 4 TO 6 SERVINGS

This has the same smoky taste as the eggplant puree on page 93, with the additional flavor of tahini and the textures and colors of the tomato and green pepper. It makes a beautiful addition to a buffet.

 2 pounds (2 medium-large) eggplant
   juice of 1 to 2 lemons (to taste)
 2 garlic cloves, minced or put through a press
 4 tablespoons plain low-fat yogurt
 2 tablespoons tahini
   salt and freshly ground pepper
 1 tomato, chopped
 1 green pepper, minced
 2 tablespoons chopped fresh parsley
   crudités, pita, or croutons for serving

Preheat the oven to 450 degrees. Cut the eggplants in half and score on the cut side with a sharp knife, down to the skin but not through it. Place the eggplants cut side down on an oiled baking sheet and bake for 20 to 30 minutes, until charred and shriveled. Remove from the heat and allow to cool.

Remove the eggplant flesh from the skins, discard seeds, and mash flesh to a puree in a mortar and pestle, blender, or food processor. Stir in the lemon juice, garlic, yogurt, tahini, salt and pepper to taste, tomato, and green pepper. Mound in a bowl and sprinkle the parsley over the top. Serve with *crudités* and/or pita or croutons. This dish will keep in the refrigerator for 3 or 4 days.

PER PORTION:

Calories	78	Protein	3 G
Fat	3 G	Carbohydrate	12 G
Sodium	20 MG	Cholesterol	1 MG

PUREED WHITE BEANS

MAKES 4 TO 6 SERVINGS

You can use any kind of dried white beans for this puree. If you use the large broad beans, remove their skins after soaking.

- ½ pound dried white beans, washed and picked over
- 1 quart water
- 1 small onion, chopped
- 3 garlic cloves, minced or put through a press
- 1 bay leaf
  salt and freshly ground pepper
  juice of 1 large lemon
- ¼ teaspoon paprika
- 1 tablespoon olive oil
- 2 to 3 tablespoons chopped fresh parsley or dill
  crudités and/or toasted pita triangles for serving

Soak the beans for several hours in 3 times their volume of water (use bottled water if your tap water is hard). Drain the beans and combine in a large saucepan with the water, onion, 2 of the garlic cloves, and the bay leaf. Bring to a boil, reduce heat, cover, and simmer until very tender, 1 to 1½ hours.

Drain the beans, retaining some of the cooking liquid, and mash with a fork or in a mortar and pestle, blender, or food processor. If you wish, moisten with some of the cooking liquid. Season to taste with salt and pepper. Place in a bowl or mound on a plate.

Combine the lemon juice, paprika, remaining garlic clove, and olive oil. Pour over the beans. Sprinkle with parsley or dill.

Serve the puree warm or chilled, with *crudités*, toasted pita triangles, or both. The beans will keep for 3 or 4 days in the refrigerator. Add the herbs shortly before serving and sprinkle with additional lemon juice if desired.

PER PORTION:

Calories	154	Protein	9 G
Fat	3 G	Carbohydrate	25 G
Sodium	7 MG	Cholesterol	0

LENTIL SALAD
WITH CUMIN VINAIGRETTE

MAKES 4 SERVINGS

Lentil salads are ubiquitous in France and in the Middle East. This is my version, with a low-fat yogurt vinaigrette seasoned with cumin.

FOR THE LENTILS:

  1 tablespoon safflower or vegetable oil
  1 small onion, chopped
  2 garlic cloves, minced or put through a press
  ½ pound lentils, washed and picked over
  3 to 4 cups water
  1 bay leaf
    salt

FOR THE DRESSING AND SALAD:

    juice of 1 large lemon
  2 tablespoons wine or cider vinegar
  1 teaspoon Dijon mustard
  1 small garlic clove, minced or put through a press
  ½ teaspoon ground cumin
  ¾ cup plain low-fat yogurt
    salt and freshly ground pepper

  1 green pepper, chopped
  4 scallions, both white and green parts, thinly sliced
  2 to 3 tablespoons chopped cilantro
    lettuce leaves and tomato wedges for garnish

PREPARE THE LENTILS:

Heat the oil in a large heavy-bottomed saucepan or casserole and sauté the onion with 1 clove of the garlic until the onion is tender. Add the lentils, water, remaining garlic, and bay leaf and bring to a boil. Reduce heat, cover, and simmer 45 minutes, adding more water if necessary, until the lentils are tender but not mushy. Add salt to taste. Drain and retain the liquid for another use.

PREPARE THE DRESSING:

While the lentils are cooking, mix together the lemon juice, vinegar, mustard, garlic, and cumin. Stir in the yogurt and add salt and pepper to taste. Toss with the lentils and chill for 2 hours or more in the refrigerator.

Toss the lentils with the green pepper, scallions and chopped cilantro. Adjust seasonings and serve over lettuce leaves. Garnish with tomato wedges.

Without the addition of the green pepper and cilantro, this salad will keep for 2 to 3 days in the refrigerator. Add the pepper and cilantro shortly before serving.

PER PORTION:

Calories	271	Protein	19 G
Fat	5 G	Carbohydrate	40 G
Sodium	77 MG	Cholesterol	3 MG

LABNA

MAKES 1 CUP

Labna is a thick cream-cheese-like cheese served all over the Middle East. It is made by draining yogurt overnight in a sieve lined with a fine tea towel or piece of muslin. You can use plain low-fat yogurt and obtain a cream cheese with very little fat. You can also drain the yogurt for less time to obtain a thick, creamy yogurt, which is desirable for cucumber salads like *tzatziki* (page 85) and *cacik* (page 102). In the Middle East salt is added to the yogurt, but salt is optional here.

> 2 cups plain low-fat yogurt
> salt (optional)
> freshly ground pepper or paprika (optional)
> chopped fresh mint or dill (optional)

Line a sieve with fine muslin or cloth and pour in the yogurt. Place over a bowl, refrigerate, and let drain overnight.

Transfer the thickened yogurt, now *labna*, to a bowl and season to taste with salt, pepper or paprika and, if you wish, chopped fresh mint or dill.

Serve as a dip with vegetables or spread on bread.

PER 1-TABLESPOON PORTION:

Calories	15	Protein	1 G
Fat	.42 G	Carbohydrate	1 G
Sodium	14 MG	Cholesterol	2 MG

DICED VEGETABLE AND YOGURT SALAD

MAKES 4 TO 6 SERVINGS

This is a typical Mediterranean salad, the usual accompaniment to meals I ate in Yugoslavia, and always on the buffet in Egypt. I've substituted yogurt for the more authentic olive oil.

FOR THE SALAD:
- 1 small cucumber, peeled and chopped
- 1 green pepper, chopped
- 4 tomatoes, chopped
- 4 scallions, chopped
- 1 tablespoon chopped fresh dill

FOR THE DRESSING:
- juice of 1 large lemon
- 1 small garlic clove, minced or put through a press
- ½ cup plain low-fat yogurt
- salt and freshly ground pepper

Toss together the vegetables and dill. Mix together the lemon juice and garlic. Stir in the yogurt and combine well. Add salt and pepper to taste. Serve at once or chill and serve. This salad will keep for 1 hour in the refrigerator.

PER PORTION:

Calories	40	Protein	2 G
Fat	.54 G	Carbohydrate	8 G
Sodium	23 MG	Cholesterol	1 MG

BLACK-EYED PEA AND TOMATO SALAD

MAKES 4 SERVINGS

This is one of the many salads that often adorned the buffets on the boat I took up the Nile. I have altered the Egyptian version, substituting plain low-fat yogurt for olive oil.

FOR THE SALAD:

- 1 cup dried black-eyed peas, washed and picked over
- ½ small onion, chopped
- 2 large garlic cloves, minced or put through a press
- 1 quart water
- 1 bay leaf
  salt
- 2 large ripe tomatoes, diced
- 1 to 2 green chili peppers (to taste), seeded and minced

FOR THE DRESSING:

- 5 tablespoons fresh lemon juice
- ½ to ¾ teaspoon ground cumin (to taste)
- 1 small garlic clove, minced or put through a press
- ½ cup plain low-fat yogurt
  salt and freshly ground pepper

- 4 heaped tablespoons chopped fresh parsley or cilantro
  handful fresh spinach, chopped (optional)
  lettuce leaves for the bowl

PREPARE THE SALAD:

Combine the black-eyed peas, onion, garlic, water, and bay leaf and bring to a boil. Reduce heat, cover, and simmer 30 to 35 minutes, until the beans are cooked through but not mushy. Add salt to taste halfway through the cooking. Drain and discard the bay leaf. Toss the beans with the tomatoes and chili peppers.

PREPARE THE DRESSING:

Mix together the lemon juice, cumin, garlic, yogurt, and salt and pepper to taste.

Toss the salad with the dressing and refrigerate several hours.

Just before serving, toss with the parsley or cilantro and the spinach if desired. Adjust seasonings. Line a bowl or platter with lettuce leaves, top with the salad, and serve. The salad will hold for 2 or 3 days without the fresh herbs and spinach, which should be added just before serving.

PER PORTION:

Calories	192	Protein	13 G
Fat	1 G	Carbohydrate	35 G
Sodium	41 MG	Cholesterol	2 MG

EGYPTIAN TOMATO SALAD

MAKES 4 TO 6 SERVINGS

This is one of my favorite Egyptian salads. Finely minced chili pepper is what makes it unique.

1 ½ pounds (6 or 7 medium) tomatoes, cut into wedges
4 to 5 tablespoons fresh lemon juice (juice of 1 large
      lemon) to taste
1 green chili pepper, finely minced
3 tablespoons cilantro or parsley, very finely minced
2 tablespoons olive oil
    salt and freshly ground pepper to taste

Place the tomatoes in a bowl or on a platter. Combine the remaining ingredients and toss with the tomatoes. Serve at once or chill and serve. The salad will keep for 2 or 3 hours in the refrigerator.

PER PORTION:

Calories	67	Protein	1 G
Fat	5 G	Carbohydrate	7 G
Sodium	10 MG	Cholesterol	0

SALATA FASOLIA
(Egyptian White Bean Salad)

MAKES 4 TO 6 SERVINGS

This salad was often on the buffet in Egypt. There's a similar one in Greece, made with the larger broad white beans and seasoned with lemon and olive oil, but without cumin and cilantro. In France the same dish would be made using a vinaigrette, but in the Middle East lemon and olive oil are used in equal proportions, and the beans are seasoned further with chopped parsley or cilantro, garlic, onion, and sometimes cumin. I substitute either cooking liquid from the beans or plain low-fat yogurt for some of the olive oil in my diet version of the recipe.

½ pound dried white beans, washed and picked over
1 onion, chopped
3 garlic cloves, minced or put through a press
1 quart water
1 bay leaf
  salt
6 to 8 tablespoons fresh lemon juice (to taste)
½ teaspoon cumin (optional)
  freshly ground pepper
1 tablespoon olive oil
4 to 6 tablespoons cooking liquid from the beans, plain
      low-fat yogurt, or a combination
4 spring onions, both white and green parts, thinly
      sliced
3 to 4 tablespoons chopped fresh parsley or cilantro (to
      taste)
2 tomatoes, cut into wedges, for garnish

Soak the beans in 3 times their volume of water (use bottled water if your tap water is hard) for several hours and drain. Combine with the onion, 2 of the garlic cloves, the water, and the bay leaf and bring to a boil. Reduce heat, cover, and simmer 1 hour or until the beans are tender. Add salt to taste at the end of the cooking time. Drain the beans and retain the cooking water. Place the beans in a bowl and discard the bay leaf.

Combine the lemon juice, cumin, remaining garlic clove, salt and pepper to taste, olive oil, and cooking liquid from the beans and/or yogurt. Toss with the beans. Cover and refrigerate until ready to serve. Just before serving, toss with the spring onions and herbs and garnish with the tomatoes.

The salad will keep, without the fresh herbs, for 2 to 3 days in the refrigerator. Add the herbs just before serving.

PER PORTION:

Calories	169	Protein	10 G
Fat	3 G	Carbohydrate	28 G
Sodium	11 MG	Cholesterol	0

SALATA BALADI (Egyptian Salad)

MAKES 6 SERVINGS

This is typical of vegetable salads served all over the Middle East and Greece. In Greece feta cheese is added; in Egypt a similar white cheese might or might not be added. I have substituted plain low-fat yogurt for the olive oil used in the authentic version.

3 tomatoes, cut into medium dice
1 small onion, cut into thin rings
2 green peppers, seeded and diced
1 medium-sized or ½ large cucumber, diced
4 tablespoons chopped fresh parsley
4 tablespoons fresh lemon juice
1 garlic clove, minced or put through a press
½ cup plain low-fat yogurt
salt and freshly ground pepper

Toss together the tomatoes, onion, green peppers, cucumber, and parsley in a salad bowl.

Mix together the lemon juice, garlic, yogurt, and salt and pepper to taste. Toss with the salad. Chill until ready to serve or serve right away. The salad will hold for 2 or 3 hours in the refrigerator.

PER PORTION:

Calories	41	Protein	2 G
Fat	.58 G	Carbohydrate	8 G
Sodium	21 MG	Cholesterol	1 MG

CACIK (Turkish Cucumber Salad)

MAKES 4 SERVINGS

Another Mediterranean cucumber and yogurt salad, this Turkish version has a refreshing minty flavor.

1 European cucumber, unpeeled, *or* 2 American
      cucumbers, peeled if bitter
   salt
1 cup plain low-fat yogurt (thickened as for *tzatziki,*
      page 85, if desired)
2 to 3 garlic cloves (to taste), minced or put through a
      press
   freshly ground pepper
1 tablespoon chopped fresh mint

Chop the cucumber into very small dice and place in a colander. Sprinkle with salt and let sit 30 minutes. Rinse and pat dry.

Combine the yogurt, garlic, pepper to taste, and mint and toss with the cucumbers. Add more salt to taste if desired. Refrigerate until ready to serve. The dish will hold for several hours in the refrigerator.

PER PORTION:

Calories	54	Protein	4 G
Fat	1 G	Carbohydrate	8 G
Sodium	177 MG	Cholesterol	3 MG

SPINACH AND YOGURT SALAD

MAKES 4 TO 6 SERVINGS

When I came across this recipe in Claudia Roden's *A New Book of Middle Eastern Food,* I really was convinced that I had learned to cook in that part of the world in another lifetime. I had made this combination often, just off the top of my head, when I cooked for heart patients in 1980 at Dean Ornish's cardiology study in Texas. The dish was requested often and has always been a favorite of mine.

1 pound fresh spinach, stemmed and washed, *or* ½
      pound frozen chopped spinach, thawed
½ cup plus 1 tablespoon plain low-fat yogurt
   juice of 1 lemon
1 garlic clove, minced or put through a press
   salt and freshly ground pepper to taste

If you're using fresh spinach, wash and wilt in its own liquid in a skillet over medium-high heat. Stir over the heat for about 5 minutes, then remove from the heat, squeeze out some of the liquid, and chop fine. If you're using thawed frozen spinach, squeeze out liquid. Mix spinach with the remaining ingredients. Allow to cool before serving.

The salad will keep for a day in the refrigerator.

PER PORTION:

Calories	27	Protein	3 G
Fat	.51 G	Carbohydrate	4 G
Sodium	58 MG	Cholesterol	1 MG

PILAKI
(Turkish Cooked Vegetable Salad)

MAKES 4 SERVINGS

When you cook the vegetables for this salad, they release their sweet-tasting juices, which combine with the lemon juice to make a delicious dressing.

- 1 tablespoon olive oil
- 2 medium-sized onions, sliced
- 2 garlic cloves, minced or put through a press
- 2 large tomatoes, sliced
- 4 green peppers, sliced
- ¾ teaspoon cumin seed
- ⅛ teaspoon cayenne pepper
- ¾ cup water
  salt and freshly ground pepper
  juice of 1 large lemon
- 1 tablespoon chopped fresh parsley

Heat the oil over medium heat in a large nonstick skillet and add the onions and garlic. Sauté for a few minutes, until the onions begin to soften, and add the tomatoes, green peppers, and cumin seed. Sauté, stirring, for about 5 minutes.

Stir in the cayenne and water and bring to a simmer. Reduce the heat and simmer the vegetables, uncovered, for about 15 minutes or until the water is evaporated, stirring from time to time. Season to taste with salt and pepper and remove from the heat. Allow to cool, then cover and chill. Just before serving, stir in the lemon juice and parsley. The salad will keep, up to the adding of the lemon juice and parsley, for a day or two in the refrigerator.

PER PORTION:

Calories	83	Protein	2 G
Fat	4 G	Carbohydrate	12 G
Sodium	10 MG	Cholesterol	0

RECIPES FROM NORTH AFRICA

HARISSA

MAKES ABOUT ⅓ CUP

Harissa is the fiery-hot pepper puree used to season North African dishes like couscous and many of the salads on pages 108–118. Part of the ritual of eating couscous involves stirring a little bit of *harissa* into the soup broth that you will ladle onto your couscous. In many couscous restaurants in Paris, this is done by the waiter, who will ask you how you like your couscous—hot, medium-hot, or mild—and will stir the appropriate amount of *harissa* into your ladleful of the broth. Even a little bit of this condiment goes a long way.

Harissa is imported from North Africa in jars and tubes and is available in imported-food stores, usually anyplace you can get couscous. But you can also make it yourself—just be sure to wear rubber gloves.

    1   ounce dried hot red chili peppers
    1   teaspoon caraway seed
    ½   teaspoon cumin seed
    ½   teaspoon coriander seed
    2   garlic cloves, peeled
    ¼   teaspoon salt
    1   tablespoon water
    4   tablespoons olive oil

Place the dried peppers in a bowl and pour on hot water to cover. Let soak for at least 1 hour. Meanwhile, grind the spices together in a spice mill.

Drain the peppers, pat dry with paper towels, and chop. Then grind or mash together with the garlic, spices, and salt in a spice mill or mortar and pestle until you have a thick paste. Add the water and 3 tablespoons of the olive oil, mix well, and transfer to a jar. Spoon the remaining olive oil over the top, cover tightly, and refrigerate. It keeps for months.

PER 1-TEASPOON PORTION:

Calories	37	Protein	0
Fat	4 G	Carbohydrate	1 G
Sodium	34 MG	Cholesterol	0

TUNISIAN MINCED PEPPER SALAD

MAKES 4 SERVINGS

Everything is chopped so fine that this is more like a relish than a salad. It would be a nice topping for *carta di musica* (page 41) or crisp pitas.

- 3 large red peppers
- 1 hot red or green pepper (optional)
- 4 garlic cloves, peeled
- 1½ teaspoons ground coriander
  juice of 1 large lemon
- 1 tablespoon olive oil
  salt to taste

Trim the peppers and remove the seeds and membranes. Cut into small pieces and either mince together with the garlic in a food processor or mash together in a mortar and pestle. Transfer to a bowl and add the remaining ingredients. Toss together well and serve or chill and serve. The salad will keep for a day in the refrigerator.

COOKED MINCED PEPPER SALAD

Proceed as above, but don't add the olive oil to the salad. Heat it in a large frying pan and sauté the mixture until the peppers are crisp-tender. Transfer to a bowl and refrigerate until ready to serve. Garnish with chopped fresh parsley. This variation will keep for 2 or 3 days in the refrigerator.

PER PORTION:

Calories	56	Protein	1 G
Fat	4 G	Carbohydrate	6 G
Sodium	3 MG	Cholesterol	0

ZUCCHINI AJLOUKE

MAKES 4 SERVINGS

An *ajlouke* is a coarse pureed cooked vegetable dish served as an hors d'oeuvre or first course in Tunisia, usually at room temperature or chilled. Traditionally, olive oil is added to the dish, but I don't think it's necessary here, as the zucchini is quite moist.

 2 medium-sized zucchini (about ¾ pound), cleaned and
 thinly sliced
 ¼ teaspoon *harissa* (page 106), *or* 2 pinches cayenne
 pepper
 juice of ½ to 1 lemon (to taste)
 2 garlic cloves, minced or put through a press
 ½ teaspoon ground caraway
 ½ teaspoon ground coriander
 salt and freshly ground pepper to taste

Steam the zucchini for 10 to 15 minutes, until quite tender. Drain and refresh under cold water. Press out as much water as possible and transfer to a bowl.

Using a fork, crush the zucchini and add the remaining ingredients. Correct seasonings, transfer to a serving dish, and serve or chill and serve. The zucchini will keep for a day or two in the refrigerator.

PER PORTION:

Calories	19	Protein	1 G
Fat	.38 G	Carbohydrate	4 G
Sodium	5 MG	Cholesterol	0

EGGPLANT AJLOUKE
(Tunisian Eggplant Puree)

MAKES 4 SERVINGS

This is similar to the other eggplant purees in this collection, but the texture is coarser, and the Tunisian version is very *picante* because of the *harissa*.

  1 ½ pounds (2 medium-small) eggplant
  ⅛ to ¼ teaspoon *harissa* (page 106) or cayenne pepper
       (to taste)
  1 garlic clove, minced or put through a press
    juice of ½ to 1 lemon (to taste)
  ½ teaspoon ground caraway
  4 tablespoons plain low-fat yogurt
  1 red pepper, minced
    salt
    crudités or crisp pita for serving (optional)

Preheat the broiler and roast the eggplant until uniformly charred and tender. Remove from the heat, and when cool enough to handle, remove the skin and gently squeeze out the liquid. Place in a bowl or food processor fitted with the steel blade and mash with the *harissa* or cayenne, the garlic, lemon juice, and caraway. Stir in the yogurt and minced red pepper and add salt to taste. Transfer to a bowl and serve or chill and serve with *crudités* or crisp pita bread. The puree will keep for 2 to 3 days in the refrigerator.

PER PORTION:

Calories	55	Protein	3 G
Fat	.64 G	Carbohydrate	12 G
Sodium	18 MG	Cholesterol	1 MG

CARROT AND POTATO AJLOUKE
(Tunisian Mashed Carrots and Potatoes)

MAKES 4 SERVINGS

This is a pretty, spicy *ajlouke*. The optional potatoes make the dish slightly more substantial. Both fresh and dried coriander are used here, each contributing its unique flavor.

1 cup water
4 sprigs cilantro
1 dried hot red pepper
1 teaspoon coriander seed
1 pound carrots, peeled and sliced
1 medium-sized potato, peeled and diced
  juice of 1 large lemon
1 teaspoon ground caraway
⅛ to ¼ teaspoon *harissa* (page 106) or cayenne pepper
    (to taste)
2 tablespoons plain low-fat yogurt
  salt to taste
2 tablespoons chopped cilantro or fresh parsley

Place the water, cilantro sprigs, hot red pepper, and coriander seed in the bottom part of a steamer and the carrots and potato above. Steam, covered, for 30 minutes, until the vegetables are quite tender.

Refresh the vegetables under cold water, drain thoroughly, and transfer to a bowl. Crush with a fork or wooden spoon or coarsely puree in a food processor fitted with the steel blade, and mix in the remaining ingredients except the cilantro. Correct seasonings and transfer to a serving dish. Sprinkle with the additional cilantro and serve or chill and serve. The salad will keep for 2 to 3 days in the refrigerator.

PER PORTION:

Calories	60	Protein	2 G
Fat	.64 G	Carbohydrate	13 G
Sodium	43 MG	Cholesterol	0

PUMPKIN AJLOUKE
(Tunisian Pumpkin Puree)

MAKES 4 SERVINGS

Here is another spicy, pretty Tunisian *ajlouke* that is slightly sweet because of the pumpkin. Like all the others, it's simple to make and marvelous to eat.

- 1 pound pumpkin flesh
  juice of 1 lemon
- 2 garlic cloves, minced or put through a press
- ¼ teaspoon *harissa* (page 106) or cayenne pepper
- 1 scant teaspoon ground caraway
- 1 teaspoon ground coriander
- 2 tablespoons plain low-fat yogurt
  salt to taste
  crudités or crisp pita triangles for serving

Steam the pumpkin for 20 minutes or until tender. Refresh under cold water and drain. Gently squeeze out excess water.

Place the pumpkin in a bowl and mash with a fork or mortar and pestle. Blend in the remaining ingredients. Correct seasonings and transfer to a serving dish. Serve chilled or at room temperature, with *crudités* or crisp pita triangles. The puree will keep for 2 or 3 days in the refrigerator.

PER PORTION:

Calories	43	Protein	2 G
Fat	.58 G	Carbohydrate	10 G
Sodium	9 MG	Cholesterol	0

TUNISIAN GRILLED VEGETABLE SALAD

MAKES 4 SERVINGS

This salad has a marvelous roasted flavor and will keep for a few days in the refrigerator.

3 large ripe tomatoes
2 large green peppers
1 large red pepper
6 large garlic cloves, unpeeled
  juice of 1 large lemon
1 garlic clove, minced or put through a press
  salt and freshly ground pepper

Grill the tomatoes, peppers, and unpeeled garlic under a broiler or over a burner flame until uniformly charred, turning often. Remove from the heat and place the peppers in a plastic bag. Remove the skin from the tomatoes when they are cool enough to handle and place in a wide bowl or baking dish. Cut into small pieces in the bowl so that you don't lose the juice.

When the peppers are cool enough to handle, remove the skins and seeds, rinse, and pat dry. Chop and add to the tomatoes.

Squeeze the garlic out of its skin over the peppers and tomatoes. If the flesh isn't soft, chop it very fine.

Add the lemon juice, minced or pressed garlic, and salt and pepper to taste. Toss together well. Serve warm or cold.

PER PORTION:

Calories	53	Protein	2 G
Fat	.59 G	Carbohydrate	12 G
Sodium	13 MG	Cholesterol	0

TUNISIAN CAULIFLOWER
AND POTATO SALAD

MAKES 6 SERVINGS

Spicy with *harissa*, paprika, and cumin or caraway, this is a substantial winter salad. It makes a nice lunch with pita or other whole-grain bread.

2   medium-sized potatoes, scrubbed
1   small head cauliflower, broken into florets
2   to 3 garlic cloves (to taste), minced or put through a
       press
    juice of 1 large lemon
⅛   teaspoon *harissa* (page 106) or cayenne pepper
½   teaspoon paprika
1   teaspoon ground cumin or caraway
½   cup plain low-fat yogurt
    salt
2   hard-cooked eggs, peeled and chopped
    chopped fresh parsley or cilantro for garnish

Steam the potatoes until tender, about 20 minutes. Add the cauliflower for the last 5 to 10 minutes, depending on how crunchy you like it. Refresh under cold water and drain. Slice the potatoes.

In a salad bowl, mix together the garlic, lemon juice, *harissa*, paprika, cumin or caraway, yogurt, and salt to taste. Toss with the potatoes, cauliflower, and hard-cooked eggs. Serve warm or chilled, garnished with parsley or cilantro. The salad will keep for 2 or 3 days in the refrigerator.

PER PORTION:

Calories	109	Protein	6 G
Fat	3 G	Carbohydrate	17 G
Sodium	56 MG	Cholesterol	92 MG

SPICY CARROT SALAD

MAKES 4 SERVINGS

The seasonings in this salad come from a Tunisian carrot salad, in which the carrots are cooked and tossed with a similar sauce. Since I like grated carrot salads, I've come up with my own version. It's one of my favorites, lemony and *picante.*

        juice of 1 large lemon
    1   tablespoon cider or white wine vinegar
    2   garlic cloves, minced or put through a press
    ⅛ to ¼ teaspoon *harissa* (page 106) or cayenne pepper
    ½   teaspoon caraway seed or ground caraway
    ½   teaspoon ground cumin
    1   tablespoon olive oil
    3   tablespoons plain low-fat yogurt
        salt to taste
    1   pound (about 5 medium) carrots, peeled and grated
    2 to 3 tablespoons chopped cilantro

Combine the lemon juice, vinegar, garlic, *harissa,* and spices in a salad bowl and mix together well. Stir in the olive oil and yogurt and add salt to taste. Toss with the carrots and cilantro and serve or chill and serve. This salad will keep for a day or two in the refrigerator, but the cilantro should be added close to serving time.

PER PORTION:

Calories	89	Protein	2 G
Fat	4 G	Carbohydrate	13 G
Sodium	45 MG	Cholesterol	1 MG

TUNISIAN BEET AND POTATO SALAD

MAKES 4 SERVINGS

Beets and potatoes make a nice combination in this pink and red salad. The caraway adds a distinctive flavor.

    2 large beets, peeled
    2 large potatoes, scrubbed
    2 tablespoons cider or white wine vinegar
    2 tablespoons fresh lemon juice
    1 garlic clove, minced or put through a press
    2 teaspoons caraway seed, slightly crushed in a mortar
          and pestle
       salt and freshly ground pepper
    1 tablespoon olive oil
    3 tablespoons plain low-fat yogurt
    2 tablespoons chopped fresh parsley for garnish

Steam the beets and potatoes until they are both tender (the potatoes will take about 15 to 20 minutes, the beets 20 to 30). You can steam them together or separately.

Meanwhile, mix together the vinegar, lemon juice, garlic, caraway seed, salt and pepper to taste, olive oil, and yogurt in a salad bowl.

When the potatoes are cooked, refresh under cold water, drain, slice thin, and toss with the dressing. When the beets are tender, refresh under cold water, drain, dice, and gently toss with the potatoes. Correct seasonings, cover, and chill. Just before serving, garnish with the parsley. It will keep for 2 days in the refrigerator—it will also turn very pink.

PER PORTION:

Calories	151	Protein	4 G
Fat	4 G	Carbohydrate	27 G
Sodium	53 MG	Cholesterol	1 MG

TUNISIAN COOKED VEGETABLE SALAD

MAKES 8 GENEROUS SERVINGS

This is also called "Friday Night Salad" in Tunisia. In Moslem countries, Friday is the day of rest, so dinner might consist of an easy salad made from the week's leftover vegetables. You can use whatever other vegetables you have on hand.

2 medium-sized carrots, diced
½ small head cauliflower, broken into florets
2 turnips, diced
2 medium-sized boiling or new potatoes, scrubbed and diced
¼ head cabbage, shredded
juice of 1 to 2 lemons (to taste)
½ to 1 teaspoon *harissa* (page 106) *or* ¼ to ½ teaspoon cayenne pepper (to taste)
1 garlic clove, minced or put through a press
1 teaspoon ground caraway
½ teaspoon ground coriander
salt to taste
1 tablespoon olive oil
4 tablespoons plain low-fat yogurt

Place the carrots, cauliflower, turnips, potatoes, and cabbage in a steamer and steam 15 minutes or until tender. Meanwhile, combine the remaining ingredients in a salad bowl and mix well.

Refresh the vegetables under cold water and drain well. Toss with the dressing, correct seasonings, chill, and serve cold. This salad will keep for 3 or 4 days in the refrigerator.

PER PORTION:

Calories	90	Protein	3 G
Fat	2 G	Carbohydrate	16 G
Sodium	47 MG	Cholesterol	0

TUNISIAN ZUCCHINI SALAD

MAKES 4 SERVINGS

Another simple, refreshing North African salad, delicately seasoned with fresh lemon juice, olive oil, and cumin.

    1 pound zucchini, scrubbed and thinly sliced
       juice of 1 large lemon
    1 garlic clove, minced or put through a press
    ¾ teaspoon ground cumin
       salt and freshly ground pepper to taste
    1 tablespoon olive oil
    1 tablespoon plain low-fat yogurt (optional)
       chopped cilantro or fresh parsley for garnish (optional)

Steam the zucchini until tender and bright green, 5 to 10 minutes. Refresh under cold water and drain.

Mix together the remaining ingredients in a salad bowl and toss with the zucchini. Chill and serve, garnished, if you wish, with chopped cilantro or parsley. This salad will keep for a day or 2 in the refrigerator.

PER PORTION:

Calories	51	Protein	1 G
Fat	4 G	Carbohydrate	5 G
Sodium	4 MG	Cholesterol	0

TUNISIAN POTATO SALAD WITH CUMIN

MAKES 4 SERVINGS

I've always loved the combination of potatoes and cumin. So, apparently, have the Tunisians.

1½ pounds new or boiling potatoes, unpeeled
⅛ to ¼ teaspoon *harissa* (page 106) or cayenne pepper
      (to taste)
  1 teaspoon ground cumin
    juice of 1 large lemon
  1 teaspoon olive oil
  3 tablespoons plain low-fat yogurt (optional)
    salt to taste
  2 tablespoons chopped cilantro or fresh parsley
      (optional)

Steam or boil the potatoes until tender, about 15 to 20 minutes. Meanwhile, combine the remaining ingredients in a bowl and mix well.

When the potatoes are cooked, refresh under cold water, drain, cut into dice, and toss with the dressing. Serve warm or chill and serve. The potato salad will keep for 2 or 3 days in the refrigerator, without the cilantro or parsley, which should be added close to serving time.

PER PORTION:

Calories	151	Protein	4 G
Fat	2 G	Carbohydrate	32 G
Sodium	13 MG	Cholesterol	0

MOROCCAN CARROT SALAD

MAKES 4 TO 6 SERVINGS

  1 pound (about 5) carrots, peeled and grated
¾ cup minced fresh parsley
    pinch sea salt
  1 tablespoon orange flower water
1½ teaspoons mild-flavored honey (such as clover or acacia)
    juice of 2 lemons
½ teaspoon ground cumin
    leaf lettuce for the platter or bowl

Combine the carrots, parsley, and sea salt. Stir together the orange flower water, honey, lemon juice, and cumin. Just before serving, toss with the carrots. Line a platter or bowl with lettuce leaves, top with the carrots, and serve. The salad will hold for an hour or two in the refrigerator but is best tossed just before serving.

PER PORTION:

Calories	40	Protein	1 G
Fat	.17 G	Carbohydrate	10 G
Sodium	49 MG	Cholesterol	0

MOROCCAN ORANGE SALAD

MAKES 4 SERVINGS

This would be a refreshing first course for a substantial North African couscous (pages 217–224). The bright red, pungent pomegranate seeds contrast beautifully with the oranges.

  6 navel oranges
  1 tablespoon orange flower water
  ⅛ to ¼ teaspoon ground cinnamon (to taste)
  1 teaspoon mild-flavored honey (such as clover or acacia)
    pinch freshly grated nutmeg
    chopped fresh mint for garnish
    pomegranate seeds for garnish

Cut away the skin and white pith of the oranges by rotating a small sharp knife held at an angle against the orange. Hold over the salad bowl as you do this so you can catch the juice. Slice the oranges into rounds.

Combine the orange flower water, cinnamon, and honey and toss with the oranges. Sprinkle with a little nutmeg and chill or serve at once, garnishing with fresh mint and pomegranate seeds. This will hold for several hours in the refrigerator.

PER PORTION:

Calories	102	Protein	2 G
Fat	.19 G	Carbohydrate	26 G
Sodium	2 MG	Cholesterol	0

ORANGE AND GRATED CARROT SALAD

MAKES 4 TO 6 SERVINGS

This too would make a light first course, with couscous to follow.

- 2 navel oranges
- 1 pound (about 5) carrots, peeled and grated
- 1 teaspoon ground cinnamon
- 3 tablespoons fresh lemon juice
- 1 teaspoon orange flower water
  pinch salt
- 1 tablespoon chopped fresh mint

Cut away the skin and white pith of the oranges by rotating against a small sharp knife held at an angle against the orange. Hold over the salad bowl as you do this so you can catch the juice. Now cut the sections of the orange away from the membranes, still holding above the bowl, by running the knife between the membranes and the edges of the orange sections. Place in the bowl and toss with the carrots, cinnamon, lemon juice, and orange flower water. Add a little salt and refrigerate until ready to serve. It will hold for several hours. Just before serving, toss with the mint.

PER PORTION:

Calories	53	Protein	1 G
Fat	.17 G	Carbohydrate	13 G
Sodium	46 MG	Cholesterol	0

MOROCCAN TOMATO AND HOT PEPPER SALAD

MAKES 4 TO 6 SERVINGS

This unique, *picante* salad combines roasted sweet green peppers with fresh fiery-hot ones. The cucumber has a welcome cooling effect.

4 green peppers
4 large ripe tomatoes, peeled, seeded, and diced
1 cucumber, peeled, seeded, and diced
2 to 3 teaspoons minced fresh chili peppers (to taste),
     seeds and membranes removed
   salt and freshly ground pepper
   juice of ½ large lemon (more to taste)
1 to 2 garlic cloves (to taste), minced or put through a
     press
¼ to ½ teaspoon ground cumin (to taste)
1 tablespoon olive oil
2 tablespoons plain low-fat yogurt (optional)
2 to 3 tablespoons chopped fresh parsley or cilantro

Roast the green peppers under the broiler or over a gas burner until uniformly charred. Place in a plastic or paper bag and allow to cool. Remove the charred skin, rinse, pat dry, remove seeds and membranes, and dice.

Toss together the tomatoes, diced roasted peppers, cucumber, and chili peppers. Add salt and pepper to taste.

Mix together the lemon juice, garlic, cumin, olive oil, and yogurt. Toss with the vegetables. Just before serving, toss with the parsley or cilantro. Serve at room temperature or chilled. It will keep for a day or two in the refrigerator, but add the parsley or cilantro just before serving.

PER PORTION:

Calories	60	Protein	2 G
Fat	3 G	Carbohydrate	9 G
Sodium	13 MG	Cholesterol	0

NORTH AFRICAN BEET SALAD

MAKES 6 SERVINGS

This pretty Moroccan salad has the characteristic seasonings: orange flower water, sweet spices like cinnamon and nutmeg, or earthy ones like cumin.

    2 pounds beets, trimmed
       juice of 1 large lemon
    ½ teaspoon ground cumin
    ½ teaspoon paprika
    ¼ teaspoon ground cinnamon
    1 tablespoon orange flower water
    2 tablespoons olive oil
       salt and freshly ground pepper
    2 tablespoons chopped fresh parsley
       leaf or romaine lettuce for the bowl

Wash the beets and place on a plate in a steamer. Steam until tender, about 20 to 30 minutes. Set aside the liquid that accumulates on the plate and refresh the beets under cold water. Peel and slice.

Toss the beets with the lemon juice, cumin, paprika, cinnamon, orange flower water, olive oil, and the steaming liquid that accumulated on the plate. Add salt and pepper to taste, cover, and chill. It will keep a day or two in the refrigerator.

Just before serving, toss with parsley. Line a bowl or platter with the lettuce leaves, top with the beets, and serve.

PER PORTION:

Calories	88	Protein	2 G
Fat	5 G	Carbohydrate	11 G
Sodium	73 MG	Cholesterol	0

CHAPTER THREE

SOUPS

In Provence all of my friends who are great cooks (in other words, all of my friends in Provence) make delicious soups.

During the harvest at Lulu and Lucien Peyraud's Bandol winery, Domaine Tempier, soup is often served for dinner. Lunch is the big meal, to fortify for the hard work of harvesting grapes, and dinner is light, to ensure a good night's sleep. Lulu Peyraud can whip up a delicious soup in no time—she has enough work as it is feeding 25 people lunch every day. She makes one of the many *Provençal* garlic soups, or a simple tomato soup with vermicelli, a *pistou*, or a vegetable *potage*. They are always light and fragrant restoratives after a hard day's work.

I've also seen Christine Picasso transform parsley, potatoes, and water into the most beautiful, heartwarming soup (page 149), and Patricia Wells makes the best *pistou* I've ever tasted.

It's traditional in Europe to have an evening soup rather than a big supper. It's also a wise course for the dieter. If you consume the bulk of your calories earlier in the day, you will burn off more of them. Soup tends to be filling because of the liquid; one bowl can satisfy. Nathan Pritikin, famous for his weight-loss programs for heart patients, used to say, "If you want to lose weight, eat soup." And how pleasurable eating a warm soup in the evening can be.

Soups in southern Europe tend to be light vegetable soups or fish soups. Often no stock other than water is used, although I often use a garlic broth (page 142) or a light chicken stock (page 152). For Italian *minestrone* (page 128), which can be a meal in itself, I substitute soaking liquid from dried mushrooms for meat stock.

In the Middle East and North Africa many of the soups are heartier fare, thick and sustaining with legumes—lentils, chick-peas, white beans, or black-eyed peas—and pungent with the spices of the East, such as cumin, coriander, cardamom, and cinnamon. I've taken liberties with many of these soups and removed fatty meat from some of the traditional recipes. With the legumes and spices, they don't need the meat to be protein-rich and delicious.

HEARTY SOUPS

TUSCAN BEAN AND VEGETABLE SOUP

MAKES 6 SERVINGS

This is a thick, hearty bean soup with lots of mineral-rich dark, leafy greens. The soup is thickened by pureeing some of the beans.

- ½ pound dried white beans, washed and picked over
- 1 quart water
- 1 bay leaf
- salt
- 1 tablespoon olive oil
- 2 medium-sized yellow onions, chopped
- 4 large garlic cloves, minced or put through a press
- 2 celery stalks, diced
- 3 medium-sized carrots, peeled and diced
- 4 medium-sized potatoes, diced
- 1 pound tomatoes, chopped
- 3 pounds Swiss chard, stems removed, leaves cleaned and chopped
- 1 pound kale, stems removed, leaves cleaned and chopped
- ½ head Savoy cabbage, finely shredded
- 1 tablespoon tomato paste
- 1 dried hot red chili pepper
- 1 teaspoon dried thyme
- 5 to 6 cups water
- the cooking water from the beans
- salt and freshly ground pepper
- 12 slices whole-wheat Tuscan bread (page 24) or Crusty Country Bread (page 35)
- 1 additional large garlic clove, cut in half

Soak the beans overnight in 3 times their volume of water (use bottled water if your tap water is hard), drain, and combine with 1 quart water in a soup pot or large saucepan. Bring to a boil, add the bay leaf, reduce heat, cover, and simmer 1 to 2 hours, until tender. Add salt to taste to the cooking liquid, drain the beans, and retain the cooking liquid. Puree half the beans in some of their cooking liquid in a blender or food processor fitted with the steel blade and set aside.

Heat the olive oil in a large heavy-bottomed soup pot over low heat and add the onion and half the garlic. Sauté, stirring, for about 5 minutes and add the celery and carrots. Sauté, stirring, another 10 minutes, and add all the remaining vegetables, tomato paste, chili pepper, whole cooked beans, thyme, 5 cups water, and cooking liquid from the beans. Add some salt, bring to a simmer, cover, and simmer 1 hour. If the vegetables aren't covered, add another cup of water. Stir in the pureed beans and the remaining garlic and mix well. Taste and add salt and pepper to taste and more thyme or garlic if you wish. This soup will keep for 5 days in the refrigerator and freezes well, too.

Toast the Tuscan bread and rub each piece with garlic. Place in each soup bowl, ladle in the hot soup, and serve.

Note: You could also use the pink Italian cranberry beans for this soup, and you can enrich the flavor, if you wish, by adding a Parmesan rind or two to the simmering soup.

PER PORTION:

Calories	515	Protein	25 G
Fat	5 G	Carbohydrate	102 G
Sodium	544 MG	Cholesterol	0

PUREE OF WHITE BEAN SOUP

MAKES 6 SERVINGS

This has always been a household favorite. It's an elegant soup, thick and garlicky.

- 1 **pound dried white beans (great northern, navy, or small white), washed and picked over**
- 1 **tablespoon olive or vegetable oil**
- 1 **onion, chopped**
- 1 **leek, white part only, washed and sliced**
- 3 **garlic cloves, minced or put through a press**
- 2 **quarts water**

1 small potato, peeled and diced
¼ teaspoon dried thyme
1 bay leaf
  salt
½ cup nonfat milk, plus up to ½ cup more if desired
  freshly ground pepper
  juice of 1 large lemon
¼ cup chopped fresh parsley for garnish
4 slices whole-wheat bread, such as Crusty Country
      Bread, page 35, toasted, for garnish

Soak the beans overnight in 3 times their volume of water (use bottled water if your tap water is hard). Heat the oil in a large heavy-bottomed soup pot or casserole and add the onion, leek, and 1 clove of the garlic. Sauté until the onion is tender.

Drain the beans and add, along with 2 quarts fresh water, the remaining garlic, the potato, thyme, and bay leaf. Bring to a boil, reduce heat, cover, and simmer 1½ to 2 hours or until the beans are tender. Add salt to taste and remove the bay leaf.

Puree the soup in a blender in batches until smooth. Return to the pot and stir in the milk. Thin out with more milk if desired. Heat through and add pepper to taste. Stir in the lemon juice, taste and adjust seasonings, and serve, topping each bowl with a generous sprinkling of parsley and a whole-wheat crouton. The soup will keep 4 or 5 days in the refrigerator, before adding the lemon juice and parsley. It freezes well, also. Leftovers will keep 4 or 5 days.

WHITE BEAN PUREE

For an equally elegant puree, follow the recipe through removal of the bay leaf. Drain the beans and puree through a food mill or in a food processor. Thin out as desired with milk and season to taste with lemon juice and freshly ground pepper. Transfer to a buttered serving dish and keep warm in a 250-degree oven until ready to serve. Garnish with chopped fresh parsley.

PER PORTION:

Calories	343	Protein	21 G
Fat	3 G	Carbohydrate	60 G
Sodium	108 MG	Cholesterol	1 MG

SPRINGTIME MINESTRONE WITH BASIL

MAKES 6 TO 8 SERVINGS

This soup was inspired by a *minestrone* I ate in southern Italy; it was the best *minestrone* I've ever eaten in a restaurant anywhere. It was thick with spring vegetables, sweet peas, chard, turnips, and different kinds of beans. The broth was a meat broth but not at all greasy; I have achieved a similar meaty broth by combining soaking water from dried mushrooms with my garlic broth. This soup gets better over time. I made it in quantity for a party once, and we had the leftovers for the next four days—it tasted better each day. Definitely try to make the soup a day before you serve it.

The addition of the large quantity of basil, garlic, and Parmesan at the end makes this soup reminiscent of the French *pistou*. An authentic *pistou* would have a paste of basil, garlic, tomatoes, and lots of olive oil added at the end. Here we have the good flavor of the basil without the calories of the extra olive oil. The Parmesan rinds add depth to the flavor with almost no extra calories.

FOR THE BEANS:

    1 **cup dried white beans, washed and picked over**
    ½ **cup *borlotti* (cranberry) beans (optional)**
    6 **cups water**
    4 **garlic cloves, minced or put through a press**
    1 **bay leaf**
    1 **teaspoon salt (more or less to taste)**

FOR THE SOUP:

    ½ **ounce dried *porcini* mushrooms**
    2 **cups warm water (enough to cover mushrooms)**
    1 **tablespoon olive oil**
    1 **large onion, chopped**
    5 **garlic cloves, minced or put through a press**
    2 **leeks, white part only, cleaned and sliced**
    2 **carrots, sliced**
    2 **celery stalks, sliced**
    ½ **small head green cabbage, shredded**
    2 **quarts garlic broth (page 142)**
    2 **Parmesan rinds, wrapped in cheesecloth with 1 bay leaf and 2 sprigs thyme**
    3 **medium-sized potatoes, scrubbed and diced**
    2 **medium-sized turnips, peeled and diced**

  1 14-ounce can tomatoes, with juice, chopped
 ½ teaspoon thyme
 ½ teaspoon oregano
 ½ cup pasta, either broken spaghetti, shells, or
       orecchiette (optional)
  1 cup fresh peas or thawed frozen petite peas
 ½ pound green beans, cut into 1-inch lengths
  2 cups Swiss chard, shredded
  1 medium-sized zucchini, thinly sliced (optional)
     salt and freshly ground pepper
     pinch cayenne pepper (optional)
  1 additional large garlic clove, finely minced or put
       through a press
 ½ cup chopped fresh basil
 ¼ cup chopped fresh parsley
 ⅓ cup freshly grated Parmesan cheese for the table
       (optional)

PREPARE THE BEANS:

Soak the white beans overnight in 1 quart water and the cranberry beans overnight in 2 cups water (use bottled water if your tap water is hard). Drain and cook in 6 cups water along with the garlic and bay leaf. Bring to a boil, reduce heat, cover, and simmer 1 hour or until tender. Add 1 teaspoon salt toward the end of the cooking time. Remove the bay leaf and drain, retaining the liquid.

PREPARE THE SOUP:

Place the mushrooms in a bowl and pour on warm water to cover. Let soak 30 minutes. Drain, retaining the soaking water, and squeeze the mushrooms dry. Rinse the mushrooms thoroughly in several rinses of cold water, chop, and set aside. Strain the soaking liquid through a strainer lined with a double thickness of kitchen towels and set aside.

Meanwhile, heat the olive oil over medium-low heat in a large heavy-bottomed soup pot and sauté the onion, half the garlic, and the leeks until tender and translucent, about 5 to 10 minutes. Add the carrots, celery, and cabbage and continue to sauté 5 to 10 minutes, stirring so the vegetables don't brown. Add the remaining garlic, the mushrooms and their soaking liquid, the garlic broth, the cheesecloth with the Parmesan rinds and herbs, the potatoes, the turnips, and the tomatoes and bring to a boil. Reduce heat, cover, and simmer 45 minutes. Add the beans and 1 cup of their cooking broth (more to taste), thyme, and oregano and continue to cook another ½ hour to an hour. Fifteen minutes before serving, add the pasta and peas to the simmering soup. Ten minutes before serving, add the green beans, chard, and zucchini to the simmering broth. Remove the cheesecloth with the Parmesan rinds and herbs.

Taste the soup and adjust seasonings, adding salt, a generous amount of pepper, more garlic, and the optional pinch of cayenne if desired. Stir in the last clove of garlic, the basil, and the parsley, and serve. Sprinkle Parmesan over the top if you wish.

Note: Another way to assure that the green vegetables retain their vibrant color and remain crunchy is to steam them separately and add them to the soup along with the basil just before serving.

The soup can be made a day ahead, up to the addition of the basil and parsley, which should be added just before serving. You can eat the leftovers for a week, or freeze them.

PER PORTION:

Calories	257	Protein	12 G
Fat	3 G	Carbohydrate	50 G
Sodium	985 MG	Cholesterol	0

MEATLESS HARIRA (Moroccan Ramadan Soup)

MAKES 8 SERVINGS

An authentic *harira* contains lamb and sometimes chicken, so maybe I shouldn't give this thick potage that name. It is, however, based on recipes in Moroccan cookbooks. Rich with spices and legumes, it makes a filling meal.

½ cup dried chick-peas, washed and picked over
½ cup dried white beans, washed and picked over
2 tablespoons safflower oil
2 medium-sized yellow onions, chopped
1 teaspoon ground turmeric
¼ teaspoon powdered saffron
1 teaspoon freshly ground black pepper
1 teaspoon ground cinnamon
¼ teaspoon ground ginger
¾ cup chopped celery leaves and stalks
2 tablespoons finely chopped cilantro
½ cup finely chopped fresh parsley
2 pounds fresh (8 to 10) tomatoes, peeled, seeded, and
    chopped, or canned tomatoes
¾ cup lentils, washed and picked over

2½ quarts water
    salt and freshly ground pepper
½ cup fine *vermicelli* or cooked rice or wheat berries
 1 egg, beaten
    juice of ½ to 1 lemon (to taste)
    lemon slices, ground cinnamon, and chopped cilantro
        for garnish

Soak the chick-peas and white beans overnight or for several hours in 3 times their volume of water (use bottled water if your tap water is hard).

Heat the oil over low heat in a heavy-bottomed soup pot and sauté the onion for 5 to 10 minutes, stirring, until tender and beginning to color. Add the spices, celery, cilantro, and parsley and sauté, stirring, for another 2 to 3 minutes. Add the tomatoes and continue to cook, stirring occasionally, over medium-low heat for another 10 to 15 minutes. Drain the chick-peas and white beans and add to the pot along with the lentils and 2½ quarts of water; bring to a boil. Reduce heat and simmer, partially covered, for 1½ hours, or until the beans are thoroughly tender. Season to taste with salt and pepper. Mash some of the beans against the side of the pot with a wooden spoon to thicken the broth slightly. At this point the soup can be held in the refrigerator for 3 or 4 days, or frozen.

About 5 minutes before serving, stir in the *vermicelli*. Meanwhile, mix together the egg and lemon. When the *vermicelli* is cooked, turn off the heat and quickly stir in the egg-lemon mixture. Serve at once, garnished with lemon slices, a light sprinkling of cinnamon, and chopped cilantro.

PER PORTION:

Calories	249	Protein	13 G
Fat	6 G	Carbohydrate	39 G
Sodium	36 MG	Cholesterol	34 MG

WHITE BEAN SOUP WITH TOMATOES, ZUCCHINI, AND BASIL

MAKES 6 TO 8 SERVINGS

This white bean soup is a colorful combination, studded with tomatoes and zucchini and sprinkled with bright fresh basil. It's a spring/summer soup, lighter than the pureed white bean soup on page 126, with half the beans.

½ pound dried white beans (great northern or navy
    beans), washed and picked over
1 tablespoon olive oil
1 large onion, chopped
3 to 4 garlic cloves, minced or put through a press
2 quarts water
    a *bouquet garni* consisting of 1 bay leaf, 1 sprig
        parsley, and 1 sprig thyme tied together
½ pound new potatoes, washed and diced
1 pound tomatoes, peeled, seeded, and cut into small dice
1 tablespoon tomato paste
¼ to ½ teaspoon dried thyme (to taste)
    salt
½ pound (2 medium) zucchini, diced
    freshly ground pepper
3 tablespoons minced fresh basil (more to taste)
    fresh lemon juice to taste (optional)
4 tablespoons freshly grated Parmesan cheese for garnish

Soak the beans overnight in 2 quarts water (use bottled water if your tap
water is hard). Drain.

Heat the oil in a large heavy-bottomed soup pot and add the onion and
half the garlic. Sauté over medium-low heat until the onion is translucent.

Add the beans, 2 quarts fresh water, the *bouquet garni*, and the diced
potatoes; bring to a boil. Reduce heat, cover, and simmer 1 hour.

Add the remaining garlic, the tomatoes, tomato paste, thyme, and salt to
taste and simmer another 30 minutes, or until the beans are tender. Remove
the *bouquet garni*, add the zucchini and pepper to taste, and simmer another 10
to 15 minutes, until the zucchini is cooked through but retains a bright green
color.

Just before serving, stir the chopped fresh basil and lemon juice, if
desired, into the soup. Taste and adjust seasonings, adding salt, pepper,
garlic, lemon juice, or basil if desired, and serve at once. Pass Parmesan for
sprinkling over the top.

The soup will hold in the refrigerator, before adding the zucchini, for 3 or
4 days, or can be frozen. The zucchini and remaining ingredients should be
added close to serving time. Leftovers will keep for 3 or 4 days, but the colors
will fade.

PER PORTION:

Calories	171	Protein	10 G
Fat	3 G	Carbohydrate	28 G
Sodium	85 MG	Cholesterol	2 MG

SOUPE BASQUE

MAKES 4 SERVINGS

This is based on a recipe in Elizabeth David's *Mediterranean Food.*

- ½ pound dried white beans, washed and picked over
- 1 tablespoon olive oil
- 1 onion, chopped
- 2 garlic cloves, minced or put through a press
- ½ pound pumpkin, peeled and chopped
- 1 small head white cabbage, chopped
- 2 quarts vegetable stock (page 140) or chicken stock (page 152)
  salt and freshly ground pepper to taste
- 1 teaspoon dried thyme
- 1 to 2 additional garlic cloves (to taste), minced or put through a press (optional)

Soak the beans overnight in 3 times their volume of water (use bottled water if your tap water is hard).

Heat the oil in a heavy-bottomed soup pot and sauté the onion and garlic over medium heat, stirring, until the onion begins to color. Add the remaining ingredients except the salt, pepper, thyme, and additional garlic and bring to a boil. Reduce heat, cover, and cook 2 to 3 hours. Add salt to taste, pepper, and thyme after the first hour. Shortly before serving, taste and add more garlic if you wish. Adjust seasonings and serve with Crusty Country Bread (page 35). The soup will keep for 3 or 4 days in the refrigerator and freezes well.

PER PORTION:

Calories	368	Protein	19 G
Fat	4 G	Carbohydrate	68 G
Sodium	616 MG	Cholesterol	0

SPICY ITALIAN CHICK-PEA SOUP

MAKES 6 SERVINGS

This soup is very simple to make; the ingredients are staples you should have on hand in the pantry. This filling, slightly *picante* soup makes a satisfying, warming winter meal.

- 1 pound dried chick-peas, washed and picked over
- 2 quarts water
- 1 tablespoon olive oil
- 1 large onion, chopped
- 3 large garlic cloves (more to taste), minced or put through a press
- 1 pound (4 to 5) fresh or canned tomatoes, chopped
- 4 tablespoons tomato paste
- 1 rind of Parmesan cheese (optional)
- 1 bay leaf
- 1 small dried hot red pepper, such as cayenne
- ½ teaspoon dried thyme
- ½ teaspoon dried oregano
- salt and freshly ground pepper
- chopped fresh parsley for garnish

Soak the chick-peas overnight in 3 times their volume of water (use bottled water if your tap water is hard).

Combine the soaked chick-peas with 2 quarts water, bring to a boil, reduce heat, and simmer, covered, for 1 hour. Set aside.

Heat the olive oil in a heavy-bottomed soup pot and sauté the onion with 1 clove of the garlic until the onion is tender. Add the chick-peas and their water, the tomatoes, tomato paste, Parmesan rind, bay leaf, and hot red pepper and bring to a boil. Reduce heat, cover, and simmer 1 to 2 hours, until the beans are tender. Add the thyme, oregano, salt and pepper to taste, and hot pepper and more garlic if you wish, and continue to simmer another 20 minutes. Remove the Parmesan rind and bay leaf; serve garnished with chopped fresh parsley. The soup will keep up to 5 days in the refrigerator and freezes well.

PER PORTION:

Calories	333	Protein	16 G
Fat	7 G	Carbohydrate	54 G
Sodium	111 MG	Cholesterol	0

PUREED LENTIL SOUP

MAKES 6 SERVINGS

This is just one of many lentil soups you will find throughout the Mediterranean. You can vary its texture by pureeing only half the lentils, or you can puree the entire quantity for a smooth, creamy *potage*. I prefer the latter.

1 tablespoon olive oil
1 large onion, chopped
4 garlic cloves, minced or put through a press
1 celery stalk, chopped
2 cups green or brown lentils, washed and picked over
2 quarts water
1 bay leaf
 salt and freshly ground pepper
 juice of ½ to 1 lemon (to taste; optional)
1 to 2 teaspoons ground cumin (to taste)
2 to 3 tablespoons chopped fresh parsley (to taste) for
    garnish
 garlic croutons for garnish (*crostini,* page 53)

Heat the oil in a heavy-bottomed soup pot and sauté the onion and garlic until the onion begins to color. Add the celery and sauté another few minutes. Add the lentils, water, and bay leaf. Bring to a boil, reduce heat, cover, and cook 30 to 40 minutes, until the lentils are tender. Add salt and pepper to taste, lemon juice if you wish, and the cumin. Simmer another 5 to 10 minutes. Remove the bay leaf.

Remove the soup from the heat and puree all of it or some of it in a blender or through the fine blade of a food mill. Return to the pot and heat through, stirring. If the soup seems too watery, simmer a bit longer to reduce, making sure to stir often so that it doesn't stick to the bottom of the pot. Adjust seasonings and serve, garnished with parsley and garlic croutons. The soup will keep 3 to 5 days, refrigerated. It also freezes well.

PER PORTION:

Calories	252	Protein	19 G
Fat	3 G	Carbohydrate	40 G
Sodium	15 MG	Cholesterol	0

MOROCCAN CHICK-PEA SOUP

MAKES 4 TO 6 SERVINGS

The farther south you go in the Mediterranean region, the more complex and intriguing the flavors become. This chick-pea soup is quite unlike the European chick-pea dishes; pungent with spices and fiery with *harissa*, it is almost like an Indian curry.

1 cup dried (½ pound) chick-peas, washed and picked over
½ cup chopped fresh parsley
¼ teaspoon freshly ground black pepper
¼ teaspoon powdered saffron
¼ teaspoon ground turmeric
¼ teaspoon ground ginger
1 teaspoon ground cumin
⅓ cup grated onion
1 tablespoon tomato paste
1 large potato, unpeeled and diced
¼ to ½ teaspoon *harissa* (page 106) or cayenne pepper
     (to taste)
2 quarts water
  salt
¼ cup fresh lemon juice (optional)
¼ cup chopped cilantro

Soak the chick-peas overnight or for several hours in 3 times their volume of water (use bottled water if your tap water is hard); drain.

Combine the soaked beans with all the other ingredients except the salt, lemon juice, and cilantro and bring to a boil. Reduce heat and simmer, partially covered, for 1½ hours, until the beans are tender. Add salt to taste. Remove 2 cups of the soup and puree in a blender; return to the pot and mix well.

Just before serving, stir in the lemon juice if desired and the cilantro and correct seasonings.

The soup will keep 3 to 5 days in the refrigerator, but add lemon juice and cilantro just before serving. It also freezes well.

PER PORTION:

Calories	161	Protein	8 G
Fat	2 G	Carbohydrate	28 G
Sodium	37 MG	Cholesterol	0

HUMMUS SOUP

MAKES 6 SERVINGS

Since I love all the flavors of *hummus*, I decided to see if they would translate into a soup. They do. This tastes best if served the day after it's made.

½ pound chick-peas, washed and picked over
6 cups water
½ teaspoon ground turmeric
1 teaspoon ground cumin
½ teaspoon ground coriander
  pinch saffron threads
1 teaspoon salt (more to taste)
2 large garlic cloves, peeled (more to taste)
  juice of 2 lemons (4 to 6 tablespoons lemon juice; to
      taste)
2 tablespoons tahini
1 cup plain low-fat yogurt, plus additional for garnish
  lemon wedges for garnish

Soak the chick-peas overnight in 3 times their volume of water (use bottled water if your tap water is hard).

Drain the chick-peas and combine with the water, turmeric, cumin, and coriander in a large heavy-bottomed soup pot. Bring to a boil and add the saffron. Cover, reduce heat, and simmer 1 hour. Add the salt and continue to simmer another hour or until the beans are tender.

Blend the soup to a smooth puree in a blender or food processor along with the garlic, lemon juice, and tahini. Pour back into the pot and whisk in the yogurt. Thin out, if you wish, with water or additional yogurt. Taste and adjust seasonings.

Heat through and serve, topping each bowl with a spoonful of yogurt and garnishing with a lemon wedge for squeezing over the soup. The soup will keep for 3 or 4 days in the refrigerator and can be frozen.

PER PORTION:

Calories	199	Protein	10 G
Fat	5 G	Carbohydrate	27 G
Sodium	287 MG	Cholesterol	2 MG

HOT YOGURT SOUP
WITH BARLEY AND CORIANDER

MAKES 4 TO 6 SERVINGS

Fragrant and hearty yogurt soups, served hot or cold, are common in the Middle East. The yogurt is stabilized by mixing it with cornstarch, so it doesn't curdle when it cooks.

½ cup barley, washed
2 cups water
   pinch salt
1 tablespoon cornstarch
2 tablespoons water
2½ cups plain low-fat yogurt
1 tablespoon safflower oil
1 medium-sized onion, finely chopped
2 garlic cloves, minced or put through a press
3 cups garlic broth (page 142) or vegetable stock
   (page 140)
   salt and freshly ground pepper
1 bunch cilantro, chopped

Combine the barley and 2 cups water in a saucepan and bring to a boil. Add a pinch of salt, reduce heat, cover, and simmer 40 minutes or until the barley is tender. Pour off any water that has not evaporated and set the barley aside.

Dissolve the cornstarch in the 2 tablespoons water in a bowl and stir into the yogurt.

Heat the oil over medium heat in a heavy-bottomed soup pot and sauté the onion and garlic until the onion begins to brown. Turn down the heat and stir in the yogurt mixture. Heat through gently for a few minutes, stirring. Stir in the stock and the barley and bring slowly to a bare simmer. Do not boil. Add salt to taste and lots of pepper. Stir in the cilantro. Taste, adjust seasonings, and serve. This soup will hold, before adding the cilantro, for a day or two in the refrigerator.

PER PORTION:

Calories	161	Protein	8 G
Fat	4 G	Carbohydrate	24 G
Sodium	371 MG	Cholesterol	6 MG

PAPPA AI POMODORI
(Bread and Tomato Soup)

MAKES 4 TO 6 SERVINGS

The Italians really are culinary geniuses. Who else could have come up with such a delicious way to get rid of stale bread? This is one of their tastiest inventions; it's called a soup, but really it's got the texture of a mush, so thick it can be served on a plate. And it's a very savory mush at that, fragrant with basil and tomatoes. I first tasted this dish at a marvelous Italian restaurant in New York called Da Silvano. I think they called it a tomato soup there, because if they'd called it a bread soup they probably wouldn't have had many takers.

        1   tablespoon olive oil
        1   small onion, chopped
        4   garlic cloves, coarsely chopped
    1 ½   pounds (6 or 7) ripe tomatoes, quartered
        3   tablespoons tomato paste
            pinch cayenne pepper or hot pepper flakes
        2   tablespoons coarsely chopped or torn fresh basil
        1   pound whole-wheat or white bread, preferably a coarse
                country variety (such as Crusty Country Bread on
                page 35) a few days old if possible, cut into cubes
        5   cups garlic broth (page 142) or water
            salt and freshly ground pepper

Heat the oil in a large heavy-bottomed soup pot over low heat and sauté the onion and garlic gently for 10 to 15 minutes, being careful not to brown. Add the tomatoes, tomato paste, and cayenne and continue to simmer 20 minutes, stirring occasionally. Add the basil, bread, stock, and salt to taste and simmer 10 to 15 minutes, stirring and mashing the bread with a wooden spoon from time to time and being careful that the bread doesn't scorch on the bottom of the pot. Add lots of freshly ground pepper, adjust the salt, cover, and remove from the heat. Serve warm, at room temperature, or chilled, on plates or in bowls. The soup will keep 1 or 2 days in the refrigerator.

PER PORTION:

Calories	254	Protein	10 G
Fat	5 G	Carbohydrate	47 G
Sodium	932 MG	Cholesterol	2 MG

VEGETABLE STOCK

MAKES 2 QUARTS

This is a mild, fragrant stock that makes an excellent base for soups. The vegetables can be prepared quickly, and the stock requires no skimming. The stock freezes well.

- 2 quarts plus 1 cup water
- 2 large onions, peeled and quartered
- 6 large garlic cloves, peeled
- 2 large carrots, peeled and coarsely sliced
- 2 large potatoes, scrubbed and quartered
- 2 leeks, white part only, cleaned and thickly sliced
- 2 celery stalks, thickly sliced
    a *bouquet garni* made with 1 bay leaf, a couple of
        sprigs of parsley, and a few sprigs of thyme
- 12 whole peppercorns
- 1 teaspoon salt (more to taste)

Combine all the ingredients in a large soup pot and bring to a boil. Reduce heat, cover, and simmer 1 to 2 hours. Strain and discard the vegetables.

Note: For a "meatier"-tasting stock, add 1 tablespoon soy sauce and a couple of dried mushrooms, soaked for 30 minutes in warm water and rinsed thoroughly. Strain the mushroom soaking liquid through a strainer lined with kitchen towels and add to the stock.

PER 1-CUP PORTION:

Calories	42	Protein	1 G
Fat	.10 G	Carbohydrate	9 G
Sodium	288 MG	Cholesterol	0

GARLIC SOUPS

AÏGO BOUÏDO (*Provençal Garlic Soup*)

MAKES 4 SERVINGS

There are so many versions of garlic soup that I filled a chapter with them in my garlic cookbook, *Garlic Cookery*. "*Aïgo bouïdo sauva la vido*," says an old *Provençal* maxim, and I think this soup *could* save one's life. Garlic does have restorative powers, and this fragrant *potage* can be made in minutes.

    5 cups water
    6 large garlic cloves, minced or put through a press
    1 to 2 teaspoons salt (to taste)
    ½ teaspoon dried thyme
    4 fresh sage leaves, chopped, *or* ½ teaspoon dried
    1 bay leaf
    1 egg
    2 tablespoons chopped fresh parsley
    6 to 8 *crostini* (page 53)

Bring the water to a boil and add the garlic, salt, thyme, sage, and bay leaf. Simmer 10 to 15 minutes. Adjust seasonings.

Beat the egg in a bowl and ladle in some hot soup. Stir together, then stir back into the soup. Serve at once, topping each bowl with parsley and a *crostini* or two.

PER PORTION:

Calories	235	Protein	8 G
Fat	7 G	Carbohydrate	37 G
Sodium	1,139 MG	Cholesterol	69 MG

GARLIC SOUP MADRILENO

MAKES 4 TO 6 SERVINGS

In France, garlic soup is served in the home but rarely in restaurants. In Spain, however, I almost always found *sopa de ajo* on Spanish restaurant menus.

- 1 tablespoon olive oil
- 6 large garlic cloves, peeled
- 1 pound (4 to 5) tomatoes, coarsely chopped
- 1 small bay leaf
- ½ teaspoon paprika
- 5 cups boiling water
  salt and freshly ground pepper
- 4 to 6 *crostini* (page 53)
- 2 tablespoons chopped fresh parsley

Heat the oil in a soup pot and sauté the garlic over medium heat until it begins to brown, about 5 minutes. Add the tomatoes, bay leaf, and paprika and continue to sauté 10 minutes over moderate heat, stirring occasionally.

Pour in the boiling water and add salt to taste. Simmer, covered, 15 minutes. Remove the bay leaf and puree the soup through the medium disk of a Mouli food mill. Return to the pot. Add salt and pepper to taste, heat through, and serve, topping each bowl with a *crostini* and chopped fresh parsley. The soup will keep a day or two in the refrigerator.

PER PORTION:

Calories	144	Protein	4 G
Fat	5 G	Carbohydrate	22 G
Sodium	156 MG	Cholesterol	0

GARLIC BROTH

MAKES 6 CUPS

I often use this stock for my soups. It is very fragrant, and it can often be used interchangeably with chicken broth.

2 heads garlic, cloves separated and peeled
6 cups water
1 bay leaf
2 parsley sprigs
2 thyme sprigs *or* ¼ teaspoon dried thyme
1 to 2 teaspoons salt (to taste)

Combine all the ingredients in a stockpot and bring to a boil. Reduce heat, cover, and simmer 1 hour. Strain. Keep on hand in the refrigerator for soups or freeze. The broth will keep for 4 to 5 days in the refrigerator and can be frozen for up to 3 months.

PER 1-CUP PORTION:

Calories	18	Protein	1 G
Fat	.06 G	Carbohydrate	4 G
Sodium	551 MG	Cholesterol	0

GARLIC SOUP WITH POACHED EGGS, FROM SEVILLE

MAKES 6 SERVINGS

Serve this fragrant soup for a light supper, with a crisp green salad, and you'll all sleep well; garlic is a soporific.

6 cups water
1 tablespoon tomato paste
8 large garlic cloves, minced or put through a press
1 to 2 teaspoons salt (to taste)
½ teaspoon dried thyme
4 fresh sage leaves, chopped, *or* ½ teaspoon dried
1 bay leaf
freshly ground pepper
6 *crostini* (page 53), rubbed with garlic and brushed lightly with olive oil
6 eggs
2 tablespoons chopped fresh parsley for garnish

Bring the water to a boil and add the tomato paste, garlic, salt, thyme, sage, and bay leaf. Simmer 10 to 15 minutes. Add pepper to taste and adjust seasonings.

Meanwhile, poach the eggs in a separate pan. Place a poached egg on a *crostini* in each serving bowl and ladle in the soup. Sprinkle with parsley and serve.

PER PORTION:

Calories	192	Protein	10 G
Fat	8 G	Carbohydrate	21 G
Sodium	867 MG	Cholesterol	273 MG

AVGOLEMONO (Egg-Lemon Soup)

MAKES 4 SERVINGS

This is on menus all over Greece. The soup traditionally calls for chicken stock, but I like the fragrance of garlic broth (page 142). I have reduced the number of eggs usually called for.

    1 quart garlic broth (page 142)
    2 eggs
    ½ cup fresh lemon juice
    1 cup cooked brown or other rice
       salt and freshly ground black pepper
    4 tablespoons chopped fresh parsley
       thin lemon slices for garnish

Bring the garlic broth to a simmer.

Beat the eggs in a bowl and beat in the lemon juice. Stir a ladleful of the soup into this mixture, then transfer to the soup pot. Heat through but do not boil, or the eggs will curdle. Adjust salt and pepper to taste.

Divide the rice among the soup bowls and spoon in the soup. Garnish with parsley and lemon slices and serve.

PER PORTION:

Calories	125	Protein	5 G
Fat	3 G	Carbohydrate	20 G
Sodium	587 MG	Cholesterol	137 MG

GREEN BEAN AND GARLIC SOUP

MAKES 4 SERVINGS

This is a variation on *Provençal* garlic soup. The green beans simmer along with the garlic and give the broth a sweet, soothing flavor.

- 6 cups water
- 1 teaspoon salt (to taste)
- 1 thyme sprig *or* ¼ teaspoon dried thyme
- 1 bay leaf
- 1 teaspoon olive oil
- 10 garlic cloves, minced or put through a press
- ½ pound green beans, trimmed and cut into 1½-inch lengths
- 1 egg
  freshly ground pepper
- 3 tablespoons chopped fresh parsley
  whole-wheat croutons or *crostini* (page 53), cut into small pieces (optional)

Combine the water, salt, thyme, bay leaf, and olive oil in a soup pot and bring to a boil. Reduce the heat to a simmer and squeeze in the garlic. Add the green beans and simmer, uncovered, for 10 minutes. Adjust seasonings.

Beat the egg in a bowl and ladle in some of the simmering soup. Stir together and return to the pot, stirring all the while. Add pepper to taste and correct seasonings. Serve at once, distributing the beans evenly and topping each portion with chopped fresh parsley and *crostini* if desired.

PER PORTION:

Calories	58	Protein	3 G
Fat	3 G	Carbohydrate	7 G
Sodium	573 MG	Cholesterol	69 MG

LIGHTER SOUPS

MADAME TARDIEU'S WINTER TOMATO SOUP WITH VERMICELLI

MAKES 4 SERVINGS

The Drôme is a relatively untraveled "department" of France, just north of the Vaucluse, where I usually go when I visit Provence. It's hilly wine and olive country; to reach it you get off the autoroute north of Avignon and head east, toward Nyons. The twisting country roads are dotted with vineyards and olive groves, and the mountains of the Drôme try their best to protect one from the *mistral*, that crazy *Provençal* wind that blows down the Rhône Valley like a blue norther.

Georgette and Paul Tardieu moved to this part of France from Avignon 20 years ago to farm. Neither of them knew the first thing about farming, but they have learned over the years, and at their Domaine de la Gautière they produce the best honey and olives I've ever tasted, marvelous olive oil and preserves, and a very good table wine. Georgette Tardieu is an incredibly talented and energetic cook.

I went to Domaine de la Gautière to talk to Georgette about the food she serves to workers during the grape harvest, as Kermit Lynch, an American wine importer, had told me she was an excellent cook. Georgette had just broken her leg (she fell off a ladder while harvesting olives), and the fact that she couldn't rush around was driving her crazy. So she was happy to talk about food with me for two days, and at mealtime she would hobble to the kitchen to whip up something extraordinary. The first night, she served this tomato and *vermicelli* soup and the simple pizza on page 210. As we ate, Georgette talked passionately about cooking, while her husband looked on with the loving eyes of a man who knows how lucky he is to have married such a great cook. "You have to use all of your senses when you cook," she said. "The way a dish tastes at any given moment has much to do with its temperature. The soup we're eating now can't be served too hot, or you'll lose the flavors of the garlic, onions, and herbs and the fresh flavor of the tomatoes. I added garlic three times, at the beginning with the onions, in the middle of the cooking, and at the end, because I kept tasting and kept feeling it needed a bit more of something. You have to keep tasting." I couldn't agree more.

1   28-ounce can tomatoes
1   tablespoon olive oil
1   onion, minced
4   garlic cloves (more to taste), minced or put through a press
    salt and freshly ground pepper
½   teaspoon dried marjoram (more to taste)
½   cup *vermicelli*

Drain the tomatoes and retain the liquid. Return the liquid to the can and add enough water to fill the can. Put the tomatoes through the medium disk of a food mill into a bowl or puree and put through a sieve; set aside.

Heat the oil in a heavy-bottomed soup pot and sauté the onion with 2 cloves of the garlic until the onion is tender. Add the tomato puree and cook 10 minutes, stirring. Add the remaining garlic and the liquid from the tomatoes. Add salt and pepper to taste and the marjoram. Bring to a simmer and add the *vermicelli*. Cook until the pasta is *al dente*. Taste again, add more garlic if desired, correct seasonings, and serve—not too hot. The soup will keep up to 3 days in the refrigerator and can also be frozen—in either case, add the *vermicelli* just before serving.

PER PORTION:

Calories	136	Protein	4 G
Fat	4 G	Carbohydrate	22 G
Sodium	325 MG	Cholesterol	0

SOUPE À LA CORIANDRE

MAKES 4 SERVINGS

I am always impressed by the ability French women have to carry recipes in their heads and rattle them off in conversation. One day a friend asked me if I had ever eaten coriander soup. Her Tunisian mother-in-law had taught it to her, and she passed it on to me on the spot. Her version contained meat, but I have developed my own recipe without meat, and I love it. When I passed her in the street a few weeks later, and told her I had worked out a recipe for *soupe à la coriandre*, *"mais végétarienne,"* she shook her head disapprovingly. "You can't make it without meat," she said, and walked off in a huff. Well, judge for yourself; I think the tomatoes, spices, and cilantro give this soup plenty of flavor.

    2 bunches cilantro
    1 tablespoon olive oil
    1 onion, chopped
    2 garlic cloves, minced or put through a press
    1 teaspoon ground cumin
1 ½ teaspoons paprika
    1 32-ounce can tomatoes, with juice, chopped
    1 quart water
    4 tablespoons tomato paste
      sea salt and freshly ground pepper
  ½ cup *vermicelli*
      pinch cayenne pepper
      juice of 1 lime (more to taste)
    2 tablespoons cilantro leaves for garnish

Tie the bunches of cilantro together with a string so you can remove them after the soup simmers. Heat the olive oil in a large heavy-bottomed soup pot or casserole and sauté the onion over medium-low heat until tender.

Add the garlic, cumin, and paprika, sauté a minute, and add the tomatoes and their juice, the water, the tomato paste, the cilantro, and sea salt and freshly ground pepper to taste. Bring to a simmer, cover, and simmer 30 minutes.

Remove the soup from the heat. Take out the cilantro bunches and discard, then put the soup through a food mill or blend in a food processor or blender. Return to the heat, bring back to a simmer, and add the *vermicelli*. Cook until *al dente*, adjust seasonings, and stir in the cayenne and lime juice. Sprinkle with the additional cilantro and serve at once. The soup will keep 2 or 3 days in the refrigerator and can also be frozen—in either case, don't add the *vermicelli* and cilantro until just before serving.

PER PORTION:

Calories	171	Protein	7 G
Fat	5 G	Carbohydrate	29 G
Sodium	518 MG	Cholesterol	0

CHRISTINE'S POTATO AND PARSLEY SOUP

MAKES 4 SERVINGS

This potato and parsley soup is one of the most surprising soups I've ever eaten, and it's extremely quick, easy, and cheap to prepare. My friend Christine Picasso served it to us one time when I visited her in Provence. In her inimitable way, she whipped it up behind our backs (she claims she doesn't ever cook a dish that is time-consuming). The bright green color is striking, and the soup is rich without being heavy or fatty. All that parsley, combined with the potatoes, makes for a very healthy dish, as both are packed with vitamins and minerals, and parsley is a great tonic.

    1 quart water
    1 pound (3 medium) potatoes, peeled and quartered
    1 onion, quartered
    5 whole garlic cloves, peeled
       salt and freshly ground pepper
    1 large bunch parsley, washed, stems removed
    1 to 1½ cups low-fat milk (depending on how thick you want it)

Combine the water, potatoes, onion, garlic, and salt to taste in a saucepan or soup pot and bring to a boil. Cover, reduce heat, and simmer 45 minutes or until the potatoes and onion are quite tender. Remove from the heat and puree along with the parsley. Add the milk and return to the soup pot. Heat through, stirring. Taste, add salt and pepper to taste, and serve. Good with toasted bread. The soup will keep for a day in the refrigerator.

PER PORTION:

Calories	132	Protein	6 G
Fat	2 G	Carbohydrate	25 G
Sodium	61 MG	Cholesterol	6 MG

PUREE LEONTINE

MAKES 4 TO 6 SERVINGS

This lovely, fragrant bright green soup is based on a recipe from Elizabeth David's classic, *Mediterranean Food*. I imagine that it's named for a cook named Leontine.

2 pounds leeks, white part only
2 tablespoons olive oil
salt and freshly ground pepper
1 squeeze fresh lemon juice
1 cup spinach leaves, well washed
1 cup sweet green peas
1 cup shredded lettuce
5 cups water
1 tablespoon finely chopped fresh parsley
1 tablespoon finely chopped fresh mint

Clean the leeks by cutting in half lengthwise and running under cold water until all the dirt is gone. Pat dry and cut into thick slices.

Heat the olive oil in a heavy-bottomed soup pot over low heat and add the leeks. Add a little salt and pepper and a squeeze of lemon, cover, and cook, stirring often, over low heat for about 20 minutes. Add the spinach, peas, and lettuce, stir for a couple of minutes, and add the water and more salt to taste. Bring to a boil, reduce heat, cover, and simmer 5 to 10 minutes or until the vegetables are thoroughly tender but still bright. Remove from the heat and puree in a blender or food processor fitted with the metal blade. Return to the pot and again season to taste with salt and pepper. Just before serving, stir in the chopped herbs. The soup will hold for a day in the refrigerator.

PER PORTION:

Calories	106	Protein	3 G
Fat	5 G	Carbohydrate	14 G
Sodium	23 MG	Cholesterol	0

STRACCIATELLA WITH SPINACH

MAKES 4 SERVINGS

Stracciatella is a Roman soup made with chicken stock, eggs, semolina, and Parmesan. It's a very quick, easy soup; the chicken broth simmers for about 10 minutes, then you swirl in the egg, beaten with the semolina and Parmesan, which shred through the soup like Chinese egg drops. Here I've added spinach (you can use other green vegetables as well) and a touch of garlic.

    5 cups defatted chicken stock (page 152)
    1 to 2 large garlic cloves (to taste), minced or put
        through a press
    2 large eggs
      generous pinch freshly grated nutmeg
    1 tablespoon semolina
    3 tablespoons freshly grated Parmesan cheese
      salt and freshly ground pepper
    4 ounces fresh spinach, washed, stemmed, and torn into
        small pieces

Remove ¼ cup of the chicken stock and place the rest in a soup pot. Add the garlic, bring to a gentle simmer, and simmer 10 to 15 minutes. Meanwhile, beat the eggs in a bowl and stir in the nutmeg, semolina, and Parmesan. Add a pinch of salt and pepper to taste and stir in the reserved chicken stock.

About 3 minutes before serving, add the spinach to the simmering chicken stock. Now gradually drizzle in the egg mixture, stirring slowly all the while with a wooden spoon. Simmer the soup for 1 minute more and serve.

PER PORTION:

Calories	130	Protein	7 G
Fat	7 G	Carbohydrate	11 G
Sodium	143 MG	Cholesterol	141 MG

HAMUD (Chicken Soup with Lemon)

MAKES 6 SERVINGS
ALLOW 1 DAY OF ADVANCE PREPARATION TIME (TO MAKE THE CHICKEN STOCK)

I have a friend whose family was in the matzo business; he always used to say, "So when are you going to make me some chicken soup?" One day I made this light, lemony *potage* for him. He was in heaven; it was even better than his grandmother's, he said, even without her matzo balls. The recipe is based on an Egyptian soup called *hamud*, which I found in Claudia Roden's *A Book of Middle Eastern Food*.

The chicken stock here can be used wherever chicken stock is called for in other soups.

FOR THE STOCK:

    carcass and giblets of 1 chicken, very fresh, plus 2 to
        4 extra wings
1 carrot, sliced
1 onion, quartered
5 garlic cloves, peeled and crushed
    a *bouquet garni* made with 1 bay leaf, a couple of
        sprigs of thyme, and a couple of sprigs of parsley
1 celery stalk, sliced
2 quarts plus 1 cup water
½ teaspoon peppercorns
    salt to taste

FOR THE SOUP:

    the chicken stock
4 celery stalks, with leaves, sliced
2 leeks, white part only, cleaned and sliced
3 garlic cloves, thinly sliced
    salt and freshly ground pepper
    juice of 1 to 2 lemons (to taste)
½ pound (2 medium) zucchini, sliced
½ cup uncooked rice, cooked
3 tablespoons chopped cilantro

THE FIRST DAY: MAKE THE STOCK.
Crack the chicken bones slightly with a hammer and combine with the remaining ingredients in a soup pot. Bring to a boil and skim off any scum that rises. Reduce heat, cover, and simmer for 1 to 2 hours. Strain and remove pieces of chicken from the bones. Place the chicken in a bowl and

refrigerate, along with the stock, overnight. Discard the bones and debris. The next day, remove the stock from the refrigerator and skim off any fat that has risen to the surface.

THE SECOND DAY: MAKE THE SOUP.
      Combine the chicken stock and chicken, celery, leeks, garlic, salt and pepper to taste, and lemon juice; bring to a simmer. Simmer gently for 45 minutes and add the zucchini. Simmer another 10 to 15 minutes, then stir in the rice and cilantro. Taste and adjust seasonings before serving. This soup will hold for a day or two before adding the cilantro and can also be frozen. As a leftover it will keep another few days.

PER PORTION:

Calories	139	Protein	3 G
Fat	3 G	Carbohydrate	26 G
Sodium	36 MG	Cholesterol	0

SPINACH OR SWISS CHARD SOUP WITH YOGURT

MAKES 4 SERVINGS

This is an Egyptian recipe, usually made with an indigenous dark leafy vegetable much like Swiss chard. My version is adapted from Claudia Roden's recipe in *A Book of Middle Eastern Food.*

      1 pound fresh spinach or chard leaves, stemmed and
              washed, *or* ½ pound thawed frozen chopped spinach
      1 onion, chopped
      2 garlic cloves, minced or put through a press
      1 tablespoon olive oil
      1 leek, white part only, cleaned and chopped, *or* 4
              spring onions, chopped
      ½ cup uncooked rice
      1 quart water
         salt and freshly ground pepper
      2 cups plain low-fat yogurt
      1 to 2 additional garlic cloves, crushed or put through a press
         fresh lemon juice (optional)

If using fresh spinach or chard, wash and tear or cut into large pieces or ribbons.

Sauté the onion and 2 garlic cloves in the olive oil over low heat until softened and beginning to color. Add the spinach or chard and the leek or spring onions and sauté gently for about 5 minutes. Add the rice, water, and salt and pepper to taste; bring to a boil. Reduce heat and simmer gently for about 15 minutes or until the rice is cooked through but still *al dente*.

Meanwhile, beat together the yogurt and additional garlic. Remove the soup from the heat and beat in the yogurt. Heat through but do not boil, or the soup will curdle. Correct seasonings, add lemon juice if you wish, and serve. Leftovers will keep in the refrigerator a day or two.

PER PORTION:

Calories	222	Protein	10 G
Fat	6 G	Carbohydrate	34 G
Sodium	148 MG	Cholesterol	7 MG

TURKISH BORSCHT

MAKES 6 SERVINGS

This is a thick, warming vegetable soup, tangy with lemon juice and fragrant with fresh dill.

- 1 tablespoon olive oil
- 2 medium-sized onions, chopped
- 4 garlic cloves, minced
- 1 pound beets, peeled and chopped
- ½ pound cabbage, shredded
- 2 celery stalks, sliced
- 2 carrots, scrubbed and chopped
- 3 medium-sized potatoes, scrubbed and diced
- 1 green pepper, seeded and chopped
- 4 tomatoes, *or* 1 14-ounce can, drained and chopped
- 2 quarts water
- salt and freshly ground pepper
- ½ teaspoon crushed dill seed
- juice of 1 large lemon
- 3 tablespoons chopped fresh dill
- 1 cup plain low-fat yogurt for garnish

Heat the oil over low heat in a large heavy-bottomed soup pot and add the onion and garlic. Sauté until the onion begins to soften, and add the other vegetables. Cook, stirring, for 5 minutes. Add the water and bring to a boil. Add salt to taste, plenty of freshly ground pepper, and the dill seed. Cover, reduce heat, and cook 1 hour. Stir in lemon juice and the dill and adjust seasonings.

Serve, topping each serving with a large spoonful of plain low-fat yogurt. The soup will keep for up to 5 days in the refrigerator and freezes well.

PER PORTION:

Calories	184	Protein	7 G
Fat	3 G	Carbohydrate	35 G
Sodium	105 MG	Cholesterol	2 MG

COLD SOUPS

GAZPACHO ANDALUZ

MAKES 4 SERVINGS

When I went to Andalusia, *gazpacho* was the dish I kept wanting to eat again and again. Every restaurant served a slightly different variation, each with different garnishes. They were always refreshing and cold, and in June in southern Spain that is the kind of food one craves.

When I got back to France, I began reading about *gazpacho* and found about seven variations. I tried them all, then mixed and revised, and finally I came up with something that best matches the Andalusian *gazpacho* I most enjoyed.

FOR THE SOUP BASE:

    2 thick slices stale French bread, crusts removed
    1 pound (4 to 5) ripe tomatoes, peeled
    2 to 4 garlic cloves (to taste), peeled
    1 tablespoon olive oil
    1 to 2 tablespoons wine vinegar (to taste)
       salt and freshly ground pepper
    1 cup ice-cold water
       optional additions: 1 small scallion, chopped, *or*
           2 tablespoons chopped Spanish onion
  ½ to 1 teaspoon paprika (to taste)
  ½ teaspoon crushed cumin seed
    2 tablespoons chopped fresh basil

FOR THE GARNISH:

    1 small cucumber, peeled and finely diced
    1 red or green pepper, seeds and membranes removed,
       finely diced
    1 hard-cooked egg, diced (optional)
    4 tablespoons finely chopped onion
  ½ cup diced *crostini* (page 53)

Soak the bread in water to cover for 5 to 10 minutes, until soft. Squeeze out the water.

Using a mortar and pestle or a blender, blend together all the ingredients for the soup base until smooth. Adjust seasonings and chill several hours. The soup must be very cold.

Garnish each bowlful of soup with a heaping spoonful of each of the garnishes. This soup will hold for a day or two in the refrigerator.

PER PORTION:

Calories	180	Protein	5 G
Fat	6 G	Carbohydrate	29 G
Sodium	210 MG	Cholesterol	1 MG

CHILLED YOGURT/CUCUMBER SOUP

MAKES 4 SERVINGS

Cooling yogurt soups are standard fare in most of the hot Middle Eastern countries, and this one is a good choice for an extremely hot day anywhere—it takes only a few minutes to prepare and is very soothing. My version is based on a Turkish recipe, but I have seen similar recipes from Iran and Egypt.

- 1 long European cucumber *or* 2 smaller cucumbers, peeled
- 2 garlic cloves, minced or put through a press
- 1 quart plain low-fat yogurt
- ½ cup cold water
- 2 tablespoons chopped fresh mint
- 4 to 5 tablespoons fresh lemon juice (to taste)
  salt and freshly ground pepper to taste
- 1 tablespoon chopped mint for garnish
- 1 lemon, sliced paper-thin, for garnish

If you're using a food processor, mince the cucumber and garlic together, using the pulse action, until the cucumber is minced very small or like a coarse puree. Add the remaining ingredients except garnishes and blend together in the food processor just until everything is amalgamated. You don't want to lose the texture of the cucumber. Taste and adjust seasonings. Chill several hours. Serve with an ice cube in each bowl and garnish with fresh chopped mint and thin slices of lemon.

If you're mixing the soup by hand, chop the cucumber very fine or grate it.

Whisk together the yogurt and water and stir in the cucumber, garlic, mint, lemon juice, and salt and pepper.

Chill and serve as above. The soup will keep up to 3 days in the refrigerator.

PER PORTION:

Calories	165	Protein	13 G
Fat	4 G	Carbohydrate	21 G
Sodium	166 MG	Cholesterol	14 MG

BLENDER GAZPACHO

MAKES 6 TO 8 SERVINGS

This refreshing soup is great to have on hand in the summer. Make a big bowl of it at the beginning of the week; it keeps well in the refrigerator for at least 3 days.

1 ½ pounds (6 to 7) ripe tomatoes, peeled
1 to 2 garlic cloves (to taste)
½ onion
1 carrot, coarsely chopped
1 small cucumber, peeled and coarsely chopped
1 green pepper, seeded and coarsely chopped
2 parsley sprigs
3 to 4 tablespoons chopped fresh basil (to taste; optional)
   juice of 1 to 2 lemons (to taste)
   salt and freshly ground pepper
3 to 4 cups V-8 or tomato juice

Blend together all the ingredients in a blender until smooth. Chill several hours. Adjust seasonings. The soup will keep for a couple of days in the refrigerator.

PER PORTION:

Calories	51	Protein	2 G
Fat	.25 G	Carbohydrate	12 G
Sodium	374 MG	Cholesterol	0

HOT OR COLD PROVENÇAL TOMATO SOUP WITH BASIL

MAKES 4 TO 6 SERVINGS

I learned this recipe from Lulu Peyraud at Domaine Tempier. It's one of the many easy, delicious soups she often makes for dinner. We ate it hot in the fall, but I've also enjoyed it chilled in the summer.

1	tablespoon olive oil
1	small onion *or* 3 shallots, chopped
5	garlic cloves, minced or put through a press
2	pounds (8 to 10) tomatoes, chopped
3	cups water or garlic broth (page 142)
	salt and freshly ground pepper
8	large fresh basil leaves
¼	cup pearl barley or tapioca
	juice of ½ lemon (optional for chilled version)
2	tablespoons slivered fresh basil for garnish

Heat the oil in a large heavy-bottomed soup pot and add the onion or shallots and half the garlic. Cook gently over medium heat about 5 minutes, then add the tomatoes and remaining garlic. Cook for 10 minutes, stirring often.

Add the water or garlic broth, the basil leaves, and salt and pepper to taste; bring to a simmer. Cover and simmer 15 minutes.

Add the pearl barley or tapioca and cook 15 minutes, until the grains are tender.

Remove from the heat and puree through the fine blade of a food mill. Adjust salt. If serving hot, ladle into bowls. If serving cold, refrigerate until thoroughly chilled.

Just before serving, stir in the lemon juice (if desired when serving cold). Adjust seasonings and serve, garnishing each bowl with the additional basil. The soup will keep in the refrigerator for 2 or 3 days, without the final addition of lemon juice and basil.

PER PORTION:

Calories	85	Protein	3 G
Fat	3 G	Carbohydrate	14 G
Sodium	14 MG	Cholesterol	0

FISH SOUPS

FISH FUMET

MAKES 1 QUART

A *fumet* is a light fish broth that is often used as a base for fish soups and stews. It's very easy to make. You can get fish trimmings from fish markets.

1 pound fish trimmings (heads and bones), rinsed
1 onion, quartered
1 carrot, sliced
1 celery stalk, sliced
1 leek, white part only, cleaned and sliced
2 garlic cloves, peeled
2 parsley sprigs
1 bay leaf
1 thyme sprig
1 quart water
  salt
1 cup dry white wine

Combine the fish trimmings, onion, carrot, celery, leek, garlic, parsley, bay leaf, thyme, water, and salt to taste in a large soup pot or saucepan and bring to a simmer over medium heat. Skim off all the bitter foam that rises. Continue to skim until no foam remains, then cover, reduce heat, and simmer 15 minutes. Add the wine and simmer 15 minutes, covered. Remove from the heat and strain at once through a fine sieve or a strainer lined with cheese-cloth. Don't cook any longer than this, or the *fumet* will be bitter. You can keep the *fumet* for a day in the refrigerator.

PER 1-CUP PORTION:

Calories	39	Protein	3 G
Fat	.19 G	Carbohydrate	6 G
Sodium	132 MG	Cholesterol	11 MG

AÏGO-SAU AND ROUILLE

MAKES 4 TO 6 SERVINGS

This is a simple *Provençal* fish soup, served with a *rouille*, a mayonnaise-like mixture that actually doesn't contain much oil, at least in this version. Unlike *bouillabaisse*, aïgo-sau takes very little time to make, and you can use whatever fish are available. The recipe comes, via Alan Davidson's *Mediterranean Seafood*, from Reboul's classic *La Cuisinière Provençale.*

FOR THE SOUP:

> 2 pounds mixed small white fish, such as sea bass,
>   bream, gray mullet, snapper, sole, cod, and
>   whiting, cleaned and cut into large chunks
>
> 4 to 6 potatoes (to taste), scrubbed and sliced
>
> 1 onion, thinly sliced
>
> 2 tomatoes, peeled and chopped
>
> 6 to 8 garlic cloves (to taste), minced or put through a press
>   a *bouquet garni* made with bay leaf, a couple of fennel
>   stalks, a few sprigs of thyme, celery leaves, and parsley
>   boiling water to cover
>   salt and freshly ground pepper to taste

FOR THE ROUILLE:

> 2 small red peppers
>
> 4 garlic cloves
>
> 2 thick slices French bread, crusts removed, soaked in water
>
> 2 tablespoons olive oil
>   up to 1 cup broth from the soup
>   salt and cayenne pepper
>
> 6 slices *crostini* (page 53) (more to taste)

PREPARE THE SOUP:

Combine all the ingredients for the soup, except salt and pepper, in a casserole and bring to a boil. Cook over medium-high heat 30 minutes or until the fish is cooked through and the broth fragrant. Season to taste.

PREPARE THE ROUILLE:

While the soup is cooking, remove the seeds and membranes from the red peppers and simmer for 5 minutes in salted boiling water. Pound the garlic and red peppers together with a mortar and pestle or food processor until you have a paste. Squeeze the bread dry and pound it into the garlic and peppers. Dribble in the olive oil and work it in with the pestle, then work in about ½ cup of the broth from the fish or enough to give the mixture a mayonnaise-like consistency. Season to taste with salt and cayenne.

TO SERVE:

There are two ways to serve this. Traditionally, the fish is served separately on a plate, and the broth is served in a bowl with croutons topped with dollops of the *rouille*. But it's just as good, in my opinion, if you serve the fish and soup together in a wide bowl, topped with the croutons and *rouille*.

PER PORTION:

Calories	363	Protein	19 G
Fat	7 G	Carbohydrate	56 G
Sodium	337 MG	Cholesterol	24 MG

PROVENÇAL FISH SOUP

MAKES 4 TO 6 SERVINGS

Although this heady soup isn't a *bouillabaisse*, it is decidedly Mediterranean, with all the garlic, the saffron, and the special perfume of the orange peel that is added close to the end of the cooking. I often serve it at dinner parties, because everything up to the addition of the fish can be prepared in advance.

FOR THE SOUP:

- 1 tablespoon olive oil
- 1 large onion, chopped
- 4 garlic cloves (more to taste), minced
- 2 28-ounce cans tomatoes, with juice, seeded and chopped
- 2 tablespoons tomato paste
- ½ to 1 teaspoon dried basil (to taste) *or* 1 tablespoon minced fresh
- ½ to 1 teaspoon dried thyme (to taste)
- 1 recipe fish *fumet* (page 160)
- 1 bay leaf
  salt
- ¾ pound (4 medium) new potatoes, diced
- 1 pound (4 small) zucchini, sliced
  fresh corn from 2 to 3 ears (optional)
  freshly ground pepper
  pinch or 2 cayenne pepper *or* ¼ teaspoon hot pepper flakes

2 wide strips orange zest
  generous pinch saffron threads
2 to 2½ pounds fish fillets or steaks, such as any
  combination of cod, striped bass, monkfish, tilefish,
  snapper, redfish, bream, turbot, or conger, cut into
  2-inch cubes

FOR THE GARNISH:
  ½ pound mussels or clams (enough for 4 per serving)
  1 cup dry white wine
  ½ cup water
  3 tablespoons chopped fresh parsley
  lemon wedges

Heat the olive oil in a large heavy-bottomed soup pot or casserole and sauté the onion with the garlic until the onion is tender. Add the tomatoes, tomato paste, dried basil (fresh basil goes in later), and thyme and simmer 15 minutes. Add the *fumet*, bay leaf, and salt to taste. Bring to a simmer and cook, uncovered, for 30 minutes. Add the potatoes, cover, and simmer 10 to 15 minutes (you cover the soup now because you want to cook the vegetables without letting any more of the liquid evaporate) or until the potatoes are cooked through but still have some texture. Add the zucchini, corn, and basil if using fresh; cover and simmer 15 minutes or until the zucchini is tender. Add pepper and cayenne and adjust seasonings, adding salt, garlic, or more herbs if you wish. At this point you may remove the soup from the heat and let it sit until shortly before serving, when you will bring it back to a simmer and cook the fish.

While the stew is simmering, prepare the mussels. Clean them well in several rinses of cold water (see instructions for cleaning mussels, page 166). Bring the wine and water to a boil in a large lidded pot and add the mussels or clams. Steam 5 minutes or until the shells open, shaking the pan once to distribute evenly. Remove from the heat, drain, and set aside. Discard any that have not opened.

Fifteen to 20 minutes before serving, bring the soup to a simmer and add the orange zest and saffron. Adjust seasonings and add water if the broth seems too thick or if there's not enough of it to cover the seafood. If you add water, adjust the seasonings again. Add the fish, cover, and simmer 10 minutes, until the flesh is opaque and falls apart. Serve at once, garnishing each bowl with mussels or clams, chopped fresh parsley, and a lemon wedge.

PER PORTION:

Calories	274	Protein	37 G
Fat	4 G	Carbohydrate	22 G
Sodium	280 MG	Cholesterol	84 MG

TUNISIAN FISH SOUP

MAKES 8 SERVINGS

This hearty fish soup is seasoned with the exotic spices of North Africa. It would also make a great topping for *couscous*.

2 pounds grouper, cleaned and thickly sliced
2 pounds redfish or sea bass, cleaned and thickly sliced
  the heads of the fish
1 tablespoon olive oil
1 large onion, chopped
2½ quarts water
8 large garlic cloves, minced or put through a press
3 medium-sized carrots, peeled and sliced
1 celery stalk, with leaves, sliced
½ teaspoon *harissa* (page 106) or cayenne pepper (optional)
1 tablespoon tomato paste
½ teaspoon ground cumin (more to taste)
½ teaspoon ground caraway
½ teaspoon ground coriander
1 teaspoon paprika
  salt and freshly ground pepper to taste
1 small bunch parsley, chopped
¼ teaspoon powdered saffron
3 to 4 tablespoons chopped cilantro
  lemon wedges for garnish

Rinse the fish and fish heads and set aside.

Heat the olive oil in a large heavy-bottomed soup pot and sauté the onion over medium heat until it begins to color. Add the fish heads and stir together for about 5 minutes. Add 1 quart of the water, bring to a boil, and skim off any foam that rises. Reduce heat and simmer 30 minutes.

Strain the broth through a strainer over a bowl or another casserole. Using a wooden spoon, press the onions and fish heads against the sides of the strainer to extract as much juice as possible.

Return the broth to the soup pot and add the remaining ingredients except the fish, cilantro, and lemon. Bring to a simmer over medium heat and simmer 30 minutes, covered.

About 15 minutes before serving, add the fish to the broth. Simmer 10 to 15 minutes, until the fish is opaque and tender. Stir in the cilantro and correct the seasonings.

TO SERVE:

In Tunisia the fish is removed from the broth and placed on a platter, and the soup is served in wide soup bowls. I think it's easier to place slices of fish in each wide soup bowl and ladle the soup over, garnishing with lemon wedges. Pass the extra fish slices on a platter, garnished with lemon wedges.

PER PORTION:

Calories	126	Protein	17 G
Fat	3 G	Carbohydrate	7 G
Sodium	88 MG	Cholesterol	34 MG

EGG-LEMON SOUP IN FISH BROTH

MAKES 6 SERVINGS

This delicious Greek soup is practically identical to the *avgolemono* on page 144, but instead of using garlic broth or chicken stock you use fish *fumet*.

> 2 quarts fish *fumet* (page 160; double the recipe)
> salt and freshly ground pepper
> 1 cup uncooked rice
> 2 eggs, beaten
> juice of 1 large lemon
> chopped fresh parsley for garnish

Bring the fish *fumet* to a boil, correct seasonings, and add the rice. Simmer over medium-low heat until the rice is cooked *al dente*, about 20 minutes. While the rice is cooking, beat the eggs in a bowl and stir in the lemon juice.

When the rice is done, ladle some of the hot broth into the egg-lemon mixture and stir together. Return this mixture to the soup pot, stir, and heat through without boiling. Top each serving with chopped fresh parsley.

PER PORTION:

Calories	193	Protein	8 G
Fat	2 G	Carbohydrate	34 G
Sodium	201 MG	Cholesterol	106 MG

ITALIAN MUSSEL SOUP

MAKES 6 SERVINGS

Here mussels are cooked in a gutsy tomato broth, slightly piquant because of the cayenne. It makes a fine supper on a cold winter night.

    4 quarts mussels
    2 tablespoons olive oil
    4 large *or* 8 small shallots, chopped
    4 garlic cloves, minced or put through a press
    3 pounds tomatoes, chopped, *or* 2 28-ounce cans with
            juice, chopped
    ¼ to ½ teaspoon dried oregano (to taste)
    ¼ teaspoon dried thyme (more to taste)
    1 cup dry white wine
       pinch cayenne pepper
       generous pinch saffron threads
       freshly ground pepper
       salt (if necessary; the mussels release salt)
    ¼ cup chopped fresh parsley for garnish

TO CLEAN MUSSELS (CAN BE DONE WHILE THE BROTH IS SIMMERING):
Place the mussels in a large bowl of cold water. Brush them with a wire brush and pull out their beards. Drain the water and fill the bowl again, adding 2 tablespoons salt or vinegar. Let sit 15 minutes. The mussels will spit out much of their sand because they don't like the salt or vinegar. Drain, rinse in fresh water, brush the mussels once more, and discard any that have broken shells or are opened. Soak one more time for 15 minutes in vinegar-water or salt water; drain and rinse.

TO MAKE THE BROTH:
Heat the olive oil in a large casserole or soup pot that is big enough to eventually accommodate all the mussels. Add the shallots and garlic and cook over low heat until the shallots are tender. Add the tomatoes and stir together well. Add the oregano and thyme, bring to a simmer, cover, and cook 20 to 30 minutes. Add the white wine, cayenne, saffron, and pepper to taste and bring to a boil. Add the mussels, cover, and cook 5 minutes, shaking the pot or stirring the mussels (whichever is easier) halfway through the cooking to ensure even cooking. After 5 minutes the mussels should be opened; if not, cook a little longer, until they are all open. Discard any unopened

ones. Immediately remove from the heat. Spoon the mussels into wide soup bowls, taste the broth, and add salt only if necessary. Spoon the broth over the mussels, sprinkle with parsley, and serve.

PER PORTION:

Calories	206	Protein	18 G
Fat	8 G	Carbohydrate	17 G
Sodium	399 MG	Cholesterol	37 MG

SOPA DE PEIX
(Mallorcan Fish Broth with Rice)

MAKES 4 TO 6 SERVINGS

This simple, fragrant soup from Mallorca is usually strained before adding the rice. In my version I don't strain it, because I like the taste of the vegetables and parsley. So mine is more of a *potage* than the traditional broth. In Mallorca they use a fish called *picarel*, but bream or snapper will do. You could also use monkfish.

    1 tablespoon olive oil
    3 shallots, chopped
    4 garlic cloves, minced or put through a press
    3 medium-sized tomatoes, chopped
       handful Swiss chard leaves, chopped
    1 small bunch parsley, chopped
    2 pounds bream, snapper, or monkfish, cleaned and cut
          into steaks or fillets
 1 ½ quarts water
       salt
    ½ cup uncooked rice
       pinch saffron threads
    2 garlic cloves, finely minced or put through a press
    2 tablespoons finely chopped fresh parsley

Heat the olive oil in a heavy-bottomed soup pot or casserole and sauté the shallots and garlic until tender. Add the tomatoes, chard, and parsley and continue to sauté over medium-low heat for 15 minutes, stirring. Add a little water if the mixture sticks.

Add the fish and cook for a few minutes, then add the water and salt to taste. Bring to a simmer and simmer 15 to 30 minutes or until the fish is cooked through.

Remove the fish from the soup and bring the soup to a boil. Add the rice and saffron, reduce the heat, and simmer 20 minutes or until the rice is cooked *al dente*. Stir the fish back into the soup, breaking it up into flakes with a fork or wooden spoon, and add the additional garlic and parsley. Adjust seasonings and serve.

PER PORTION:

Calories	151	Protein	12 G
Fat	3 G	Carbohydrate	18 G
Sodium	49 MG	Cholesterol	18 MG

CHAPTER FOUR

PASTA AND PIZZA

If I were forced to eat one Mediterranean cuisine for the rest of my life, I'd choose the food of Italy without hesitation. I could live happily on pasta, pizza, and salads, and I know I wouldn't gain an ounce. These delicious dishes provide healthy, fast-burning complex carbohydrates, and as long as you don't toss the pasta with too much olive oil or rich, creamy sauces, and you don't drown your pizzas in oil and smother them with cheese, they're no threat to the dieter.

I gathered most of these recipes on trips through Italy. Before going to each region I read up on the food in Waverly Root's *The Food of Italy*, then looked for the dishes that interested me.

When I went to Palermo, I got very lucky. After a long day of traveling I checked into a small hotel near the railroad station and went out to have a bite to eat. One block from the hotel I stumbled into a tiny hole-in-the-wall *hostaria* called the Antica Hostaria Toti. Had I not known what dishes I was looking for, I would have passed this restaurant by, as it was very plain and not exactly spotless. But on the menu were all the Sicilian specialties I wanted to try: pasta with tuna, with sardines, with broccoli, with eggplant, with artichokes. Right by the door was a refrigerated case with the catch of the day, and there was no doubt that the fish was impeccably fresh.

I walked into the *hostaria* and sat down; the cook, whose name was Filippo, came out to take my order. In my strange Italian, which is more like Spanish with an Italian accent accompanied by lots of hand waving, I asked many specific questions about each dish. Filippo was obviously passionate about his *métier*, and he sat down to tell me all about the cuisine of Palermo. That night I ate an exquisite dish of *penne* with a spicy tuna and tomato sauce. My pleasure was so obvious that Filippo offered to take me to the market with him the next day and to teach me some *Palermese* dishes. So I watched Filippo make dishes like the *penne* or *rigatoni* with tuna and tomato sauce on page 176, the *fusilli* with artichokes and *porcini* mushrooms on page 180, and the *spaghetti alla Trapanese* on page 179. Filippo gave me several other recipes, including the complicated and intriguing Sicilian dish *pasta con sarde* (pasta with sardines; page 174). His recipes were very precise, so he might not approve of the changes I've made, even though all I've really done is to reduce the quantities of olive oil.

Pasta is the all-time healthy fast food. You need so few ingredients to make a sensational, filling meal out of pasta or pizza. It's easy to improvise, using whatever vegetables you might have on hand for a sauce: a can of tomatoes and some garlic, leftover vegetables and a little cottage cheese, dried *porcini* mushrooms, or just garlic and a little olive oil. I recently gave an impromptu dinner party and served a delicious pizza topped with leftover *ratatouille* (page 66) as the main course. Homemade pizza, because of the crust, requires foresight, but only one out of three times, if you make the quick *Provençal* pizza on page 210 or the crust on page 201 and freeze the other two thirds of the dough. Frozen pizza dough will thaw in two to three hours;

then it's just a question of pressing it into a pizza pan, covering it with a topping, and baking in a hot oven.

I serve all of the pasta dishes in this chapter as a main course and choose appetizers or salads from Chapter Two or skip the first course and follow the pasta with a big tossed green salad. The pizzas can be served in the same way, or you can cut them into smaller pieces and serve them as a first course, followed by fish, chicken, or a hearty soup.

PASTA

SPINACH PASTA

MAKES 4 MEDIUM-SIZED SERVINGS

This is my favorite homemade pasta, mostly because of its appealing bright green color. It goes beautifully with any tomato-based sauce.

> 5 to 6 ounces fresh spinach leaves
> 1 large egg
> 3 tablespoons very finely chopped flat-leaf parsley
> 3 ounces (about ¾ cup) whole-wheat flour or
>   whole-wheat pastry flour
> 4 ounces (about 1 cup) unbleached white flour
> ¼ teaspoon salt

Stem the spinach, wash several times, and dry thoroughly. Chop in a food processor or by hand until very fine, almost a puree. Measure out ⅓ cup (a tablespoon more is fine). Beat the egg and mix in the spinach and parsley.

Mix together the flour and salt. *If you're using a food processor,* add the egg/spinach/parsley mixture and process until the dough comes together. Add a little water, a teaspoon at a time, if it seems too dry. Sometimes the dough won't actually come together in the food processor, but will form a grainy, damp mixture. If the mixture feels damp to you, don't add more water, but scrape this mixture out of the food processor bowl and gather into a ball. If it seems too wet, you can add flour as you knead.

If you're mixing the dough by hand, mix the flour and salt together, make a mound on your work surface, make a well in the center, and add the egg/spinach/parsley mixture to the well. Using a fork, beat the egg mixture with one hand while you gradually brush flour in from the sides of the well with the other. When all the flour has been incorporated into the egg mixture, brush away the hard pieces of dough that got away and form the dough into a ball.

Knead for about 10 minutes, wrap in plastic, and let rest for 30 minutes.

Roll out the dough as thin as possible without tearing it (for me the thinnest setting for whole-wheat pastas is number 4). Cut into the desired shape. Let dry for 30 minutes before cooking. Or to store for future use, lay the pasta on a baking sheet, dust lightly with flour and dry thoroughly. Store in canisters. The pasta can also be frozen. Allow to dry 30 minutes, then place in plastic bags and seal. Transfer directly from the freezer to boiling water to cook.

To cook, bring 3 or 4 quarts of water to boil in a large pot. Add 2 teaspoons salt, a drop of oil, and the pasta. It should float to the top in about 30 seconds (unless it is thoroughly dry, in which case it will be *al dente* in a few minutes). Drain at once, top with sauce, and serve.

PER PORTION:

Calories	201	Protein	8 G
Fat	2 G	Carbohydrate	38 G
Sodium	177 MG	Cholesterol	69 MG

WHOLE-WHEAT PASTA

MAKES 4 MEDIUM-SIZED SERVINGS

Pasta made partially with whole-wheat flour has a nutty, rich flavor.

> 3 ounces (about ¾ cup) whole-wheat flour or
> whole-wheat pastry flour
> 4 ounces (about 1 cup) unbleached white flour
> ¼ teaspoon salt
> 2 large eggs

Mix together the flour and salt. *If you're using a food processor,* add the eggs and process until the dough comes together. Add a little water, a teaspoon at a time, if it seems too dry. Sometimes the dough won't actually come together in the food processor, but will form a grainy, damp mixture. If the mixture feels damp to you, don't add more water, but scrape this mixture out of the food processor bowl and gather into a ball. If it seems too wet, you can add a little flour to the board as you knead.

If you're mixing the dough by hand, mix the flour and salt together, make a mound on your work surface, make a well in the center, and add the eggs to the well. Using a fork, beat the eggs with one hand while you gradually brush flour in from the sides of the well with the other. When all the flour has been incorporated into the eggs, brush away the hard pieces of dough that got away and form the dough into a ball.

Knead for about 10 minutes, wrap in plastic and let rest for 30 minutes.

Roll out the dough as thin as possible without tearing it (for me the thinnest setting for whole-wheat pastas is number 4). Cut into the desired shape. Let dry for 30 minutes before cooking.

To cook, bring 3 or 4 quarts of water to boil in a large pot. Add 2 teaspoons salt, a drop of oil, and the pasta. It should float to the top in about 30 seconds (unless it is thoroughly dry, in which case it will be *al dente* in a few minutes). Drain at once, top with sauce, and serve.

PER PORTION:

Calories	213	Protein	9 G
Fat	3 G	Carbohydrate	37 G
Sodium	171 MG	Cholesterol	137 MG

PASTA CON SARDE
(Pasta with Sardines, Palermos Style)

MAKES 6 SERVINGS

This is one of Palermo's most famous dishes. When I first tasted it, I was totally mystified by the sauce. Once I saw the recipe I understood why: it's a very complex, intriguing dish. The main ingredients are fresh sardines (canned may be substituted, although fresh are preferable) and chopped wild fennel, for which the tops of fennel bulbs may be substituted; but there are other ingredients in the sauce that give it all of its depth and mystery: currants, pine nuts, saffron, anchovies, and onion. Because I find our bulb fennel tops less anisy than the Sicilian wild fennel, I have included an optional table-spoon of Pernod, which you would never find in an authentic recipe for the dish. I have also reduced the amount of anchovies and olive oil; the authentic sauce is quite rich, but I don't miss the extra olive oil. All the correct flavors are there.

This dish can also be baked, as in the variation that follows the master recipe. In this version the pasta and sauce are tossed together, topped with bread crumbs, and baked in a *gratin* dish.

Note: Try this dish with small fresh herrings or smelts if you can't find fresh sardines and don't like the canned ones. If you use canned sardines, rinse the oil off under cold tap water before you begin.

    2 pounds fresh sardines, cleaned and boned,* or canned
          sardines, rinsed
  ½ pound wild fennel stalks or fresh fennel bulb tops
    2 tablespoons olive oil
    1 small onion, chopped
    2 anchovy fillets
    1 tablespoon Pernod or pastis (optional)
    2 tablespoons pine nuts
 2½ tablespoons dried currants
  ¼ teaspoon powdered saffron *or* ½ teaspoon saffron
          threads dissolved in 1 tablespoon water
      salt and freshly ground pepper
    2 tablespoons fresh lemon juice
    1 teaspoon salt
  ¾ pound *bucatini* or *perciatelli* or spaghetti
    4 tablespoons toasted bread crumbs (for baked version)

Bring a pot of salted water to a gentle boil and add the sardines. Simmer 5 minutes, drain, and set aside.

Bring another large pot of water to a boil and add the fennel. Cook 10 minutes, remove the fennel, and retain the cooking liquid, which you will use for the sauce and for cooking the pasta. Chop the fennel fine.

Heat the olive oil in a large skillet and add the onion and anchovy fillets. Cook until the onion is golden, stirring, and add the sardines and fennel. Cook, stirring, over low heat for 5 minutes; the sardines will break apart. Add the Pernod or pastis, cook, stirring, for a minute, then gradually add 2 cups of the fennel cooking water, a ladleful at a time, until you have a medium-thick sauce. Add the pine nuts, currants, saffron, and salt and pepper to taste. Cook, stirring often, over low heat for 20 minutes. Add the lemon juice, taste, and adjust seasonings.

Bring the remaining fennel cooking water to a boil in a large pot and add a teaspoon of salt. Add the pasta and cook *al dente*. Drain and toss in a warm serving dish with a ladleful of the sauce. Spoon onto individual plates, top each serving with additional sauce, and serve.

*To clean and bone the sardines: Snap off the head of the sardine and pull away most of the innards with it. Tear off the center back fin from the tail end toward the head, pulling off the little bones attached to it along with it. Run your thumb along the belly, scooping out the remaining intestines, and open out the sardine so it is flat. Gently loosen the spine and ribs from the flesh and pull away toward the tail, pulling the tail off with them. Rinse and drain. Pat dry.

BAKED PASTA WITH SARDINES

Preheat the oven to 400 degrees. Toss the pasta with all of the sauce and transfer to an oiled baking dish. Sprinkle with the bread crumbs and bake for 20 minutes or until the bread crumbs brown.

PER PORTION:

Calories	408	Protein	19 G
Fat	14 G	Carbohydrate	51 G
Sodium	145 MG	Cholesterol	36 MG

PENNE OR RIGATONI WITH FRESH TUNA AND TOMATO SAUCE

MAKES 6 SERVINGS

This is one of the simplest and most satisfying pasta dishes served by my Sicilian mentor, Filippo, at his little restaurant in Palermo. He sautéed a couple of slices of fresh tuna in olive oil with lots of chopped garlic, broke it up with a spoon, poured in a bottle of tomato concentrate, added lots of pepper, *ecco!* Since we don't have the good tomato concentrate found in Italy, I use a homemade tomato sauce, not as concentrated as his (and frankly, I prefer mine).

One of the most impressive aspects of the Palermo fish markets is the sheer quantity and size of the tuna. Fresh tuna may be harder to find in America. Therefore, I have worked out two versions of this dish, one with fresh tuna and one with canned.

FOR THE TOMATO SAUCE:
- 1 tablespoon olive oil
- 3 or 4 garlic cloves (to taste), minced or put through a press
- 1 small onion, minced
- 3 pounds fresh or canned tomatoes (without juice)
- 1 tablespoon tomato paste
- salt and freshly ground pepper
- pinch sugar

FOR THE TUNA AND COMPLETED SAUCE:
- 1 pound fresh tuna steaks
- 1 tablespoon olive oil
- 3 large garlic cloves, chopped
  the tomato sauce
- ¼ teaspoon hot pepper flakes (optional)
  salt and freshly ground pepper
- 1 pound *penne* or *rigatoni*

PREPARE THE TOMATO SAUCE:

Heat the olive oil in a heavy-bottomed saucepan over low heat and add the garlic and onion. Sauté, stirring, until the onion is just turning gold and add the tomatoes and tomato paste. Bring to a simmer. Add salt and pepper to taste and a pinch of sugar; simmer over medium heat for 20 minutes, stirring often. Remove from the heat and puree through the medium blade of a food mill or in a food processor. Set aside.

PREPARE THE TUNA AND COMPLETE THE SAUCE:

Remove the skins from the tuna steaks and cut the meat off the center bone. Sauté the garlic in the olive oil over medium heat in a large heavy-bottomed nonstick frying pan or casserole for 2 minutes. Add the tuna and sauté, stirring with a wooden spoon for about 5 minutes, until the tuna has become grayish on the surface and the garlic is golden. Break the tuna into small pieces with a wooden spoon and add the tomato sauce and hot red pepper flakes. Bring to a simmer and cook, stirring often, for 10 to 15 minutes. Taste and adjust seasonings.

Bring a large pot of water to a boil, add salt, and cook the pasta *al dente*. Drain and toss with a ladleful of the sauce. Spoon onto warm plates, top each serving with the remaining sauce, and serve.

PENNE OR RIGATONI WITH CANNED TUNA AND TOMATO SAUCE

Substitute 2 9-ounce cans water-packed tuna for the fresh tuna. Do not add it to the oil with the garlic, but crumble it into the sauce and proceed as in master recipe.

PER PORTION:

Calories	477	Protein	29 G
Fat	10 G	Carbohydrate	68 G
Sodium	70 MG	Cholesterol	29 MG

PASTA WITH BROCCOLI, PALERMO-STYLE

MAKES 6 SERVINGS

Broccoli and pasta make one of my favorite combinations. This version comes from Sicily and includes the typically *Palermese* combination of anchovies, currants, pine nuts, and saffron. With all these flavors, the addition of Parmesan cheese isn't necessary.

    4   pounds broccoli, leaves and stems trimmed
        salt
    1   tablespoon olive oil
    1   small onion, chopped
    2   anchovy fillets, rinsed and chopped
    2   tablespoons dried currants
    1   tablespoon pine nuts
  ¼   teaspoon powdered saffron *or* ½ teaspoon threads
        freshly ground pepper
    1   pound *bucatini*

Trim away the stems of the broccoli and break into florets. Quarter the florets if large.

Bring a large pot of water to a rolling boil; add some salt and the broccoli. Cook 10 minutes and remove from the water (which you will use for the sauce and pasta) with a slotted spoon. Set aside the cooking water and the broccoli.

Heat the olive oil over medium heat in a large heavy-bottomed skillet and add the onion and anchovy fillets. Sauté, stirring, until the onion is golden. Add the broccoli and a ladleful of its cooking water, plus the currants, pine nuts, and saffron. Add a little salt and pepper and simmer for 5 to 10 minutes.

Meanwhile, bring the remaining broccoli cooking water to a rolling boil, adding more water if necessary. Add a teaspoon of salt and the *bucatini*. Cook *al dente* and drain. Toss with half the sauce in a casserole over low heat, then spoon onto warm plates and top each portion with the remaining sauce.

PER PORTION:

Calories	372	Protein	16 G
Fat	5 G	Carbohydrate	69 G
Sodium	283 MG	Cholesterol	1 MG

SPAGHETTI ALLA TRAPANESE

MAKES 6 SERVINGS

This typical Sicilian dish comes from Trapani, courtesy of my friend Filippo in Palermo. The *picante* tomato sauce can be prepared very quickly.

>   2 pounds ripe tomatoes, peeled
>   1 tablespoon olive oil
>   6 garlic cloves, thinly sliced
>   ¼ to ½ teaspoon hot pepper flakes *or* 1 hot red pepper,
>   crumbled (more to taste)
>   pinch freshly grated nutmeg
>   salt
>   10 large fresh basil leaves, cut into slivers
>   ¾ to 1 pound spaghetti
>   4 basil leaves, cut into slivers, for garnish

Cut the tomatoes in half, gently scoop out the seeds, and set aside.

Heat the oil over medium heat in a large heavy-bottomed frying pan or casserole and add the garlic. Sauté for about a minute and add the tomatoes, hot pepper, salt to taste, and basil. Crush the tomatoes with the back of a spoon and cook over medium-high heat for 5 minutes. Add a little nutmeg, adjust seasonings, and set aside.

Bring a large pot of water to a boil, add salt, and cook the spaghetti *al dente*. Drain and toss with the tomato sauce. Spoon onto plates and sprinkle additional basil over each serving. Serve at once.

PER PORTION:

Calories	285	Protein	9 G
Fat	3 G	Carbohydrate	54 G
Sodium	8 MG	Cholesterol	0

FUSILLI WITH ARTICHOKES AND PORCINI MUSHROOMS

MAKES 6 SERVINGS

The original Sicilian version of this dish includes a fair amount of smoked bacon, which gives the sauce a rich, meaty flavor. In my version *porcini* mushrooms and their soaking water yield a rich-tasting, earthy sauce.

2 ounces dried *porcini* mushrooms
2 cups warm water
4 medium-sized artichokes
1 lemon, cut in half
1 tablespoon olive oil
1 onion, chopped
4 garlic cloves, minced or put through a press
½ cup dry white wine
1 pound ripe tomatoes, peeled, seeded, and chopped
1 bay leaf
  salt and freshly ground pepper
2 tablespoons chopped fresh parsley
1 pound *fusilli*
3 tablespoons freshly grated Parmesan cheese for garnish

Place the *porcini* mushrooms in a bowl and pour the warm water over them. Let sit 30 minutes.

Meanwhile, prepare the artichokes. Cut off the ends and break off the outer leaves until you reach the light green and purple inner leaves. Using a paring knife, trim away all the dark green from the bottom and immediately rub the newly exposed surface with lemon juice. Slice off the purple tops, cut away the furry chokes, and again rub the exposed parts with a cut lemon. Now quarter the artichoke bottoms lengthwise and slice the quarters lengthwise as thin as possible. Toss with lemon juice and set aside.

Squeeze the mushrooms over the soaking liquid and rinse thoroughly in several changes of water. Squeeze dry and chop. Strain the soaking liquid through a strainer lined with paper towels and set aside.

Heat the olive oil over medium heat in a large heavy-bottomed frying pan or casserole and add the onion and half the garlic. Sauté, stirring until the onion is almost golden, and add the remaining garlic, the artichokes, and the chopped *porcini*. Stir together for about a minute and add the wine. Turn up the heat and cook, stirring, until the wine has almost evaporated. Add the tomatoes and mushroom stock, bay leaf, and salt and pepper to taste. Bring to a simmer, reduce heat, cover, and cook 20 to 30 minutes over low heat.

Taste and adjust seasonings, adding garlic, salt, or pepper if you wish. Stir in the parsley.

Bring a large pot of water to a boil, add salt, and cook the *fusilli al dente*. Drain, toss with the sauce, and serve at once. Pass Parmesan and sprinkle if desired over each serving.

PER PORTION:

Calories	409	Protein	15 G
Fat	5 G	Carbohydrate	80 G
Sodium	138 MG	Cholesterol	2 MG

SPAGHETTI ALLA CARRETTIERA

MAKES 4 SERVINGS

This spicy dish is one of the simplest *Palermese* recipes from my friend Filippo, minus a large fraction of the olive oil he would use.

- 3 tablespoons olive oil
- 4 large garlic cloves, finely minced
- 6 heaped tablespoons finely chopped flat-leaf parsley
- ¼ to ½ teaspoon hot pepper flakes (to taste)
- 1 teaspoon salt
- ¾ pound spaghetti
- 4 tablespoons freshly grated Parmesan cheese (optional)

Heat the oil over low heat in a skillet and gently sauté the garlic until golden. Add 4 tablespoons of the parsley and the hot pepper flakes, stir together for a minute, and remove from the heat.

Bring a large pot of water to a boil, add salt, and cook the spaghetti *al dente*. Drain and toss in a warm serving dish with the garlic mixture. Add the remaining parsley, stir together, and serve at once, passing the Parmesan in a bowl if desired.

PER PORTION:

Calories	413	Protein	11 G
Fat	11 G	Carbohydrate	66 G
Sodium	5 MG	Cholesterol	0

SPAGHETTI WITH SWEET PEAS AND TOMATO SAUCE

MAKES 4 SERVINGS

I have never tasted peas sweeter than Sicilian peas in April. I used to buy them in the market and snack on them during the day. They were so tender and sweet that I liked them raw; cooking them longer than 5 minutes seems a shame, and I was sorry to see that they were overcooked in most of the local restaurants. If you can't get really fresh, really sweet peas—and chances are you can't—substitute defrosted frozen petite peas.

1½ pounds fresh peas, shelled, *or* 1½ cups thawed frozen
    petite peas
1 tablespoon olive oil
2 garlic cloves, minced or put through a press
3 pounds (12 to 15) tomatoes, diced
1 tablespoon tomato paste
   pinch sugar
   salt and freshly ground pepper
2 tablespoons chopped fresh basil
¾ pound spaghetti
¼ cup freshly grated Parmesan cheese (optional)

If using fresh peas, steam the peas 5 minutes or until tender but still bright green.

Heat the oil in a heavy-bottomed casserole over low heat and sauté the garlic for 1 minute. Add the tomatoes, tomato paste, sugar, and salt to taste and cook, stirring often, over medium heat, for 20 minutes. Add pepper to taste and the basil. Adjust seasonings, adding more garlic or salt if you wish. Stir in the peas.

Bring a large pot of water to a boil, add salt, and cook the spaghetti *al dente*. Drain, toss with the tomato/pea sauce, and serve, passing the Parmesan on the side.

PER PORTION:

Calories	468	Protein	17 G
Fat	5 G	Carbohydrate	90 G
Sodium	65 MG	Cholesterol	0

SPAGHETTI WITH BROCCOLI, PINE NUTS, AND PARMESAN

MAKES 4 TO 6 SERVINGS

Another broccoli and pasta combination, this is simpler than the Sicilian version and can be thrown together in minutes.

    1 large bunch broccoli (about 2 pounds), broken into
           florets
    2 tablespoons olive oil
    2 large garlic cloves, minced or put through a press
    1 tablespoon pine nuts
       salt and freshly ground pepper
    1 teaspoon salt
  ¾ pound whole-wheat spaghetti
    3 tablespoons chopped fresh parsley
  ¼ cup freshly grated Parmesan cheese

Steam the broccoli for 5 to 10 minutes, until crisp-tender. Refresh under cold water and set aside.

Bring a large pot of water to a boil.

Meanwhile, heat 1 tablespoon of the olive oil in a wide heavy-bottomed skillet over low heat and gently sauté the garlic and pine nuts until the garlic is golden. Add the broccoli and stir together over low heat until the broccoli is heated through. Set aside. Season to taste with salt and freshly ground pepper.

When the water comes to a boil, add 1 teaspoon salt, the remaining oil, and the spaghetti. Cook the pasta *al dente*, drain, and toss at once with the broccoli mixture, the parsley, and Parmesan. Serve at once on warm plates.

PER PORTION:

Calories	275	Protein	15 G
Fat	5 G	Carbohydrate	45 G
Sodium	102 MG	Cholesterol	3 MG

PASTA E FAGIOLI

MAKES 4 TO 6 SERVINGS

It's amazing how much you can do with 3 large tomatoes and a few other ingredients. Once I rented a house with four friends on a sunny island off the coast of Yugoslavia. We drove there via Italy, stopping in northern Yugoslavia to board a ferryboat. By the time we got to our island, all we wanted to do was swim; after a cold, gray spring in Paris we were ready for the sun and sea. So we spent our first afternoon lazing on the rocks, beginning our summer tans, swimming, and working up an appetite.

But we had not done any serious marketing upon our arrival, and none of us really wanted to leave the cove to go into town. So with what provisions we did have I set about making dinner.

We had bought tomatoes, onions, garlic, peppers, Parmesan, and fruit the morning before in the Italian city of Vicenza, and upon arriving at the island we had picked up a few provisions, including chick-peas and pasta. So our first dinner was *paste e fagioli*, made with the 3 scrumptious, juicy tomatoes left over from Italy, the chick-peas, and spaghetti. We ate it at our outside table, overlooking the Adriatic, and nothing could have been better.

This is a slightly more elaborate version of that dish, which depended on our only herb, oregano. And you needn't restrict yourself to chick-peas— white beans are more commonly used, and kidney beans are delicious.

½ pound dried white beans (great northern, navy, or small white),
    kidney beans, or chick-peas, washed and picked over
1 tablespoon olive or vegetable oil
1 large onion, chopped
4 garlic cloves, minced or put through a press
2 quarts water
1½ pounds fresh or canned tomatoes, with juice, coarsely
    chopped
1 tablespoon tomato paste
1 bay leaf
1 small dried hot red pepper
  salt and freshly ground pepper
1 teaspoon dried oregano
¼ to ½ teaspoon dried thyme (to taste)
¼ to ½ teaspoon dried rosemary (to taste)
6 ounces small macaroni, *fusilli*, broken spaghetti, or *fettuccine*
2 tablespoons chopped fresh parsley
¼ cup freshly grated Parmesan cheese (optional)

Soak the beans overnight in 1 quart water (use bottled water if your tap water is hard). Drain.

Heat the oil in a large heavy-bottomed soup pot or casserole and sauté the onion with half the garlic until the onion is tender. Add the beans and water and bring to a boil. Add the tomatoes, tomato paste, bay leaf, and another garlic clove; cover, reduce heat, and simmer 1 hour. Add the hot pepper and simmer another 30 minutes or until the beans are tender.

Remove the bay leaf and add the remaining garlic, salt and pepper to taste, oregano, thyme, and rosemary. Simmer 15 minutes.

Mash some of the beans against the side of the pot with the back of a wooden spoon to thicken the sauce. Adjust seasonings.

Bring a large pot of water to a rolling boil. Add some salt and the pasta and cook *al dente*. Drain thoroughly and stir into the beans. Add the parsley and serve, passing the Parmesan if desired.

Note: You can also make this dish using canned beans. Substitute 2 14-ounce cans beans for the dried beans and water. Make the tomato sauce: Sauté the onion and garlic in the olive oil until tender, add the tomatoes, tomato paste, and herbs, and simmer 1 hour, stirring often. If you are using fresh tomatoes, add 1 cup water. Stir in the hot pepper and the beans and proceed with master recipe.

PER PORTION:

Calories	308	Protein	16 G
Fat	5 G	Carbohydrate	53 G
Sodium	115 MG	Cholesterol	3 MG

SPINACH FETTUCCINE WITH WILD AND FRESH MUSHROOMS

MAKES 4 TO 6 SERVINGS

This dish was inspired by a visit I made to northern Italy during the height of the *porcini* season. I came home with a few pounds of dried mushrooms, a treasure that brightened the next few months.

You might be puzzled by the presence of soy sauce in the recipe. It's not a Mediterranean tradition, but my own. When I cook mushrooms, I sometimes add a little soy sauce to bring out their "meaty" flavor.

1 ounce dried mushrooms, preferably *porcini* (*cèpes*)
  boiling water to cover
1 tablespoon olive oil
2 shallots, chopped
2 garlic cloves, minced or put through a press
1 pound fresh cultivated or wild mushrooms (such as
    oyster mushrooms or fresh *porcini*), cleaned and
    sliced
¼ cup dry white wine
1 tablespoon soy sauce
¼ to ½ teaspoon dried thyme (to taste)
¼ to ½ teaspoon chopped dried rosemary (to taste)
  salt and freshly ground pepper
2 tablespoons chopped fresh parsley
¾ pound spinach *fettuccine*
¼ cup freshly grated Parmesan cheese

Soak the dried mushrooms in boiling water to cover for 15 to 30 minutes. Drain and retain the soaking water. Rinse the mushrooms thoroughly, squeeze dry, and chop. Set aside.

Heat the oil in a wide heavy-bottomed nonstick skillet over medium heat and sauté the shallot with 1 clove of the garlic until tender. Add the fresh mushrooms and remaining garlic and sauté over medium-high heat until they begin to release liquid, 5 to 10 minutes. Add the chopped dried mushrooms, the wine, and the soy sauce and continue to sauté, stirring, until tender and aromatic. Stir in the thyme and rosemary, ½ cup of the soaking liquid from the mushrooms, and salt and freshly ground pepper to taste. Raise heat and cook until the mushrooms are slightly glazed and a little liquid remains in the pan. Stir in the parsley and set aside.

Fill a large pot with water and add to it the remaining soaking liquid from the dried mushrooms. Bring to a boil, add salt and a little oil, and cook the *fettuccine al dente*. Drain and toss at once with the mushrooms and the Parmesan. Serve on warm plates.

PER PORTION:

Calories	297	Protein	12 G
Fat	5 G	Carbohydrate	48 G
Sodium	256 MG	Cholesterol	57 MG

SPINACH FETTUCCINE WITH SORREL CHIFFONADE AND WHOLE ROASTED GARLIC CLOVES

MAKES 4 SERVINGS

This dish was inspired during a weekend I spent with the food writer Patricia Wells at her beautiful country house in Provence. The sorrel came from the garden, and the thyme and rosemary grew wild all around the house. I love the sharp taste of the sorrel with the sweet-pungent baked garlic and the delicate homemade pasta.

½ to 1 head garlic (to taste) cloves separated and peeled
2 tablespoons olive oil
¼ teaspoon dried thyme, *or* ¾ teaspoon fresh
¼ teaspoon dried rosemary
    salt and freshly ground pepper
    homemade spinach *fettuccine* for 4 (page 172)
1½ cups fresh sorrel leaves, washed, dried, and cut
      crosswise into thin slivers (*chiffonade*)
¼ cup freshly grated Parmesan cheese

Preheat the oven to 450 degrees, or have a fire in your fireplace or a grill ready. Oil a double thickness of aluminum foil or a single thickness of heavy-duty foil, about 10 inches square. Place the garlic cloves on the foil and sprinkle with thyme, rosemary, and salt and pepper to taste. Drizzle with a little more olive oil, using about 1 tablespoon in all, and fold the foil over the garlic, crimping and sealing the edges tightly. Bake in the hot oven or on the coals for 20 to 30 minutes. Remove from the heat and keep in the foil until ready to toss with the pasta.

Have a large bowl or casserole warming in a warm oven.

Bring a large pot of water to a boil. Add salt and the pasta and cook *al dente*, which should take about half a minute if the pasta is fresh. When it comes to the surface, it is ready. Drain and toss at once with the garlic, sorrel chiffonade, the remaining tablespoon of olive oil, and the Parmesan. Add freshly ground pepper to taste and serve at once.

PER PORTION:

Calories	311	Protein	12 G
Fat	11 G	Carbohydrate	43 G
Sodium	293 MG	Cholesterol	73 MG

SPAGHETTI WITH NEAPOLITAN TOMATO SAUCE

MAKES 4 SERVINGS

Some of the best things in life are the simplest. This dish will be only as good as the tomatoes that go into it.

2 teaspoons olive oil
1 to 1½ pounds (4 to 7) ripe tomatoes (to taste), peeled, seeded, and chopped
1 garlic clove, minced or put through a press
    pinch sugar
    salt and freshly ground pepper
1 tablespoon slivered fresh basil
¾ pound spaghetti

Heat the oil and add the tomatoes, garlic, sugar, and salt and pepper to taste. Cook over medium heat for 20 minutes. Add the basil and adjust seasonings.

Cook the spaghetti *al dente* in a large pot of salted boiling water. Drain, toss with the tomato sauce, and serve.

PER PORTION:

Calories	361	Protein	12 G
Fat	4 G	Carbohydrate	70 G
Sodium	12 MG	Cholesterol	0

SPAGHETTI WITH EGGPLANT AND TOMATO SAUCE

MAKES 4 SERVINGS

This dish comes from Sicily, where eggplant is abundant. There the eggplant is fried in a lot of oil and then cooked in the tomato sauce. I bake the eggplant separately to avoid using so much oil and mix it into the tomato sauce once it is cooked.

1 pound (1 large) eggplant, peeled and cut into ½-inch
    dice
 salt
2 tablespoons olive oil
4 garlic cloves, minced or put through a press (more to
    taste)
1 small onion, minced
3 pounds fresh or canned tomatoes (without juice)
1 tablespoon tomato paste
 salt and freshly ground pepper
 pinch sugar
1 to 2 tablespoons chopped fresh basil (to taste)
¾ pound spaghetti
¼ cup freshly grated Parmesan cheese (optional)

Preheat the oven to 450 degrees.

Sprinkle the eggplant with salt and let sit in a colander for 30 minutes. Rinse and shake dry in a kitchen towel. Place in an oiled baking dish and toss with 1 tablespoon of the olive oil. Cover tightly with foil or a lid and place in the hot oven. Bake 30 minutes or until tender.

Meanwhile, make the tomato sauce. In the remaining tablespoon of olive oil, sauté the garlic and onion in a heavy-bottomed casserole over low heat until the onion is just turning gold. Add the tomatoes and tomato paste. Bring to a simmer. Add salt and pepper to taste and a pinch of sugar, simmer, uncovered, over medium heat, stirring often, for 20 minutes. Put through a food mill or puree in a food processor and return to the pot. Adjust seasonings, adding more garlic, salt, or pepper if you wish. Stir in the cooked eggplant and the basil.

Bring a large pot of water to a boil, add salt, and cook the spaghetti *al dente*. Drain, toss with the sauce, and serve, passing the Parmesan at the table if desired.

PER PORTION:

Calories	469	Protein	15 G
Fat	9 G	Carbohydrate	86 G
Sodium	63 MG	Cholesterol	0

ORECCHIETTE WITH BROCCOLI RAAB

MAKES 4 SERVINGS

Broccoli raab has always been popular in Italy and is becoming more common in the United States. It looks like thin, leafy broccoli stalks with tiny buds and tastes like a cross between broccoli and dark leafy greens like mustard or turnip greens. I came across this delicious dish in southern Italy. *Orecchiette* means "ears," and this pasta has the shape of little shell-like ears. It's perfect for the sauce, which lodges in the hollows of the pasta, making every bite burst with the pungent flavor of the broccoli raab.

1 pound broccoli raab
2 tablespoons olive oil
4 large garlic cloves, minced or put through a press
  the steaming water from the broccoli raab
  salt and freshly ground pepper
1 teaspoon olive oil
½ pound *orecchiette*
¼ cup freshly grated Parmesan cheese

Peel any thick stems of broccoli raab, then coarsely chop the stems, flowers, and leaves. Place in a steamer above boiling water and steam, covered, for 5 minutes. Remove from the heat, transfer to a food processor or food mill fitted with a medium blade, and puree. Retain the steaming water.

Heat the olive oil in a wide frying pan over medium-low heat and add the garlic. Sauté until it begins to turn golden, then add the pureed broccoli raab. Stir together for 3 to 5 minutes over medium heat and moisten with 2 to 4 tablespoons of the steaming water. Season to taste with salt and freshly ground pepper and set aside. Heat through once more just before you drain the pasta, adding a little more of the steaming water if it seems dry.

Bring a large pot of water to a rolling boil; add salt, a teaspoon of oil, and the *orecchiette*. Cook for about 8 to 10 minutes, stirring from time to time, or until *al dente* (*orecchiette* take a fairly long time to cook). Drain, toss at once with the broccoli raab and the Parmesan, and serve.

PER PORTION:

Calories	333	Protein	12 G
Fat	10 G	Carbohydrate	51 G
Sodium	161 MG	Cholesterol	5 MG

SPAGHETTI WITH FISH BROTH

MAKES 4 TO 6 SERVINGS

This dish is a perfect example of simple, heady peasant cuisine, where nothing is wasted. At the busy Palermo restaurant where I first encountered it, a large pot of fish stock including the heads and bones of the daily catch was always going so that the pasta could be cooked right in the broth. At home you would have to make too much fish broth in order to have enough liquid for the pasta, so I suggest you cook the spaghetti separately and then ladle on the broth. But if you happen to have a large pot of fish stock on hand, do cook the pasta in it.

    2 pounds fish heads and carcasses
    1 head garlic, cloves separated, mashed, and peeled
    1 onion, quartered
    1 carrot, sliced
    1 leek, white part only, cleaned and sliced
    1 celery stalk, sliced
    1 tablespoon olive oil
      a *bouquet garni* made with 1 bay leaf, a couple of thyme
          sprigs, and a couple of parsley sprigs tied together
    5 cups water
      salt and freshly ground pepper
    2 garlic cloves, put through a press
    1 pound spaghetti
    ½ cup finely chopped parsley

Combine the fish, whole crushed cloves of garlic, onion, carrot, leek, celery, olive oil, *bouquet garni*, and water. Bring to a boil. Skim off any foam that rises. Add salt and pepper to taste, reduce heat, cover, and simmer 30 minutes. Strain and return to the pot. Add the remaining garlic, taste, and adjust salt and pepper. Set aside.

Bring a large pot of water to a boil and cook the spaghetti *al dente*. Bring the fish stock to a boil. Lift out the spaghetti with a strainer and divide among bowls. To serve, spoon a couple of ladlefuls of the broth and sprinkle a tablespoon or two of parsley over each helping.

PER PORTION:

Calories	334	Protein	12 G
Fat	3 G	Carbohydrate	63 G
Sodium	91 MG	Cholesterol	7 MG

FETTUCCINE WITH UNCOOKED TOMATOES

MAKES 4 TO 6 SERVINGS

This is a summer dish, to be made with the juiciest, sweetest tomatoes you can find.

- 8 ripe tomatoes, seeded and diced
- 3 to 4 tablespoons chopped fresh basil (to taste)
- 3 to 4 tablespoons chopped fresh parsley (to taste)
- 3 tablespoons capers, rinsed
- 1 garlic clove, minced or put through a press
- 2 tablespoons olive oil
- ¼ cup (1 ounce) freshly grated Parmesan cheese
  salt and freshly ground pepper to taste
- 1 teaspoon salt
- ¾ pound *fettuccine*

Bring a large pot of water to a boil.

Meanwhile, toss the tomatoes, basil, parsley, capers, garlic, 1 tablespoon of the olive oil, and Parmesan together in a bowl. Add salt and freshly ground pepper to taste.

When the water reaches a rolling boil, add a teaspoon of salt, the remaining oil, then the pasta. Cook *al dente*, drain, and toss at once with the vegetable mixture. Serve at once on warm plates.

PER PORTION:

Calories	293	Protein	11 G
Fat	6 G	Carbohydrate	49 G
Sodium	203 MG	Cholesterol	57 MG

SPAGHETTI WITH MUSSELS

MAKES 4 TO 6 SERVINGS

This delicious pasta couldn't be lighter or easier. Basically it's *moules à la marinière* taken from their shells and tossed with their cooking liquid and spaghetti.

3 quarts mussels, cleaned

1 onion *or* 4 shallots, minced

2 to 3 garlic cloves (to taste), minced

2 cups dry white wine

1 cup water

4 parsley sprigs

½ bay leaf

6 peppercorns

¼ to ½ teaspoon dried thyme (to taste)

1 tablespoon olive oil

2 garlic cloves, minced or put through a press

6 tablespoons chopped fresh parsley

salt and freshly ground pepper

¾ pound spaghetti

4 tablespoons freshly grated Parmesan cheese (optional)

Clean the mussels (see page 166).

Combine the onion or shallots, 2 or 3 minced garlic cloves, wine, water, parsley sprigs, bay leaf, peppercorns, and thyme in a very large lidded pot or wok and bring to a boil. Boil 1 or 2 minutes and add the mussels. Cover the pot tightly and cook over high heat for 5 minutes. Shake the pot firmly several times during the cooking to distribute the mussels evenly and ensure even cooking. If the pot is too heavy to do this effectively, stir a couple of times with a long-handled spoon. The mussels are ready when their shells have opened; this takes about 5 minutes. Discard any mussels that have not opened.

Drain the mussels and retain the cooking liquid. Strain this liquid and divide into 2 equal portions. Add 1 portion to a large pot of water in which you will cook the spaghetti.

Remove the mussels from their shells and set aside.

Heat the oil in a large frying pan and sauté the garlic until golden over medium-low heat. Add the mussels, their remaining cooking liquid, and the parsley; taste and adjust salt and pepper and heat through.

Meanwhile, bring the water to a boil, add salt, and cook the spaghetti *al dente*. Drain and toss with the mussels and their liquid. Serve at once in warm wide bowls. Pass the Parmesan if desired.

PER PORTION:

Calories	346	Protein	21 G
Fat	6 G	Carbohydrate	49 G
Sodium	367 MG	Cholesterol	31 MG

GREEN LASAGNE WITH MUSHROOMS AND BROCCOLI

MAKES 6 TO 8 SERVINGS

Lasagne can be rich and heavy, or it can be feather-light, like this one. The *béchamel* here is made with nonfat milk and very little butter, and the pasta is rolled as thin as paper—so different from thick, heavy commercial noodles. The colors are gorgeous, and the *lasagne* tastes sublime. You'll feel like you're splurging.

FOR THE PASTA:

- 3 ounces whole-wheat pastry flour
- 4 ounces unbleached white flour
- ¼ teaspoon salt
- 1 large egg
- ⅓ cup spinach, washed, dried, and finely chopped

FOR THE FILLING:

- 1 ounce dried *porcini* mushrooms
- 2 cups boiling water
- 1 pound (1 bunch) broccoli, broken into florets
- 2 tablespoons olive oil
- 2 medium shallots
- 4 garlic cloves, minced or put through a press
- 1½ pounds fresh cultivated mushrooms, trimmed, rinsed, dried, and sliced
- 3 tablespoons dry red or white wine
- 1 tablespoon soy sauce
- 1 teaspoon fresh *or* ½ teaspoon dried thyme
- ½ teaspoon chopped fresh or crumbled dried rosemary
  salt and freshly ground pepper
- 2 to 3 tablespoons chopped fresh parsley (to taste)

FOR THE BÉCHAMEL:

- 1½ tablespoons butter
- 3 cups skimmed milk
- 2½ tablespoons unbleached white flour
- 4 tablespoons freshly grated Parmesan cheese
  salt and freshly ground white pepper
  pinch freshly grated nutmeg

FOR THE LASAGNE:

    butter for the *lasagne* pan

1½ **cups freshly grated Parmesan cheese**

    the pasta, mushroom/broccoli filling, and *béchamel*

PREPARE THE PASTA:

Mix up the pasta dough, following the directions on page 172, and wrap in plastic. Set aside or refrigerate while you prepare the remaining ingredients. (*Note:* You might not need all the pasta dough if you roll it very thin. However, one-egg pasta doesn't make quite enough. Freeze any leftover dough.)

BEGIN PREPARING THE FILLING:

Place the dried *porcini* in a bowl and pour on 2 cups boiling water. Let sit while you prepare the *béchamel.*

Blanch the broccoli in plenty of boiling water, or steam for 5 minutes, and set aside in a bowl.

PREPARE THE BÉCHAMEL:

Melt the butter over low heat in a heavy-bottomed saucepan. Combine 2 cups of the milk and the flour in a blender jar and blend at high speed for 1 minute. Add the remaining milk and mix well. (Don't blend all the milk at once, or the liquid will splash out of the blender jar.) Add to the butter and bring to a boil over medium-low heat, stirring constantly. Simmer for about 10 minutes, until the sauce is quite thick. Stir in the Parmesan and season to taste with salt, white pepper, and nutmeg. Cover with parchment or a lid and set aside. Don't worry if a film forms over the surface, as you can whisk it away later.

FINISH PREPARING THE FILLING:

Drain the soaked dried mushrooms over a bowl. Strain the soaking liquid again through a strainer lined with a paper towel or through a paper coffee filter. Set aside. Rinse the soaked *porcini* thoroughly to remove all sand and grit and squeeze dry in a clean kitchen towel or in paper towels. Chop coarsely if they're very large.

Heat the olive oil in a large frying pan and add the shallots and half the garlic. Sauté until the shallots are tender; add the remaining garlic and the dried and fresh mushrooms (you may have to do this in batches; in this case, divide the shallots and garlic evenly among batches). Sauté for about 5 minutes, until the mushrooms release some of their liquid, and add the wine and the soy sauce. Sauté for about 10 minutes, stirring often, until the mushrooms are juicy and aromatic. Add the thyme, rosemary, and salt and pepper to taste toward the end of the cooking time. Add ½ cup of the soaking liquid from the mushrooms and turn up the heat to high. Cook, stirring, until the mushrooms are glazed. Taste, adjust seasonings, and remove from the heat. Stir in the parsley.

Place the remaining soaking liquid in a saucepan and reduce over high heat to ½ cup. Stir this into the *béchamel*. If this makes your *béchamel* too thin, simmer over low heat, stirring often, until it reaches the desired thickness.

ROLL OUT THE PASTA:

Roll out the pasta very thin (number 5 setting, or number 4 if it tears at number 5) and cut into wide strips that will fit your *lasagne* pan. Allow to dry for 15 minutes on a lightly floured board or kitchen towel.

ASSEMBLE THE LASAGNE:

When assembling the *lasagne*, you need to work fairly quickly, so get everything organized before you begin. Butter your *lasagne* pan generously and have your *béchamel*, mushrooms, broccoli, and Parmesan within reach. Stir ½ cup of *béchamel* into the mushrooms and ½ cup into the broccoli.

Cook only a few noodles at a time, enough for 1 layer. Bring a large pot of water to a boil, add salt and a drop of oil, and cook the *lasagne* noodles, a few at a time, just until they float to the surface of the pot, in about 10 to 20 seconds. Remove from the water and cool in a bowl of cold water. Drain on clean dish towels. Don't let the noodles sit too long on the towels once drained, or they'll become sticky.

Place the noodles in a layer on the bottom of the dish, overlapping very slightly. Spread a thin layer of *béchamel* over this and top with a thin layer of the mushrooms. Sprinkle on some Parmesan. Cook the next batch of pasta and repeat the layers, this time substituting broccoli for the mushrooms. You should have about 5 to 6 layers of pasta, alternating mushrooms and broccoli. The last layer of pasta will be the top layer of the lasagne. Spread a thin layer of *béchamel* over the top and sprinkle with Parmesan. Cover with foil until ready to bake. At this point you can refrigerate the mixture for several hours, covered with foil.

Preheat the oven to 400 degrees. Bake *lasagne* for 20 to 25 minutes or until the top is browned and bubbling. Remove from the heat and let sit for about 10 minutes before serving. You can also turn off the oven and keep the *lasagne* warm in the oven while eating your first course. Leftovers are particularly good.

PER PORTION:

Calories	350	Protein	19 G
Fat	15 G	Carbohydrate	37 G
Sodium	705 MG	Cholesterol	61 MG

PASTA PRIMAVERA WITH ROASTED RED PEPPERS

MAKES 6 SERVINGS

This pasta salad explodes with the colors and flavors of springtime. It makes a beautiful first course for a spring or early summer meal.

- 3 red peppers
- 1 pound asparagus
- 3 tablespoons olive oil
- 2 garlic cloves, minced or put through a press
  about ⅛ teaspoon coarse salt
- 1 bunch basil
- 1 pound fresh peas, shelled, *or* 1 cup thawed frozen peas
- ½ pound spinach, herb, or whole-wheat pasta
- ½ cup chopped fresh parsley, preferably Italian flat-leaf
- 2 ounces (½ cup) freshly grated Parmesan cheese
  salt and freshly ground pepper
  radish roses for garnish

Roast 2 of the red peppers, either under a broiler or above a burner flame, turning until all sides are charred. Remove from the heat and place in a paper bag or damp towel. Allow to cool.

Meanwhile, cut off the tips of the asparagus, about 2 inches from the top. Trim off the tough base of the asparagus and cut the remaining stalks into pieces about ½ inch long. Keep the tops separate from the stalks. Cut the remaining red pepper into thin lengthwise strips and cut these strips in half or into thirds.

When the roasted peppers are cool enough to handle, remove the skins and pat dry. Remove the stems, seeds, and membranes and cut into thin strips. Place in a bowl and toss with 1 tablespoon of the olive oil, 1 of the garlic cloves, the coarse salt, and 8 large leaves basil, cut into slivers. Toss together, cover, and refrigerate for at least 1 hour.

Mince the remaining basil. Steam the peas, asparagus tips, and asparagus stalks separately, just until crisp-tender, about 5 minutes for the asparagus, 5 to 10 minutes for the peas. Refresh under cold water.

Bring a large pot of water to a boil, add salt, and cook the pasta *al dente*. Drain and toss with the remaining olive oil, which you have mixed with the remaining garlic clove. Refrigerate until shortly before ready to serve or leave at room temperature if serving soon.

Shortly before serving, toss the pasta with the steamed peas, asparagus stalks, sliced raw pepper, minced basil, parsley, Parmesan, and salt and pepper to taste. Serve on individual plates and top each portion with a spoonful of roasted red peppers. Place spears of asparagus and a few radishes on the side and serve.

PER PORTION:

Calories	292	Protein	12 G
Fat	12 G	Carbohydrate	36 G
Sodium	159 MG	Cholesterol	42 MG

MIDDLE EASTERN PASTA WITH LENTILS

MAKES 4 TO 6 SERVINGS

Italy isn't the only country where you can get great pasta. Here is just one of the many pungent Middle Eastern noodle recipes I've come across.

½ pound brown or green lentils, washed and picked over
3 cups water
1 bay leaf
  salt
1 tablespoon olive oil
2 onions, chopped
3 large garlic cloves, minced or put through a press
1 teaspoon ground coriander
1½ teaspoons ground cumin
  pinch cayenne pepper
  freshly ground black pepper
12 ounces spaghetti or *tagliatelle* noodles
2 tablespoons plain low-fat yogurt

Combine the lentils, water, and bay leaf and bring to a boil. Reduce heat, cover, and simmer 30 to 40 minutes or until the lentils are tender but not mushy. Add salt to taste toward the end of the cooking.

Heat the olive oil in a heavy-bottomed frying pan and sauté the onions until tender and beginning to color. Add the garlic, coriander, and cumin and continue to sauté a couple of minutes, stirring. Stir this mixture into the lentils and add cayenne and black pepper to taste.

Bring a large pot of water to a boil, add some salt, and cook the noodles *al dente*. Drain and add to the lentils. Add the yogurt, toss together, and serve at once.

PER PORTION:

Calories	375	Protein	18 G
Fat	4 G	Carbohydrate	68 G
Sodium	10 MG	Cholesterol	0

PIZZA

THREE-HOUR PIZZA DOUGH

MAKES 1 12- TO 15-INCH CRUST TO SERVE 6

This recipe is based loosely on one from Alice Waters. If you want to make just one pizza and haven't begun far enough in advance to wait the many hours required by the crust on page 201, use this recipe. It makes a delicious, crunchy crust.

FOR THE SPONGE:
- ¼ cup lukewarm water
- 2 teaspoons active dry yeast
- ¼ cup whole-wheat flour

FOR THE DOUGH:
- ½ cup plus 1 tablespoon lukewarm water
- 1 tablespoon olive oil
- ½ teaspoon salt
- 1 cup whole-wheat pastry flour
- ¾ cup unbleached white flour

Mix the ingredients for the sponge and let sit, covered, in a warm place, for 30 minutes.

Add the lukewarm water and olive oil; mix well. Add the salt, then stir in the whole-wheat pastry flour, then the white flour.

Scrape out of the bowl and knead on a lightly floured surface for 10 to 15 minutes. The dough will be sticky, but keep flouring your hands and add only enough flour to prevent sticking to the kneading surface.

Shape the dough into a ball and place in an oiled bowl; turn so the greased side is up. Cover and let rise for 2 hours.

Punch the dough down and let rise again for 40 minutes.

Turn the dough out onto a lightly floured surface and roll out thin or press out and stretch with your hands. Line an oiled pizza pan and shape an attractive ridge around the edge with the overhanging dough.

Preheat the oven to 500 degrees for 30 minutes. Use a baking stone if you have one.

Spread the topping of your choice over the pizza dough and bake 20 to 30 minutes.

PER PORTION:

Calories	167	Protein	4 G
Fat	3 G	Carbohydrate	46 G
Sodium	182 MG	Cholesterol	0

FIVE- TO EIGHT-HOUR PIZZA DOUGH

MAKES 3 14- TO 15-INCH CRUSTS TO SERVE 18

This crust is based on Carol Field's recipe. Her dough has less yeast than the preceding one and rises for a much longer time. It's my favorite pizza crust, with its slightly sour taste and very crisp texture. Make sure you bake the pizzas at the highest possible temperature to get the best texture. You can freeze whatever raw dough you don't use if you want to make only one pizza. Frozen dough will thaw in about 2 hours, and how convenient it is to have it on hand. It can be frozen for up to 6 months.

2½ teaspoons (1 envelope) active dry yeast
2 cups lukewarm water
1 teaspoon salt
1 tablespoon olive oil
3 cups whole-wheat pastry flour
2 to 3 cups unbleached white flour
   additional olive oil for shaping dough

Dissolve the yeast in the water and let stand 10 minutes. Stir in the salt and olive oil, then whisk in the whole-wheat pastry flour, a cup at a time. Stir in 2 cups of the unbleached flour, a cup at a time, and turn out onto a floured surface or knead in the bowl, adding more unbleached flour as necessary. *If you're kneading by hand,* knead until elastic, about 10 to 15 minutes (it will still be rather sticky). *If you're using an electric mixer,* mix together the ingredients with the paddle, then change to the dough hook and knead for 10 minutes.

Shape the dough into a ball and place in an oiled bowl; turn the dough so the greased side is up. Cover loosely with plastic wrap and/or a damp towel and let rise at room temperature for from 4 to 8 hours. If the dough doubles in size before this, punch it down. It needs the time to develop its full flavor.

To shape, oil your hands and the top of the dough. Punch down and turn out onto a floured work surface. Cut into 3 equal pieces (freeze whatever you might not use). Shape each piece into a ball and let rest under a kitchen towel for 30 minutes.

Oil 3 14- to 15-inch pizza pans or baking sheets. Place the pieces of dough in the pans and press and stretch with your hands, keeping them oiled so the dough doesn't stick. Press out to a circle ⅛ inch thick with a thick edge. Pinch the overhang to make an attractive edge. The dough can stand, covered with a towel, for up to an hour before being topped and baked.

Preheat the oven to 525 to 550 degrees. If possible, heat baking tiles or a baking stone in the oven for 30 minutes before baking the pizza.

Cover pizza with the topping of your choice and place the pizza pans on top of the tiles or baking stone in the oven. Bake until the edges of the dough are browned, 20 to 30 minutes. If you're using cheese, don't add until halfway through the baking, or it will burn.

PER CRUST:

Calories	142	Protein	3 G
Fat	1 G	Carbohydrate	31 G
Sodium	106 MG	Cholesterol	0

PIZZA WITH SWEET PEPPERS

MAKES 1 15-INCH PIZZA (6 SERVINGS)

This is a very pretty, easy-to-make pizza. The peppers can be sautéed hours in advance and reheated gently just before baking.

1 recipe three-hour pizza dough (page 200) *or* ⅓ recipe
    five- to eight-hour pizza dough (page 201)
1 tablespoon olive oil
1 pound (3 large) red peppers, seeded and thinly sliced
1 pound (3 large) yellow peppers, seeded and thinly sliced
2 garlic cloves, minced
1 tablespoon fresh thyme *or* 1 teaspoon dried
    salt and freshly ground pepper
    hot pepper flakes to taste (optional)

Defrost the pizza dough if frozen.

Heat the oil in a heavy-bottomed or nonstick frying pan and sauté the peppers and garlic together, stirring, for about 10 minutes, until they are softened but still have some texture. Stir in the thyme and add salt and pepper to taste and the hot pepper flakes if desired.

Preheat the oven to 500 to 550 degrees. Use a baking stone if possible and heat for 30 minutes. Roll out the dough and line an oiled pizza pan. Top with the peppers. Bake 20 to 25 minutes, until the crust is browned. Remove from the oven and serve.

PER PORTION USING 3-HOUR CRUST:

Calories	221	Protein	5 G
Fat	5 G	Carbohydrate	38 G
Sodium	188 MG	Cholesterol	0

PER PORTION USING 5-HOUR CRUST:

Calories	196	Protein	5 G
Fat	4 G	Carbohydrate	36 G
Sodium	127 MG	Cholesterol	0

EGGPLANT, TOMATO, AND BASIL PIZZA

MAKES 1 12- TO 15-INCH PIZZA (6 SERVINGS)

This pizza always transports me to southern Italy. A more authentic version would have you sauté the eggplant in lots of oil, but I get around that by roasting it in a very hot oven. The slices don't look as neat as fried slices, but their flavor is more intense.

1 **recipe three-hour pizza dough (page 200)** *or* ⅓ **recipe**
    five- to eight-hour pizza dough (page 201)
1 **pound (1 large) eggplant**
6 **garlic cloves, minced**
2 **tablespoons olive oil**
1 **pound (4 to 5) tomatoes, seeded and chopped**
3 **tablespoons chopped or shredded fresh basil**
    pinch cayenne pepper or hot pepper flakes
    salt and freshly ground pepper

203

Defrost the pizza dough if frozen.

Preheat the oven to 450 degrees. Brush a baking sheet with olive oil. Cut the eggplants in half lengthwise and make a long slash down the middle, being careful not to cut through the skin. Place cut side down on the baking sheet and bake in the hot oven for 20 to 30 minutes, until the skin is shriveled and the eggplant tender. Remove from the heat and allow to cool, then slice crosswise.

Sauté the garlic in 1 tablespoon of the olive oil over low heat until it begins to color. Add the tomatoes and stir together over low heat for about 5 minutes. Stir in the basil, cayenne or hot pepper flakes, and salt and pepper to taste.

Preheat the oven to 500 to 550 degrees. Roll out the pizza dough and line an oiled pan. Spread with the tomato sauce and top with the eggplant. Brush the eggplant with the remaining tablespoon of oil and a little of the sauce so that it doesn't get too dry when you bake it. Bake 20 to 25 minutes, until the crust is brown and crisp, and serve.

PER PORTION USING 3-HOUR CRUST:

Calories	242	Protein	6 G
Fat	7 G	Carbohydrate	40 G
Sodium	192 MG	Cholesterol	0

PER PORTION USING 5-HOUR CRUST:

Calories	217	Protein	5 G
Fat	6 G	Carbohydrate	37 G
Sodium	132 MG	Cholesterol	0

PIZZA WITH FRESH AND WILD MUSHROOMS

MAKES 1 15-INCH PIZZA (4 SERVINGS)

This is another recipe inspired by my travels in northern Italy during the *porcini* season.

   1 recipe three-hour pizza dough (page 200) *or* ⅓ recipe
       five- to eight-hour pizza dough (page 201)
   2 ounces dried *porcini* mushrooms (or *cèpes*)

1 quart warm water
2 tablespoons olive oil
4 garlic cloves, minced or put through a press
½ pound fresh cultivated mushrooms, cleaned, trimmed,
  and thinly sliced
4 tablespoons white wine
1 tablespoon soy sauce
½ teaspoon dried thyme (more to taste)
½ teaspoon crumbled dried rosemary (more to taste)
  salt and freshly ground pepper
3 tablespoons chopped fresh parsley

Defrost the pizza dough if frozen.

Soak the dried mushrooms in the warm water for 30 minutes. Lift the mushrooms from the soaking water and gently squeeze over the soaking liquid. Place in a bowl and rinse thoroughly in several changes of water. Squeeze dry again and chop coarsely. Strain the soaking water through a strainer lined with paper towels or cheesecloth.

Heat 1 tablespoon of the olive oil over medium heat in a large heavy-bottomed skillet and add half the garlic. Sauté, stirring, until it begins to turn golden, in a couple of minutes, and add the dried and fresh mushrooms. Sauté, stirring, for about 5 minutes, until the mushrooms begin to release their liquid, and add the white wine and soy sauce. Sauté, stirring, until the wine has just about evaporated and add the soaking liquid from the mushrooms, the thyme, the rosemary, the remaining garlic, and salt and pepper to taste. Turn up the heat and continue to cook, stirring, until most of the liquid has evaporated and the mushrooms are glazed. Stir in the parsley and remove from the heat.

Preheat the oven to 450 to 500 degrees. Roll out the pizza dough and line a pan. Spread the mushrooms over the top. Brush with the remaining tablespoon of olive oil. Bake in the preheated oven for 20 to 25 minutes, until the crust is brown and crisp. Remove from the heat and serve.

PER PORTION USING 3-HOUR CRUST:

Calories	250	Protein	6 G
Fat	8 G	Carbohydrate	41 G
Sodium	362 MG	Cholesterol	0

PER PORTION USING 5-HOUR CRUST:

Calories	225	Protein	5 G
Fat	6 G	Carbohydrate	38 G
Sodium	301 MG	Cholesterol	0

SICILIAN PIZZA

MAKES 1 15-INCH PIZZA (4 SERVINGS)

This pizza was inspired by the incredible produce I saw in the Palermo market, the Vucciria. An authentic Sicilian pizza would also contain anchovies, olives, and cheese, but this lower-calorie version is every bit as enticing. The tomato sauce is the classic Sicilian *sfinciuni* (the word for Sicilian pizza) sauce, adapted from Carol Field's recipe. You could substitute another tomato sauce, such as the one on page 182 or 238, for this one.

> 1 recipe three-hour pizza dough (page 200) *or* ⅓ recipe
> five- to eight-hour pizza dough (page 201)

FOR THE ONION/TOMATO SAUCE:
> 1 pound (3 medium or 2 large) yellow onions, chopped
> 1 quart water
> 3 tablespoons tomato paste
> 1 anchovy, chopped

FOR THE REST OF THE TOPPING:
> ½ pound (1 small) eggplant, sliced, peeled if desired
> 1 medium-sized fennel bulb, chopped
> 2 large garlic cloves, chopped
> 1 tablespoon olive oil
>   salt and freshly ground pepper
> 1 medium-sized jar (8 to 12 artichoke hearts) or can
>   artichoke hearts packed in water, chopped
> 2 tablespoons capers, rinsed
> 2 tomatoes, seeded and chopped
> 1 teaspoon dried oregano
> 2 teaspoons chopped fresh rosemary *or* 1 teaspoon dried

Defrost the dough if frozen.

First make the sauce: Combine the onions, water, tomato paste, and anchovy in a saucepan, bring to a simmer, cover, and simmer 1 hour. Uncover and simmer another 45 minutes to an hour, until the sauce is thick.

Meanwhile, preheat the oven to 425 degrees. Toss together the eggplant, fennel, garlic, olive oil, and salt and pepper to taste in a baking dish. Cover tightly with foil and bake 30 minutes or until tender. Check and stir from time to time.

Raise the oven temperature to 500 to 525 degrees. Roll out the dough and line an oiled 15-inch pizza pan or a baking pan. Spread the onion/tomato sauce over the top, then top with the baked eggplant and fennel and the artichoke hearts, capers, tomatoes, herbs, and more salt and pepper to taste. Bake 20 to 25 minutes, until the crust is brown.

PER PORTION USING 3-HOUR CRUST:

Calories	259	Protein	8 G
Fat	6 G	Carbohydrate	47 G
Sodium	396 MG	Cholesterol	0

PER PORTION USING 5-HOUR CRUST:

Calories	234	Protein	7 G
Fat	4 G	Carbohydrate	44 G
Sodium	335 MG	Cholesterol	0

PIZZA WITH ROASTED TOMATO SAUCE AND MUSSELS

MAKES 1 15-INCH PIZZA (4 SERVINGS)

Here ripe tomatoes are baked until they blacken, which might sound strange, but they become very sweet. Then they are cooked on top of the stove until you have a very thick, dense, intensely flavored puree.

    1 recipe three-hour pizza dough (page 200) *or* ⅓ recipe
          five- to eight-hour pizza dough (page 201)
  10 medium-sized ripe tomatoes
        about 2½ dozen mussels, cleaned (page 166)
    2 tablespoons olive oil
    1 onion, chopped
    4 garlic cloves, minced
    3 tablespoons chopped fresh parsley

Defrost the pizza dough if frozen.
    Preheat the oven to 450 degrees. Place the tomatoes in an oiled roasting pan and bake, uncovered, for about 45 minutes to an hour, until blackened. Remove from the oven and puree, skins and all, through the coarse blade of a Mouli food mill.

Meanwhile, steam the mussels in a little water or white wine for 5 minutes, until their shells open. Remove from the heat. Discard any that have not opened and remove the mussels from their shells. Set aside.

Heat 1 tablespoon of the oil in a heavy-bottomed saucepan or casserole and sauté the onion and garlic over low heat until the onion begins to color. Add the tomato puree and bring to a simmer. Cook, uncovered, for 20 to 40 minutes or longer, until the sauce is a thick paste. Stir often to prevent sticking. Season to taste with salt and freshly ground pepper.

Preheat the oven to 500 to 550 degrees. Spread the tomato sauce over the pizza crust. Place in the oven and bake 10 minutes. Scatter the mussels and parsley over the pizza, drizzle on the remaining olive oil, and bake another 10 minutes or until the crust is brown. Serve at once.

PER PORTION USING 3-HOUR CRUST:

Calories	269	Protein	8 G
Fat	8 G	Carbohydrate	43 G
Sodium	249 MG	Cholesterol	5 MG

PER PORTION USING 5-HOUR CRUST:

Calories	244	Protein	8 G
Fat	6 G	Carbohydrate	40 G
Sodium	189 MG	Cholesterol	5 MG

SPINACH AND RED PEPPER TORTA RUSTICA

MAKES 8 TO 10 SERVINGS

This double-crusted deep-dish tart is as exciting to look at as it is to eat, with its multicolored dark green, red, and light green layers. The crust is a yeasted pizza dough with a rich, nutty flavor. It takes a while to make, so serve it for a dinner party on a weekend and dazzle your guests.

FOR THE PIZZA DOUGH:

- 2½ teaspoons (1 envelope) active dry yeast
- 2¼ cups lukewarm water
- 2 teaspoons salt
- 1 tablespoon olive oil
- 2 cups whole-wheat flour
- 2½ cups unbleached white flour, plus more as necessary for kneading

FOR THE FILLING:

    4 10-ounce packages frozen spinach

    1 tablespoon olive oil

    1 onion, minced

    2 garlic cloves, minced or put through a press

  ½ teaspoon dried thyme

  ½ teaspoon crumbled dried *or* 1 teaspoon minced fresh
          rosemary

    3 eggs

  ½ cup freshly grated Parmesan cheese
      salt and freshly ground pepper

    4 large red peppers *or* 1 1-pound jar good-quality
          peeled red peppers, drained

    1 cup fresh basil leaves, washed and dried

    1 pound low-fat cottage cheese

    2 tablespoons chopped fresh parsley

    1 additional egg for egg wash (optional)

PREPARE THE DOUGH:

Dissolve the yeast in the water in a large bowl. Add the salt and olive oil and stir in the whole-wheat flour, a cup at a time. Stir in the unbleached flour, a cup at a time, and turn out onto a lightly floured board. Knead 10 to 15 minutes, adding unbleached flour as necessary to prevent sticking, until the dough is smooth and elastic.

Oil the bowl and form the dough into a ball. Place in the bowl, seam side up, then turn so oiled side is up. Cover with a damp towel or loosely with plastic wrap and let rise in a warm spot until doubled in bulk, about 2 hours.

Punch down the dough and turn out onto a lightly floured surface. Knead for a few minutes, then remove one third of the dough for the top crust. Roll out the remaining two thirds into a circle large enough to line a 10-inch springform pan and leave an overhang. It should be about ¼ inch thick. Place in the refrigerator while you prepare the filling.

PREPARE THE FILLING:

Thaw the spinach or cook according to the directions on the package. Squeeze out extra moisture and set aside.

Heat the olive oil in a large skillet and sauté the onion with the garlic until the onion is tender, about 5 minutes. Add the spinach, thyme, and rosemary and stir together. Cook for a couple of minutes and remove from the heat.

Beat 2 of the eggs in a bowl; stir in ¼ cup of the Parmesan and the spinach mixture. Season to taste with salt and pepper and set aside.

Place the peppers under a broiler or directly over a gas burner flame and cook on all sides until the skin is charred. Place in a plastic or paper bag and let sit until cool enough to handle. Remove the skins and rinse under cold water. Carefully cut in half lengthwise, remove seeds and membranes, and open the peppers out flat.

Chop the basil finely in a food processor or with a large knife. Mix together with the cottage cheese, the remaining egg, the remaining Parmesan, and the parsley. Season to taste with salt and freshly ground pepper.

To assemble the tart, roll out the bottom two thirds of the dough and line a buttered 10-inch springform pan with the edges hanging over by 1 inch. Layer on half the spinach, then half the peppers, then all of the cottage cheese mixture, then the remaining peppers, and finally the remaining spinach. Roll out the top crust and place over the filling, then fold in the overhanging edges and pinch the crusts together.

Preheat the oven to 375 degrees. Brush the assembled tart with beaten egg and bake 45 minutes or until puffed and brown. Remove from the heat and let cool 10 to 15 minutes. Carefully remove the springform pan and serve, cut into wedges, or allow to cool and serve at room temperature. Refrigerate any leftovers and reheat in a moderate oven.

PER PORTION:

Calories	367	Protein	21 G
Fat	8 G	Carbohydrate	56 G
Sodium	824 MG	Cholesterol	88 MG

GEORGETTE TARDIEU'S PROVENÇAL PIZZA

MAKES 4 TO 6 SERVINGS

Georgette Tardieu served me this pizza with her winter tomato soup with *vermicelli* (page 146) one night at her *Provençal* farm. I watched her put together the simple yeastless crust in minutes; it's a pizza you can make on the spur of the moment. Try it with some of the toppings in this chapter as well as this tomato sauce.

FOR THE QUICK WHOLE-WHEAT PIZZA CRUST:
   2 cups whole-wheat pastry flour
   ½ teaspoon salt

1   teaspoon baking powder
½   teaspoon baking soda
½   cup plus 2 tablespoons water (more as needed)
2   tablespoons olive oil

FOR THE TOMATO SAUCE:
1   tablespoon olive oil
2   to 3 garlic cloves, minced or put through a press
2   pounds fresh or canned and drained tomatoes, seeded
        and chopped
1   tablespoon tomato paste
    salt
1   teaspoon dried oregano
½   teaspoon dried thyme or 1 teaspoon fresh
    pinch ground cinnamon
    freshly ground pepper

FOR THE ADDITIONAL TOPPINGS:
¼   cup freshly grated Parmesan or Gruyère cheese
1   cup sliced fresh mushrooms, sautéed for 2 minutes in
        2 teaspoons olive oil
1   onion, sliced into rings
1   green pepper, sliced into rings
1   zucchini, thinly sliced and sautéed for 2 minutes in 2
        teaspoons olive oil
    hot pepper flakes
    additional garlic, minced or put through a press

PREPARE THE CRUST:
Mix together the flour, salt, baking powder, and baking soda. Add the
water and work in with your hands, then add the oil and work it in (this can
also be done in an electric mixer or food processor). The dough will be stiff
and dry. Oil a 10-inch pie pan, pizza pan, or quiche pan. Roll out the dough
about ¼ inch thick and line the pan. Since the dough is stiff, this will take
some elbow grease. Just keep pounding down with the rolling pin and rolling
out until you get a nice flat, round dough. Don't worry if it tears; you can
always patch it together. Pinch a nice border around the top edge and
refrigerate until ready to use. (The pizza crust can also be frozen for up to 3
months at this point. Defrost before continuing.)

PREPARE THE TOMATO SAUCE:
Heat the oil in a heavy-bottomed frying pan or casserole and sauté the
garlic for about 1 minute. Add the tomatoes and tomato paste and bring to a

simmer. Add salt to taste and cook, uncovered, for about 30 minutes over medium-low heat, stirring occasionally. Add the oregano and thyme and cook another 10 minutes. Add the cinnamon and pepper to taste. Taste and correct seasonings, adding salt, garlic, or herbs if you wish. Set aside.

TOP AND BAKE THE PIZZA:
Preheat the oven to 450 degrees. Spread the tomato sauce over the crust. Add the toppings of your choice. Bake in the preheated oven for 15 to 20 minutes or until the crust is brown and crisp.

PER PORTION:

Calories	294	Protein	7 G
Fat	12 G	Carbohydrate	42 G
Sodium	433 MG	Cholesterol	3 MG

PISSALADIÈRE

MAKES 6 SERVINGS

This is not the first time I've included a *pissaladière* in a cookbook, but a Mediterranean cookbook would be incomplete without a recipe for this *Provençal* onion pizza. There are many versions of this recipe; some cooks make it in a pastry crust, but for this book a pizza crust is better because it's lower in fat, and I prefer it anyway. Traditional *pissaladière* is garnished with anchovies and black olives, but I have left out the olives and used only a few anchovies for the diet version.

   1 recipe three-hour pizza dough (page 200) *or* ⅓ recipe
         five- to eight-hour pizza dough (page 201)
   1 tablespoon olive oil (more as necessary)
   4 pounds (8 large or 12 medium) onions, very thinly
         sliced
   ¼ cup red wine
   ¼ teaspoon dried thyme (more to taste)
      salt and freshly ground pepper
   6 anchovy fillets, rinsed

Defrost the pizza dough if frozen.
Meanwhile, heat the olive oil over low heat in a large nonstick skillet.

Add the onions and cook, stirring from time to time, until they are translucent. Add the wine and thyme and cook gently, stirring occasionally, for 1 to 1½ hours, until they are golden brown and beginning to caramelize. Add salt and freshly ground pepper to taste. The onions should not brown or stick to the pan. Add water if necessary.

Preheat the oven to 500 degrees. Roll out the dough, line the pizza pan with it, and top with the onions. Cut the anchovies in half and make crisscrosses over the onions. Bake the *pissaladière* in the preheated oven for 20 to 25 minutes or until the crust is browned and crisp. Remove from the heat and serve hot or let cool and serve at room temperature.

PER PORTION USING 3-HOUR CRUST:

Calories	300	Protein	9 G
Fat	6 G	Carbohydrate	54 G
Sodium	337 MG	Cholesterol	2 MG

PER PORTION USING 5-HOUR CRUST:

Calories	275	Protein	8 G
Fat	5 G	Carbohydrate	51 G
Sodium	276 MG	Cholesterol	2 MG

CHAPTER FIVE

GRAINS, BEANS, STUFFED VEGETABLES, AND FATTA

Most of the recipes in this section are hearty main dishes, and I have a weakness for all of them—fragrant, glistening vegetable and seafood *risottos*; pungent couscous with fish, chicken, or vegetables; comforting, bright yellow polenta with tomato sauce and mushrooms; saffron-hued *paella*; garlicky chick-pea stews. Grains and legumes are the foods that most of the world's population survives on, and all around the Mediterranean basin people have been cooking them up into the most mouth-watering dishes for centuries.

In Paris, going out for *couscous* is the equivalent of going out for Mexican food; I always love it, but I always come home feeling bloated. That's why I prefer to make *couscous* at home now; my recipes are low in fat, and I use about half as much salt as the Parisian cooks pour on. Serving a dish like *couscous* at home is a real event; my friends are always delighted with the ritual and with the food. Dishes like *paella* and *risotto* are also for special occasions. *Risotto*, which must be served as soon as it's ready, is right for an intimate dinner for two or four, while *paella* is a party dish. You may be surprised to find these dishes in a diet cookbook, but my versions have considerably less oil, butter, and/or cream or cheese than the traditional recipes. To my palate they are just as delicious.

The other dishes here, the beans and grains, are tasty, economical dishes that are great for everyday eating. They are the staple foods of the eastern Mediterranean and the Middle East. One of the most beautiful sights in Egypt is the baskets filled with red lentils, *ful*, black-eyed peas, yellow fava beans, brown lentils, barley, wheat, and rice in markets everywhere. In Greece the *tavernas* offer delicious purees of split yellow peas, large white beans stewed with tomatoes, and rice seasoned with cumin and curry. Stuffed vegetables are standard fare, the stuffing always based on rice.

This is satisfying food that nourishes and sustains. It is especially useful to the dieter, because there is no way that you can go hungry eating these dishes.

COUSCOUS

COUSCOUS WITH PUMPKIN AND FAVA BEANS

MAKES 10 TO 12 SERVINGS

This is a delicious vegetable *couscous*. The pumpkin gives it a very pretty color.

½ pound dried broad white beans (favas), washed and
     picked over
1 tablespoon olive oil
2 onions, sliced thin
6 large garlic cloves, minced or put through a press
1 bay leaf
2 quarts water
   salt and lots of freshly ground pepper
4 tomatoes, peeled and chopped
4 medium-sized potatoes, diced
4 medium-sized carrots, peeled and thickly sliced
4 turnips, peeled and diced
1 pound pumpkin, peeled and cut into large pieces
½ teaspoon paprika (more to taste)
½ teaspoon ground coriander
½ teaspoon *harissa* (page 106) or cayenne pepper
½ teaspoon ground cinnamon
1½ pounds *couscous*
   additional *harissa* (page 106)
   chopped cilantro for garnish

Soak the beans overnight or for several hours in 3 times their volume of water (use bottled water if your tap water is hard) and drain.

Heat the oil in the bottom part of a *couscousière* or in a heavy-bottomed soup pot or casserole and sauté the onion and half the garlic over medium-low heat until the onion is tender and beginning to color. Add the beans, bay leaf, and water. Bring to a boil, reduce heat, and simmer 1 hour. Add salt to taste and all the remaining ingredients except the *couscous*, additional *harissa*, and cilantro and continue to simmer for an hour. Adjust seasonings.

Prepare the *couscous* according to the directions on page 224. Place in the top part of the *couscousière*, above the broth, or heat through in the oven.

Serve the *couscous* in flat wide bowls or on plates and spoon over the vegetables, beans, and broth, seasoning, if you wish, with additional *harissa*. Sprinkle some cilantro over each serving.

PER PORTION:

Calories	363	Protein	15 G
Fat	2 G	Carbohydrate	72 G
Sodium	45 MG	Cholesterol	0

VEGETABLE COUSCOUS

MAKES 6 TO 8 SERVINGS

This is the way I eat *couscous* in Paris restaurants, where the vegetables and broth are spooned over the *couscous* and the meat comes separately.

¾ pound dried chick-peas, washed and picked over
1 tablespoon olive oil
1 large *or* 2 small onions, sliced
3 to 4 garlic cloves, minced or put through a press
1 green pepper, sliced
2 leeks, white part only, cleaned and sliced
2 celery stalks, coarsely sliced
1 28-ounce can tomatoes, without the liquid, coarsely
    chopped
2 quarts water
1 bay leaf
1 fresh *jalapeño* or other hot green chili pepper, seeded
    and sliced
½ teaspoon saffron threads
½ pound turnips, peeled and quartered or cut into sixths
    if large
¾ pound (3 to 4) carrots, thickly sliced
    salt and freshly ground pepper
    cayenne pepper

¾ to 1 pound *couscous*
1½ cups shelled fresh or thawed frozen peas
  1 pound (4 small) zucchini, sliced
  1 tablespoon olive oil (if heating the couscous in a
      frying pan)
  1 bunch cilantro, chopped
    harissa (page 106) for garnish
    lemon wedges for garnish

Soak the chick-peas overnight in 3 times their volume of water (use bottled water if your tap water is hard). Drain.

Heat the olive oil in a large heavy-bottomed soup pot. Add the onion, half the garlic, and the green pepper; sauté until the onion begins to soften. Add the chick-peas, leeks, celery, canned tomatoes, water, bay leaf, and hot green chili. Bring to a boil. Reduce heat, cover, and simmer 1 hour. Add the saffron, remaining garlic, turnips, carrots, and salt and pepper to taste; cover and simmer another hour. Add cayenne to taste and adjust seasonings. Transfer to a *couscousière* if you are using one. At this point you can set the soup aside for several hours.

Thirty minutes before you wish to serve, place the *couscous* in a large bowl or a casserole and gradually sprinkle on about 2 cups water. Let it sit, stirring with a wooden spoon or between your palms and fingers every 5 minutes or more to prevent the *couscous* from lumping, for 15 minutes.

Meanwhile, bring the soup back to a simmer and add the shelled peas and zucchini. When the *couscous* is tender (add a little more water if you think it's necessary), add salt to taste and heat it through in either the top part of your *couscousière*, a strainer, or a steamer that fits tightly over your soup pot, or in a tablespoon of olive oil in a frying pan. Simmer the soup 10 to 15 minutes, until the zucchini and peas are cooked through but still bright. Stir in the cilantro.

To serve, spoon the *couscous* into warmed wide flat soup bowls and ladle on a generous helping of the soup. Pass *harissa* and lemon wedges with a small bowl of broth so that people can dissolve the *harissa* in a spoonful before adding it to the couscous.

PER PORTION:

Calories	422	Protein	19 G
Fat	3 G	Carbohydrate	81 G
Sodium	224 MG	Cholesterol	0

FISH COUSCOUS

MAKES 6 TO 8 SERVINGS

This recipe is hearty, spicy, and delicious. It's great for a party because much of the dish, up to the final steaming of the *couscous* and the addition of the fish and green vegetables, is prepared ahead. The dish consists of a rich vegetable/fish soup, slightly *picante* because of the addition of a hot fresh green chili pepper, which is spooned out over the steamed *couscous*. Guests have the option of firing up their *couscous* with the chili/tomato paste called *harissa* (available in imported food stores; or make your own—page 106). Use the precooked variety of *couscous*, available packaged in most supermarkets, to save yourself hours of fussing with the more authentic variety.

FOR THE FISH STOCK:
- 3 pounds fish heads and bones
- 2 quarts water
- 1 onion, peeled and quartered
- 1 large carrot, thickly sliced
- 1 celery stalk, sliced
- 2 large garlic cloves, peeled
- 1 leek, white part only, cleaned and sliced
- 6 peppercorns
  a *bouquet garni* made with 1 bay leaf, 2 sprigs thyme, and 2 sprigs parsley
- 1 cup dry white wine
  salt

FOR THE VEGETABLE SOUP AND COUSCOUS:
- 1 tablespoon olive oil
- 1 large *or* 2 small onions, sliced
- 3 to 4 garlic cloves (to taste), minced or put through a press
- 1 green pepper, sliced
- ½ pound dried chick-peas, washed and picked over, and soaked overnight in 3 times their volume of water (use bottled water if your tap water is hard), then drained
- 1 leek, white part only, cleaned and sliced
- 2 celery stalks, sliced
- 1 28-ounce can tomatoes, without the liquid, coarsely chopped
- 1 quart water

1 bay leaf
1 fresh *jalapeño* or other hot green chili pepper, seeded
     and sliced
  the fish stock
½ teaspoon saffron threads
½ pound (3 medium) turnips, peeled and quartered or
     cut into sixths if large
¾ pound (3 to 4) carrots, thickly sliced
  salt and freshly ground pepper
  cayenne pepper
1 cup shelled fresh or thawed frozen peas
½ pound (2 small) zucchini, sliced
2 pounds (or a little more) gray mullet, redfish, or cod,
     cut into 6 or 7 steaks
¾ to 1 pound *couscous*
1 tablespoon olive oil (if heating the *couscous* in a
     frying pan)

FOR THE GARNISH:
1 bunch cilantro, chopped
  harissa (page 106)
  lemon wedges

PREPARE THE FISH STOCK:

Combine all of the ingredients except wine and salt in a large soup pot and bring to a simmer. Skim off all the foam that rises. Continue to skim until no more foam remains, then cover, reduce heat, and simmer 30 minutes. Add the white wine and simmer another 20 minutes. Remove from the heat and strain. Add salt to taste and set aside.

PREPARE THE SOUP AND COUSCOUS:

Heat the olive oil in a large heavy-bottomed soup pot. Add the onion, half the garlic, and the green pepper; sauté until the onion begins to soften. Add the chick-peas, leek, celery, canned tomatoes, water, bay leaf, hot green chili, and bring to a boil. Reduce heat, cover, and simmer 1 hour. Add the fish stock, saffron, remaining garlic, turnips, carrots, and salt and freshly ground pepper to taste; cover and simmer another hour. Add cayenne to taste and adjust seasonings. Transfer to a *couscousière* if you are using one. At this point you can set the soup aside for several hours.

Thirty minutes before you wish to serve, place the *couscous* in a large bowl or a casserole and gradually sprinkle on about 2 cups water and salt to taste. Let it sit, stirring with a wooden spoon or between your palms and fingers every 5 minutes or more to prevent the *couscous* from lumping, for 15 minutes.

Meanwhile, bring the soup back to a simmer and add the shelled peas, zucchini, and fish steaks. When the *couscous* is tender (add a little more water if you think it's necessary), add salt to taste and heat it through in the top part of your *couscousière*, or in a strainer or steamer that fits tightly over your soup pot, or in a tablespoon of olive oil in a frying pan. Simmer the soup 10 to 15 minutes, until the fish is opaque and flakes with a fork and the zucchini is cooked through but still bright.

To serve, spoon the *couscous* into warmed wide flat soup bowls and ladle on a generous helping of the soup, making sure that everybody gets a fish steak. Sprinkle on chopped fresh cilantro; pass *harissa* and lemon wedges, with a small bowl of broth so that people can dissolve the *harissa* in a spoonful before adding it to the couscous.

Note: The couscous can also be reheated in a covered baking dish in a 350-degree oven for 15 to 20 minutes.

PER PORTION:

Calories	528	Protein	39 G
Fat	8 G	Carbohydrate	74 G
Sodium	352 MG	Cholesterol	61 MG

SAVORY CHICKEN COUSCOUS

MAKES 6 TO 8 SERVINGS

In addition to serving this savory, lemony *couscous* in the traditional manner, with the grain spooned out onto each plate and topped at the table with the chicken, broth, and vegetables, you can serve the dish as a casserole by placing the grains in a large serving dish and topping with the chicken, etc., then allowing each person to add extra broth seasoned with *harissa* or cayenne to his or her serving. This dish is very easy to make; both the chicken *tagine* and the *couscous* will hold, separately, for hours.

FOR THE CHICKEN TAGINE:
    1   **chicken, about 2½ to 3 pounds, cut into 8 pieces**
    1   **tablespoon olive oil**

  2 large onions, sliced
  4 to 6 garlic cloves (to taste), minced or put through a
        press
  2 carrots, sliced
  2 turnips, peeled and diced
  2 celery stalks, sliced
  1 teaspoon ground cumin
  ½ teaspoon ground ginger
  ½ teaspoon ground turmeric
  1 bay leaf
  1 cup dry white wine
2½ cups defatted chicken stock (page 152)
     salt
  1 teaspoon paprika
  1 cup cooked chick-peas
  ¼ teaspoon powdered saffron
  ½ pound (2 small) zucchini, sliced
  3 to 4 tablespoons fresh lemon juice (more to taste)
     freshly ground pepper
     cayenne pepper
  ¼ cup chopped cilantro
  2 tablespoons chopped fresh parsley

FOR THE COUSCOUS:
  ¾ pound *couscous*
  2 cups defatted chicken stock (page 152) or vegetable
        stock (page 140)
     harissa, cilantro leaves, and lemon slices for garnish

PREPARE THE CHICKEN TAGINE:
   Remove the skin from as many pieces of chicken as possible.

   Heat the olive oil in a large flameproof casserole over medium heat and sauté the onions and garlic, stirring, until the onions are tender, about 5 to 10 minutes. Add the carrots, turnips, and celery, and sauté another couple of minutes.

   Add the chicken, cumin, ginger, turmeric, bay leaf, white wine, chicken stock, and salt to taste; stir together and bring to a simmer. Simmer gently for 45 minutes to an hour, stirring occasionally, until the chicken is very tender and falling off the bones. Add the paprika, chick-peas, saffron, zucchini, and lemon juice; simmer another 15 minutes, until the zucchini is tender but still bright green. Taste and add salt, pepper, and cayenne to taste. Stir in the cilantro and parsley just before serving.

PREPARE THE COUSCOUS:

Oil an attractive ovenproof serving dish (I use a large, oval earthenware *gratin* dish). Place the *couscous* in the dish and pour on the chicken broth. Let sit for 10 minutes, by which time the *couscous* will be tender and will have absorbed the liquid. Now rub the *couscous* between your fingers and thumbs to separate the grains. If not serving right away, cover and keep warm in a low oven. Or place in the top part of a *couscousière*, above the simmering chicken *tagine.*

When you are ready to serve, bring the chicken *tagine* to a simmer, fluff the *couscous* once more with a spoon, and spoon onto plates. Ladle the chicken and vegetables and some of the broth over each plate of *couscous*, being careful not to drown the *couscous* in the broth. Leave enough broth in the pot so that each guest gets an extra ladleful to mix with the spicy *harissa* and ladle over the *couscous*. Garnish with cilantro and lemon slices and pass the extra broth with the *harissa*.

To season with the *harissa*, stir a very small spoonful into a ladleful of broth and spoon over the *couscous* (⅛ teaspoon in a ladleful of broth will be mildly hot, ¼ teaspoon hot, and more will be very hot, so ask guests what their preference is).

If you are not using the *harissa*, you can make your *couscous* slightly *picante* by adding cayenne to the broth and spooning the extra broth over each serving.

PER PORTION:

Calories	355	Protein	25 G
Fat	6 G	Carbohydrate	50 G
Sodium	101 MG	Cholesterol	52 MG

RED COUSCOUS

MAKES 4 SERVINGS

This spicy dish is a nice idea for using up leftover *couscous*. Serve on the side with steamed vegetables and fish.

      1   tablespoon olive oil
      4   garlic cloves, minced or put through a press
    ¼   teaspoon *harissa* (page 106) and 2 teaspoons tomato
              paste dissolved in ½ cup water
    ½   teaspoon paprika
    ½   teaspoon ground caraway
          salt
          juice of ½ to 1 lemon (to taste)
    ¼   cup water
      3   cups leftover cooked *couscous*

Heat the oil in a lidded frying pan or casserole and sauté the garlic over low heat for about 2 minutes, stirring. Add the *harissa* and tomato paste dissolved in water, the paprika, the caraway, and salt to taste; bring to a simmer. Cover and simmer 5 minutes, stirring often. Add the lemon juice, the additional water, and the *couscous*. Mix together well, correct seasonings, and transfer to a warm serving dish.

PER PORTION:

Calories	197	Protein	6 G
Fat	4 G	Carbohydrate	34 G
Sodium	24 MG	Cholesterol	0

RICE DISHES, RISOTTO

When I go to most cities in Italy, I concentrate on pasta, but in Venice my mouth waters for *risotto*. Rice is the staple of the Veneto and surrounding northern regions of Italy. It's called Arborio rice and is roundish with a marvelous chewy texture. The only other rice I've had that is somewhat similar comes from the Camargue, in southern France.

The Italian *risotto* is rich, creamy, and elegant. Mine tastes rich, too, but it's less fattening than traditional *risotti*. Eash chewy grain of rice, suspended in an unctuous mixture of broth and a *little* Parmesan, is distinct. The effect on your taste buds is explosive, as all the savory flavors of the broth and additions to the *risotto*, anything from peas to wild mushrooms to lemon to seafood, circulate through your mouth as you chew the perfectly *al dente* rice.

I discovered the wonders of this dish almost by accident, at my first meal in Venice. In a small, unassuming family *trattoria*, where the waiter sang as he served, a seafood *risotto* was placed in front of me. The rice had been cooked in a tomato-infused fish broth, and various bits of fish and shellfish, each with its own distinct flavor—mussels, clams, little squid, shrimp, crayfish—had been cooked along with it. The Parmesan stirred in at the end of the cooking melted around and between the little nubbins and oozed luxuriously into every bite. Never had rice, the lowly grain that feeds so many people on this globe, been so magnificent. Ten years later I had a similar seafood *risotto* in Venice, also on the night I arrived, very hungry after a very long journey, and it was equally satisfying.

On another trip to Venice, during *Carnevale* in the cold month of February, I ate a different *risotto* every day. My friends were only too eager to accompany me (it is a dish that most restaurants won't prepare for fewer than two people). I sampled different seafood *risotti*, one a gray-black color, made with inky cuttlefish, whose fresh, satisfying flavor pervaded the dish without overpowering it. I ate a creamy *risotto* packed with *porcini*, the wild Italian mushrooms, another with red beans, one with zucchini, and another with red chicory. With *risotto* I drank northern Italian wines, light reds like Merlot or young Chiantis, sometimes more substantial reds like Bardolinos or Valpolicellas, or refreshing whites from the region, Pinot Grigio, Tocai, Soave.

When I came home from Venice that time, I took out my Italian cookbooks and began to experiment with recipes. I found more than 30 to work with, and of course there are many more than that.

A successful *risotto* begins with a flavorful broth, either meat, chicken, vegetable, or fish. Traditionally, the rice is first sautéed in butter and oil, but

I use just a little oil, just enough to coat the grains. Then the rice is cooked slowly in the broth. Usually a little wine is added and cooked with the rice until it evaporates, before the broth is added. The simmering broth is added a little at a time, and the rice is stirred over medium heat until it absorbs most of the liquid. Then another ladleful (about ½ cup) is added, and you continue to stir. Your goal is to have the rice *al dente*, cooked through but still firm to the bite. This takes about 30 minutes with Italian Arborio rice; if you use another rice, the *risotto* won't be as creamy or chewy. Most recipes include freshly grated Parmesan cheese, which is added just before the end of the cooking. When it's done, the *risotto* should be creamy, because not all the broth is absorbed. It must be served at once, as the rice continues to swell and will absorb the remaining liquid, changing the quality of the dish.

LEMON RISOTTO

MAKES 2 SERVINGS AS A MAIN DISH OR 4 AS A SIDE DISH

This is a very elegant *risotto*, with its tart, lemony flavor. It would make a good side dish with grilled or baked fish, as well as a delicious starter.

    4 cups vegetable stock (page 140), garlic broth (page
          142), or defatted chicken stock (page 152)
    1 tablespoon olive oil
    ½ small onion, minced
    2 garlic cloves, minced or put through a press
    1 cup Italian Arborio rice, washed
    ¼ cup dry white wine
       salt
       juice of 1 large lemon (4 to 5 tablespoons)
       grated zest of ½ lemon
    1 egg, beaten
    ¼ cup freshly grated Parmesan cheese (or more)
       freshly ground pepper

Have the stock simmering in a saucepan.

Heat the oil in a wide heavy-bottomed frying pan and sauté the onion and garlic over medium-low heat until the onion is golden. Add the rice and continue to sauté, stirring, until all the grains are separate and coated with oil.

Stir in the white wine and salt to taste and cook over medium heat, stirring all the while. The wine should bubble, but not too quickly. You want some of the flavor to cook into the rice before it evaporates.

When the wine has just about evaporated, stir in a ladleful of the stock. It should just cover the rice and should bubble slowly like the wine. Cook, stirring constantly, until it is just about absorbed. Add another ladleful of the stock and continue to cook in this fashion, not too fast but not too slow, adding more broth when the rice is almost dry. After 25 to 35 minutes the rice should be cooked *al dente*, firm to the bite.

Beat together the lemon juice, lemon zest, egg, and Parmesan. Add another ladleful of stock so that the rice is not completely dry and remove from the heat. Immediately stir in the lemon mixture. Taste and adjust seasonings, adding salt and pepper to taste. Return to the heat and stir for a few seconds, then serve at once.

PER MAIN-DISH PORTION:

Calories	594	Protein	17 G
Fat	14 G	Carbohydrate	99 G
Sodium	844 MG	Cholesterol	147 MG

RISOTTO AI FUNGHI

MAKES 3 TO 4 SERVINGS AS A MAIN DISH

This dish is most luxurious when you can find the real fresh *porcini* (from Italy) or *cèpes* (from France). If your search proves fruitless, make the *risotto* anyway, using a combination of fresh cultivated mushrooms and dried imported ones—it will still be delicious. The dried mushrooms will give the *risotto* the rich, savory flavor it needs.

Although the Italians would never use soy sauce in a recipe, I find that the addition of this ingredient brings out the meaty flavor of the mushrooms.

    1 ounce imported dried wild mushrooms, preferably
        porcini or *cèpes*
    2 cups boiling water
    1 quart vegetable stock (page 140) or defatted chicken
        stock (page 152)
    2 tablespoons olive oil

2 shallots *or* ½ small onion, chopped

3 garlic cloves, minced or put through a press

½ pound fresh cultivated or wild mushrooms, cleaned
and thickly sliced

1 ½ cups Italian Arborio rice

½ teaspoon dried thyme

¼ teaspoon chopped dried rosemary *or* ½ to 1 teaspoon
chopped fresh

½ cup dry white wine

1 tablespoon soy sauce
salt and freshly ground pepper

¼ to ½ cup freshly grated Parmesan cheese (to taste)

2 tablespoons chopped fresh parsley

Place the dried mushrooms in a bowl and pour on boiling water to cover. Let sit 30 minutes while you prepare the remaining ingredients.

Drain the mushrooms and retain the soaking liquid. Strain this through a sieve lined with paper towels and combine with the vegetable or chicken stock. Bring this stock to a simmer in a saucepan.

Rinse the soaked mushrooms thoroughly, squeeze dry, and chop.

Heat the oil in a large heavy-bottomed lidded saucepan or skillet and sauté the shallot or onion with the garlic until tender and translucent. Add the chopped dried and sliced fresh mushrooms and sauté over medium heat, stirring, for 5 minutes. Add the rice, thyme, and rosemary and sauté with the mushrooms until all of the grains are coated with oil and the liquid from the mushrooms. Add the wine and soy sauce and sauté, stirring, until almost all the liquid is absorbed.

When the wine has just about evaporated, stir in a ladleful of the stock. It should just cover the rice and should bubble slowly like the wine. Cook, stirring constantly, until it is just about absorbed. Add another ladleful of the stock and continue to cook in this fashion, not too fast but not too slow, adding more broth when the rice is almost dry. Continue to add stock, a ladleful at a time, and stir the rice until the rice is cooked *al dente*, firm to the bite. This should take about 35 minutes in all. Add another ladleful of stock so that the rice is not completely dry, stir for a minute or two, add plenty of freshly ground pepper, and remove from the heat.

Taste the rice and adjust salt. Stir in the Parmesan and the parsley, combine well, and serve at once.

PER PORTION:

Calories	441	Protein	12 G
Fat	10 G	Carbohydrate	75 G
Sodium	729 MG	Cholesterol	7 MG

RISOTTO WITH SWISS CHARD

MAKES 2 SERVINGS AS A MAIN DISH

When I visit my friend Christine in Provence, I always return with sacks of Swiss chard from her garden. Christine doesn't like the dark leafy green vegetable, because it reminds her too much of World War II and just after the war, when chard was one of the only things they had to eat. Her gardener has his own reasons for growing it, and I for one appreciate them, because I love chard. This *risotto*, slightly bitter with the chard, reminds me a little of the red chicory *risotto* I've eaten in Venice.

> 1 quart vegetable stock (page 140) or defatted chicken
>   stock (page 152)
> 2 tablespoons olive oil
> ½ small onion, minced
> 2 garlic cloves, minced or put through a press
> 1 cup Italian Arborio rice, washed
> ¼ cup dry white wine
>   salt
> 2½ cups Swiss chard, leaves only, cut into julienne strips
> ½ teaspoon crumbled dried rosemary
>   freshly ground pepper
>   juice of ½ large lemon (2 tablespoons)
> ¼ cup freshly grated Parmesan cheese (or more)

Have the stock simmering in a saucepan.

Heat the oil in a wide heavy-bottomed frying pan and sauté the onion and garlic over medium-low heat until the onion is golden. Add the rice and continue to sauté, stirring, until all the grains are separate and coated with oil.

Stir in the white wine and salt to taste and cook over medium heat, stirring constantly. The wine should bubble, but not too quickly; some of its flavor should cook into the rice before it evaporates.

When the wine has just about evaporated, stir in a ladleful of the stock. It should just cover the rice and should bubble slowly like the wine. Cook, stirring constantly, until it is just about absorbed. Add another ladleful of the stock and continue to cook in this fashion, not too fast but not too slow, adding more broth when the rice is almost dry. After 25 minutes, stir in the chard and rosemary and continue to add stock, a ladleful at a time, and stir the rice until the rice is cooked *al dente*, firm to the bite. This should take another 10 minutes or so. Add another ladleful of stock so that the rice is not completely dry, stir for a minute or two, and remove from the heat.

Add plenty of freshly ground pepper. Combine the lemon juice and Parmesan; stir into the rice. Correct seasonings, return to the heat, and stir for a few seconds. Serve at once.

PER PORTION:

Calories	308	Protein	8 G
Fat	9 G	Carbohydrate	50 G
Sodium	452 MG	Cholesterol	5 MG

SEAFOOD RISOTTO

MAKES 4 TO 6 SERVINGS

This dish is based on the memory of the *risotto* I have twice eaten upon arriving, hungry, in Venice. The Venetian version includes different kinds of seafood, including squid and fish, and more oil than mine.

    1 pound (¾ quart) mussels
    1 pound littleneck clams
    1 cup dry white wine
    3 cups water
    4 garlic cloves, peeled and crushed
       pinch dried thyme
       salt and freshly ground pepper
    1 pound shrimp, peeled and deveined
    1 tablespoon olive oil
    1 small onion *or* 2 shallots, minced
    3 garlic cloves, minced or put through a press
    3 tomatoes, peeled, seeded, and chopped
 1 ½ cups Italian Arborio rice
    1 quart stock from the mussels and clams
    2 tablespoons chopped fresh parsley

Clean the mussels and the clams. Brush, rinse, and pull out the mussels' beards. Discard any mussels or clams with broken shells or any that are open.

Place in a bowl of cold water and add a tablespoon of salt or a tablespoon of vinegar. Let sit 10 minutes. Rinse under cold water, brushing once more, and soak another 10 minutes. Rinse again.

Combine the white wine, water, crushed garlic cloves, and thyme in a large lidded pot. Add the mussels and clams and bring to a boil. Cover the pot tightly and cook over high heat for 5 minutes or until the mussels and clams open. Drain and retain the liquid. Rinse the shellfish under cold water and remove from the shells, putting the clams in one bowl and the mussels in another. Coarsely chop the clams. Strain the cooking liquid through a strainer lined with paper towels or cheesecloth. You should have at least a quart; add water if necessary to make a quart. Add salt and pepper to taste. Place in a saucepan and bring to a simmer.

Chop the shrimp into fairly small pieces and set aside.

Heat the oil over medium-low heat in a wide heavy frying pan and sauté the onion or shallot and the remaining garlic until the onion begins to color. Add the tomatoes and salt and pepper to taste; continue to sauté, stirring often, for about 10 minutes. Add the rice and stir to coat with the mixture. Cook, stirring, for a minute or two. Now begin adding the simmering stock, a ladleful or two at a time, and cook, stirring until each ladleful is just about absorbed. The stock should just cover the rice and should be bubbling but not boiling too quickly. After 15 minutes, add the shrimp and stir into the rice. Continue adding stock and cooking until the rice is cooked *al dente*, another 10 minutes or so. When the rice is *al dente*, add a final ladleful of stock, stir in the mussels, clams, and parsley, and adjust seasonings. Serve at once.

PER PORTION:

Calories	301	Protein	20 G
Fat	4 G	Carbohydrate	44 G
Sodium	170 MG	Cholesterol	103 MG

OTHER RICE DISHES

RICE PILAF WITH CUMIN OR CURRY

MAKES 4 SERVINGS

This is just one of several Mediterranean rice pilafs. Similar dishes can be found all over Greece and the Middle East. This version goes very nicely with fish or chicken.

- 1 tablespoon olive oil
- 1⅓ cups brown or Italian Arborio rice
- 1½ teaspoons ground cumin or curry powder
- 2 tablespoons fresh lemon juice
- ¼ teaspoon salt

Bring about 3 cups water to boil in a kettle.

Meanwhile, heat the olive oil in a heavy-bottomed lidded saucepan over medium heat and add the rice. Cook, stirring, for 3 to 4 minutes, until the grains are coated with oil and beginning to smell toasty.

Add enough boiling water to cover by 1½ inches. Add the cumin or curry powder, the lemon juice, and the salt and reduce the heat to low.

Bring to a boil over low heat and cook, uncovered, until small craters form on the surface and you can no longer see water. This should take 15 to 20 minutes if the heat is low. Cover tightly and remove from the heat. Let sit, covered, for 20 to 25 minutes. The rice should be cooked. If the rice is cooked but any water remains, boil off the water without disturbing the rice. Taste and adjust seasonings, adding salt or lemon juice if you wish, and serve with vegetables or beans.

PER PORTION:

Calories	256	Protein	5 G
Fat	5 G	Carbohydrate	49 G
Sodium	142 MG	Cholesterol	0

SPANISH RICE

MAKES 6 SERVINGS AS A SIDE DISH

Very similar to a *paella* without the fish, this savory, pretty rice dish would make a good side dish to accompany grilled fish.

> 1 quart vegetable stock (page 140), chicken stock (page 152), or garlic broth (page 142)
> 1 tablespoon olive oil
> ½ onion, minced
> 4 large garlic cloves, minced or put through a press
> 1½ cups rice
> 1 green pepper, cut into thin strips
> 1 red pepper, cut into thin strips
> 3 tomatoes, seeded and chopped
> ¼ cup dry white wine
> ½ teaspoon saffron threads
> 1 cup shelled fresh peas
> salt and freshly ground pepper

Have the stock simmering in a saucepan.

Heat the oil in a large heavy-bottomed lidded frying pan or casserole and add the onion and garlic. Cook, stirring, until the onion is tender. Add the rice and cook, stirring, for 1 minute. Add the peppers and tomatoes and stir together for a couple of minutes.

Add the wine and continue to stir until the liquid is absorbed. Add the simmering stock and the saffron, bring to a slow boil over medium heat, and cook for 25 minutes. Add the peas and continue to cook until all the liquid is absorbed or until the rice is cooked *al dente* and the peas cooked through, about 10 more minutes. Pour off any stock that remains, add salt and pepper to taste, and serve.

PER PORTION:

Calories	261	Protein	6 G
Fat	3 G	Carbohydrate	53 G
Sodium	202 MG	Cholesterol	0

TIAN DE COURGETTES
(Zucchini and Rice Terrine)

MAKES 6 TO 8 SERVINGS

This is a simple but unforgettable rice and zucchini terrine from Provence, called a *tian* after the name of the casserole it is traditionally cooked in. A *Niçoise* specialty, it is one of my favorite *Provençal* dishes. I was glad to discover how easy it is to make at home. The rice gives the dish its special chewy texture.

> 1 tablespoon olive oil
> 1 onion, minced
> 2 pounds (8 small) zucchini, finely chopped
> 1 to 2 garlic cloves (more to taste), minced or put
>   through a press
> 2 eggs, beaten
> 2 ounces Gruyère cheese, grated (½ cup)
> 2 tablespoons freshly grated Parmesan cheese
> ½ cup chopped fresh parsley
> ½ cup raw short-grain brown or Italian Arborio rice, cooked
> ¼ to ½ teaspoon dried thyme (to taste)
>   salt and freshly ground pepper

Preheat the oven to 375 degrees and oil a nonstick loaf pan or a 1½-quart casserole.

Heat the olive oil in a large heavy-bottomed skillet and sauté the onion over medium-low heat until tender. Add the zucchini and the garlic and sauté over a low flame, stirring often, for 10 minutes. Remove from the heat.

Beat the eggs in a large bowl and stir in the cheeses, parsley, rice, thyme, and sautéed vegetables. Add salt and freshly ground pepper to taste. Turn into the prepared baking dish. Bake 40 to 60 minutes (it will take up to 60 minutes in a loaf pan), until firm. Remove from the heat. Serve hot, warm, or cold, cut into slices or squares.

To store, cover with plastic wrap or foil and keep in the refrigerator for up to a day.

PER PORTION:

Calories	134	Protein	7 G
Fat	6 G	Carbohydrate	14 G
Sodium	76 MG	Cholesterol	77 MG

ARROZ A LA MARINERA
(Valencian Fish Paella)

MAKES 8 GENEROUS SERVINGS

Paella is a luxurious dish. Even when it isn't rich, it seems so. My introduction to this bright yellow combination of rice and seafood (and in this case chicken) was in a beach town south of Barcelona; from my balcony I could see the *paellas* coming out to the tables on the terrace of the restaurant next door. The heady aromas would waft up, and we could never contain ourselves for very long. Night after night we ate *paella* for dinner; we would always feel uncomfortably full afterward, but the next night we'd be at it again. This *paella*, however, doesn't have a fraction of the oil and chicken fat that traditional Spanish *paellas* normally contain. The recipe comes from Valencia, and unlike many heartier *paellas*, which often combine chicken, fish, and sausage, this one contains only fish and shellfish. Naturally, in Valencia they use Valencia rice, a small round-grain rice, but I use either Italian Arborio rice or Carolina rice (which will result in a lighter, slightly less *al dente paella*) for mine. I recommend using a nonstick skillet for this dish.

1 quart fish *fumet* (page 160)
3 tablespoons olive oil
¾ pound monkfish fillets or steaks, bones removed, cut into chunks
¾ pound squid and cuttlefish or squid only, cleaned and cut into strips
2 onions, chopped
3 to 4 garlic cloves (more to taste), minced or put through a press
1 green pepper, sliced
1 red pepper, sliced
4 tomatoes, peeled and chopped
1½ teaspoons paprika
2 cups Carolina, Italian Arborio, or Valencia rice salt and freshly ground pepper
1¼ pounds lobster or crayfish, shrimp, and mussels, cleaned and left in their shells
¾ teaspoon saffron threads

Have the fish stock simmering in a saucepan.
Heat 2 tablespoons of the oil over medium heat in a large heavy-bottomed skillet, preferably nonstick. Add the monkfish, squid, and cuttlefish and sauté

until the fish begins to color, about 5 minutes. Transfer to a plate. Add the remaining tablespoon of oil and the onions and garlic. Sauté until the onion is golden and add the peppers. Sauté for about 5 minutes and add the tomatoes and paprika. Sauté for about 5 minutes, then add the sautéed fish and the rice. Stir together well and add the fish stock. Add salt and pepper to taste, bring to a simmer, simmer 3 minutes, and stir in the lobster or crayfish, the shrimp, the mussels, and the saffron.

Simmer, uncovered, over medium-low heat for 20 to 25 minutes, until all the liquid has been absorbed. Stir occasionally so that the rice doesn't stick to the bottom of the pan. Adjust seasonings and serve.

Note: This can be prepared a couple of hours ahead of time and reheated in a medium oven.

PER PORTION:

Calories	346	Protein	22 G
Fat	7 G	Carbohydrate	48 G
Sodium	162 MG	Cholesterol	127 MG

POLENTA

BAKED POLENTA WITH TOMATO SAUCE AND MUSHROOMS

MAKES 4 SERVINGS

Polenta is the Italian version of cornmeal mush, but there's nothing mushy about it. A hearty, comforting northern Italian dish, it has sustained me through many afternoons of strenuous cross-country skiing.

Making polenta requires energy and elbow grease. You stir the cornmeal in simmering water for 20 minutes without stopping, as it thickens and stiffens. By the end you have worked up an appetite and a blister on your thumb. You pour the cooked polenta out onto a platter and top it with a sauce, or you allow it to cool, as in this recipe, slice it up, and bake it in a casserole. In Italy, polenta slices are often grilled or fried.

This recipe is easy to put together once you've made the polenta, and the dish can be assembled and held for a day or two in the refrigerator. The bubbling tomato sauce, topped with a savory mixture of sautéed fresh and dried mushrooms and a small amount of Gruyère, blends beautifully with the polenta. The Gruyère may be omitted for a lower-fat version.

FOR THE POLENTA:
- 5 cups water, plus additional boiling water in a kettle
- 1 teaspoon salt
- ½ pound (about 1⅓ cups) coarse stone-ground cornmeal

FOR THE TOMATO SAUCE:
- 1 tablespoon olive oil
- 1 small onion, chopped
- 2 large garlic cloves, minced or put through a press
- 1 28-ounce can tomatoes without the juice, seeded and chopped
- 1 teaspoon tomato paste
  salt
- ¼ to ½ teaspoon dried thyme (to taste)
  freshly ground pepper

FOR THE MUSHROOMS:

> ½ cup imported dried wild mushrooms, such as *porcini* or
>   *cèpes*, soaked in boiling water to cover for ½ hour
> 1 tablespoon olive oil
> ½ pound fresh cultivated mushrooms, cleaned, trimmed,
>   and sliced
> 1 to 2 garlic cloves (to taste), minced or put through a
>   press
> 2 tablespoons red wine
> 1 teaspoon soy sauce (optional)
> ¼ teaspoon dried thyme
> ¼ teaspoon crumbled dried rosemary
>   salt and freshly ground pepper

FOR THE FINAL CASSEROLE:

> oil for the baking dish
> 2 ounces Gruyère cheese, grated (about ½ cup; optional)

The tomato sauce and mushroom topping can be prepared before or after you prepare the polenta, as long as you give the polenta time to cool (30 minutes) so that it slices easily. The wild mushrooms need to soak about 30 minutes to soften, so it's a good idea to start them before you begin the polenta

COOK THE POLENTA:

Brush a clean large cutting board or platter with olive or vegetable oil. Bring the 5 cups of water to a rolling boil in a deep heavy pot. Have additional water simmering in a kettle. Add the salt and reduce the heat so the water is just boiling—a little higher than a simmer. Using a long-handled wooden spoon, stir the water constantly in one direction while you add the cornmeal in a very slow stream, so slow that you can see the individual grains. To do this, pick up the cornmeal by handfuls and let it run through your fingers. The mixture will become harder and harder to stir as you add all the cornmeal. Never stop stirring. If it seems extremely thick, add boiling water from the kettle, a little at a time.

Once all the cornmeal has been added, continue to stir in the same direction for 20 minutes. The polenta should come away from the sides of the pan when it's done. It may seem done before the 20 minutes are up, but the cornmeal won't be cooked properly and won't have a creamy consistency. Keep adding small ladlesful of boiling water as it becomes impossible to stir. When it is done, it will have the consistency of very thick Cream of Wheat, and a spoon should stand up when stuck into the middle.

Pour or scrape the polenta out of the pot onto the oiled cutting board or platter. Allow to cool.

PREPARE THE TOMATO SAUCE:

In a heavy-bottomed saucepan, heat the olive oil over medium heat and add the onion and 2 garlic cloves. Sauté, stirring, until the onion is tender and translucent, then add the tomatoes, tomato paste, and salt to taste. Bring to a simmer, cover, and reduce the heat. Simmer 30 minutes, stirring from time to time, adding the thyme halfway through the cooking. Add freshly ground pepper, taste, and adjust seasonings. Set aside.

PREPARE THE MUSHROOM TOPPING:

Meanwhile, drain the dried mushrooms, rinse thoroughly, dry, and chop. Heat the olive oil in a skillet and sauté the sliced fresh mushrooms and the garlic until the mushrooms begin to release their liquid. Add the chopped dried mushrooms, the wine, soy sauce, thyme, and rosemary, and add salt and pepper to taste. Sauté over medium-high heat for another 3 to 5 minutes, until tender and aromatic. Remove from the heat.

ASSEMBLE THE CASSEROLE:

Preheat the oven to 375 degrees. Oil a 1½- to 2-quart baking dish and place a small spoonful of tomato sauce on the bottom. Cut the cooled polenta into ½-inch slices using a sharp stainless-steel knife (or a string, the way Italians do it), and place a layer of slices in the baking dish. Top with half the tomato sauce and sprinkle with half the cheese. Repeat the layers with the remaining polenta and tomato sauce. Spread the sautéed mushrooms over top and sprinkle on the remaining cheese.

Bake in the preheated oven for 30 minutes, until bubbling and beginning to brown. If you wish, pass under a broiler for 3 minutes before serving. Serve at once.

PER PORTION:

Calories	424	Protein	13 G
Fat	15 G	Carbohydrate	62 G
Sodium	938 MG	Cholesterol	16 MG

POLENTA WITH WILD MUSHROOM RAGOÛT

MAKES 6 SERVINGS

This is a luxurious polenta inspired by my travels in northern Italy during the wild-mushroom season. The polenta is transferred to a board or serving dish, topped with a rich mushroom *ragoût*, and served right away.

- 5 cups water, plus additional boiling water in a kettle
- 1 teaspoon salt
- ½ pound (about 1⅓ cups) coarse stone-ground cornmeal
- 1 recipe mushroom *ragoût* (page 320)
- 3 to 4 tablespoons freshly grated Parmesan cheese (to taste; optional)
- 2 tablespoons finely chopped fresh parsley for garnish

Using the water, salt, and cornmeal, make the polenta according to the instructions on page 239. Have a warm serving dish or platter or an oiled board ready, because once it is cooked in the pot it will be ready to serve. When the polenta is thick and creamy, pour or scrape it out of the pot onto the oiled cutting board or warm serving dish or platter. Make a depression in the top and pour on the mushroom *ragoût*. Sprinkle with Parmesan if you wish and with parsley and serve at once.

PER PORTION:

Calories	227	Protein	6 G
Fat	5 G	Carbohydrate	40 G
Sodium	679 MG	Cholesterol	0

OTHER GRAINS

CHICK-PEAS WITH BULGUR

MAKES 6 TO 8 GENEROUS SERVINGS

This is a fragrant, hearty Middle Eastern pilaf. The cinnamon and allspice give it a sweet flavor.

- ¾ pound chick-peas, washed and picked over
- 1 tablespoon olive oil
- 2 medium-sized onions, sliced
- 6 cups water
- 1 bay leaf
- 2 teaspoons ground allspice
- 2 tomatoes, peeled and chopped
- 1 tablespoon tomato paste
  salt and freshly ground pepper
- 8 ounces (1⅓ cups) bulgur
- ½ teaspoon ground cinnamon (more to taste)
- ¾ cup plain low-fat yogurt (optional)

Soak the chick-peas overnight or for several hours in 3 times their volume of water (use bottled water if your tap water is hard). Drain.

Heat the olive oil in a large heavy-bottomed soup pot or casserole and add the onions. Sauté until tender and add the chick-peas, water, bay leaf, allspice, tomatoes, and tomato paste. Bring to a boil, reduce heat, cover, and simmer 1½ to 2 hours, until the beans are tender. Add salt and pepper to taste. Stir in the bulgur, cover, and turn off the heat. After 20 minutes, check to see if the bulgur has absorbed the liquid and become tender; cook a little longer if it has not. Adjust seasonings and serve, sprinkling cinnamon over each serving and accompanying with plain low-fat yogurt.

PER PORTION:

Calories	288	Protein	11 G
Fat	5 G	Carbohydrate	52 G
Sodium	31 MG	Cholesterol	0

LENTILS AND BULGUR PILAF

MAKES 6 TO 8 SERVINGS

This is a simple and hearty dish from Lebanon.

- ½ pound lentils, washed and picked over
- 5½ cups water
- 2 garlic cloves, minced or put through a press
- 1 bay leaf
- 1 teaspoon ground cumin
  pinch cayenne pepper
  salt and freshly ground pepper
- 6 ounces (1 cup) bulgur
- 2 large onions, thinly sliced
- 1 tablespoon olive oil
- 2 tablespoons chopped fresh parsley or cilantro
- ½ cup plain low-fat yogurt for topping

Soak the lentils in the water in a large casserole for 1 hour. Add the garlic, bay leaf, and cumin and bring to a boil. Reduce the heat and simmer 20 to 30 minutes, until tender. Toward the end of cooking, add the cayenne and salt and pepper to taste.

Stir the bulgur into the lentils (there should be plenty of liquid left), cover, and turn off the heat. Let sit for 20 to 30 minutes, until the bulgur has absorbed the liquid from the lentils and become tender.

Meanwhile, sauté the onions in the olive oil over low heat in a nonstick skillet until almost caramelized.

Taste the bulgur and lentils and adjust seasonings. Transfer to a serving platter and sprinkle on the onions and parsley or cilantro. Serve topped with plain low-fat yogurt, with a crisp green salad on the side.

PER PORTION:

Calories	212	Protein	11 G
Fat	3 G	Carbohydrate	38 G
Sodium	15 MG	Cholesterol	1 MG

BELILA

MAKES 6 SERVINGS

Among my favorite Egyptian dishes is *belila*, cooked whole-wheat berries in milk. *Belila* is served as a dessert as well as breakfast. The authentic dessert version is much sweeter than this one, the wheat berries heated through in a sugary syrup. It's often served with little dishes of currants, flaked almonds, and powdered sugar on the side. In my version I have sweetened the milk (skimmed) with a little honey and spice and left out the powdered sugar.

Belila will keep for up to 3 days in the refrigerator, so you can make it in the evening and heat it up for breakfast.

½ pound (1 cup) wheat berries
3 cups water
2 cups skimmed milk
1 tablespoon honey
½ teaspoon ground cinnamon
¼ to ½ teaspoon freshly grated nutmeg (to taste)
½ teaspoon vanilla extract
1 tablespoon orange flower water
1 apple, chopped

Soak the wheat berries overnight in water to cover and drain. Combine with the water and bring to a boil. Reduce heat, cover, and simmer about 1 hour, until the skins split. Drain.

Heat the milk and stir in the honey, cinnamon, nutmeg, vanilla, and orange flower water. Add the wheat and stir until the milk just reaches the simmering point. Serve, topping each portion with chopped apple.

PER PORTION:

Calories	189	Protein	8 G
Fat	2 G	Carbohydrate	37 G
Sodium	46 MG	Cholesterol	2 MG

BEANS

FUL MEDAMES

MAKES 4 TO 6 SERVINGS

Ful (also spelled *foul* or *fool*), or *ful medames*, are the small, thick-skinned brown beans that are the national dish of Egypt. They are as ubiquitous there as *frijoles* are in Mexico, but unlike Mexican beans, *ful medames* are not refried in lard, but mashed after the beans have been cooked, then mixed with olive oil, lemon juice, and various seasonings (in this lightened version I have omitted the olive oil).

Ful has sustained Egyptians at least since the pharaohs. Like beans and corn *tortillas* in Mexico, the brown beans eaten with whole-wheat *baladi* bread (pita made with coarse whole-wheat flour) provide a cheap and efficient source of protein in a very poor country. Yet "the dish of the pharaohs" knows no social barriers; it's as much a staple in middle- and upper-class homes as it is for the peasants in the fields. Most Egyptians eat *ful medames* for breakfast; Mohammed, our taxi driver in Cairo, told us that there is an Arabic expression that means *"ful* is like cement in the stomach"—not exactly an enticing simile; "sticks to your ribs" would be more appropriate. Mohammed says that a breakfast of *ful medames* and *baladi* bread will keep him going until dinner, when he might eat the same thing again, with grilled meat and *tahina* or eggplant salad. In fact, it's not surprising to see these beans at breakfast, lunch, and dinner.

I tried the *ful* at every restaurant that offered it when I visited Egypt, and it was never the same. Sometimes it was thick and spicy, sometimes watery and bland, to be seasoned as desired at the table. I watched Egyptians mash their beans with a fork, pour on olive oil, and sprinkle on salt and onion, and copied them, turning my bland beans into a much tastier dish.

At a busy lunchtime place in Cairo, the *ful medames* was already mashed, salted, and doused with olive oil (*drowned* might be a more appropriate description). Here it was quite tasty (you could avoid some of the oil by not mixing it into the beans); it made up part of a delicious meal consisting of falafel, *baladi* bread, *tahina*, rice, and pickled vegetables, all served on a tin tray divided into compartments, the kind I used to get in elementary school cafeterias.

The Sheraton Hotels in Egypt make a great show of *ful medames*. The beans are served from huge brass urns that are heated over a gas flame. The vessel is tilted toward you, and you spoon out your beans with a big brass ladle. Beside the urn are bowls of spices—cumin and hot chili powder (I've read that cinnamon is used in some places, but I've never seen it)—to mash and stir into the beans with olive oil. On top go chopped onion, tomato, peppers, and garlic, a squeeze of lime, *tahina*, and parsley, and a beaker of olive oil is served (in my diet version the beaker of olive oil is omitted).

Egyptian brown beans can be found in Greek markets. If you can't find them, substitute fava beans or kidney beans.

FOR THE BEANS:

 1 pound dried Egyptian brown beans, washed and
 carefully picked over (the ones I brought back
 from Egypt were about 5 percent stones and
 sticks, so make sure you take a good look)
 1 tablespoon olive oil
 1 large onion, chopped
 4 to 6 garlic cloves (to taste), minced or put through a
 press
 2 quarts water
 1 bay leaf
 1 tablespoon tomato paste (optional)
 2 dried hot chili peppers (more to taste)
 2 teaspoons ground cumin
 salt and freshly ground pepper

FOR THE GARNISH:

 ground cumin
 ground chilies (hot or mild)
 2 lemons or limes, cut into wedges
 4 tablespoons chopped cilantro or fresh parsley
 1 small onion, minced (optional)
 a few garlic cloves, chopped
 2 tomatoes, minced
 1 small sweet pepper *or* 2 hot peppers, minced
 whole-wheat pita for serving, page 40

Soak the beans in 3 times their volume of water for 8 hours or overnight (use bottled water if your tap water is hard). Drain.

Heat the olive oil in a large heavy-bottomed soup pot or casserole and add the onion and 2 of the garlic cloves. Sauté over medium heat until the onion begins to soften. Add the beans, water, another garlic clove, the bay leaf, tomato paste if desired, chilies, and cumin; bring to a boil. Reduce heat, cover, and simmer 2 hours, until the beans are soft. Toward the end of the cooking, add salt and pepper to taste and the remaining garlic to taste. When the beans are tender and aromatic, remove from the heat and discard the bay leaf.

If the *ful* is very wet, drain off some of the liquid (keep it for soups). To thicken, mash half the beans in a food processor or mortar and pestle or with a potato masher. Do not *puree* the beans, just mash them to retain their texture. Stir back into the whole beans and continue to mash together a little more with a potato masher or wooden spoon. The mixture should be thick and just a little soupy, not stiff like *frijoles*.

Serve the beans in bowls or on plates and pass the garnishes, which people can sprinkle on to their taste. The citrus juice adds a particularly nice touch. Mash the beans further with your fork if you wish. Serve with whole-wheat pita bread (page 40), either soft or crisped in the oven. *Ful* will keep for 4 or 5 days in the refrigerator and can be frozen.

PER PORTION:

Calories	303	Protein	21 G
Fat	4 G	Carbohydrate	51 G
Sodium	13 MG	Cholesterol	0

MIDDLE EASTERN LENTILS WITH SPINACH

MAKES 4 TO 6 SERVINGS

Lentils and other beans go nicely with spinach. You can also make this dish with Swiss chard.

½ pound (1⅓ cups) brown lentils, washed and picked over
1 small onion, chopped
3 garlic cloves, minced or put through a press
3 cups water
1 bay leaf
 salt and freshly ground pepper
1 pound fresh spinach
½ teaspoon ground coriander
1 teaspoon ground cumin (more to taste)

Combine the lentils, onion, 2 of the garlic cloves, water, and bay leaf in a saucepan and bring to a boil. Reduce heat, cover, and simmer 30 minutes, until the lentils are tender. Add salt and freshly ground pepper to taste.

Meanwhile, stem and wash the spinach. Chop and wilt in its own liquid in a large frying pan. Drain the lentils, retaining some of the liquid, discard the bay leaf, and add the lentils to the spinach. Stir together, moisten with some of the cooking liquid from the lentils, and add the coriander, cumin, remaining garlic, and more salt and pepper to taste. Stir together over medium heat for about 5 minutes and serve. The dish will keep for a day or two in the refrigerator.

PER PORTION:

Calories	146	Protein	12 G
Fat	.64 G	Carbohydrate	25 G
Sodium	48 MG	Cholesterol	0

WHITE BEANS À LA PROVENÇALE

MAKES 4 SERVINGS AS A SIDE DISH

White beans go beautifully with tomatoes, garlic, thyme, and basil. This is a lovely combination of *Provençal* flavors.

½ pound dried white beans (great northern, navy, or
    small white), washed and picked over, *or* 3 cups
    canned
2 tablespoons olive oil (if using dried beans)
1 onion, chopped
2 garlic cloves, minced or put through a press
1 quart water
1 bay leaf
    salt
¾ pound (3 medium) fresh or canned (drained) tomatoes,
    peeled and chopped
¼ teaspoon dried thyme *or* ½ to 1 teaspoon fresh (to
    taste)
1 to 2 tablespoons chopped fresh basil (to taste)
    freshly ground pepper
    fresh lemon juice (optional)

IF YOU'RE USING DRIED WHITE BEANS:

Soak the beans in 1 quart water overnight or for several hours (use bottled water if your tap water is hard). Drain.

Heat 1 tablespoon of the oil in a large heavy-bottomed saucepan or casserole and sauté the onion and 1 clove of the garlic until the onion is tender. Add the beans along with 1 quart fresh water and the bay leaf. Bring to a boil, reduce heat, cover, and simmer 1½ hours or until the beans are tender. Add salt to taste, remove the bay leaf, drain, and retain the cooking liquid.

Heat the remaining oil in a wide heavy-bottomed skillet or casserole and sauté the remaining garlic over medium heat for 1 minute. Add the tomatoes, thyme, and more salt to taste and bring to a simmer. Simmer 10 minutes, then add the beans, ½ cup of their cooking liquid, and the basil. Cover and simmer 15 to 20 minutes. Adjust seasonings, adding pepper to taste and lemon juice if you wish. Remove from the heat and serve as a side dish.

IF YOU'RE USING CANNED BEANS:

Drain the canned beans and retain the liquid. Add enough water to measure ½ cup.

Heat 1 tablespoon of olive oil over medium heat in a wide heavy-bottomed skillet or casserole and sauté the onion with 2 garlic cloves until the onion is tender. Add the tomatoes and thyme and proceed as above.

The beans will keep for a couple of days in the refrigerator, but don't add the basil until shortly before serving.

PER PORTION:

Calories	275	Protein	14 G
Fat	8 G	Carbohydrate	40 G
Sodium	15 MG	Cholesterol	0

POTAJE DE GARBANZOS
(Spanish Chick-Pea and Tomato Stew)

MAKES 6 SERVINGS

This is a thick soup, almost a stew, that can be served as a hearty main dish with whole-grain bread and a salad. Canned beans, with their liquid, can be substituted for dried (3 19-ounce cans is about right).

 1 pound dried chick-peas, washed and picked over
 6 cups water
    salt
 1 tablespoon olive oil
 1 large onion, chopped
 4 large garlic cloves, minced or put through a press
1½ teaspoons paprika
 1 pound ripe fresh or canned tomatoes with the juice,
       peeled, seeded, and chopped
 1 bay leaf
 3 tablespoons tomato paste
 2 medium-sized boiling potatoes, diced
 1 teaspoon dried thyme
 1 teaspoon dried oregano
 2 cups broth from cooking the beans
    freshly ground black pepper
    cayenne pepper
    chopped fresh parsley for garnish

Soak the beans for several hours in 3 times their volume of water (use bottled water if your tap water is hard). Drain and cook, covered, in 6 cups water for 1 to 2 hours, until tender. Add salt to taste and cook 10 minutes. Drain and retain 2 cups of the broth.

In a heavy-bottomed casserole, heat the olive oil and sauté the onion and garlic over medium-low heat until the onion is tender, about 5 to 10 minutes. Add the paprika, stir together, and add the tomatoes, bay leaf, and tomato paste. Simmer over medium heat, stirring often, for 10 minutes.

Add the potatoes, thyme, oregano, broth from the chick-peas, the chick-peas, and more salt to taste. Bring to a boil, reduce the heat, cover, and simmer 30 minutes, until the potatoes are tender. Add plenty of black pepper, cayenne to taste, and serve, garnishing each bowl with chopped fresh parsley.

This dish will keep for up to 5 days in the refrigerator and freezes well.

PER PORTION:

Calories	377	Protein	17 G
Fat	7 G	Carbohydrate	64 G
Sodium	93 MG	Cholesterol	0

SPICY LENTILS WITH PEPPERS AND TOMATOES

MAKES 6 TO 8 SERVINGS

Lentils have been a staple in the Middle East since biblical times. There are many different dishes; this spicy one and the lentil recipes that follow are just a sampling.

¾ pound (2 cups) brown or green lentils, washed and picked over
6 cups water
1 bay leaf
 salt
1 tablespoon olive oil
1 large onion, chopped
2 garlic cloves, minced or put through a press
1 green pepper, seeded and chopped
2 hot chili peppers, seeded and finely chopped
1½ pounds ripe fresh or canned tomatoes (without the juice), peeled and sliced
 freshly ground pepper
3 to 4 tablespoons chopped cilantro (to taste)
 juice of ½ lemon (optional)

Combine the lentils, water, and bay leaf in a large heavy-bottomed saucepan and bring to a boil. Reduce heat, cover, and simmer 30 to 40 minutes, until the lentils are tender. Add salt to taste. Drain and retain some of the cooking liquid.

Heat the oil in a large heavy-bottomed skillet or casserole and add the onion and garlic. Sauté over medium-low heat until the onion is tender and beginning to color. Add the green pepper and chili peppers and sauté another 5 to 10 minutes, until the pepper is tender, and add the tomatoes and drained lentils. Add a little bit of cooking liquid from the lentils if the mixture seems dry. Simmer over medium-low heat for 15 minutes. Season to taste with more salt and pepper, stir in the cilantro and lemon juice if desired, and serve, or allow to cool and serve chilled.

This dish will keep for 3 to 5 days in the refrigerator.

PER PORTION:

Calories	189	Protein	13 G
Fat	2 G	Carbohydrate	31 G
Sodium	12 MG	Cholesterol	0

MIDDLE EASTERN LENTILS
WITH VEGETABLES

MAKES 6 TO 8 SERVINGS

This is a hearty lentil and vegetable stew seasoned with coriander, cumin, lots of garlic, and a touch of cayenne.

    1 pound (1⅓ cups) brown or green lentils, washed and picked over
    1 quart water
    1 bay leaf
    3 celery stalks
    2 carrots, sliced
    ½ pound (2 medium) leeks, trimmed, cleaned, and sliced
    1 pound tomatoes, peeled and chopped
    ½ pound zucchini, sliced
       salt and freshly ground pepper
    1 teaspoon crushed coriander seed
    1½ teaspoons crushed cumin seed
       pinch cayenne pepper
    1 tablespoon olive oil
    1 large onion, thinly sliced
    3 to 4 large garlic cloves (to taste), minced or put
          through a press
    3 to 4 tablespoons chopped cilantro (to taste)
       juice of 1 lemon

Soak the lentils in the water in a large casserole for 1 hour. Bring to a boil, add the bay leaf, cover, and simmer for 20 minutes, until just about tender. Add the celery, carrots, leeks, tomatoes, zucchini, salt and pepper to taste, coriander seed, cumin seed, and cayenne; continue to simmer 15 minutes, until the vegetables are tender and the liquid is just about absorbed.

Meanwhile, heat the olive oil in a frying pan and sauté the onion until golden. Add the garlic, cook a few minutes, stirring, and stir into the lentils. Taste and adjust seasonings. Transfer to a serving dish and sprinkle with the cilantro and lemon juice or sprinkle with the cilantro and lemon juice and serve from the casserole.

This dish will keep in the refrigerator, without the addition of the lemon and cilantro, for 3 or 4 days.

PER PORTION:

Calories	155	Protein	10 G
Fat	2 G	Carbohydrate	26 G
Sodium	31 MG	Cholesterol	0

EGYPTIAN RICE AND LENTILS

MAKES 4 TO 6 SERVINGS

This rice and lentil pilaf could be a hearty main dish and looks beautiful on a platter surrounded by tomatoes—baked or raw—and dark green leafy vegetables.

- 6 ounces (1 cup) brown lentils, washed and picked over
- ¾ teaspoon salt
- 1 tablespoon plus 1½ teaspoons olive oil
- 1 large onion, ½ chopped and ½ thinly sliced
- 1 tablespoon crushed cumin seed
- ½ teaspoon ground cinnamon
- ½ cup long-grain rice
- 2 cups water
  freshly ground pepper
- ½ cup plain low-fat yogurt for topping

Soak the lentils in water to cover for 1 hour. Drain, place in a saucepan or casserole, cover with water by 2 inches, and bring to a boil. Add ½ teaspoon of the salt, reduce heat, and simmer 30 minutes, until just about tender.

In another casserole, heat 1 tablespoon of the olive oil and sauté the chopped onion until it begins to color. Add the cumin seed and cinnamon, stir together, and add the rice. Stir to coat with oil and add 2 cups water and the lentils with their liquid, plus about ¼ teaspoon salt and pepper to taste. Stir together, bring to a boil, reduce heat, cover, and cook 20 to 25 minutes or until the liquid is absorbed.

Meanwhile, brown the sliced onion in the remaining 1½ teaspoons of olive oil. When the rice and lentils are cooked, transfer to a platter and strew the browned onions over the top.

Serve with plain low-fat yogurt on the side and a big salad. It will keep for 3 or 4 days in the refrigerator.

PER PORTION:

Calories	219	Protein	11 G
Fat	4 G	Carbohydrate	35 G
Sodium	19 MG	Cholesterol	1 MG

EGYPTIAN RED LENTIL PUREE

MAKES 4 SERVINGS

Red lentils are actually a beautiful orange shade, and when they cook they become yellowish. Their flavor is milder than that of brown or green lentils. They make a lovely sight mounded high in baskets in Egyptian markets.

    1 ½ teaspoons olive oil
      1 onion, chopped
      3 large garlic cloves, minced or put through a press
    ½ pound (1 ½ cups) small red lentils (available in Indian
           import stores and some natural-foods stores),
           washed and picked over
      2 teaspoons ground cumin
    1 ½ teaspoons ground coriander
         salt and freshly ground pepper
         pinch cayenne pepper
         juice of 1 lemon (optional)

Heat the oil in a heavy-bottomed saucepan and sauté the onion and half the garlic over low heat until the onion is tender and beginning to color. Add the lentils, cumin, and coriander, cover by 1 inch with water, and bring to a simmer. Cover and simmer over low heat for 30 minutes, checking the water from time to time and adding more if the lentils dry out. Add the remaining garlic, salt and pepper to taste, and cayenne; continue to simmer until the lentils are soft and beginning to disintegrate. Mash with the back of a spoon and continue to cook until thick and savory, another 15 minutes or so, stirring often to prevent sticking, or coarsely puree in a food processor. Correct seasonings and serve, adding the lemon juice if you wish. The puree will keep 3 or 4 days in the refrigerator.

PER PORTION:

Calories	222	Protein	17 G
Fat	3 G	Carbohydrate	35 G
Sodium	9 MG	Cholesterol	0

FASOULIA
(Stewed Beans with Tomato and Garlic)

MAKES 4 SERVINGS AS A SIDE DISH OR 2 AS A MAIN DISH

This delicious Greek bean dish is sometimes served hot, sometimes at room temperature. The beans are bathed in a thick tomato puree, which is a reduction of their cooking liquid, and seasoned with garlic, oregano, and the ubiquitous onion (optional in my version). You can use either fava beans or the giant white beans of the same shape, which the French call *soissons*. Favas have an outer skin that must be removed after soaking. Don't remove the skins from the white beans, or the beans will fall apart when you cook them.

½ pound (1½ cups) dried giant white or fava beans,
    washed and picked over
1 quart water
4 large garlic cloves, minced or put through a press
1 bay leaf
3 heaped tablespoons tomato paste
1 teaspoon dried oregano
  salt
  juice of 1 large lemon (more to taste)
  freshly ground pepper
2 tablespoons chopped fresh parsley
½ small onion, chopped (optional)

Soak the beans overnight in 3 times their volume of water (use bottled water if your tap water is very hard).

Drain the beans. If using favas, remove outer shells. Combine the beans in a large saucepan with the water, garlic, bay leaf, and tomato paste. Bring to a boil. Reduce heat, cover, and simmer 45 minutes. Add the oregano and salt and simmer another 15 to 30 minutes or until the beans are tender but not mushy. Uncover and raise the heat. Reduce the liquid until the beans are bathed in a thick tomato puree. Remove from the heat.

Add the lemon juice and freshly ground pepper to taste. Adjust salt. Allow to cool or serve hot. Serve garnished with chopped fresh parsley and the chopped onion if desired.

This dish will keep for 3 to 5 days in the refrigerator.

PER MAIN-DISH PORTION:

Calories	437	Protein	32 G
Fat	2 G	Carbohydrate	78 G
Sodium	277 MG	Cholesterol	0

TURKISH-STYLE BEANS WITH TOMATOES

MAKES 6 SERVINGS

This dish can be made with kidney beans, white beans, or even pintos. It's delicious served hot or cold.

1 pound red kidney beans, white beans, or pinto beans, washed and picked over
2 bay leaves
2 quarts water
salt
1 tablespoon olive oil
2 large onions, chopped
4 to 5 garlic cloves (to taste), minced or put through a press
1½ pounds (6 or 7) ripe tomatoes, peeled and chopped
1 teaspoon paprika
pinch cayenne pepper *or* 1 dried hot red pepper
freshly ground pepper
3 tablespoons chopped fresh parsley or cilantro
2 tablespoons chopped fresh basil or cilantro for garnish
lemon wedges for serving (optional)

Soak the beans overnight in 3 times their volume of water.

Drain the beans and place in a large soup pot with 1 of the bay leaves and the water. Bring to a boil, reduce heat, cover, and simmer 1½ to 2 hours, until tender. Add salt to taste, drain, and retain 1 cup of the cooking liquid.

Heat the oil over medium-low heat in a heavy-bottomed casserole and add the onions and half the garlic. Sauté for about 5 minutes, until the onion is tender and beginning to color, and add the tomatoes, remaining garlic, and more salt to taste. Simmer, uncovered, over medium-low heat for 30 minutes, stirring often. Add the beans, 1 cup of their cooking liquid (or more to taste), the paprika, the remaining bay leaf, the cayenne or hot red pepper, and the 3 tablespoons chopped parsley or cilantro. Simmer for another 20 minutes. Adjust seasonings.

Turn onto a serving platter or dish, garnish with the 2 tablespoons chopped basil or cilantro, and serve, or allow to cool and serve at room temperature, passing lemon wedges on the side. The beans will keep 3 to 5 days in the refrigerator.

PER PORTION:

Calories	317	Protein	20 G
Fat	3 G	Carbohydrate	55 G
Sodium	29 MG	Cholesterol	0

CHICK-PEAS WITH SPINACH

MAKES 6 SERVINGS

This is another typical Middle Eastern dish, combining beans and spinach. There are several versions of chick-peas with spinach, some calling for dried mint and paprika, others for crushed coriander seed and cumin. This one combines ideas from several recipes.

½ pound (1 cup) dried chick-peas, washed and picked over
6 cups water
  salt
1 pound fresh spinach, stemmed
1 tablespoon olive oil
1 onion, chopped
1 teaspoon crushed coriander seed
  freshly ground pepper
  juice of ½ lemon
2 large garlic cloves, crushed or put through a press
1 cup plain low-fat yogurt
1 teaspoon dried mint *or* 2 teaspoons chopped fresh
  paprika

Soak the chick-peas for several hours in 3 times their volume of water (use bottled water if your tap water is hard). Drain and combine with 6 cups water in a large pot. Bring to a boil, reduce heat, cover, and simmer 1½ to 2 hours, until tender. Add salt to taste. Drain and retain ¾ cup of the cooking liquid.

Wash the spinach but don't dry it; finely chop the leaves.

Heat the olive oil and sauté the onion with the coriander seed until tender and golden. Add the spinach and cook over medium-high heat for about 5 minutes. Add the chick-peas and about ½ cup of their liquid, season with a little more salt and pepper to taste, and simmer, uncovered, for 5 to 10 minutes, until the liquid is absorbed. Stir in the lemon juice and transfer to a serving dish.

Stir the crushed garlic into the yogurt and add the mint and salt and pepper to taste. Pour over the chick-peas and spinach and sprinkle with paprika. Serve warm or chilled. This dish will keep for a day or two in the refrigerator, and up to 4 days without the final yogurt topping.

PER PORTION:

Calories	201	Protein	11 G
Fat	5 G	Carbohydrate	29 G
Sodium	79 MG	Cholesterol	2 MG

STUFFED VEGETABLES

Stuffed vegetables are one of the brilliant inventions of Mediterranean cuisines. They are everywhere in Greece and the Middle East, adorning buffets and *taverna* menus. They are not only a beautiful way to display a delicious stuffing, but an ingenious vehicle for leftovers as well. In most Mediterranean countries the stuffed vegetables often have meaty fillings and are drenched with oil, partly because they sit in very oily baking dishes for hours. That's what makes them different from these light diet versions; the oil isn't necessary. You can fill vegetables with the stuffings that follow or use leftovers from the other grain and bean dishes in this chapter. Just make sure to add lots of fragrant herbs and spices.

POMODORI AL RISO

MAKES 4 SERVINGS

This is an Italian version of stuffed tomatoes. Its success depends on delicious, perfectly ripe tomatoes.

    4 large firm tomatoes
    6 heaped tablespoons Italian Arborio rice
    4 garlic cloves, minced or put through a press
       salt and freshly ground pepper
   12 fresh basil leaves, cut into slivers
    3 tablespoons chopped fresh parsley
   ½ teaspoon dried oregano
    4 tablespoons freshly grated Parmesan cheese

Preheat the oven to 375 degrees. Oil a baking dish large enough to hold all the tomatoes.

Cut the tomatoes across the top, about one third of the way down from the stems, saving the top for a lid. Squeeze out the seeds and discard. Scoop out the pulp, chop, and mix together with the rice, garlic, salt and pepper to taste, basil, parsley, oregano, and Parmesan. Fill the tomatoes and replace the lid. Place in the baking dish, cover, and bake 1 hour. Remove from the heat and let sit a few minutes or allow to cool completely before serving.

The tomatoes will hold for a day in the refrigerator and can be reheated.

PER PORTION:

Calories	149	Protein	6 G
Fat	2 G	Carbohydrate	27 G
Sodium	129 MG	Cholesterol	5 MG

TOMATOES AND ZUCCHINI STUFFED WITH LENTIL AND BULGUR PILAF

MAKES 4 TO 6 SERVINGS

4 to 6 firm ripe tomatoes
½ recipe lentil and bulgur pilaf (page 243)
4 to 6 small zucchini
plain low-fat yogurt for garnish (optional)
chopped fresh parsley and mint for garnish

Preheat the oven to 350 degrees. Oil a baking dish large enough to hold all the vegetables.

Cut the tops off the tomatoes, about ½ inch down from the stems, scoop out the seeds with a small spoon, and discard. Gently scoop out some of the flesh, chop, and mix with the pilaf.

Cut the zucchini in half lengthwise and steam for 5 minutes. Scoop out the inner flesh to within ¼ inch of the edges and chop the flesh. Stir into the pilaf.

Carefully fill the tomatoes and zucchini with the pilaf and place in the baking dish. Cover and heat through for 15 minutes. Top with a spoonful of yogurt if you wish and sprinkle on parsley and mint just before serving. These will hold for a day in the refrigerator and can be reheated.

PER PORTION:

Calories	174	Protein	10 G
Fat	2 G	Carbohydrate	32 G
Sodium	21 MG	Cholesterol	1 MG

RICE AND TOMATO STUFFING
FOR VEGETABLES

ENOUGH FOR 2 POUNDS VEGETABLES (TOMATOES, EGGPLANT, PEPPERS, OR ZUCCHINI) TO MAKE 6 SERVINGS

This typical Middle Eastern stuffing is one of my favorites.

- ½ pound (2 to 3) tomatoes, finely chopped
- 1 tablespoon olive oil
- 1 onion, finely chopped
- 1 to 2 garlic cloves (to taste), minced or put through a press
- 1 hot green chili pepper, minced (optional)
- ½ cup uncooked rice
- ½ cup finely chopped fresh parsley or cilantro
- 4 to 6 tablespoons chopped fresh mint, dill, or both (to taste)
  salt and freshly ground pepper
- 2 to 4 tablespoons fresh lemon juice (to taste)
- ½ teaspoon ground cinnamon or allspice

Combine all the ingredients and stuff vegetables according to the recipes on pages 258–263. The stuffed vegetables will keep for a day in the refrigerator.

PER PORTION:

Calories	93	Protein	2 G
Fat	2 G	Carbohydrate	16 G
Sodium	6 MG	Cholesterol	0

STUFFED EGGPLANT

MAKES 6 SERVINGS

My favorite stuffing for this succulent dish is the rice and tomato stuffing above. You can also use several of the grain dishes in this chapter, such as the lentil and bulgur pilaf on page 243 or the chick-peas with bulgur on page 242.

2 pounds (6 small *or* 3 medium) eggplant
  salt
1 teaspoon olive oil
5 tomatoes, chopped
3 tablespoons tomato paste
4 large garlic cloves, minced or put through a press
  freshly ground pepper
  juice of 1 large lemon
  filling of your choice (such as Rice and Tomato
    Stuffing for Vegetables on page 260)

Cut the tops off the eggplants at the stem end, about ½ inch down, retaining the stem ends to use as stoppers. Cut a flat edge along the bottom of the eggplants so they will stand upright in a pot. Using a small knife or grapefruit spoon, carefully cut or scoop out the inner flesh to within ½ inch of the skin and the bottom edge. Chop the scooped-out pulp and place in a colander. Sprinkle both the inside of the eggplants and the chopped pulp with salt and let sit for 30 minutes. Rinse and pat dry. Meanwhile, make the stuffing.

Steam the eggplant pulp and the shells for 15 minutes. Remove from the heat, and when the shells are cool enough to handle, stuff with the filling, just three-quarters full, as the rice will expand when it cooks. Invert the tops and stopper the open ends with them (the stem will be inside).

Brush the bottom of a pot large enough to accommodate the stuffed eggplants with the olive oil. Toss together the chopped tomatoes, tomato paste, steamed eggplant pulp, and garlic. Add salt and pepper to taste. Place the stuffed eggplants on top of this mixture in the pan. You can lay them down or stand them up, whichever way they fit. Add the lemon juice and enough water so that the liquid covers about a third of the eggplants and bring to a simmer. Cover and simmer 45 minutes or until the rice is thoroughly cooked.

Remove the eggplants from the pot and place on a plate. Remove the tops. Turn up the heat and reduce the sauce until it is thick and fragrant. Correct seasonings and pour over the eggplants. Allow to cool to room temperature or serve hot. The stuffed eggplants will keep for a day in the refrigerator.

PER PORTION:

Calories	78	Protein	3 G
Fat	1 G	Carbohydrate	17 G
Sodium	79 MG	Cholesterol	0

STUFFED ZUCCHINI

MAKES 6 SERVINGS

These pretty stuffed zucchini are cooked in a mixture of tomatoes, tomato paste, and water, like the stuffed eggplant on page 260. I like them best cooled to room temperature. Tender baby zucchini stuffed this way would make a nice first course or lunch dish.

- 2 pounds (8) small or medium-sized zucchini
  salt
  filling of your choice (such as Rice and Tomato
      Stuffing for Vegetables on page 260)
- 1 teaspoon olive oil
- 5 large tomatoes, chopped
- 3 tablespoons tomato paste
- 1 cup water
  juice of 2 large lemons
- 4 garlic cloves, minced or put through a press
  freshly ground pepper
- 2 tablespoons chopped fresh mint

Cut the stem end off the zucchini and carefully scoop out the pulp to within ¼ to ½ inch of the skin, using an apple corer or small spoon. Set aside the pulp and use for a salad or stew. Lightly salt the inside of the zucchini and fill three-quarters full with the filling of your choice.

Brush the bottom of a large deep casserole with olive oil. Combine the tomatoes, tomato paste, water, juice of 1 of the lemons, and the garlic. Add more salt and pepper to taste. Lay the stuffed zucchini on top of this mixture in the casserole.

Bring to a simmer, cover the casserole, reduce heat, and simmer 30 to 45 minutes, until the rice is cooked. Remove from the heat. Serve hot or at room temperature, with a little sauce from the pan spooned over. Just before serving, add the juice of the remaining lemon and sprinkle on the mint. The zucchini will keep for a day in the refrigerator.

PER PORTION:

Calories	59	Protein	3 G
Fat	.55 G	Carbohydrate	13 G
Sodium	80 MG	Cholesterol	0

STUFFED TOMATOES AND GREEN PEPPERS

MAKES 6 SERVINGS

Stuffed tomatoes and peppers are the vegetables one is most likely to find in Greek *tavernas*, where they are served at room temperature.

- 6 medium-sized or large green peppers
- 6 large, firm ripe tomatoes
  filling of your choice (such as Rice and Tomato
    Stuffing for Vegetables on page 260)
- 1 teaspoon olive oil
- 3 tomatoes, chopped
- 3 tablespoons tomato paste
- 4 large garlic cloves, minced or put through a press
  salt and freshly ground pepper
  juice of 1 large lemon
- 2 tablespoons fresh chopped parsley, mint, or cilantro

Cut the tops off the peppers and whole tomatoes, about ½ inch from the ends. Save the ends, which will serve as caps. Scoop out the seeds and membranes from the peppers and discard. Scoop out the tomato pulp, finely chop, and set aside.

Stuff the peppers and tomatoes with the filling. Replace the tops.

Brush the bottom of a pot large enough to accommodate the stuffed vegetables with the olive oil. Toss together the reserved tomato pulp, chopped tomatoes, tomato paste, and garlic. Add salt and freshly ground pepper to taste. Place the stuffed tomatoes and peppers on top of this mixture in the pan. Add the lemon juice and enough water so that the liquid comes about one quarter of the way up the sides of the vegetables and bring to a simmer. Cover and simmer 45 minutes or until the rice is thoroughly cooked.

Remove the tomatoes and peppers from the pot and place on a plate. Remove the tops. Turn up the heat and reduce the sauce until it is thick and fragrant. Correct seasonings and pour over the vegetables. Allow to cool to room temperature or serve hot. Sprinkle with the herbs just before serving. The vegetables will keep for a day in the refrigerator.

PER PORTION:

Calories	78	Protein	3 G
Fat	2 G	Carbohydrate	16 G
Sodium	85 MG	Cholesterol	0

FATTA (PITA CASSEROLES)

Some of the most intriguing and delicious dishes I ate in Egypt were *fatta* (singular, *fattet*), dishes made with crisp pita breads broken up into small pieces, soaked in a tasty stock, and topped with any one of a number of delicious foods, plus thickened yogurt. *Fatta* are an ingenious way to use stale pita bread. Sometimes they have meat toppings, but more often they are topped with beans or vegetables. These are hearty dishes and very easy to make; serve with a salad, and you have a meal.

FATTET WITH EGGPLANT AND DRIED MUSHROOMS

MAKES 6 TO 8 SERVINGS

This *fattet* is my own invention. I wanted to substitute something for the traditional lamb and lamb stock that was less fatty but equally savory. Dried mushrooms are my solution; you would never find them in a traditional Middle Eastern recipe, but they're delicious and "meaty" here.

2 ounces dried *porcini* mushrooms
3 cups boiling water
2 pounds (2 large) eggplant
1 tablespoon olive oil
2 garlic cloves, minced or put through a press
1 teaspoon ground allspice
2 tablespoons dry white wine
1 tablespoon soy sauce
 salt and freshly ground pepper
2 whole-wheat pita breads (page 40)
1½ cups plain low-fat yogurt
2 teaspoons tahini
1 small garlic clove, crushed or put through a press
1 tablespoon chopped fresh mint or parsley (optional)

Place the dried mushrooms in a bowl and pour on the 3 cups boiling water. Let sit for at least 30 minutes.

Preheat the oven to 425 degrees. Cut the eggplants in half lengthwise and score down to the skin but not through it. Place cut side down on an oiled baking sheet and bake 20 minutes or until the skin is shriveled and the eggplants softened. Remove from the heat and dice when cool enough to handle.

Drain the mushrooms and retain the water. Squeeze the mushrooms over the water, then strain the water through a strainer lined with cheesecloth or paper towels. Rinse the mushrooms thoroughly, squeeze dry, and cut up if very large.

Heat the olive oil in a large nonstick heavy-bottomed frying pan or casserole and sauté the dried mushrooms with the garlic over medium heat for 5 minutes. Add the eggplant, allspice, and white wine and continue to sauté 5 to 10 minutes, stirring. Add the soaking liquid from the mushrooms and the soy sauce and bring to a simmer. Simmer 15 minutes. Season to taste with salt and pepper.

Open up the pita breads and toast in the oven until crisp and brown. Break into pieces and line an oiled baking dish. Top with the eggplant/mushroom mixture.

Beat together the yogurt, tahini, and small garlic clove. Pour over the eggplant and mushrooms. Sprinkle with mint or parsley and serve.

Note: If you want a hotter dish, heat it in a moderate oven. Leftovers will keep for a couple of days in the refrigerator.

PER PORTION:

Calories	151	Protein	6 G
Fat	4 G	Carbohydrate	25 G
Sodium	305 MG	Cholesterol	3 MG

FATTET WITH CHICKEN

MAKES 6 TO 8 SERVINGS

The best way to make the low-calorie version of this lemony, savory dish is to cook the chicken the day before or several hours before you make the *fattet* so that you can refrigerate and defat the stock. Then just reheat the stock and chicken before you make the dish. I also love this *fattet* cold; the yogurt on the top becomes like thick white cheese.

FOR THE CHICKEN STOCK:
      1 medium-sized chicken, cut into pieces
1 ½ to 2 quarts water (enough to cover the chicken)
      1 bay leaf
      1 onion, quartered
      4 garlic cloves, crushed
         salt
         juice of 3 lemons
         seeds from 2 cardamom pods, ground to a powder
         freshly ground pepper

FOR THE RICE AND FATTET:
      4 cups plain low-fat yogurt
      1 tablespoon vegetable or safflower oil
      1 large onion, chopped
      6 ounces (1 cup) *basmati* rice, rinsed
      1 teaspoon ground cinnamon
      1 teaspoon ground allspice
         salt and freshly ground pepper
      3 whole-wheat pita breads (page 40)
      4 garlic cloves, pounded in a mortar and pestle or put
            through a press

PREPARE THE STOCK:

Combine the chicken, water to cover, bay leaf, onion, garlic, and salt to taste; bring to a boil. Skim off any foam and add the lemon juice, cardamom, more salt, and pepper to taste. Simmer gently for 1 hour, until the chicken is very tender and almost falls off the bones. Remove the chicken from the stock, strain the stock, and refrigerate for several hours or overnight. Skim off the layer of fat that forms at the top. Set aside 1 ½ cups of the stock for soaking the pita and the rest for cooking the rice. Skin and bone the chicken, tear into pieces and set aside.

PREPARE THE RICE AND FATTET:

Place the yogurt in a sieve lined with muslin or a thin dish towel and let drain for about an hour.

Meanwhile, heat the oil in a heavy-bottomed saucepan and sauté the onion until tender and beginning to color. Add the rice, cinnamon, allspice, and salt and pepper to taste; cover by an inch with the chicken stock set aside for the rice (add some water if there isn't enough). Bring to a simmer, cover the pan, and cook over low heat for 15 to 20 minutes or until the rice is tender and the liquid absorbed.

Open up the pita bread and toast in the oven until brown and crisp. Oil a baking dish or casserole and crumble the bread into it. Spread the rice over the bread and top with the chicken pieces. Heat the remaining chicken stock to a simmer and pour on enough to moisten the pita bread.

Beat the 4 cloves pounded or pressed garlic into the thickened yogurt. Spread over the chicken and serve.

Note: You can reheat this dish in a medium oven (350 degrees) if you want to eat it hot. Leftovers will keep a couple of days in the refrigerator.

PER PORTION:

Calories	351	Protein	27 G
Fat	7 G	Carbohydrate	45 G
Sodium	326 MG	Cholesterol	59 MG

CHICK-PEA FATTET

MAKES 6 SERVINGS

This is one of my favorites. The lemony chick-peas are perfect with the pita and garlicky yogurt. The dish is almost like a *hummus* casserole.

    1 ½ cups dried chick-peas, washed and picked over
      6 cups water
         salt
    2 ½ cups plain low-fat yogurt
      2 whole-wheat pita breads (page 40)
      1 large garlic clove
         juice of 1 ½ lemons
     ½   teaspoon ground cumin
      3 garlic cloves, minced or put through a press
      2 teaspoons tahini (optional)
         freshly ground pepper
      1 to 2 tablespoons dried or fresh mint leaves (to taste;
             optional)

Soak the beans in water to cover (use bottled water if your tap water is hard) for several hours or overnight, then drain and combine with the water in a large pot. Bring to a boil, reduce heat, cover, and simmer 1 ½ to 2 hours, until the beans are very soft. Add salt to taste at the end of the cooking.

Meanwhile, drain the yogurt for about an hour in a strainer lined with muslin or a thin dish towel.

Open out the pita breads and toast in a hot oven until crisp and brown. Oil a 2-quart baking dish, break the pita into pieces, and line the dish.

Drain the beans and retain the cooking liquid. Coarsely puree half of them, or pound in a mortar and pestle, along with the juice of 1 lemon, 1 large garlic clove, the cumin, and ½ cup of the cooking liquid. Add salt to taste.

Place the drained yogurt in a bowl and beat in the 3 garlic cloves, tahini, and pepper.

Squeeze the juice of ½ lemon into the cooking liquid from the beans and sprinkle about ½ to ¾ cupful over the broken-up pita bread (enough to moisten the bread). Top with the chick-pea puree. Spread the remaining chick-peas over the puree and top with the yogurt. Crush the dried mint or sprinkle the fresh mint over the top and serve. Leftovers will keep about 3 days in the refrigerator.

PER PORTION:

Calories	320	Protein	17 G
Fat	6 G	Carbohydrate	52 G
Sodium	244 MG	Cholesterol	6 MG

CHAPTER SIX

FISH, CHICKEN, AND RABBIT

I've combined the fish, chicken, and rabbit recipes in one chapter because they are all low-fat foods that are very high in animal protein and excellent choices for the dieter. Always remove the skin from the chicken pieces before cooking to reduce the fat content dramatically. Rabbit is a very tasty and lean meat, and there is no skin to remove. In Europe it has always been popular, and now it's beginning to be appreciated in America. In addition to being such a healthy meat, it's incredibly easy to prepare.

It's obvious from the contents of this chapter that I am most passionate about fish, which is such a vital element in the life and cuisines of the Mediterranean. No matter where you go in the Mediterranean, you are never too far away from the sea. It's fascinating to see how different cultures apply different cooking techniques and spices to the same fish. The same red mullet that is grilled and served with a tomato sauce in Italy or France will be seasoned with cumin in North Africa; tuna served with a garlicky tomato and caper sauce in Provence is brought forth with a fiery-hot tomato sauce seasoned with paprika, cayenne, cumin, and lots of parsley in Algeria. Grilled swordfish steaks in Italy are sauced with lemon, capers, and garlic; in Turkey they are marinated with onion, garlic, and coriander seeds and sauced with lemon juice, yogurt, parsley, and a pinch of cinnamon. A Spanish *escabeche* of sardines contains saffron; not so in Provence.

Mediterranean fish markets are as colorful as the vegetable markets. In Venice there is a wealth of squid, cuttlefish, sea urchins, and shellfish. In Palermo it was the huge tuna that were unforgettable; I've never seen so many or so big. When I was staying on the tiny Greek island of Simi, near Rhodes and not far from Turkey, one day a boat brought in an enormous swordfish, and all morning long the fishermen worked at cutting up the fish while villagers waited for their portions. Everyone in the village ate well that night.

The fish called for in these pages are fish you can obtain easily in the United States, such as mullet, cod, swordfish, mackerel, tuna, snapper, bream, John Dory, and halibut. The oilier fish, like tuna and swordfish, are higher in calories than the light-fleshed fish like snapper and bream, but their fats are unsaturated fats, and they contain Omega-3 oil, a substance that is thought to lower cholesterol levels in humans. Tuna and swordfish happen to be my favorite fish, which might account for the number of recipes in which they occur.

The first group of fish recipes are the fish stews that you find in every Mediterranean country. I haven't included the most famous one, the French *bouillabaisse*, because it's a complicated dish to make and requires fish that are hard to come by in the United States. Instead I've opted for the easier and equally delicious *Provençal* fish soup on page 162. I always serve these stews as main courses, preceding them with appropriate salads or starters (from Chapter Two) and following them with a light, fruity dessert. I find that they are convenient and will keep in the refrigerator for two to three days.

The next batch of recipes are grilled fish dishes. This is my favorite way to eat fish; my husband still adores it after eating practically nothing but grilled fish for six months while he was losing weight. If you don't have a grill, a broiler will work just as well for all of these recipes, but you won't get the charcoal taste. You will find many new ideas for seasonings, marinades, and sauces. European grilled fish tends to be simpler than the Middle Eastern dishes; whereas a French or Italian recipe might ask you to marinate the fish in lemon juice, a little olive oil, and garlic and serve it very simply, perhaps with lemon, capers, and garlic, in the Middle East the marinade might contain yogurt and spices as well as onion and garlic, and the sauce will probably be pungent with Eastern spices and lots of herbs. Lemons are the universal accompaniment; in Europe the fishmongers always slip a few lemons into the bag along with your purchase.

Finally, there is a miscellany of raw, baked, and poached fish recipes, many of which have been inspired by dishes I've eaten on my travels. The main difference between these recipes and the authentic dishes is in the quantities of oil used. Especially in North Africa, Spain, Greece, and the Middle East, authentic recipes call for much more olive oil than is actually necessary for a dish to be succulent and good.

All of the recipes here—the chicken, rabbit, and fish—are easy, all are delicious, and they all make perfect main dishes for family dining or entertaining.

FISH STEWS

SIMPLE SPANISH FISH STEW

MAKES 4 SERVINGS

This is one of the easiest fish stews I've ever cooked. You pound together garlic, tomato, and parsley in a mortar and pestle, sauté the mixture with some paprika, and add water and fish, which you cook for a mere 15 minutes.

You will need a mortar and pestle for this recipe. You can't use a food processor, because it won't pound the ingredients together correctly for a really pungent, thick paste.

- 4 large garlic cloves, peeled
- 3 parsley sprigs
  salt
- 1 tomato, peeled
- 1 tablespoon olive oil
- ½ teaspoon paprika
- 2 pounds red snapper or bream, cleaned, filleted, cut
    into chunks, and lightly salted
  freshly ground pepper
- 3 to 4 cups water (just enough to cover the fish)
- 4 to 6 *crostini* (page 53)

In a mortar and pestle, pound together the garlic and parsley with a little salt until you have a paste. Add the tomato and work into the paste.

Heat the olive oil over medium-low heat in a heavy-bottomed casserole and sauté the paste, stirring, for about 3 minutes. Add the paprika and the fish, stir together, and add water to cover. Bring to a boil, add more salt and pepper to taste, and boil for 5 minutes. Reduce heat and simmer another 5 to 10 minutes or until the fish is cooked through. Adjust seasonings and serve in flat wide soup bowls. Float *crostini* on the top.

PER PORTION:

Calories	320	Protein	21 G
Fat	10 G	Carbohydrate	38 G
Sodium	347 MG	Cholesterol	27 MG

A FISH STEW FROM SOUTHERN ITALY

MAKES 4 SERVINGS

Here is another simple fish stew. The original recipe, from Bari, contains black olives and a great deal of olive oil. I've taken out the oily olives, substituted some white wine for most of the oil, and added hot pepper flakes.

- 1 tablespoon olive oil
- 3 large garlic cloves, minced or put through a press
- 1½ pounds ripe fresh or canned tomatoes (with juice), peeled and chopped
- 1 small bunch parsley, chopped
- ¼ to ½ teaspoon hot pepper flakes (to taste; optional)
  salt
- ½ cup dry white wine
- 4 large (about 6 ounces each) thin steaks grouper or other firm-fleshed fish
  freshly ground pepper

Heat the olive oil in a large heavy-bottomed casserole and sauté the garlic over medium-low heat until golden. Add the tomatoes, parsley, hot pepper flakes, and some salt. Bring to a simmer and cook, stirring, for 10 minutes. Add the white wine, bring back to a simmer, add the fish steaks, and cook for 5 to 10 minutes, until they are cooked through. Season to taste with more salt and pepper to taste. To serve, place a piece of fish on each plate and spoon the sauce over.

ITALIAN FISH STEW WITH POTATOES

To the master recipe, add 2 medium-sized unpeeled potatoes, sliced. Add them to the garlic when you add the tomatoes, but let this mixture simmer for 20 minutes or until the potatoes are tender. Add the white wine, simmer another 5 minutes, then add the fish and proceed as in master recipe.

PER PORTION:

Calories	231	Protein	35 G
Fat	6 G	Carbohydrate	10 G
Sodium	116 MG	Cholesterol	63 MG

MOULES À LA MARINIÈRE
(Mussels Steamed in White Wine)

MAKES 4 TO 6 SERVINGS

France, Spain, and Italy all have their own versions of these simple steamed mussels. *Moules à la Marinière* is one of my favorite meals, served with crusty bread, a nice green salad, and a cold glass of white or rosé wine.

4 quarts mussels, cleaned
1 onion *or* 4 shallots, minced
2 to 3 garlic cloves (to taste), minced or put through a
    press
2 cups dry white wine
4 parsley sprigs
½ bay leaf
6 peppercorns
¼ to ½ teaspoon dried thyme (to taste)
3 tablespoons fresh lemon juice
4 tablespoons chopped fresh parsley

Clean the mussels (see page 166).

Combine the onion or shallots, garlic, wine, parsley sprigs, bay leaf, peppercorns, and thyme in a very large lidded pot or wok and bring to a boil. Boil a minute or two and add the mussels. Cover the pot tightly and cook over high heat for 5 minutes. Shake the pot firmly several times during the cooking to distribute the mussels evenly and ensure even cooking. If the pot is too heavy to do this effectively, stir a couple of times with a long-handled spoon. The mussels are ready when their shells have opened; this takes about 5 minutes. Discard any mussels that haven't opened.

Spoon the mussels into wide soup bowls. Add the lemon juice to the broth, bring to a boil again, and pour over the mussels. Sprinkle with parsley and serve. The mussels are eaten by pulling them from the shells with the fingers, an empty shell, or a small fork, so you'll need bowls for empty shells as well as finger bowls. Use leftover mussels in salads and pasta. They'll keep for a day or two in the refrigerator.

PER PORTION:

Calories	126	Protein	16 G
Fat	3 G	Carbohydrate	8 G
Sodium	382 MG	Cholesterol	37 MG

GRILLED FISH

GRILLED FISH À LA MAROCAINE

MAKES 4 SERVINGS

This *picante*, pungent Moroccan marinade can be used for any fish suitable for grilling or broiling and can also be used to marinate fish before baking. It's good with firm white-fleshed fish.

       12 garlic cloves
       ½ teaspoon coarse salt
        1 bunch cilantro
        1 tablespoon paprika
        1 tablespoon ground cumin
           pinch cayenne pepper
           juice of 2 large lemons
        1 teaspoon olive oil
        4 6-ounce halibut, bream, monkfish, or snapper steaks
               or 1 whole 2-pound fish, cleaned, scales left on
               but scored several times on the sides
           additional cilantro for garnish

   Pound together the garlic, salt, cilantro, paprika, cumin, and cayenne. Stir in the lemon juice and olive oil. Marinate fish steaks or whole fish in this for several hours, turning from time to time.
   Grill the fish for 4 minutes for each ½-inch thickness, turning halfway through. Baste with the marinade, and serve at once, garnished with additional cilantro. Chill leftovers and serve cold the next day.

PER PORTION:

Calories	235	Protein	38 G
Fat	6 G	Carbohydrate	8 G
Sodium	292 MG	Cholesterol	54 MG

GRILLED RED MULLET WITH LIGHT TOMATO SAUCE

MAKES 6 SERVINGS

Red mullet is a popular fish all over the Mediterranean, from France to Greece to Lebanon. In Provence the fish is most often pan-fried or grilled and served very simply, with lemon juice and olive oil or possibly a light tomato sauce. In the Middle East and Spain the recipes can become more intriguing with various spices and other seasonings.

FOR THE FISH AND MARINADE:

    6 small or medium (about 6 to 8 ounces each) red
        mullet, cleaned, but livers left in (the livers are
        very tasty and add flavor to the cooked fish)
      salt and freshly ground pepper
    1 tablespoon olive oil
      juice of 1 large lemon

FOR THE SAUCE:

    1 tablespoon olive oil
 1½ pounds ripe fresh tomatoes
      pinch sugar
      salt and freshly ground pepper

FOR THE GARNISH:

    2 garlic cloves, finely minced
    3 tablespoons finely minced parsley
      additional lemon juice (optional)

MARINATE THE FISH:

Sprinkle the fish with salt and pepper to taste. Toss with the olive oil and lemon juice and marinate for 15 minutes.

PREPARE THE SAUCE:

Meanwhile, heat the olive oil over low heat and add the tomatoes, sugar, and salt and pepper to taste. Simmer over low heat for 10 minutes.

BROIL AND GARNISH THE FISH:

Prepare a grill or broiler. Brush the fish with the marinade and grill until crisp on both sides, about 5 minutes per side. Baste a few times during the cooking. Transfer the fish to a platter and sprinkle with the garlic, parsley, and lemon juice if you wish. Spoon the tomato sauce alongside each fish or pass separately. Leftovers can be eaten cold the next day.

PER PORTION:

Calories	206	Protein	24 G
Fat	9 G	Carbohydrate	6 G
Sodium	88 MG	Cholesterol	59 MG

GRILLED RED MULLET WITH CUMIN

MAKES 4 SERVINGS

This is a Tunisian version of the grilled red mullet I so often eat when I'm in the south of France. Small whitings can be substituted for red mullets.

- 4 small or medium-sized red mullets (about ½ pound each), cleaned, scales left on
  - juice of 1 lemon
- 2 garlic cloves, crushed or put through a press
- ½ teaspoon ground cumin (more to taste)
  - salt and freshly ground pepper
- 2 tablespoons olive oil
  - lemon wedges for serving

Mix together the lemon juice, garlic, cumin, salt and pepper to taste, and olive oil. Marinate the fish in this mixture for 15 minutes, turning occasionally.

Grill or broil the fish for about 3 to 4 minutes on each side, basting once with the marinade. Serve at once with lemon wedges. Chill any leftovers and serve cold or at room temperature the next day.

PER PORTION:

Calories	205	Protein	23 G
Fat	11 G	Carbohydrate	1 G
Sodium	79 MG	Cholesterol	59 MG

GRILLED MACKEREL WITH CUMIN

MAKES 4 SERVINGS

This Tunisian version of grilled mackerel can be *picante*, with the addition of *harissa*, or not, depending on your taste. Either way, it will be pungent with garlic, lemon, and cumin.

> juice of 1 large lemon
> 3 tablespoons plain low-fat yogurt
> 2 garlic cloves, crushed or put through a press
> 1 teaspoon ground cumin
> ⅛ teaspoon *harissa* (page 106) or cayenne pepper
>   dissolved in 2 tablespoons water (optional)
> salt and freshly ground pepper
> 2 pounds mackerel (4 small, 2 medium, *or* 1 large fish),
>   cleaned
> lemon wedges for garnish

Combine the lemon juice, yogurt, garlic, cumin, *harissa*, and salt and pepper to taste in a dish large enough to hold the fish. Marinate the fish in this mixture for 30 minutes, turning from time to time.

Prepare a grill or broiler and grill the fish for 4 minutes for each ½-inch of thickness, turning the fish over halfway through the cooking and basting from time to time. Serve with lemon wedges.

PER PORTION:

Calories	288	Protein	26 G
Fat	19 G	Carbohydrate	2 G
Sodium	129 MG	Cholesterol	94 MG

GRILLED RED MULLET WITH ROMESCO SAUCE

MAKES 4 SERVINGS

Romesco sauce is a spicy sauce from Tarragona, Spain. The authentic recipe includes more roasted almonds than my diet version, so the texture of mine is slightly different, but the taste of the roasted almonds comes through.

FOR THE FISH:

> 4 red mullet, about ½ pound each, cleaned, scales left
>   on
> salt and freshly ground pepper
> 1 tablespoon olive oil
>   juice of 1 large lemon
> 2 tablespoons chopped fresh parsley

FOR THE SAUCE:

> 1 small onion, chopped
> 1 tablespoon olive oil
> 1 tablespoon roasted skinned almonds*
> 6 garlic cloves
> 1 fresh hot red pepper *or* ½ teaspoon hot pepper flakes
>   or cayenne pepper
> 5 medium-sized ripe fresh tomatoes, peeled, seeded, and
>   chopped
> 2 teaspoons vinegar or fresh lemon juice
>   salt

PREPARE THE FISH:

Toss the fish with salt and pepper to taste, olive oil, lemon juice, and parsley; let them marinate for a couple of hours.

PREPARE THE SAUCE:

Sauté the onion in the olive oil until tender. Remove from the heat. In a mortar and pestle or a food processor, pound together or puree the roasted almonds, garlic, hot red pepper, sautéed onion, and tomatoes. Work in the vinegar or lemon juice and add salt to taste. If you want a more elegant-looking sauce, puree through the fine blade of a food mill or a blender.

Grill the fish for 4 minutes for each ½-inch thickness, turning halfway through, and serve the sauce on the side.

Leftovers can be stored in the refrigerator and served, cold, the next day.

PER PORTION:

Calories	256	Protein	26 G
Fat	13 G	Carbohydrate	11 G
Sodium	93 MG	Cholesterol	59 MG

*Roast skinned almonds in a dry pan over medium heat until they smell toasty. Remove from heat.

SPICY GRILLED SEA BASS

MAKES 6 TO 8 SERVINGS

This is a Lebanese recipe, which I have altered by bringing in more spices (inspired by an Iraqi recipe) and reducing the oil. If you can't find sea bass, use snapper or bream.

        1   whole 2- to 3-pound sea bass, cleaned
            salt and freshly ground pepper
        1   small onion, chopped
        4   garlic cloves, peeled
       ¼   teaspoon salt
        1   tablespoon paprika
       ¼   teaspoon cayenne pepper
       ¼   teaspoon fenugreek seed, crushed
     1 ½   teaspoons cumin seed, crushed
            1-inch piece fresh gingeroot, peeled and sliced
        1   small bunch parsley, leaves only
        1   small bunch cilantro, leaves only
        1   tablespoon olive oil
            juice of ½ lemon
        1   teaspoon tahini
       ½   cup plain low-fat yogurt
            lemon wedges for serving

Salt and pepper the fish and score a few times on both sides.

Place the remaining ingredients except the lemon wedges in a blender and blend to a paste.

Prepare a grill or broiler. Brush the fish with a thick layer of the paste on one side and grill on that side for 10 to 15 minutes (the cooking time in all will be 5 minutes for each ½ inch of thickness of the fish, measuring at the thickest point, and grilling for an equal amount of time on both sides). Turn the fish over and brush the other side with the paste. Grill until the fish is crisp and flakes easily with a fork.

Transfer to a platter and serve with remaining sauce and lemon wedges.

PER PORTION:

Calories	98	Protein	12 G
Fat	4 G	Carbohydrate	4 G
Sodium	127 MG	Cholesterol	24 MG

GRILLED SWORDFISH WITH CAPERS, LEMON, AND GARLIC

MAKES 4 SERVINGS

The inspiration for this dish comes from one served at Villa Cheta in Acquafredda on the south coast of Italy. After three deliciously filling first courses—sardines with lemon and mint, *crostini* with peppers and chicken livers, and a marvelous *minestrone*—these thin, vibrantly seasoned grilled swordfish steaks arrived, and who could resist? The chef used anchovies and oil in his sauce, but I think capers, lemon juice, and garlic make a nice, simple condiment for the tasty swordfish. Have the steaks cut thin and don't grill them for a second too long.

    4   ½-inch-thick swordfish steaks, 4 to 6 ounces each
    1   tablespoon plus 1 teaspoon olive oil
        salt and freshly ground pepper
    1   to 2 garlic cloves (to taste), minced
    2   heaped tablespoons capers
    6   tablespoons fresh lemon juice

Prepare a grill or preheat the broiler. Brush the swordfish steaks on both sides with 1 tablespoon of the olive oil and lightly salt and pepper.

Pound the garlic in a mortar and pestle and add the capers. Mash together with the garlic and add the lemon juice and 1 teaspoon olive oil. Blend together well. Season to taste with pepper.

Grill the fish or broil 3 to 4 inches from the flame for 2 to 2½ minutes on each side. Don't cook any longer, or the fish will be too dry. Remove from the heat. Spoon the caper/lemon mixture over each steak. Serve hot or allow to cool and serve. Chill leftovers and serve cold or at room temperature the next day.

PER PORTION:

Calories	219	Protein	28 G
Fat	10 G	Carbohydrate	2 G
Sodium	265 MG	Cholesterol	55 MG

GRILLED SARDINES

MAKES 4 SERVINGS

There is nothing simpler or more satisfying than very fresh sardines grilled over aromatic wood. I have vivid memories of eating them for the first time in a friend's house in Provence, on a rainy day in February. They were bought that morning in Marseille, and the buyer insisted that winter was the best time for sardines because they were burning off a lot of their fat.

Finding fresh sardines in America is a little difficult, but when you see them, and they're very fresh, snap them up and try this succulent dish. Or use other small oily-fleshed fish, such as herring or mackerel.

olive oil for the grill
24 to 48 sardines (6 to 12 per person, depending on
the size), cleaned if large (the tiny ones are usually
already cleaned)
salt

Prepare a fire in your grill, indoors or outdoors, and oil the grill rack with olive oil. Place the sardines on it; grill small sardines for 1 minute on each side, large sardines for 2½ minutes on each side. The fish should fall apart easily but not be dry. Season to taste with salt.

Eat with your fingers, removing the skins, which are not very digestible. Accompany with country bread and a big salad or serve as a first course.

PER PORTION:

Calories	312	Protein	21 G
Fat	25 G	Carbohydrate	0
Sodium	102 MG	Cholesterol	79 MG

GRILLED TUNA STEAKS WITH ALGERIAN TOMATO SAUCE

MAKES 4 SERVINGS

These grilled tuna steaks have a completely different character from those in the preceding *Provençal* recipe. They are marinated in a pungent, highly seasoned marinade and sauced with a *picante* tomato sauce.

FOR THE MARINADE AND FISH:

½ bunch parsley
1 small onion, sliced
½ teaspoon paprika
¼ teaspoon cayenne pepper
½ teaspoon ground cumin
¼ teaspoon freshly ground pepper
¼ teaspoon salt
   juice of 2 large lemons
4 tuna steaks, 4 to 6 ounces each

FOR THE SAUCE:

1 tablespoon olive oil
2 pounds (8 to 10) tomatoes, chopped
2 garlic cloves, minced or put through a press
1 teaspoon paprika
¼ teaspoon cayenne pepper (more or less to taste)
   pinch freshly ground black pepper
½ teaspoon ground cumin
½ bunch parsley, finely chopped
   salt

Pound together the ingredients for the marinade in a mortar and pestle or blend in a food processor. Transfer to a baking dish and marinate the tuna steaks in it for at least an hour, turning occasionally.

Meanwhile, combine the ingredients for the sauce in a saucepan and simmer over medium heat for 30 minutes or until thick. Correct seasonings.

Grill the tuna steaks, just searing them on both sides, so that they are still rare in the middle (about 3 minutes per side). Remove from the heat, top with the tomato sauce, and serve. Leftover sauce will keep for a few days in the refrigerator and can be frozen.

PER PORTION:

Calories	297	Protein	36 G
Fat	11 G	Carbohydrate	14 G
Sodium	158 MG	Cholesterol	54 MG

SWORDFISH BROCHETTES

MAKES 6 SERVINGS

This dish is served in both Turkey and Egypt. If you can't find swordfish, another firm-fleshed fish, such as halibut or tuna, will work.

     2 pounds swordfish
     4 tablespoons fresh lemon juice
     2 tablespoons olive oil
     1 tablespoon grated onion
  1 ½ teaspoons paprika
     ½ teaspoon ground cumin (more to taste)
     ½ teaspoon salt
     6 bay leaves
        thick lemon slices
    12 tomatoes, cut in half
        lemon juice for garnish
        chopped fresh parsley for garnish

Cut the fish into pieces about 1 ½ by 2 inches.

Prepare a marinade by mixing together the lemon juice, olive oil, grated onion, paprika, cumin, salt, and bay leaves. Toss the fish in this marinade, cover, and marinate for 4 to 6 hours.

Light a fire or preheat a broiler, and when it is ready, skewer the fish through the long side of the pieces, alternating lemon slices and tomatoes between pieces of fish.

Grill the fish, brushing often with the marinade and turning until uniformly cooked; this should take about 5 to 10 minutes, depending on the size of the fish pieces.

Sprinkle with lemon juice and parsley and serve. Chill leftovers and serve cold.

PER PORTION:

Calories	280	Protein	32 G
Fat	11 G	Carbohydrate	14 G
Sodium	339 MG	Cholesterol	59 MG

TUNA À LA MARSEILLAISE

MAKES 4 TO 6 SERVINGS

Marseillaise sauce, which I learned from Lulu Peyraud at Domaine Tempier in Bandol, is a heady mixture of onion, garlic, tomatoes, and lots of capers. Lulu is capable of grilling 20 tuna steaks at a time and not overcooking one of them. She serves this sauce on the side. It's great with any grilled fish.

FOR THE SAUCE:

- 1 tablespoon olive oil
- 1 small *or* ½ medium-sized onion, finely chopped
- 8 garlic cloves, peeled and chopped (can be chopped or mashed along with the capers)
- ½ cup capers, rinsed and chopped in a food processor or mashed in a mortar and pestle
- 2½ pounds (10 to 12) tomatoes, chopped
    freshly ground pepper

FOR THE FISH:

- 4 to 6 tuna steaks, about 4 to 6 ounces each
    olive or safflower oil

PREPARE THE SAUCE:

Heat the olive oil in a large heavy-bottomed skillet and add the onion. Sauté for a few minutes and add the garlic and capers. Sauté, stirring for 5 minutes, and add the tomatoes. Cook over medium-low heat, stirring occasionally, for 20 to 30 minutes. Set aside.

COOK THE FISH:

The fish can be either grilled or sautéed. Brush steaks with oil and cook over aromatic wood or sauté in a nonstick skillet in 1 tablespoon olive oil over medium-high heat 4 minutes for each ½ inch thickness, turning halfway through the cooking. Watch closely, because tuna steaks will become cotton-dry if you overcook them. The steaks should remain pink in the middle.

Remove from the heat and serve immediately, topped with the tomato-caper sauce. Leftover sauce will keep for a few days in the refrigerator.

PER PORTION:

Calories	288	Protein	35 G
Fat	12 G	Carbohydrate	10 G
Sodium	364 MG	Cholesterol	54 MG

GRILLED SWORDFISH STEAKS

MAKES 6 SERVINGS

This is a Turkish recipe, and as usual, the marinade is pungent with onion, garlic, and spices.

FOR THE MARINADE AND FISH:
- 1 medium-sized onion
- juice of 1 large lemon
- 1 tablespoon olive oil
- 3 garlic cloves, peeled and crushed
- 1 tablespoon coriander seed, crushed
- pinch cayenne pepper
- salt
- 6 swordfish steaks, about 2 pounds in all

FOR THE SAUCE:
- 1 tablespoon olive oil
- 1 tablespoon plain low-fat yogurt
- 2 to 3 tablespoons fresh lemon juice (to taste)
- 2 tablespoons finely chopped parsley
- pinch ground cinnamon
- salt and freshly ground pepper

Prepare the marinade: Peel and grate the onion, then squeeze out the juice and mix with the remaining ingredients. Marinate the swordfish steaks in this mixture for 3 to 6 hours, turning occasionally.

Mix together the ingredients for the sauce.

Grill or broil the fish not more than 4 minutes for each ½ inch of thickness (I prefer it just seared on each side, for about 2½ minutes per side). Remove from the heat, transfer to a platter, and top with the sauce. Serve hot or allow to cool and serve at room temperature.

PER PORTION:

Calories	221	Protein	30 G
Fat	10 G	Carbohydrate	2 G
Sodium	139 MG	Cholesterol	59 MG

RAW, BAKED, AND POACHED FISH

TUNA CARPACCIO

MAKES 4 SERVINGS

Carpaccio, which originated at Harry's Bar in Venice, is the Italian version of steak *tartare* but is much more delicate. It consists of paper-thin slices of raw beef, usually served with a rich sauce and shaved raw mushrooms. Paris restaurants sometimes serve a first course of tuna *carpaccio*, very thin slices of raw tuna, which looks a lot like beef, with a light sauce. Tuna has always been my favorite raw fish in Japanese *sashimi*, and I like this even better, because it's so delicate—the sauce is perfect with it.

1 pound very fresh tuna fillets
2 garlic cloves, minced or put through a press
2 tablespoons capers, rinsed
   juice of 1 large lemon
3 tablespoons olive oil
2 tablespoons chopped fresh basil
1 tablespoon chopped fresh chives
   salt and freshly ground pepper

Cut the tuna into slices as thin as possible. It's easiest to do this along the natural layers of the fish. Arrange on 4 plates and refrigerate.

Using a mortar and pestle or a food processor, pound together or puree the garlic and capers. Whisk in the lemon juice and olive oil and stir in the basil, chives, and salt and pepper to taste. Pour this sauce over the fish just before serving or toss the fish with the sauce and then arrange on the plates.

PER PORTION:

Calories	260	Protein	27 G
Fat	16 G	Carbohydrate	2 G
Sodium	155 MG	Cholesterol	43 MG

EGYPTIAN BAKED FISH WITH CUMIN AND CORIANDER

MAKES 4 TO 6 SERVINGS

This lemony baked fish is seasoned—like so many Egyptian dishes—with cilantro and cumin; it can be made several hours ahead of serving, as it's eaten cold.

FOR THE FISH STOCK:

- 1 pound fish trimmings
- 1 small onion, cut in half
- 1 bay leaf
- 6 black peppercorns
- 1 tablespoon white wine vinegar
- 4 parsley sprigs
- 1 quart water
- salt

FOR THE FISH:

- salt and freshly ground pepper
- 1 tablespoon olive oil
- 1½ pounds firm white-fleshed fish fillets or steaks, such as sea bass, hake, bream, snapper, or gray mullet
- 2 large onions, finely chopped
- 2 garlic cloves, minced or put through a press
- 1½ teaspoons cumin seed, crushed
- 3 tablespoons chopped cilantro
- juice of 1 large lemon
- pinch cayenne pepper
- additional chopped cilantro for garnish

PREPARE THE STOCK:

Combine the ingredients for the stock in a large pot and bring to a simmer. Skim off the foam that rises and simmer, uncovered, for 40 minutes. Strain. Return the stock to the pot and bring to a boil. Reduce to 1 cup and set aside.

PREPARE THE FISH:

Lightly salt and pepper the fish. Preheat the oven to 400 degrees. Heat the olive oil in a flameproof baking dish large enough to hold the fish fillets and sauté the onion and garlic until the onion is tender. Add the cumin, cook over medium heat for 5 minutes, stirring, and add the cilantro. Lay the fish fillets over this mixture, pour on the reduced stock, and bring to a simmer. Cover with foil and place in the oven. Bake for 10 to 15 minutes, until the fillets are opaque and break apart easily with a fork.

Remove from the heat and sprinkle on the lemon juice and cayenne. Correct seasonings and allow to cool. Sprinkle with the additional cilantro before serving and spoon some of the sauce over each portion.

PER PORTION:

Calories	163	Protein	23 G
Fat	5 G	Carbohydrate	6 G
Sodium	120 MG	Cholesterol	50 MG

BAKED MONKFISH, HAKE, OR SWORDFISH WITH WILD MUSHROOMS

MAKES 4 SERVINGS

This recipe is based on a Marcella Hazan dish. The rich, garlicky mushroom topping calls for a firm-fleshed fish that won't fall apart when baked. (Don't use cod, sole, or flounder, which will flake too easily.) In France I have used hake, which is delicious and inexpensive, as well as the more expensive monkfish. The dish is a very "meaty" one.

- 1 ounce dried *porcini* mushrooms (or *cèpes*)
- 4 1- to 1½-inch hake, monkfish, or swordfish steaks
- 1 tablespoon olive oil plus 1 teaspoon for the baking dish
  salt and freshly ground pepper
- 4 garlic cloves, minced or put through a press
- 3 tablespoons white wine
- ¼ teaspoon dried thyme
- ¼ teaspoon crumbled dried rosemary
- 4 tablespoons chopped fresh parsley
- 5 tablespoons fresh lemon juice (more to taste)

Soak the mushrooms in 1 quart warm water for 30 minutes. Lift the mushrooms from the soaking water and gently squeeze over the soaking liquid. Place in a bowl and rinse thoroughly in several changes of water. Squeeze dry again and chop coarsely. Strain the soaking water through a strainer lined with paper towels.

If you're using monkfish steaks, pull away the skin and loosen the fish from the center bone with a fish-filleting knife, but don't detach it. Rinse the fillets (or other fish fillets) and pat dry. Brush a baking dish large enough to accommodate the steaks with olive oil and lay the fish in it in one layer. Sprinkle with salt and pepper to taste.

Heat 1 tablespoon olive oil in a large heavy-bottomed skillet over medium heat and add the garlic. Sauté, stirring, until it begins to turn golden, in a couple of minutes, and add the mushrooms. Continue to sauté, stirring, for a minute or two and add the white wine. Resume sautéing and stirring until the wine has just about evaporated. Add the soaking liquid from the mushrooms, the thyme, rosemary, and more salt and pepper to taste. Turn up the heat and continue to cook, stirring, until most of the liquid has evaporated and the mushrooms are glazed. Stir in 3 tablespoons of the parsley and remove from the heat.

Douse the fish with 1 tablespoon of the lemon juice and pour on the mushrooms so that the fish steaks are covered. Top with the remaining lemon juice.

Cover the dish and place in the refrigerator for at least 1 hour, preferably 5 to 6 hours. Remove from the refrigerator and allow to come to room temperature before baking.

Preheat the oven to 400 degrees.

Bake the fish in the upper part of the oven for 20 minutes or until the flesh is opaque all the way through. Baste with the juices in the pan halfway through the baking. Remove from the heat and sprinkle with the remaining parsley. Allow to sit for 5 minutes before serving. Leftovers will keep for a day in the refrigerator.

PER PORTION:

Calories	169	Protein	22 G
Fat	6 G	Carbohydrate	8 G
Sodium	31 MG	Cholesterol	35 MG

BAKED RED SNAPPER FROM SIMI

MAKES 6 SERVINGS

This recipe is based on a fish dish I ate at a village *taverna* on a tiny Greek island called Simi. I'm not sure the chef really used red snapper for this dish; it could have been dentex, bream, or mullet. But the important element here is the sauce, which was marvelous, if a bit on the oily side. The chef refused to give me the recipe, but I think I've figured it out, and I've reduced the amount of oil.

2 pounds red snapper fillets
salt and freshly ground pepper
juice of 1 large lemon
1 tablespoon olive oil plus 1 teaspoon for the baking dish
3 onions, chopped
2 large garlic cloves, minced or put through a press
2 pounds (8 to 10) tomatoes, chopped
½ pound fresh spinach, stemmed, washed, and coarsely chopped
1 teaspoon paprika
1 teaspoon ground cumin (more to taste)
1 tablespoon tomato paste
¼ cup water
½ cup dry white wine
1 bunch parsley, chopped

Rinse the fish and pat dry.

Preheat the oven to 375 degrees and oil a baking dish. Lay the fish in the dish, salt and pepper lightly, and pour on the lemon juice.

In a heavy-bottomed casserole or saucepan, heat the oil and sauté the onion and garlic over medium heat until the onion begins to color. Add the tomatoes, spinach, paprika, and cumin, and season to taste with salt and pepper. Dissolve the tomato paste in about ¼ cup water and add to the sauce along with the wine. Bring to a simmer, add half the parsley, and cook, uncovered, for 15 minutes. Adjust seasonings.

Pour the sauce over the fish. The fish should be completely submerged. If it isn't, add a little more water with another bit of tomato paste dissolved in it. Bake in the oven until the fish is opaque and flakes easily, about 20 to 30 minutes.

Transfer the fish to a platter and reduce the sauce until it is thick. Spoon over the fish, sprinkling with parsley and more lemon juice if you wish. Alternatively, you can allow the fish to cool in the baking dish and serve at room temperature or cold. Leftovers will keep for a day in the refrigerator.

PER PORTION:

Calories	238	Protein	35 G
Fat	5 G	Carbohydrate	14 G
Sodium	166 MG	Cholesterol	56 MG

MALLORCAN FISH BAKED WITH CHARD AND POTATOES

MAKES 4 TO 6 SERVINGS

Even though you cook this dish for an hour, until the potatoes are done, the fish doesn't dry out. All the moisture from the chard, as well as the fact that it is tightly covered, helps the fish remain succulent. This is a simple, comforting dish.

- 1 tablespoon olive oil
- 3 large potatoes, scrubbed and sliced
  salt and freshly ground pepper
- 1 large onion, chopped
- 1 bunch parsley, washed, dried, and chopped
- 2 pounds Swiss chard, leaves removed and chopped,
    stems discarded
- 2 large tomatoes, peeled and sliced
- 2 pounds thick slices or fillets of hake, bream, or
    snapper
- ¾ cup dry white wine

Preheat the oven to 350 degrees.

Spoon the olive oil over the bottom of a 3-quart baking dish and cover with the potato slices. Sprinkle with salt and pepper to taste. Toss together the chopped onion, parsley, and chard, add salt and pepper to taste, and place half of this mixture over the potatoes. Top with half the tomatoes. Lay the fish in an even layer over the tomatoes, season with salt and pepper, and top with the remaining onion/parsley/chard mixture and the tomatoes. Pour in the wine and cover tightly with foil. Bake for 1 to 1½ hours, until the potatoes are tender. Remove from the heat and serve from the baking dish. Leftovers will keep for a day in the refrigerator.

PER PORTION:

Calories	310	Protein	37 G
Fat	5 G	Carbohydrate	30 G
Sodium	418 MG	Cholesterol	56 MG

BAKED FISH EN PAPILLOTE WITH VEGETABLE JULIENNE

MAKES 4 SERVINGS

Fish baked or grilled in foil or parchment is frequently on menus in restaurants along the Mediterranean coast of France. Near Monte Carlo there's a charming town called Villefranche-sur-Mer. A small restaurant called Tante Germaine serves this delightful fish baked *en papillote* with julienned vegetables.

> 4 small whole porgy, sea bream, or flounder (¾ to 1
>   pound each), cleaned
>   salt and freshly ground pepper
> 1 tablespoon olive oil
> 1 small fennel bulb, sliced into julienne strips
> 1 carrot, peeled and sliced into julienne strips
> 2 leeks, white part only, cleaned and sliced into julienne
>   strips
> 1 zucchini, sliced into julienne strips
> 1 garlic clove, minced or put through a press
> ½ teaspoon crushed fennel seed
> 1 tablespoon Pernod or anisette
> 2 lemons, cut in half

Preheat the oven to 425 degrees. Rinse the fish, pat dry, and sprinkle lightly with salt and pepper if you wish.

Cut 4 double thicknesses of aluminum foil, large enough to accommodate the fish. Brush with olive oil. Lay a fish on each piece.

Heat the tablespoon of olive oil in a large heavy-bottomed skillet and sauté the vegetables and garlic together over medium heat for 5 minutes, stirring. Add the Pernod and fennel seed and continue to sauté, stirring, for 5 minutes. Add salt and pepper to taste.

Stuff the fish with some of this mixture and lay the remaining vegetables over the fish. Squeeze juice from half a lemon over each fish. Enclose the fish in the foil and crimp the edges together well.

Place in a baking dish and bake in the preheated oven for 20 minutes or until the fish is opaque and flakes easily. Serve at once.

PER PORTION:

Calories	189	Protein	24 G
Fat	5 G	Carbohydrate	15 G
Sodium	110 MG	Cholesterol	40 MG

SEA BREAM WITH FENNEL AND WHITE WINE

MAKES 4 SERVINGS

This recipe comes from Provence, where fish is often perfumed with fresh or dried fennel. Usually it's grilled, but here it is baked on a rack over a pan of white wine, tomatoes, and garlic. As it bakes, the fish drips into the wine mixture, which is served on the side as a sauce.

For this dish you will need a broiling pan or a baking pan with a rack fitted into it.

  1 2-pound sea bream *or* 2 to 4 smaller ones, cleaned
        and scaled
  1 small fennel bulb
  1½ teaspoons olive oil
     several thyme sprigs
     salt and freshly ground pepper
  1 cup dry white wine
  1 tablespoon olive oil
  1 tomato, sliced
  2 garlic cloves, crushed
  1 lemon, thinly sliced

Preheat the oven to 350 degrees. Make deep slashes on the back of the fish and insert the feathery tips of the fennel. Chop the remaining fennel finely and sauté over medium heat in 1½ teaspoons olive oil for about 5 to 10 minutes, stirring, until crisp-tender. Remove from the heat and insert the fennel into the fish's belly along with the thyme.

Place the fish on a rack fitted into a pan. Salt and pepper lightly, pour on the white wine, and drizzle on 1 tablespoon olive oil. Place the tomato and garlic in the pan with the white wine and spread the lemon slices over the fish. Bake 20 to 25 minutes, basting occasionally, until the fish is opaque and the flesh pulls away easily from the bone.

Transfer the fish to a platter, strain off the cooking juices, and serve on the side as a sauce. Leftovers will keep 1 day in the refrigerator.

PER PORTION:

Calories	174	Protein	23 G
Fat	7 G	Carbohydrate	6 G
Sodium	102 MG	Cholesterol	40 MG

SPANISH-STYLE ESCABECHE

MAKES 4 SERVINGS

In hot Mediterranean countries small fish are often preserved in a vinegar-based sauce, or *escabeche*. Each country has a different version of the dish. This Spanish *escabeche* is flavored with two unique, special ingredients, saffron and a pinch of ginger. In most *escabeche* recipes the fish is fried, but why not grill or broil it?

> salt and freshly ground pepper
> 1 pound sardines or other small fish
> 1 tablespoon olive oil
> 2 garlic cloves
> pinch saffron threads
> pinch ground ginger
> salt
> 4 tablespoons red wine vinegar
> 3 tablespoons water
> 1 shallot, minced
> 1 lemon, sliced
> 2 small bay leaves

Preheat your broiler or prepare a grill.

Salt and pepper the fish and toss with the olive oil.

Grill the fish for about 2½ minutes on each side. Transfer to a baking dish or casserole.

Pound the garlic in a mortar along with the saffron, ginger, and a little salt. Mix in the vinegar, water, and shallot. Toss with the fish. Add the lemon slices and bay leaves, cover, and refrigerate overnight. Correct salt and pepper before serving cold. The dish will keep for a few days in the refrigerator.

PER PORTION:

Calories	119	Protein	7 G
Fat	9 G	Carbohydrate	5 G
Sodium	35 MG	Cholesterol	26 MG

MIDDLE EASTERN SHRIMP WITH CUMIN

MAKES 4 TO 6 SERVINGS

This pungent shrimp dish comes from Turkey. It's reminiscent of a shrimp curry, especially when it's served with *basmati* rice.

1 ½ pounds shrimp in their shells
3 cups water
2 strips lemon zest
4 parsley sprigs
2 garlic cloves, crushed
6 peppercorns
handful celery leaves
1 tablespoon olive oil
1 large onion, chopped
4 additional garlic cloves, minced or put through a press
1 to 1 ½ teaspoons ground cumin (to taste)
pinch cayenne pepper
salt and freshly ground pepper
2 to 3 tablespoons chopped cilantro or fresh parsley
lemon wedges for garnish
cooked rice for serving

Peel the shrimp and place the shells in a saucepan with the water, lemon zest, parsley sprigs, 2 garlic cloves, peppercorns, and celery leaves. Bring this mixture to a boil, reduce heat, and simmer 45 minutes. Strain and measure out 1 cup of the liquid.

Heat the oil in a large heavy-bottomed frying pan and add the onion and 4 garlic cloves. Sauté over medium-low heat until the onion is tender and beginning to color and add the cumin, cayenne, salt and pepper to taste, and shrimp. Stir together for a minute or so and pour in the cup of liquid from the shells. Bring to a rapid boil, then reduce heat to a simmer and cook 10 minutes.

Transfer to a serving dish, sprinkle with the cilantro or parsley, and serve hot or allow to cool, with rice either underneath or on the side and lemon wedges for garnish. Leftovers will keep in the refrigerator for a day.

PER PORTION:

Calories	134	Protein	19 G
Fat	4 G	Carbohydrate	4 G
Sodium	139 MG	Cholesterol	140 MG

WHITINGS POACHED WITH
CARAWAY AND SPICES

MAKES 4 SERVINGS

This dish is from Tunisia, where caraway is a very popular seasoning. The authentic recipe contains about eight times more oil, but it's not necessary, as the fish is actually poached in the sauce.

   1 tablespoon olive oil
   6 garlic cloves, minced or put through a press
   ⅛ to ¼ teaspoon *harissa* (page 106) (to taste), or
        cayenne pepper (to taste), dissolved in ½ cup water
   ½ teaspoon ground caraway
   ¼ teaspoon ground coriander
   ¼ teaspoon paprika (more to taste)
   ¼ teaspoon saffron threads
     salt and freshly ground pepper
   1 cup water
   4 small whitings, cleaned and scaled, heads removed
     fresh lemon juice to taste
     lemon wedges for serving

Heat the olive oil in a wide heavy-bottomed frying pan or a flameproof casserole or baking dish large enough to accommodate the fish. Sauté the garlic for a minute or two over medium-low heat and add the *harissa* or cayenne dissolved in water, the caraway, coriander, paprika, saffron, and salt and pepper to taste. Cover and simmer 5 minutes. Add 1 cup of water and the fish and simmer gently for 10 minutes, or 5 minutes for each ½-inch thickness of the fish, turning the fish halfway through the cooking. Remove the fish with a slotted spoon and place on a platter. Strain the cooking liquid, add lemon juice to taste, and pass the sauce on the side along with lemon wedges. Leftovers will keep 1 day in the refrigerator.

PER PORTION:

Calories	150	Protein	23 G
Fat	5 G	Carbohydrate	2 G
Sodium	91 MG	Cholesterol	82 MG

BAKED FISH WITH TOMATOES AND SWEET PEPPERS

MAKES 4 SERVINGS

At Cannes, one of the great institutions is the marvelous covered market, one of the most beautiful in the Midi, and very much alive in the month of May, when the Cannes film festival is on, with fresh spring vegetables and an unbelievable array of fish. A small bistro on the old port serves delicious baked sea bream, surrounded by a sauce of tomatoes, peppers, and lots of garlic. The sauce is delicious with any of the fish suggested below.

     salt and freshly ground pepper
- 1 tablespoon olive oil plus 1 teaspoon for the baking dish
- 1 shallot, minced
- 3 large garlic cloves, minced
- ½ pound red and yellow peppers (or all one color), seeded and cut into 1- to 1½-inch pieces
- 4 ripe fresh tomatoes, peeled, seeded, and coarsely chopped
- 1 whole bream, red snapper, or salmon, about 2½ pounds
- ¼ cup dry white wine
- 12 large basil leaves, cut into thin slivers

Clean and scale the fish, leaving the skin intact. Rinse and pat dry. Sprinkle with salt and pepper to taste. Using a sharp knife, make 2 diagonal slashes, about ¼ inch deep, on each side. Preheat the oven to 400 degrees.

Heat the olive oil in a flameproof baking dish big enough to hold the fish, or in a frying pan, and add the shallot and garlic. Sauté for about 3 minutes over medium heat and add the peppers. Continue to sauté 3 minutes or so and add the tomatoes and a little salt and pepper. Resume sautéing for 3 to 5 minutes, stirring often. If you are cooking this mixture in the baking dish, push the tomatoes, etc., to the sides and lay the fish in the middle. If you have been using a frying pan, oil the baking dish, lay the fish down in it, and transfer the tomato mixture to the baking dish. Pour in the wine and cover tightly with foil. Bake in the preheated oven for 20 minutes or until the fish is opaque and flakes easily with a fork.

When the fish is done, remove from the oven and transfer to a warm serving plate. Reduce the sauce in the baking dish for a few minutes over high heat. Stir in the basil, adjust seasonings, and transfer to the serving platter, surrounding the fish with the sauce. Serve the fish, spooning a generous helping of sauce over each portion. Keep leftovers in the refrigerator and serve cold the next day.

PER PORTION:

Calories	225	Protein	32
Fat	6 G	Carbohydrate	11 G
Sodium	108 MG	Cholesterol	55 MG

TUNA STEAKS WITH FENNEL

MAKES 4 SERVINGS

This is an Italian dish. Tuna goes beautifully with fennel, which becomes sweet and fragrant as it cooks.

- 2 tablespoons olive oil
- 2 garlic cloves, minced or put through a press
- 4 small to medium-sized fennel bulbs, thinly sliced
  salt and freshly ground pepper
- 4 tuna steaks (4 to 6 ounces each), about 1 inch thick
- 1 to 2 tablespoons finely chopped fresh parsley
  lemon wedges for serving

Heat the olive oil over low heat in a wide lidded skillet and add the garlic. Cook for a few minutes, until the garlic is transparent and the oil fragrant. Add the fennel and salt and pepper to taste, cover, and sweat over low heat for 10 to 15 minutes, stirring occasionally, until tender. Set aside.

Lightly salt and pepper the tuna steaks and cook in a nonstick pan over medium-high heat for 30 to 45 seconds on each side. Place the steaks on top of the fennel in the other pan.

Cover the pan and place over medium heat. Let sweat for about 1 minute, then turn the steaks and cook 1 minute on the other side. Check for doneness by pressing the steaks with your finger. They should be slightly pink in the middle and supple and soft to the touch. Be careful not to overcook, or the tuna will be as dry as cotton.

Sprinkle on the parsley and serve with lemon wedges on the side. Leftovers will keep a day in the refrigerator.

PER PORTION:

Calories	292	Protein	35 G
Fat	14 G	Carbohydrate	5 G
Sodium	209 MG	Cholesterol	54 MG

SPICY LEBANESE-STYLE COLD FISH

MAKES 4 TO 6 SERVINGS

Fish is often allowed to cool in its cooking juices, then served with pita bread in the Middle East.

	salt
1	2-pound sea bass, snapper, or haddock, filleted (retain trimmings for stock)
2½	cups water or fish *fumet* (page 160)
1	tablespoon olive oil
2	large onions, thinly sliced
4	garlic cloves, minced or put through a press
1	teaspoon paprika
½	teaspoon ground cinnamon
⅛ to ¼	teaspoon cayenne pepper (to taste)
½	teaspoon caraway seed, lightly crushed
	freshly ground pepper
	juice of 1 to 2 lemons
2 to 3	tablespoons chopped fresh parsley or cilantro for garnish
	cooked rice or whole-wheat pita bread (page 40) for serving

Salt the fish fillets and let stand while you prepare the stock and other ingredients.

Combine the fish trimmings and water in a saucepan and bring to a boil. Skim off the foam that rises and simmer 30 minutes. Strain and reserve.

Heat the oil over medium-low heat in a heavy-bottomed flameproof casserole or baking dish large enough to accommodate all the fish in one layer. Sauté the onions and garlic until the onions are tender, about 10 minutes. Lay the fish fillets over the onions, sprinkle with all the spices plus salt and pepper to taste, and pour on the stock, which should just cover the fish (add water or white wine if it doesn't). Bring to a gentle simmer and cook for 10 to 15 minutes, until the fish is opaque and flakes easily with a fork.

Remove from the heat, pour on lemon juice, and correct the seasonings, adding salt and pepper if you wish. Allow to cool.

Before serving, sprinkle with parsley or cilantro. Serve with rice and/or pita bread (page 40). The fish will keep for a day in the refrigerator.

PER PORTION:

Calories	104	Protein	12 G
Fat	4 G	Carbohydrate	6 G
Sodium	43 MG	Cholesterol	25 MG

CHICKEN

CHICKEN KEBABS

MAKES 6 SERVINGS

You can add different vegetables, such as tomatoes, onions, and sweet peppers, to the skewers for these spicy *brochettes*.

 3 whole chicken breasts, skinned, boned, and halved
 3 garlic cloves
 ¼ teaspoon salt
 seeds from 10 cardamom pods
 1 teaspoon ground turmeric
 ½ teaspoon ground allspice
 ¼ teaspoon freshly ground pepper
 ½ teaspoon ground cumin
 juice of 3 large limes
 2 tablespoons olive oil
 4 tablespoons plain low-fat yogurt

Cut the chicken into 1½- by 2-inch pieces and place in a bowl. Pound the garlic with the salt in a mortar and pestle. Grind the cardamom in a spice grinder and add to the garlic along with the other spices. Blend together well.

Squeeze the limes and place the juice in a bowl. Whisk in the garlic/spice mixture, the olive oil, and the yogurt. Toss with the chicken and marinate for 2 to 4 hours, tossing occasionally.

Skewer the chicken, alternating with vegetables if you wish, and grill over charcoal or under a broiler for 4 to 6 minutes, turning and basting often, until golden. Serve with rice or other grains.

PER PORTION:

Calories	185	Protein	28 G
Fat	6 G	Carbohydrate	3 G
Sodium	174 MG	Cholesterol	69 MG

PROVENÇAL CHICKEN AND GARLIC, COOKED IN ROSÉ WINE

MAKES 6 SERVINGS

Use a Bandol or Côtes de Provence rosé for this very garlicky chicken dish.

   1 2½-pound chicken, cut into 8 pieces
   1 tablespoon olive oil
   8 shallots, finely minced
  24 garlic cloves, unpeeled
   ¼ cup Cognac
   2 cups dry rosé, preferably from Bandol or Provence
   2 rosemary sprigs
   2 thyme sprigs
      salt and freshly ground pepper
      chopped fresh parsley for garnish

Remove the skin from as many pieces of chicken as possible (the wings are difficult).

Heat the olive oil over medium-low heat in a large nonstick skillet and add the shallots and garlic. Cook, stirring, until the shallots begin to color. Add the chicken pieces and raise heat to medium. Cook, turning the chicken, for about 5 minutes, and add the Cognac. Continue cooking, stirring, until the Cognac evaporates. Add the rosé, rosemary, thyme, and salt and pepper to taste and bring to a simmer. Reduce heat and simmer 20 to 30 minutes, stirring and turning the chicken pieces from time to time. Remove the chicken from the pan and place on a platter. If any liquid remains, turn up the heat, bring to a boil, and pour over the chicken (reduce by half if there is as much as a cup left). Garnish with chopped fresh parsley and serve.

If the garlic cloves have become very soft, pass them in a bowl and squeeze the softened flesh out onto bread or toast. If they are not soft enough for this (this will depend on their size), discard.

Leftovers can be refrigerated and eaten cold the next day.

PER PORTION:

Calories	170	Protein	23 G
Fat	5 G	Carbohydrate	7 G
Sodium	84 MG	Cholesterol	70 MG

CHICKEN BREASTS EN PAPILLOTE

MAKES 4 SERVINGS

Despite its title, this is an Italian recipe, served in a Roman restaurant. Chicken breasts are topped with sautéed mushrooms and garlic, tomatoes, and lemon zest and baked in foil. The result is a very tasty and succulent piece of chicken.

> 2 whole boned chicken breasts, halved and pounded to
>   about ¼-inch thickness
>   salt and freshly ground pepper
> 1½ teaspoons olive oil for brushing chicken
>   1 tablespoon olive oil
>   1 shallot, minced
>   2 large garlic cloves, minced or put through a press
>   ½ pound mushrooms
>   ½ teaspoon chopped fresh rosemary *or* ¼ teaspoon dried
>   ¼ teaspoon dried thyme
>   3 tomatoes, peeled, seeded, and chopped
>   zest of 1 lemon

Preheat the oven to 375 degrees.

Sprinkle the chicken lightly with salt and pepper.

Cut 4 large double thicknesses of aluminum foil, large enough to fold loosely over each chicken breast. Brush with olive oil and set a chicken breast half on each piece.

Heat 1 tablespoon olive oil in a large heavy-bottomed skillet and sauté the shallot and garlic until the shallot is tender. Add the mushrooms and sauté, stirring, until the mushrooms begin to release some of their liquid, about 10 minutes. Add the rosemary, thyme, and tomatoes and sauté over medium heat, stirring occasionally, for another 5 to 10 minutes. Remove from the heat, stir in the lemon zest, and season to taste with salt and pepper.

Spoon some of this sauce over each of the chicken breasts. Fold the foil over the chicken breasts, crimp the edges tightly together, and bake in the preheated oven for 20 minutes. Serve in the foil.

PER PORTION:

Calories	212	Protein	29 G
Fat	7 G	Carbohydrate	8 G
Sodium	87 MG	Cholesterol	68 MG

GARLIC AND CHICKEN KEBABS

MAKES 6 SERVINGS

This recipe is an amalgamation of a couple of Middle Eastern chicken recipes, one with lots of garlic and one spicy one. Reading both recipes, I thought of adding whole cloves of garlic to the *kebabs*, so now the dish has a touch of Provence thrown in.

> 3 whole chicken breasts, skinned, boned, and halved
> 3 garlic cloves, peeled
> ¼ teaspoon salt
> 1 teaspoon paprika
> 1 teaspoon ground cinnamon
> ¼ teaspoon cayenne pepper
> juice of 1½ lemons
> 2 tablespoons olive oil
> ½ cup plain low-fat yogurt
> freshly ground pepper
> 18 to 24 whole garlic cloves, unpeeled

Cut the chicken into 1½- by 2-inch pieces.

Pound the 3 garlic cloves with the salt in a mortar and pestle and work in the paprika, cinnamon, and cayenne.

Place the lemon juice in a bowl and whisk in the olive oil, yogurt, spice mixture, and freshly ground pepper to taste.

Toss the marinade with the chicken pieces and unpeeled garlic cloves in a bowl. Let marinate for 2 to 4 hours, turning occasionally.

Prepare a grill and skewer the chicken pieces and whole cloves of garlic, using 3 to 4 cloves per *brochette*. Grill about 6 minutes about 4 inches from the heat, turning and basting, until the chicken is golden and the garlic charred.

Heat the leftover marinade and serve.

PER PORTION:

Calories	204	Protein	29 G
Fat	6 G	Carbohydrate	6 G
Sodium	182 MG	Cholesterol	70 MG

BAKED CHICKEN WITH
40 CLOVES OF GARLIC

MAKES 4 SERVINGS

This is a lusty, beautiful dish. The chicken becomes succulent and ever so fragrant as it bakes slowly in white wine with 40 unpeeled cloves of garlic. The garlic becomes mild, sweet, and soft as it cooks, and you eat it like butter on croutons. Most authentic French versions of this dish include more olive oil than mine, as well as some butter, but the results here are heavenly. I've tried various methods for this dish. Sometimes the chicken is cooked in an uncovered pan on top of the stove, but because we remove the skin here and use very little fat, the dish comes out best when the chicken is simmered in the oven in a closed pot.

   1 3- or 4-pound chicken, cut into pieces
   2 tablespoons olive oil
      salt and freshly ground pepper
  40 large, meaty garlic cloves, unpeeled
1¾ cups dry white wine
   4 thyme sprigs *or* ¼ teaspoon dried
   1 rosemary sprig *or* ¼ teaspoon dried
   8 garlic croutons (*crostini,* page 53) (without tomato)
   2 tablespoons Cognac
      chopped fresh parsley for garnish

Preheat the oven to 350 degrees. Remove the skin from the chicken pieces.

Heat the oil over medium heat in a heavy-bottomed flameproof casserole wide enough to accommodate the chicken in a single layer. Add the chicken, and salt and pepper lightly. Sauté for 5 minutes, then turn over and sauté another 5 minutes. If the bottom of the pan scorches a little, don't worry; it won't affect the flavor of the dish. Remove the chicken pieces from the pot.

Add the garlic and sauté, stirring, for 3 to 5 minutes, until beginning to brown. Again, don't worry about scorching. Spread the cloves in a single layer and return the chicken pieces to the pot. Add the wine, thyme, and rosemary and cover tightly.

Place the casserole in the oven and bake 45 minutes. Meanwhile, make the garlic croutons.

After 45 minutes, check the chicken. It should be tender and fragrant. If it isn't quite cooked through or very tender, bake another 15 minutes.

Remove the casserole from the oven. Heat the Cognac in a small saucepan and light with a match. Pour over the chicken and shake the casserole until the flames die down. Taste the sauce in the pot, adjust seasonings, and sprinkle with parsley.

To serve, place a couple of croutons on each plate, a piece of chicken or two, topped with some of the sauce in the pan, and several garlic cloves, which your guests should squeeze out onto the croutons.

PER PORTION:

Calories	555	Protein	49 G
Fat	18 G	Carbohydrate	49 G
Sodium	455 MG	Cholesterol	133 MG

CHICKEN BOUILLABAISSE

MAKES 4 SERVINGS

This savory, garlicky chicken dish has many of the flavors of a fish *bouillabaisse*—lots of garlic, onions, tomatoes, a hint of orange peel, and a *soupçon* of saffron and cayenne. The fava beans add a beautiful color to the dish, and their marvelous flavor is always welcome. The *bouillabaisse* is extremely easy to make—much easier than a fish *bouillabaisse*—and can be made ahead of time and reheated. You can omit the potatoes and serve the dish with rice, but I love the potatoes.

1 chicken, about 2 pounds, cut into 6 to 8 pieces
2 tablespoons olive oil
1 medium-sized or large onion, thinly sliced
1 leek, white part only, cleaned and sliced
2 large garlic cloves, minced or put through a press
1 pound tomatoes, peeled, seeded, and coarsely pureed
    in a food processor, *or* 1 14-ounce can Italian
    plum tomatoes, drained and chopped
2 additional garlic cloves, minced or put through a press
    salt
1 ½ cups dry white wine
2 cups defatted chicken stock (page 152)
1 bay leaf
½ teaspoon dried thyme (more to taste)

¼ teaspoon crushed fennel seed
 2 pinches saffron threads
   2-inch piece dried orange peel
 1 pound fresh fava beans, shelled
   pinch cayenne pepper
¾ pound unpeeled new potatoes, scrubbed and sliced
     (optional)
   freshly ground pepper
   lemon juice and parsley for garnish

Remove the skin from the chicken pieces.

Heat the olive oil in a heavy 3-quart (or larger) casserole and sauté the onion, leek, and 2 large garlic cloves over low heat for about 10 minutes, stirring often to prevent browning.

Add the tomatoes and additional garlic and continue to sauté over medium heat for 5 minutes. Raise heat and cook over high heat for a few more minutes, stirring.

Add the chicken, salt lightly, and stir together with the tomatoes and onions. Cover and cook 10 minutes over medium heat, turning the pieces once.

Add the wine, chicken stock, bay leaf, thyme, fennel seed, saffron, orange peel, and more salt to taste. Bring to a simmer, cover, and simmer slowly for 20 to 25 minutes or until the chicken is cooked through.

Meanwhile, blanch the fava beans in salted boiling water for 30 seconds, drain, and transfer to a bowl of cold water. Pop them out of their thick shells. Steam for 5 to 8 minutes, until tender but still bright green. Set aside.

If you are using the potatoes, steam or boil until tender, drain, and set aside.

When the chicken is done, stir in the cooked fava beans and the cooked sliced potatoes if desired. Remove the bay leaf and the orange peel and add just a hint of cayenne, just enough to lift up the flavor of the *bouillabaisse*, not enough to make it *picante*. Add pepper to taste and lemon juice if desired. Garnish with chopped fresh parsley and serve in wide soup bowls. The *bouillabaisse* will hold for a day or two in the refrigerator.

PER PORTION:

Calories	366	Protein	30 G
Fat	12 G	Carbohydrate	36 G
Sodium	110 MG	Cholesterol	76 MG

RABBIT

RABBIT COOKED IN WINE, WITH TOMATOES AND CAPERS

MAKES 6 SERVINGS

Rabbit is a light, easy meat to cook. When it's simmered for a few hours, as it is here, the meat is so tender that it just falls off the bone. This dish is served at a sensational Sardinian restaurant I ate at in Rome, Il Drappo. When I got back home, I worked out my own version.

    1   3- to 3½-pound rabbit, cut into pieces
    1   bottle dry white wine
    6   garlic cloves, peeled and crushed
    1   bay leaf
        a few thyme sprigs
    1   carrot, sliced
    1   celery stalk, sliced
    1   large onion, chopped
    3   garlic cloves, minced or put through a press
    1   tablespoon olive oil
    1   pound (4 to 5) tomatoes, peeled and chopped
    2   teaspoons dried thyme
        salt and freshly ground pepper
    4   tablespoons capers, rinsed
    2   tablespoons fresh lemon juice
    ½   teaspoon chopped fresh rosemary
        cooked rice or wide flat noodles for serving

   Rinse the rabbit pieces and pat dry. Place in a bowl and pour on the white wine. Add the 6 garlic cloves, bay leaf, thyme, carrot, and celery; marinate overnight in the refrigerator. Remove from the refrigerator and allow to come to room temperature.
   Sauté the onion and 3 garlic cloves in the oil over medium heat until the onion begins to color. Add the rabbit and the marinade with all the vegetables, the tomatoes, dried thyme, and salt and pepper to taste. Add water to

cover the rabbit, bring to a simmer over low heat, cover, and cook 2 hours, turning once or twice. Add the capers, lemon juice, and rosemary during the last half hour. The rabbit should be very tender and falling off the bone. Adjust seasonings and serve over rice or flat wide noodles. The dish will keep in the refrigerator for a couple of days.

PER PORTION:

Calories	328	Protein	43 G
Fat	12 G	Carbohydrate	10 G
Sodium	255 MG	Cholesterol	128 MG

RABBIT WITH 40 CLOVES OF GARLIC

MAKES 4 SERVINGS

This is very much like the chicken with 40 cloves of garlic on page 305, but rabbit is substituted for chicken and red wine for white. The rabbit is marinated overnight in wine to tenderize the meat before it's cooked. I have served this dish with wild rice, which isn't very Mediterranean but makes a delicious accompaniment, along with a simply steamed green vegetable and a tossed salad.

1 3- or 4-pound rabbit, cut into pieces
1 bottle hearty red wine, such as Côtes du Rhône
2 tablespoons olive oil
   salt and freshly ground pepper
40 large, meaty garlic cloves, unpeeled
4 thyme sprigs *or* ¼ teaspoon dried
1 sprig rosemary *or* ¼ teaspoon dried
   garlic croutons (*crostini*, page 53, without tomato)
   chopped fresh parsley for garnish

The day before you wish to serve this, place the rabbit in a bowl and pour on the red wine. Cover and refrigerate overnight, turning the pieces once. An hour before cooking, remove the rabbit from the refrigerator, remove the pieces from the wine, and pat dry with paper towels.

Preheat the oven to 350 degrees.

Heat the oil over medium heat in a heavy-bottomed flameproof casserole. Add the rabbit and salt and pepper lightly. Sauté for 5 minutes, then turn the pieces over and sauté another 5 minutes. (This can be done in batches if the casserole isn't wide enough to accommodate all of the rabbit pieces in a single layer.) Don't worry if the pan scorches a bit; it won't affect the flavor of the dish. Remove the rabbit from the pot.

Add the garlic and sauté, stirring, for 5 minutes, until beginning to brown. Spread in a single layer and return the rabbit pieces to the pot. Add the red wine, thyme, rosemary, and more salt and pepper to taste, and cover tightly.

Place the casserole in the preheated oven and bake 1 hour or until the rabbit pieces are falling away from the bone. Meanwhile, make the garlic croutons.

When the rabbit is very tender, remove the rabbit pieces and the garlic from the pot and place on a platter. Place the pot over high heat and reduce the wine until thick. Correct seasonings and pour over the rabbit. Sprinkle with parsley and serve, placing a couple of croutons on each plate, a piece of rabbit or two, and several garlic cloves, which are to be squeezed out onto the croutons.

PER PORTION:

Calories	767	Protein	76 G
Fat	28 G	Carbohydrate	51 G
Sodium	449 MG	Cholesterol	207 MG

RABBIT SIMMERED IN CHICKEN STOCK

MAKES 6 SERVINGS

This is a very simple recipe. The rabbit is simmered in a light chicken stock, seasoned with lots of thyme, garlic, and onions, until it is so tender that it falls off the bone. Serve with fresh pasta.

    1 tablespoon olive oil
    2 onions, finely chopped
    4 garlic cloves, minced or put through a press
    1 3- to 4-pound rabbit, cut up

1 ½ quarts defatted chicken stock (page 152)
   1 bay leaf
   2 teaspoons dried thyme (more to taste)
      salt and freshly ground pepper
 ½ to ¾ pound cooked fresh pasta for serving

Heat the oil over medium heat in a large heavy-bottomed casserole or stockpot. Add the onion and garlic and sauté until the onion is tender and beginning to color. Add the rabbit, chicken stock, bay leaf, thyme, and salt and pepper to taste. Bring to a simmer, reduce heat, cover partially, and simmer over very low heat for 1 to 2 hours, until the rabbit is very tender and falls off the bone. Adjust seasonings and serve over fresh pasta. This will keep for a couple of days in the refrigerator.

PER PORTION:

Calories	373	Protein	46 G
Fat	15 G	Carbohydrate	11 G
Sodium	98 MG	Cholesterol	138 MG

CHAPTER SEVEN

VEGETABLE SIDE DISHES AND EGGS

A market in Cannes or Palermo in the springtime is a sight to see: tomatoes of all sizes, bright red and so sweet you can eat them like apples; many kinds of small green peppers (I counted a dozen varieties in Cannes); beautiful vine-ripened red and yellow peppers; long, dark, shiny eggplants, smaller roundish ones, white eggplants; big bunches of artichokes, the little purple ones and the larger green ones, still on their stalks; zucchini and other varieties of squash, including, in Palermo, a light green squash that was about two feet long; peas as sweet as sugar, so tender that you don't need to cook them; green beans, yellow beans, snow peas; spinach and chard, little yellow and red potatoes that are also incredibly sweet; fennel, celery, carrots, baby turnips. In the central market in Athens and the Egyptian souks there are also all kinds of dark leafy greens and okra and long green beans. In Yugoslavia there isn't so much variety, but the tomatoes are the best I've ever tasted. It's worth a trip to Italy in the fall just for the wild mushrooms, the big, meaty *porcini* that are called *cèpes* in France.

It is, in the end, the vegetables that give Mediterranean cuisine its character. Interestingly enough, the most widely used vegetables are usually not indigenous to the Mediterranean; but where would these cuisines be without tomatoes, peppers, and squash, all of which came from the New World, or the eggplants that came from Asia?

Look for the freshest vegetables you can find, the most vivid and vibrant, homegrown or grown on small farms if possible. If the vegetables have no taste to begin with, alas, no amount of garlic will help.

The chapter that follows is just a smattering of the many recipes that could have been included here. I've also included a few egg dishes that combine eggs and vegetables. (If you have a cholesterol problem, I suggest that you avoid these and stick to the vegetable dishes.)

VEGETABLES

SFORMATO DI PATATE
(Italian Mashed Potato Pie)

MAKES 6 SERVINGS

You won't find this version of *sformato di patate* in Italian cookbooks; I found it in a town called Borgotaro, in the Alto Val di Taro, a hilly region northeast of Parma. I didn't go there for potatoes, but for the annual wild mushroom (*porcini*) festival. I wandered into a food shop where large vegetable tortes were on display. At first I wasn't sure what the potato torte was, as it was a rosy orange color (because a spoonful of tomato paste is blended with the mashed potatoes). I bought a wedge and nibbled happily as I continued on my way. What a nice, simple potato dish! It's easy to make and keeps for several days in the refrigerator. Serve it cut into squares or wedges, warm or at room temperature, for hors d'oeuvres, for lunch, or as a side dish.

- 2 pounds (6 medium) potatoes, peeled
  vegetable oil for the pan
- 2 tablespoons bread crumbs
- 1 tablespoon margarine, olive oil, or butter
- ½ cup 2% fat milk
- 1 egg
  about ½ teaspoon salt (to taste)
- ¼ teaspoon paprika
- 1 scant tablespoon tomato paste
- 1 large garlic clove, minced or put through a press
  freshly ground pepper
- ⅓ cup freshly grated Parmesan cheese

Cut the potatoes into chunks if they're large. Boil gently in salted water, covered, or steam until tender, about 30 minutes.

Meanwhile, preheat the oven to 350 degrees. Oil a 10-inch cake pan or quiche pan and sprinkle with bread crumbs.

When the potatoes are tender, drain and place in a bowl. Add the margarine and mash with a potato masher. Gradually blend in the milk, beating with a wooden spoon or a whisk. When the milk is incorporated, stir in the beaten egg, salt, paprika, tomato paste, garlic, and pepper to taste. Stir in ¼ cup of the Parmesan.

Transfer to the prepared pan and sprinkle the remaining Parmesan over the top. Bake in the preheated oven for 40 minutes or until the mixture is firm and the top is browned. Remove from the heat and allow to cool 15 minutes before slicing or cool completely; this also tastes good at room temperature.

PER PORTION:

Calories	180	Protein	7 G
Fat	7 G	Carbohydrate	24 G
Sodium	370 MG	Cholesterol	52 MG

SPICY ITALIAN-STYLE BROCCOLI

MAKES 4 TO 6 SERVINGS

This is a typical southern Italian dish. You can also cook broccoli raab (see page 395) the same way.

    2 pounds (2 small bunches) broccoli, broken into florets,
        stems peeled and chopped
    1 tablespoon olive oil
    2 garlic cloves, minced or put through a press
    1 small dried hot red pepper, crumbled
    1 tablespoon dry white wine
        salt and freshly ground pepper

Steam the broccoli for 10 minutes or until tender and still bright green. Drain.

Heat the olive oil over medium heat in a nonstick skillet and sauté the garlic and red pepper for 1 minute. Add the broccoli and wine and sauté, stirring, 3 to 5 minutes. Add salt and pepper to taste and serve.

PER PORTION:

Calories	65	Protein	5 G
Fat	3 G	Carbohydrate	8 G
Sodium	41 MG	Cholesterol	0

POTATO GRATIN

MAKES 6 TO 8 SERVINGS

One of my favorite dishes in France is *gratin dauphinois*, a potato *gratin* that is usually very rich. This low-fat version, which calls for skimmed milk instead of whole milk, no *crème fraîche*, and very little cheese, is just as luscious as any potato *gratin* I've eaten in France. I've added a Mediterranean twist to mine by slicing up the garlic used to season the *gratin* dish and adding it to the potatoes.

    2 large garlic cloves, cut in half lengthwise
    3 pounds (9 medium) russet or new potatoes, unpeeled
         (or peeled, according to your taste), scrubbed
         and very thinly sliced
3 ⅓ cups skimmed milk
    2 large eggs, lightly beaten
       about 1 teaspoon salt (to taste)
       freshly ground pepper
    6 tablespoons freshly grated Parmesan cheese

Preheat the oven to 400 degrees. Rub the inside of a large (about 14 by 9 by 2 inches) oval *gratin* dish all over with the cut side of the garlic.

Slice the remaining garlic into thin slivers and toss with the potatoes. Layer the potatoes and garlic in an even layer in the *gratin* dish.

Mix together the milk, eggs, and salt and pour over the potatoes. Add a generous amount of pepper.

Place in the preheated oven and bake for about 1 hour to 1 hour and 15 minutes. Every 15 minutes or so, remove the casserole from the oven and, using a knife or a wooden spoon, break up the top layer of potatoes that is drying up and getting crusty and fold it into the rest of the potatoes.

When the *gratin* is golden and the potatoes tender, sprinkle on the Parmesan and return to the heat. Bake another 15 to 20 minutes, until a golden-brown crust has formed on the top. Remove from the oven and serve.

PER PORTION:

Calories	215	Protein	10 G
Fat	3 G	Carbohydrate	36 G
Sodium	444 MG	Cholesterol	74 MG

GRATED POTATO TORTE WITH ONIONS

MAKES 6 SERVINGS

Here is another Italian potato torte. The potatoes are grated and embellished with savory onions that have been cooked slowly and browned in red wine. This can be served warm or cold and makes a fine appetizer.

    1 tablespoon olive oil
    1 pound (2 large) red or yellow onions, very thinly sliced
    ⅓ cup red wine
    ⅓ cup water
    ¼ teaspoon dried thyme
    1 pound (3 medium) potatoes, peeled
    2 tablespoons low-fat milk
    1 tablespoon flour
    1 egg
       about ½ teaspoon salt (to taste)
       pinch freshly grated nutmeg
       freshly ground pepper
    ¼ cup plus 2 tablespoons freshly grated Parmesan cheese
       olive oil for the baking dish

Heat the olive oil in a heavy-bottomed casserole over medium heat and sauté the onions, stirring, until they begin to brown, about 10 minutes. Add the wine and water, stir together, reduce heat, and cover. Simmer over low heat, stirring occasionally, for 40 minutes, until the onions are a dark reddish-brown color and smell sweet and fragrant. If the onions stick to the pan, add a little more water and remember to stir from time to time. Add the thyme and remove from the heat.

Preheat the oven to 400 degrees. Oil a 10-inch pie pan or low-sided casserole.

Grate the potatoes, using the fine grating blade.

Beat together the milk, flour, and egg. Stir in the potatoes and onions. Add the salt, nutmeg, pepper to taste, and ¼ cup of the Parmesan and mix together thoroughly. Spoon into the baking dish and spread out evenly. The mixture shouldn't be more than an inch thick; thinner is better. Sprinkle the remaining 2 tablespoons Parmesan over the top.

Bake in the preheated oven for 40 minutes or until the top and sides have a golden crust. Remove from the heat and serve hot or allow to cool and serve at room temperature, cut into wedges. This will keep for 2 or 3 days in the refrigerator.

PER PORTION:

Calories	153	Protein	6 G
Fat	7 G	Carbohydrate	18 G
Sodium	316 MG	Cholesterol	51 MG

BAKED POTATOES WITH FENNEL

MAKES 4 TO 6 SERVINGS

I'd never thought about baking potatoes with fennel until I ran across the dish in Marcella Hazan's latest book, *Marcella's Italian Kitchen*. My version has less oil than hers and no butter. The fennel becomes sweet and fragrant as it bakes with the potatoes.

salt and freshly ground pepper
1 **tablespoon olive oil**
1 **pound (2 medium) fennel bulbs**
1 **to 1½ pounds (3 to 5) boiling potatoes, scrubbed and**
     thinly sliced

Preheat the oven to 425 degrees. Lightly oil a 3-quart baking dish with olive oil.

Cut off the tops of the fennel, but retain the feathery leaves for garnish. Discard the tough or discolored outside leaves and slice into thin, lengthwise slices. If the fennel bulbs are very large, cut them in half lengthwise. Place in the baking dish, salt and pepper lightly, and toss with the olive oil. Cover the baking dish tightly with heavy-duty aluminum foil or a lid and place in the top part of the preheated oven. Bake 15 minutes, until the fennel is almost tender.

Add the potatoes to the fennel. Add salt and pepper to taste and toss well. Cover and return to the oven. Bake 20 to 30 minutes, until the potatoes are tender. Remove from the heat and serve (they can sit for a bit before serving).

PER PORTION:

Calories	101	Protein	3 G
Fat	2 G	Carbohydrate	18 G
Sodium	75 MG	Cholesterol	0

MUSHROOM RAGOÛT

MAKES 8 SERVINGS

If you can get fresh wild mushrooms for this *ragoût* it will be truly special, but it is marvelous with regular mushrooms as well, as long as you have dried mushrooms, which are necessary for the strong, "meaty" flavor. The addition of soy sauce is my own, to bring out the meaty mushroom flavor.

1 ounce imported dried wild mushrooms, such as *cèpes, porcini,* or *chanterelles*
boiling water to cover
2 tablespoons olive oil
2 large shallots *or* 1 medium onion, minced
½ pound fresh wild mushrooms, such as *porcini* or *chanterelles,* washed and shaken dry (optional)
½ pound fresh cultivated mushrooms (use 1 pound cultivated mushrooms in all if fresh wild mushrooms are unavailable), cleaned, stems trimmed at the bottom, and thickly sliced
3 to 4 garlic cloves (to taste), minced or put through a press
1 to 2 tablespoons soy sauce (to taste)
½ cup dry red wine
1 cup soaking water from the dried mushrooms
½ to 1 teaspoon dried thyme (to taste)
½ teaspoon chopped fresh or crumbled dried rosemary
1 cup vegetable stock (page 140)
salt and freshly ground pepper

Place the dried mushrooms in a bowl and pour on boiling water to cover. Let sit for 30 minutes, while you prepare the remaining ingredients.

Heat the olive oil in a large heavy-bottomed skillet and add the shallots or onions. Cook over medium-low heat, stirring often, for about 15 minutes, or until golden brown. Add the fresh wild and cultivated mushrooms, or 1 pound cultivated mushrooms if fresh wild mushrooms are not available. Stir together and sauté for 5 to 10 minutes, until they begin to release their liquid.

Meanwhile, drain the dried mushrooms and retain the liquid. Rinse the mushrooms thoroughly to remove sand, squeeze dry, and add to the skillet along with the garlic. Stir together and sauté a few minutes, adding oil if necessary. Add the soy sauce and wine and bring to a simmer.

Strain the soaking liquid from the mushrooms through a strainer lined with cheesecloth or through a coffee filter. Measure out 1 cup and add to the mushrooms along with the thyme, rosemary, and stock. Bring to a simmer, cover, and simmer 20 minutes. Uncover and raise heat to high. Reduce the liquid by half, or until the mushrooms are glazed and some liquid remains in the pan. Taste and add salt and pepper to taste, plus more garlic or herbs if desired. The *ragoût* will keep for a few days in the refrigerator and can be frozen. Reheat to simmer before serving.

PER PORTION:

Calories	67	Protein	2 G
Fat	4 G	Carbohydrate	8 G
Sodium	234 MG	Cholesterol	0

BROILED MUSHROOMS

MAKES 4 SERVINGS

You would be likely to find these juicy broiled mushrooms, fragrant with garlic, thyme, and rosemary, in a Tuscan or *Provençal* household. They make a nice first course as well as a great side dish.

1 pound mushrooms, cleaned, stems removed
1 tablespoon olive oil plus 1 teaspoon for baking sheet
3 garlic cloves, cut into thin slivers
½ teaspoon crumbled dried rosemary
¼ teaspoon dried thyme
salt and freshly ground pepper

Preheat the broiler. Oil a baking sheet.

Place the mushrooms on the baking sheet, rounded sides down. Drizzle on the olive oil and sprinkle on the garlic, rosemary, thyme, and salt and pepper to taste.

Place under the broiler, about 4 inches from the heat source, and cook 10 to 15 minutes, basting every 5 minutes with the juices released by the mushrooms. Turn the mushrooms over during the last 5 minutes. Remove from the heat and serve as a side dish or first course. Serve warm or hot. These will hold for a couple of hours once cooked, but will dry out somewhat.

PER PORTION:

Calories	62	Protein	3 G
Fat	4 G	Carbohydrate	6 G
Sodium	5 MG	Cholesterol	0

PROVENÇAL OKRA STEW

MAKES 4 SERVINGS

This is a modified version of a *Provençal* recipe. I've removed the olives that are included in the authentic recipe and reduced the olive oil. The okra retains its crunchy texture in the rich anchovy-enhanced tomato sauce.

- 1 pound okra
- ¼ cup red wine vinegar
- 1 tablespoon salt
  water to cover
- 2 tablespoons olive oil
- 2 medium onions, chopped
- 4 garlic cloves, minced or put through a press
- 1 14-ounce can Italian plum tomatoes, with liquid,
    coarsely chopped
- 2 tablespoons chopped fresh basil *or* 2 teaspoons dried
- ¼ teaspoon dried thyme
- 2 anchovy fillets, rinsed and chopped
  freshly ground pepper
  juice of 1 large lemon

Trim the ends and tips of the okra. Combine the okra, vinegar, and salt in a medium bowl and cover with water. Let sit 30 minutes, drain, rinse, and pat the okra thoroughly dry with kitchen towels.

Heat the oil in a medium-sized casserole over medium-low heat. Add the onion and half the garlic; sauté, stirring, until the onion is tender, about 5 minutes. Add the remaining garlic, the canned tomatoes, the dried herbs (fresh basil is added later), and the anchovy fillets and bring to a simmer. Simmer, uncovered, over medium-low heat for 30 minutes. Add the fresh basil if using it and the okra and simmer another 10 to 15 minutes or longer, to taste. Add freshly ground pepper to taste and the lemon juice; taste and adjust seasonings. Serve hot or cold. The stew can be held for a day in the refrigerator.

PER PORTION:

Calories	152	Protein	5 G
Fat	7 G	Carbohydrate	6 G
Sodium	1,893 MG	Cholesterol	1 MG

BROILED EGGPLANT WITH GARLIC AND ROSEMARY

MAKES 4 TO 6 SERVINGS

The slightly charred flavor of grilled or roasted eggplant is one of my favorite tastes. Although an outdoor grill is a great asset for this dish, you can achieve good results with an oven broiler. This dish is best made with long, thin eggplants.

- 2 pounds (2 large) eggplant, preferably long, thin ones
  salt
- 2 large garlic cloves, finely minced
- 1 teaspoon chopped fresh rosemary
  freshly ground pepper
- 2 tablespoons olive oil

Cut the eggplants in half lengthwise and make crosshatch incisions on the cut side, making sure not to cut through the skin. Sprinkle with salt and let sit for 30 minutes. Squeeze gently, rinse, and pat dry with paper towels.

Preheat the broiler. The eggplant should not be less than 10 inches from the heat source. Use the bottom of the oven if necessary.

Stuff the crosshatch incisions with garlic and rosemary and sprinkle on pepper to taste. Brush the cut sides of the eggplant thoroughly with olive oil.

Place the eggplant halves cut side up on the broiler pan and place in the oven. Broil for 15 to 30 minutes or until thoroughly tender, basting with olive oil halfway through. Remove from the heat. Serve hot, warm, or at room temperature. The eggplant will hold several hours before serving.

PER PORTION:

Calories	74	Protein	1 G
Fat	5 G	Carbohydrate	8 G
Sodium	5 MG	Cholesterol	0

EGGPLANT GRATIN

MAKES 4 TO 6 SERVINGS

This luscious *gratin*, which is based on Patricia Wells's version of the one that is served at Oustau de Baumanière, a famous restaurant in Les Baux-de-Provence, makes a good side dish with pasta, fish, or chicken or a marvelous main dish. Unlike most eggplant *gratins*, the eggplant isn't saturated with oil because it isn't fried, but rather baked at a high temperature.

FOR THE TOMATO SAUCE:

- 1 tablespoon olive oil
- 2 onions, chopped
- 3 large garlic cloves, minced or put through a press
- 3 pounds ripe fresh tomatoes, quartered, *or* 3 28-ounce cans tomatoes, drained and quartered
- 1 bay leaf
- 2 to 3 tablespoons chopped fresh basil, parsley, or a combination (to taste)
- ¼ to ½ teaspoon dried thyme (to taste)
- ½ teaspoon dried oregano
  pinch sugar
  salt and freshly ground pepper to taste
  pinch cayenne pepper (optional)

FOR THE GRATIN:

- 2 medium-sized eggplants (about 2 pounds)
- 1 tablespoon olive oil
  the tomato sauce
  handful of any chopped fresh herb, such as basil, chervil, thyme, rosemary, or parsley, minced
  salt and freshly ground pepper

PREPARE THE TOMATO SAUCE:

(This sauce will keep in the refrigerator for several days and freezes well.) Heat the olive oil over medium heat in a large heavy-bottomed casserole and sauté the onion and half the garlic, stirring often, until the onion is tender and golden but not brown. Add the tomatoes, remaining garlic, and remaining sauce ingredients, bring to a simmer, and cook, uncovered, for 35 to 45 minutes, stirring often. Adjust seasonings, adding garlic, salt, or more herbs if you wish, and remove the bay leaf. Press the sauce through the fine or medium blade of a food mill or through a fine-meshed sieve and set aside.

PREPARE THE GRATIN:

Preheat the oven to 450 degrees. Cut the eggplants in half lengthwise and pierce the cut side in a few places with the tip of a knife. Oil a baking sheet with the tablespoon of olive oil and place the eggplants on it, cut sides down. Bake in the hot oven for 20 minutes or until the eggplants are soft and beginning to shrivel. Remove from the heat and allow to cool, but leave the oven on.

When the eggplants are cool enough to handle, slice crosswise into thin slices. Don't worry if they don't hold their shape.

Lightly oil a 1½- to 2-quart *gratin* dish. Spoon in a thin layer of the tomato sauce. Sprinkle with some of the minced herbs and cover with a layer of the eggplant. Lightly salt and pepper the eggplant and repeat the layers until all the ingredients are used up, ending with a layer of tomato sauce.

Return to the 450-degree oven and bake for 30 to 40 minutes, until bubbling. Serve warm or at room temperature.

You can prepare the *gratin* a day ahead of time up to the baking. Bake the day of serving. Leftovers will keep several days in the refrigerator. Reheat in a moderate oven.

PER PORTION:

Calories	129	Protein	4 G
Fat	5 G	Carbohydrate	21 G
Sodium	26 MG	Cholesterol	0

PROVENÇAL TOMATO
AND PEPPER TIAN

MAKES 4 TO 6 SERVINGS

This dish should be served cold, with the vegetable juices spooned over each helping.

- 3 large red peppers
- 2 large green peppers
- 3 garlic cloves, minced or put through a press
- 1 small red onion, sliced
- 1 tablespoon olive oil
- 2 pounds (8 to 10) tomatoes, sliced
  salt and freshly ground pepper
- 1 cup chopped fresh basil
- 1 teaspoon dried thyme
- ¼ cup freshly grated Parmesan cheese
- 2 tablespoons whole-wheat bread crumbs
  additional chopped fresh basil or parsley for garnish

Roast the red and green peppers over a gas burner flame or under the broiler, turning until all the skin is charred. Place in a paper or plastic bag and allow to cool. Remove all the charred skin, rinse, and remove the seeds and membranes. Cut in lengthwise quarters, toss with 1 of the garlic cloves, and set aside.

Preheat the oven to 400 degrees. Brush a 1½-quart baking dish with olive oil.

Sauté the onion and remaining garlic in the olive oil over medium heat until the onion is tender. Set aside.

Layer a third of the tomatoes over the bottom of the baking dish. Salt and pepper lightly and top with half of the onion and garlic. Combine the basil and thyme and sprinkle a couple of tablespoons of the herbs over the tomatoes. Top with a third of the Parmesan. Next lay half the green and red peppers on top, salt and pepper, then add another layer of herbs. Repeat these layers—tomatoes, onion and garlic, herbs, Parmesan, peppers, herbs— and finish with the final third of tomatoes, Parmesan, and herbs. Sprinkle the bread crumbs over the top.

Bake 20 minutes, remove from the heat, and let sit for 15 minutes. Refrigerate for at least 2 hours and serve chilled, garnished with additional basil or parsley. Spoon the juices in the pan over each serving. This dish will keep a couple of days in the refrigerator.

PER PORTION:

Calories	107	Protein	5 G
Fat	4 G	Carbohydrate	15 G
Sodium	97 MG	Cholesterol	3 MG

SLOW-BAKED TOMATOES

MAKES 4 TO 6 SERVINGS

I learned this recipe from Lulu Peyraud, at Domaine Tempier. She served these tomatoes at one of her winery harvest lunches, and I'd never tasted such a sweet and savory version of baked tomatoes. The secret is to bake them for a very long time at low heat. By the end of the baking time they are almost caramelized.

4 to 6 large ripe fresh tomatoes, cut in half horizontally
4 to 6 teaspoons olive oil
   salt and freshly ground pepper
2 to 3 garlic cloves (to taste), minced or put through a press
3 tablespoons chopped fresh basil or parsley

Preheat the oven to 325 degrees. Place the tomatoes on a baking sheet, cut sides up. Drizzle on the olive oil and sprinkle with salt and pepper to taste.

Bake in the preheated oven for 2 to 3 hours, until the tomatoes collapse and begin to caramelize. Sprinkle with the garlic about halfway through the baking, or at the end, and sprinkle with the herbs just before serving. Serve hot or at room temperature.

PER PORTION:

Calories	59	Protein	1 G
Fat	4 G	Carbohydrate	6 G
Sodium	11 MG	Cholesterol	0

QUICK BAKED TOMATOES
À LA PROVENÇALE

MAKES 4 TO 6 SERVINGS

This is a quick version of baked tomatoes. It's juicier and less sweet than the preceding slow-baked dish. The recipe comes from my friend Marguerite Mullen, a great cook and caterer from Los Angeles.

    6 firm, large ripe tomatoes
    2 shallots, minced
    2 garlic cloves, minced
    2 tablespoons chopped fresh parsley
    2 tablespoons chopped fresh basil (optional; do *not* substitute dried)
    ½ teaspoon dried thyme
    ¼ teaspoon crushed dried rosemary
       salt and freshly ground pepper

Preheat the oven to 400 degrees.

Cut the tomatoes across the top, about ½ inch down from the stem. Gently scoop out the seeds and place upside down on a rack for 10 minutes.

Mix together the shallots, garlic, and herbs. Place the tomatoes cut side up on an oiled baking sheet or in an oiled baking pan. Lightly salt and pepper and sprinkle with the herb and garlic mixture. Bake 20 minutes in the preheated oven, until the skins burst but the tomatoes are still intact. Serve hot.

PER PORTION:

Calories	33	Protein	2 G
Fat	.31 G	Carbohydrate	8 G
Sodium	14 MG	Cholesterol	0

BAKED WHOLE HEADS OF GARLIC

MAKES 4 TO 6 SERVINGS

During the summers I've spent in Provence, I've gone wild with garlic. One of my favorite dishes is this one. If you're cooking over an open fire, wrap the bulbous heads of young summer garlic in foil and cook them in the embers; the garlic cooks to a soft, unctuous, sweet, and mildly pungent puree, to be spread on toasted bread or potatoes. It's equally delicious made in the oven. Spread on toast, this puree is great with grilled fish or chicken, as well as salads of all kinds.

> 1 tablespoon plus 1 teaspoon olive oil
> 2 large heads garlic (young elephant garlic is very good)
>   a few fresh thyme sprigs *or* ¼ to ½ teaspoon dried (to taste)
> ¼ to ½ teaspoon chopped fresh rosemary (to taste)
>   salt and freshly ground pepper

Preheat the oven to 350 degrees. Cut a large double-thick square of aluminum foil and brush with the olive oil. Place the garlic heads on the foil, brush the garlic with olive oil, and sprinkle with the herbs and salt and pepper to taste. Fold the foil up over the garlic and crimp the edges together tightly, leaving some space around the garlic. Bake in the preheated oven for 1 to 1½ hours, until the garlic is very soft.

Remove from the foil and allow to cool a little or to room temperature. Separate into individual cloves, or clumps of a few cloves each, and squeeze out the pulp onto bread or toast. Leftovers can be kept in the refrigerator and eaten cold or at room temperature.

PER PORTION:

Calories	43	Protein	2 G
Fat	2 G	Carbohydrate	8 G
Sodium	4 MG	Cholesterol	0

SWISS CHARD OR SPINACH WITH FENNEL AND HOT PEPPER

MAKES 4 TO 6 SERVINGS

Every day, on a springtime visit to southern Italy, I was introduced to at least one new vegetable dish, and usually several. This particularly delicious one was prepared by the chef at Villa Cheta in Acquafredda. The greens could have been beet greens or even kale, but Swiss chard or spinach would also be appropriate. Wild fennel grows everywhere in southern Italy and Sicily. If you can't find it, use the tops of bulb fennel.

> 2 pounds Swiss chard leaves or spinach
> 2 teaspoons olive oil
> 2 garlic cloves, minced or put through a press
> 4 tablespoons finely chopped wild fennel or the feathery
>   tops of bulb fennel
> ½ teaspoon hot pepper flakes (more to taste)
>   salt and freshly ground pepper
>   juice of ½ lemon
>   lemon wedges for serving

Separate the Swiss chard leaves or the spinach from the stalks or stems and wash thoroughly in several changes of water.

Heat the oil over medium heat in a large nonstick skillet and sauté the garlic for 1 minute. Add the greens, raise the heat to medium-high, and allow to wilt in the liquid remaining on their leaves. Stir in the fennel, hot pepper flakes, and salt and pepper to taste. Cook, stirring, for 4 or 5 minutes and remove from the heat. Toss with the lemon juice and serve, passing additional lemon wedges so people can squeeze on more juice as desired.

PER PORTION:

Calories	42	Protein	3 G
Fat	2 G	Carbohydrate	6 G
Sodium	297 MG	Cholesterol	0

TZIMMES

MAKES 6 SERVINGS

This is a modified version of the traditional Jewish sweet potato casserole, which is usually served at Passover and on other Jewish holidays. Like most of the foods adorning Jewish holiday tables, the authentic *tzimmes* (pronounced "tsimmis") is very rich. I've taken out the fats and moistened the dish with plain low-fat yogurt.

- 3 large sweet potatoes, well scrubbed
- 1 cup plain low-fat yogurt
- ½ pound (2 or 3) carrots, peeled and grated
- ½ pound (2 medium) tart apples, peeled, cored, and grated
- 2 tablespoons mild-flavored honey (such as clover or acacia)
- ⅓ cup raisins
- ¼ cup chopped walnuts or pecans
- ½ teaspoon ground cinnamon
- ¼ teaspoon ground cloves
- ¼ teaspoon freshly grated nutmeg
- ¼ teaspoon salt

Preheat the oven to 425 degrees. Prick the potatoes and bake them in their skins until thoroughly tender, about 45 minutes. Remove from the oven and reduce heat to 350 degrees.

Scoop out the potato from the peels, discard the peels, and puree the potatoes in a food processor fitted with the steel blade or through a food mill. Mix in the yogurt and set aside.

Steam the carrots for 5 minutes. Add the apples and steam 5 minutes. Remove from the heat and add the honey, raisins, walnuts, spices, and salt. Stir in the sweet potato puree and mix everything together well.

Transfer to an oiled or buttered baking dish or casserole, cover with foil or a lid, and bake in the preheated oven for 20 to 30 minutes. Serve hot. The dish will hold in the refrigerator for a couple of days. Reheat in a moderate oven.

PER PORTION:

Calories	222	Protein	5 G
Fat	4 G	Carbohydrate	44 G
Sodium	111 MG	Cholesterol	2 MG

ZUCCHINI À LA PROVENÇALE

MAKES 4 TO 6 SERVINGS

This is a spring or summer dish requiring ripe red tomatoes and tender zucchini. It's delicious served hot or cold.

    1   tablespoon olive oil
1 ½ pounds (6 small) zucchini, sliced about ¼ inch thick
    2   garlic cloves, minced or put through a press
    1   pound (4 to 5) tomatoes, chopped
        salt and freshly ground pepper
    1   tablespoon chopped fresh basil
        fresh lemon juice (if serving cold)

Heat the olive oil in a wide heavy-bottomed skillet and sauté the zucchini with the garlic over medium heat for 5 minutes. Add the tomatoes and salt and pepper to taste and bring to a simmer. Simmer over medium-low heat, stirring from time to time, for 15 to 20 minutes. Add the basil, correct seasonings, and serve, or serve it cold with a little lemon juice squeezed over the top.

PER PORTION:

Calories	54	Protein	2 G
Fat	3 G	Carbohydrate	7 G
Sodium	12 MG	Cholesterol	0

CARCIOFI ALLA ROMANA
(Roman-Style Artichokes)

MAKES 4 SERVINGS

These artichokes are stuffed with a fragrant mixture of garlic and mint, and poached in wine, to which a few more cloves of garlic have been added. All the flavors converge when you bite into each leaf. This dish works as an appetizer and makes a good side dish.

- 4 medium-sized artichokes
- 4 garlic cloves, chopped
- 4 tablespoons chopped fresh mint
- 1 cup dry white or rosé wine
- 1 bay leaf
- 2 garlic cloves, peeled and crushed
- 1 slice onion
- 1 tablespoon olive oil

Trim the artichokes by cutting off the stem and breaking off the tough bottom leaves. Using a sharp knife, cut the artichokes across the tops, about ½ inch down.

Mix together the chopped garlic and mint, and using 1 tablespoon per artichoke, stuff the artichokes by squeezing bits of the mixture between the leaves, pushing it as far down between the leaves as you can.

Combine the wine, bay leaf, crushed garlic, onion, and olive oil in a saucepan or casserole large enough to hold the artichokes and stand the artichokes in the pan. Bring to a simmer, cover, and simmer about 40 minutes or until the artichokes are tender and the leaves pull away easily.

Allow to cool and serve. Leftovers will hold for a couple of days in the refrigerator.

PER PORTION:

Calories	106	Protein	4 G
Fat	4 G	Carbohydrate	18 G
Sodium	106 MG	Cholesterol	0

FAVA BEANS WITH SWEET PEPPERS

MAKES 4 SERVINGS

This is a beautiful combination of fresh fava beans and roasted sweet red pepper, cooked gently with garlic in olive oil and white wine. It's a gorgeous side dish and is also nice with pasta.

2½ pounds unshelled fava beans
1 large *or* 2 small sweet red peppers
2 tablespoons olive oil
2 large garlic cloves, finely minced
⅓ cup dry white wine
¼ teaspoon dried thyme
  salt and freshly ground pepper
2 tablespoons fresh lemon juice

Bring a large pot of salted water to a boil while you remove the fava beans from their pods.

Meanwhile, roast the red peppers over a gas flame or under a broiler, turning until all sides are uniformly charred. Remove from the heat and place in a paper or plastic bag until cool enough to handle. Remove all the charred skin, rinse the peppers, and pat dry. Slice into thin strips, then cut the strips into 1- or 2-inch lengths.

Blanch the fava beans for 30 seconds, no longer, drain, and transfer to a bowl of cold water. Slip the beans out of their thick skins, and place in a bowl.

Heat the olive oil in a heavy-bottomed lidded skillet and gently sauté the garlic until golden, about 2 minutes. Add the fava beans and red peppers and stir together over medium heat for about 2 minutes. Add the wine and the thyme, cover, and turn heat to low. Simmer 5 to 8 minutes (I like them slightly crunchy and bright green; after they've cooked 5 minutes their color dulls and they become quite soft). Add salt and freshly ground pepper to taste, stir in the lemon juice, and serve.

PER PORTION:

Calories	179	Protein	9 G
Fat	7 G	Carbohydrate	21 G
Sodium	6 MG	Cholesterol	0

FRESH FAVA BEANS SIMMERED IN WINE

MAKES 4 SERVINGS

Broad beans, or fava beans, are popular throughout the Mediterranean. A ritual springtime *Provençal* hors d'oeuvre is young and tender fava beans, eaten raw, accompanied by thin slices of sausage and red wine. You sit around, enjoying the sunshine, the wine, and the company, and pop the beans out of their skins and into your mouth.

2½ pounds unshelled fresh fava beans
    salt
1 tablespoon olive oil
1 onion, minced
2 garlic cloves, minced or put through a press
    a few lettuce leaves, cut into *chiffonade*
½ cup dry white wine
    salt and freshly ground pepper

Remove the beans from the pods. Bring a pot of water to a boil, add salt, and drop in the beans. Boil for 30 seconds (no longer), drain, and transfer to a bowl of cold water. Using your thumbnail to slit the outer skins, pop out the beans and set aside.

Heat the oil in a casserole or covered skillet and sauté the onion over medium-low heat for 5 minutes or until tender. Add the garlic, beans, and lettuce, cover, and cook, stirring often, for 10 minutes. Add the wine, cover, and cook 10 minutes or until the beans are tender. Season to taste with salt and pepper and serve.

PER PORTION:

Calories	127	Protein	7 G
Fat	4 G	Carbohydrate	17 G
Sodium	6 MG	Cholesterol	0

CÉLERI AU CUMIN

MAKES 4 SERVINGS

I'd never thought of making a vegetable dish out of celery alone until a Tunisian friend gave me this recipe. The cumin, lemon, and celery make a delicious combination.

>   juice of 2 lemons
> 1   tablespoon olive oil
> 1   pound (1 head) celery, washed and sliced on the
>   diagonal, leaves discarded
> 3   tablespoons water
> ¾   tablespoon ground cumin
>   pinch salt
>   freshly ground pepper
>   minced fresh parsley for garnish

Heat the lemon juice and olive oil in a heavy-bottomed lidded casserole. Add the remaining ingredients except parsley, stir together well, cover, and simmer over low heat for 20 to 30 minutes, until done to your taste—after 20 minutes, the celery will still be a little crisp.

Remove from the heat, transfer to a bowl, and chill several hours. Sprinkle with parsley and serve. The celery can be kept for a day in the refrigerator and reheated.

PER PORTION

Calories	53	Protein	1 G
Fat	4 G	Carbohydrate	6 G
Sodium	123 MG	Cholesterol	0

EGG DISHES

COUCOU À L'IRANIENNE
(*Iranian Omelet with Parsley and Mint*)

MAKES 10 SERVINGS

A *coucou* is the Iranian version of a flat omelet, like a *tortilla Española*. This one is filled with a garden of parsley and mint and contains pine nuts, currants, and a little saffron. I've had *coucous* with other herbs, notably fresh chervil, and they are marvelous with the fresh soft walnuts you can buy in the fall. The eggs just barely set, and the herbs remain crunchy and fragrant. The omelet is even better served cold, a day later; the herbs hold their color and texture, so it makes great picnic fare. This version, using 18 eggs, makes a very large omelet, enough to serve 5 or 6 people at one meal and again for lunch the next day.

It's important to mix together the eggs and filling ingredients an hour or more before you cook the *coucou*. This gives the herbs time to swell—and don't chop them too fine. Accompany with a big green salad.

You can cut the quantities in half and use a smaller frying pan if you want a smaller *coucou*.

    2   large bunches parsley (about 2 to 3 cups), stems
            removed
    1   large bunch mint (1 to 1½ cups), stems removed
   18   large eggs
   ¼   cup pine nuts
   ¼   cup dried currants
        salt and freshly ground pepper
   ¼   teaspoon powdered saffron
    1   tablespoon olive oil

Wash and dry the herbs. Chop them coarsely with a knife, not in a machine (you don't want them so fine that they don't absorb the egg and swell).

Beat the eggs in a large bowl. Mix in the herbs, pine nuts, and currants, salt and pepper to taste, and saffron; cover and set aside for 1 to 2 hours in a cool place. If you store it in the refrigerator, bring to room temperature before cooking.

To cook, heat a deep, wide lidded nonstick frying pan over medium-low heat and add the olive oil. Stir the egg mixture briskly and pour into the pan. Turn the flame to low and cook, lifting the edges and turning the pan until the omelet cooks on the bottom, like a Spanish omelet. Cover the pan, place on a Flame-Tamer or asbestos pad if the flame seems too high (you don't want the bottom of the omelet to stick and burn before it's cooked through), and cook 20 minutes or until set but still a little runny on the top.

Bring to the table and serve in wedges; pass salt and peppermill. Serve a big green salad on the side. Leftovers will keep two days in the refrigerator.

PER PORTION:

Calories	189	Protein	12 G
Fat	13 G	Carbohydrate	6 G
Sodium	130 MG	Cholesterol	493 MG

BAKED TUNISIAN EGGAH

MAKES 4 TO 6 SERVINGS

The *eggah* is a Tunisian version of a Spanish omelet, but it's baked, like a quiche. It makes a nice, fragrant luncheon dish or light supper.

- 1 tablespoon olive oil
- 1 onion, thinly sliced
- 4 garlic cloves, thinly sliced
- 1 green pepper, seeded and thinly sliced
- 1 red pepper, seeded and thinly sliced
- 2 zucchini, sliced about ¼ inch thick
- 1 pound (4 to 5) ripe tomatoes, peeled and cut into wedges
- ⅛ to ¼ teaspoon cayenne pepper (to taste)
- ¾ teaspoon ground cumin
- ½ teaspoon ground coriander
- ½ teaspoon ground cinnamon
  sea salt and freshly ground pepper
- 6 eggs
- 4 tablespoons chopped fresh parsley

Heat the olive oil in a large heavy-bottomed lidded frying pan or casserole and add the onion and garlic. Sauté gently until the onion begins to soften. Add the green and red peppers and continue to sauté 5 minutes, stirring. Add the zucchini and continue to sauté 5 minutes. Stir in the tomatoes, spices, and sea salt and pepper to taste. Stir together, cover, and reduce heat. Simmer gently for 20 minutes or until the vegetables are cooked through and fragrant. If they begin to stick to the bottom of the pan, add a little water. Correct seasonings and remove from the heat.

Meanwhile, preheat the oven to 350 degrees and oil a baking dish large enough to accommodate the vegetables and eggs.

Beat the eggs in a large bowl and add the parsley. Stir in the vegetable mixture, correct seasonings again, and turn into the prepared baking dish. Cover and bake 30 minutes. Remove the cover and bake another 10 minutes or until the top is nicely browned and the eggs set. Serve at once, or allow it to cool and serve, cut into squares, as an appetizer. The *eggah* will keep a day or two in the refrigerator.

PER PORTION:

Calories	136	Protein	8 G
Fat	8 G	Carbohydrate	9 G
Sodium	79 MG	Cholesterol	274 MG

CHAPTER EIGHT

DESSERTS

Naturally, most of these refreshing desserts are inspired by the bounty of fresh fruits that grow in Mediterranean countries. Traditional sweets from these countries tend to be cloying and rich, but with all that gorgeous fruit, who needs them?

As I write I can smell the fresh peaches in a summer market in Provence. I have bought them by the case and watched them disappear quickly into fruit salads and tarts. Into fruit salads go peaches, apricots, and currants. Sometimes dessert will be just a big bowl of perfectly ripe strawberries, astonishingly sweet.

Another fruit that comes to mind at once is the fig, one of the most sensuous of foods. Figs are everywhere in the Mediterranean, where they begin to ripen in August and last through October. Sometimes they are served as a first course, with melon and Parma ham, but I prefer them for dessert, as is, or slightly poached in wine (pages 344–345).

The oranges, tangerines, and grapefruit that come from Spain, Israel, and North Africa bring sunshine and sweet, juicy desserts to my table in wintertime. All winter long we routinely pass a bowl of very sweet, seedless Moroccan or Tunisian tangerines (*clementines*) after dinner. I especially love the red-fleshed blood oranges that begin to arrive from Spain and Israel in March. Their red juice is astonishing, and their flavor is unique: more tart than other oranges, but not at all sour.

Fresh fruit is the perfect ending to a spicy or savory Mediterranean meal. You need something light, thirst-quenching and refreshing for your palate. My desserts are almost always either clean-tasting sherbets or fruit salads (the meals themselves almost always being Mediterranean in character), accompanied by *biscotti* (page 366). These crunchy cookies, made with no butter and very little sweetening, are perfect for dipping in wine and fruit marinades. When I want to serve a baked dessert, I make a very lightly sweetened tart (the diet versions are made in pizza, butterless crusts), a light *clafouti*, or a low-fat flan. My guests appreciate these finales that leave them utterly satisfied but feeling light and healthy.

Note: I use mild-flavored honey to sweeten my desserts. These are clear, light-colored honeys that don't have a strong taste that interferes with the flavors of the dish. The mildest honeys are clover and acacia. If you can't find these, and can find only darker honeys (even orange blossom, which isn't too dark, is too strong), substitute sugar or unrefined sugar for the honey called for in the recipes.

FIGS

Figs, to me, are the most sumptuous of fruits. I love all the varieties, the leaf-green ones that are pink and juicy on the inside, the dark red and deep black ones that explode with ripeness, the small figs and the large ones. They are everywhere in Mediterranean markets, piled into enticing pyramids, and the trees they grow on seem to be everywhere too.

They begin to ripen in Mediterranean countries around the middle of August and continue to abound through the middle of October. When I think of figs, I remember a lone fig tree on a dirt road in Provence on the way to a hill town about two miles from the house where I was staying. Every morning I would walk up to the town, stopping at the fig tree for a juicy breakfast on the way up and on the way back. I can still taste the fruit, and every time I buy a fig now my spirit returns to that tree.

I make fig tarts and compotes, bake them, and marinate them. But my greatest pleasure is eating them as is, when they are perfectly ripe. I've been taught to eat figs from a plate with a fork and knife, with or without the skin, but my favorite way is just to pick up a fig, open it up at the bulbous end, and eat the fruit away from the skin, leaving the skin. A Frenchman told me some time ago that this is the way a fig should be eaten, so I do it this way.

In Greece, figs are often eaten with yogurt. This too is delicious. A fig and yogurt dessert would include perhaps 3 figs per person and about ½ cup of plain low-fat yogurt, garnished with a little fresh mint. Mash some of the fruit into the yogurt, sprinkle with a little mint, and you will have a feast for dessert. Other recipes follow.

FRESH FIGS POACHED IN WINE

MAKES 4 SERVINGS

Here figs are poached in a mixture of red wine, honey, and cinnamon, then removed from the wine, and the wine is strained and reduced by about a third. The figs can then sit all day.

> 2 cups red wine, not too full-bodied
> 4 tablespoons mild-flavored honey (such as clover or
>   acacia)
> ½ teaspoon ground cinnamon (more to taste)
> ½ teaspoon vanilla extract
> 1 pound ripe fresh figs
> ½ to 1 cup plain low-fat yogurt

Combine the wine, honey, cinnamon, and vanilla and bring to a boil in a large heavy-bottomed saucepan. Meanwhile, make a lengthwise incision in each fig, but do not cut them in half all the way. The inside as well as the outside will now become infused with the heady, spicy wine and honey mixture.

Turn the wine to a simmer and drop in the figs. If they are very ripe, turn off the heat immediately and infuse for 5 to 10 minutes. If they are slightly hard, poach for 15 minutes. Carefully remove the figs from the wine with a slotted spoon and place in a flat baking dish. Strain the wine through a fine sieve and return to the pot. Bring to a boil and reduce by about a third. Pour over the figs. Allow to cool and serve, topped with a generous dollop of yogurt, or serve warm.

PER PORTION:

Calories	187	Protein	3 G
Fat	.99 G	Carbohydrate	45 G
Sodium	38 MG	Cholesterol	3 MG

FIGS POACHED IN MADEIRA

MAKES 4 SERVINGS

Nothing could be more Mediterranean than these two ingredients. When you simmer the Madeira, the fattening alcohol evaporates.

1 ½ cups Madeira
  1 pound fresh figs, cut in half
  1 tablespoon mild-flavored honey (such as clover or
        acacia)

Bring the Madeira to a simmer and simmer 5 minutes. Add the figs, simmer 5 to 10 minutes (5 minutes only if very ripe), and remove from the heat. Allow to cool in the wine and serve at room temperature or chilled.

PER PORTION:

Calories	143	Protein	1 G
Fat	.34 G	Carbohydrate	37 G
Sodium	9 MG	Cholesterol	0

PEACHES, APRICOTS, PLUMS, AND NECTARINES

NECTARINE GRANITA

MAKES 4 TO 6 SERVINGS

A *granita* is a fruit ice, made here by just pureeing the fruit with a very small amount of sweetening, folding in an egg white, and freezing until not quite solid. You break up the *granita* a few times with a fork or in a food processor during the freezing process so that it won't have too many ice crystals.

2 pounds (8 to 10) ripe, juicy nectarines
1 tablespoon mild-flavored honey (such as clover or
   acacia) or sugar
3 tablespoons fresh lemon juice
⅛ teaspoon almond extract
¼ teaspoon vanilla extract
1 egg white

Blanch the nectarines and remove the skins. Pit and cut into quarters. Puree in a food processor or blender and blend in the honey or sugar, lemon juice, almond extract, and vanilla extract.

Beat the egg white until it forms stiff peaks. Quickly beat into the nectarine puree. Transfer to a stainless steel bowl or ice trays without the dividers, cover, and place in the freezer. Every 2 to 3 hours, break up the *granita* with a fork or a food processor and return to the freezer. It should not be frozen solid when you serve it, but should break apart easily.

PER PORTION:

Calories	84	Protein	2 G
Fat	.63 G	Carbohydrate	20 G
Sodium	9 MG	Cholesterol	0

PEACH CREAM

MAKES 6 SERVINGS

How could something so creamy contain no cream? This silky dessert, just whipped peaches and an egg, is as light as a feather. It has the texture of a slightly thickened puree; you can make it up to 2 hours before you wish to serve.

- 2 pounds (8 to 10) ripe peaches
- 1 to 2 tablespoons fresh lemon juice (to taste)
- ¼ teaspoon almond extract
- ½ teaspoon vanilla extract
- 1 to 2 tablespoons mild-flavored honey (such as clover or acacia) (to taste)
- 1 egg

Drop the peaches into boiling water for 20 seconds and refresh under cold water. Remove the skins and cut peaches into quarters. Puree in a food processor or blender along with the lemon juice, almond extract, and vanilla extract. Transfer to a heavy-bottomed saucepan and add the honey. Heat through, stirring, until the mixture begins to simmer. Stir for about 5 minutes, being careful that the puree doesn't stick to the bottom of the pan. Remove from the heat and allow to cool for about 15 minutes.

Beat the egg in a bowl and stir into the puree. Return to the heat and heat through over low heat, stirring constantly, for about 3 to 5 minutes. Do not allow the mixture to come to a boil, or the egg will curdle. Transfer to individual cups or small bowls, cover, and refrigerate for an hour or two.

APRICOT CREAM

Substitute 2 pounds (8 to 10) apricots for the peaches. Do not peel.

PER PORTION:

Calories	81	Protein	2 G
Fat	1 G	Carbohydrate	18 G
Sodium	12 MG	Cholesterol	46 MG

PEACH-YOGURT SHERBET

MAKES 4 SERVINGS

This sherbet tastes rich, but it's actually very low in fat, thanks to the yogurt. The sweetening here comes from the banana, a very small amount of honey, and the natural sweetness of the peaches.

- 1 pound (4 to 5) ripe peaches
- 1 small medium-ripe banana
- 1 cup plain low-fat yogurt
- 1 tablespoon mild-flavored honey (such as clover or acacia)
- 2 teaspoons vanilla extract
  freshly grated nutmeg (optional)

Blanch the peaches in boiling water for 20 seconds. Refresh under cold water and remove the skins. Remove the pits and slice. Peel and slice the banana. Freeze the fruit in plastic bags. When frozen solid, remove from the freezer and pound to break into chunks.

Place the yogurt, honey, and vanilla in a food processor. Add the frozen fruit. Using the pulse action, process until the fruit is mashed. Then turn on the processor and blend until you have a smooth puree. Add nutmeg, if you wish, and serve. Or return to the freezer until ready to serve. If the mixture freezes solid, allow to soften for 30 minutes in the refrigerator before serving. The sherbet will keep for several weeks in the freezer.

PER PORTION:

Calories	117	Protein	4 G
Fat	1 G	Carbohydrate	24 G
Sodium	40 MG	Cholesterol	3 MG

BAKED PEACH COMPOTE

MAKES 6 SERVINGS

I've always loved the taste of baked peaches, especially peach pie. This dessert has everything delicious about peach pie, but without the fattening crust.

> 3 pounds (12 to 15) peaches
> 2 tablespoons fresh lemon juice
> 2 tablespoons mild-flavored honey (such as clover or
>   acacia)
> ½ teaspoon ground cinnamon
> ½ teaspoon freshly grated nutmeg
> ½ teaspoon vanilla extract

Preheat the oven to 350 degrees. Lightly butter a 2-quart baking dish.

Blanch the peaches in boiling water for 20 seconds. Refresh under cold water and remove the skins. Pit and slice. Toss with the remaining ingredients in the baking dish. Bake in the preheated oven for 45 minutes to an hour. Serve warm or at room temperature. The compote will keep for several days in the refrigerator.

PER PORTION:

Calories	100	Protein	1 G
Fat	.22 G	Carbohydrate	26 G
Sodium	0	Cholesterol	0

PEACH SOUP

MAKES 6 SERVINGS

This creamy peach soup can be a starter or light lunch as well as a dessert.

  3   pounds (12 to 15) unpeeled ripe peaches
  2   tablespoons mild-flavored honey (such as clover or
        acacia)
  3   tablespoons fresh lemon juice
  2   cups plain low-fat yogurt
  1   cup fresh orange juice
  ½   teaspoon vanilla extract
  ½   teaspoon ground cinnamon
  ½   teaspoon freshly grated nutmeg
  ¼   teaspoon ground cardamom

Set aside 4 of the peaches. Remove the pits from the remaining peaches and puree in a blender or food processor along with the honey and lemon juice. Transfer to a bowl and whisk in the yogurt, orange juice, vanilla, and spices. Slice the remaining peaches and add to the soup. Chill until ready to serve. The soup will keep for a few days in the refrigerator.

PER PORTION:

Calories	167	Protein	5 G
Fat	1 G	Carbohydrate	36 G
Sodium	54 MG	Cholesterol	5 MG

PEACHES IN RED WINE WITH HONEY AND CINNAMON

MAKES 6 SERVINGS

This compote is very easy to make. The wine is brought to a simmer, then spiced with cinnamon and sweetened with a bit of honey and vanilla. The peaches sweeten the wine a little more and also absorb some of the wine. It's a mouth-watering combination and a very refreshing dessert. Serve it well chilled, from a glass bowl, on a hot summer day. To serve this dish during winter, use thawed frozen peaches.

6 firm ripe peaches *or* 1½ pounds thawed frozen
    peaches
1½ cups full-bodied red wine (such as Côtes du Rhône or
    Barolo)
2 to 3 tablespoons mild-flavored honey (such as clover
    or acacia) (to taste)
½ teaspoon ground cinnamon (more to taste)
1 teaspoon vanilla extract
    fresh mint for garnish

Blanch the peaches in boiling water for 20 seconds, refresh under cold water, and remove their skins.

Heat the wine to a simmer and remove from the heat. Stir in the honey, cinnamon, and vanilla. Pour into a bowl and slice in the peaches. Refrigerate for several hours. Serve cold, garnished with fresh mint. The peaches will keep for a day in the refrigerator.

PER PORTION:

Calories	91	Protein	1 G
Fat	.11 G	Carbohydrate	23 G
Sodium	3 MG	Cholesterol	0

PEACHES AND APRICOTS WITH CURRANTS

MAKES 4 TO 6 SERVINGS

This is a dessert my friend Christine Picasso often serves in the summer.

juice of 1 lemon
1 tablespoon mild-flavored honey (such as clover or
    acacia)
4 to 6 unpeeled ripe peaches, sliced
4 to 6 unpeeled ripe apricots, sliced
2 tablespoons dried currants

Mix together the lemon juice and honey. Toss with the peaches, apricots, and currants. Chill for an hour or more and serve. The dessert will keep for 2 days in the refrigerator.

PER PORTION:

Calories	82	Protein	1 G
Fat	.20 G	Carbohydrate	21 G
Sodium	1 MG	Cholesterol	0

BAKED PLUM COMPOTE

MAKES 6 SERVINGS

Late August and early September are plum months in France, where the markets abound with multicolored piles of greengages, little yellow *mirabelles*, small deep-purple *quetsches*, and larger, red-purple plums. Each has a distinctive flavor, and I love to experiment with them, making new desserts. This easy-to-make, warm, sweet/tart compote is one of my favorites. When you bake the plums, they become sweet and syrupy all on their own. The only added sweetener is a little honey and *cassis*.

3 pounds mixed plums, halved and pitted
2 tablespoons mild-flavored honey (such as clover or
    acacia)
1 tablespoon *crème de cassis*

Preheat the oven to 350 degrees. Lightly butter a baking dish large enough to hold all the plums. Toss the plums in the dish together with the honey and *cassis*. Bake in the preheated oven for 45 minutes to an hour. Serve hot, warm, or cooled. The compote will keep about 3 days in the refrigerator.

PER PORTION:

Calories	149	Protein	2 G
Fat	2 G	Carbohydrate	35 G
Sodium	0	Cholesterol	0

FRUIT SOUP

MAKES 4 TO 6 SERVINGS

This is a refreshing summer compote, delicious hot or cold.

- 1 pound (4 to 5) peaches
- 1 pound (4 to 5) nectarines
- 2 pounds (4 to 5) plums (use several varieties if available)
- 1 pound strawberries, hulled
- 3 cups water
  juice of 1 large lemon (more to taste)
- 2 tablespoons mild-flavored honey (such as clover or acacia)
- 1 tablespoon tapioca
  chopped fresh mint for garnish

Blanch the peaches in boiling water for 20 seconds, refresh under cold water, and remove skins. Pit and slice. Pit and slice the nectarines and plums; cut the strawberries in half. Combine fruit with the water, lemon juice, and honey; bring to a simmer, cover, and simmer 15 minutes. Stir in the tapioca and continue to cook, stirring, until the mixture thickens. Remove from the heat. Serve hot or chill and serve cold, garnished with chopped fresh mint. The compote will keep a couple of days in the refrigerator.

PER PORTION:

Calories	187	Protein	3 G
Fat	2 G	Carbohydrate	46 G
Sodium	1 MG	Cholesterol	0

BERRIES

STRAWBERRY SHERBET

MAKES 4 TO 6 SERVINGS

This sherbet is very simple and light. The *crème de cassis* brings out the sweet flavor of the strawberries.

- 1 ½ pounds (2 pints) strawberries, hulled
- 2 tablespoons *crème de cassis*
- 1 tablespoon mild-flavored honey (such as clover or acacia)
- 3 to 4 tablespoons fresh lemon juice (to taste)
  fresh mint for garnish

Puree all the ingredients except mint in a blender or food processor until smooth. Freeze in an ice cream freezer or *sorbetière* or in a covered bowl. If you are freezing in a covered bowl, blend the mixture two more times before it freezes solid, to break up the ice crystals. Allow to soften for 15 to 20 minutes in the refrigerator before serving. Garnish with fresh mint. The sherbet will keep for several weeks in the freezer.

PER PORTION:

Calories	66	Protein	1 G
Fat	.40 G	Carbohydrate	13 G
Sodium	2 MG	Cholesterol	0

STRAWBERRY SOUP

MAKES 4 TO 6 SERVINGS

This is a simple *concassé* of strawberries: in other words, the berries are crushed (not pureed) and mixed with orange juice, honey, and *crème de cassis*. Into this mixture go whole or halved strawberries that have been marinated in lemon juice and honey to bring out their sweetness and flavor. It's essential to find sweet, ripe red strawberries.

> 2 pounds (2½ pints) ripe strawberries, hulled
>   juice of 1 lemon
> 2 tablespoons mild-flavored honey (such as clover
>   or acacia)
>   juice of 1 orange
> 1 tablespoon *crème de cassis*
> 2 tablespoons chopped fresh mint
>   fresh mint leaves for garnish

Divide the berries in half according to their appearance, including all crushed berries in the batch of less attractive berries. You will use this one for the *concassé*.

Cut the large berries in the prettier batch into halves or quarters and toss them with the lemon juice and 1 tablespoon honey, or more to taste. Cover and refrigerate.

Place the remaining strawberries in the bowl of your mixer or in a large bowl. Using the mixing beater, a fork, or a pestle, crush the berries to a coarse puree. Beat in the orange juice, *crème de cassis*, and 1 tablespoon honey, or more to taste. Set aside until ready to serve. This can be done hours in advance and stored in the refrigerator.

Just before serving, stir the mint into the *concassé*. To serve, ladle a generous portion of the *concassé* into each bowl. Give the whole strawberries a toss and add them to each serving. Garnish with fresh mint leaves and serve.

PER PORTION:

Calories	82	Protein	1 G
Fat	.54 G	Carbohydrate	19 G
Sodium	2 MG	Cholesterol	0

STRAWBERRIES IN ORANGE JUICE

MAKES 4 SERVINGS

This looks beautiful in a big glass bowl, and no dessert could be simpler.

    1 pound (1½ pints) fresh strawberries, hulled and cut in
        half
    2 cups fresh orange juice
    1 tablespoon chopped fresh mint

Separate about one quarter of the strawberries and crush with a fork. Mix the crushed and uncrushed strawberries with the orange juice. Chill until ready to serve and toss with the mint just before serving. The strawberries will hold for a few hours in the refrigerator.

PER PORTION:

Calories	88	Protein	2 G
Fat	.63 G	Carbohydrate	20 G
Sodium	2 MG	Cholesterol	0

STRAWBERRY-YOGURT SHERBET

MAKES 4 SERVINGS

This sherbet is slightly creamier than the sherbet on page 354 because of the added yogurt and banana. The banana adds sweetness and rich texture.

    1 pound (1½ pints) ripe strawberries, hulled
    1 small ripe banana, sliced
    2 tablespoons crème de cassis
    1 tablespoon mild-flavored honey (such as clover or acacia)
    1 to 2 tablespoons fresh lemon juice (to taste)
    ½ cup plain low-fat yogurt

Freeze the strawberries and sliced banana in plastic bags. Remove from the freezer and pound the bag to separate the strawberries and banana slices if they are stuck together. Place the strawberries and banana slices in a food processor with the other ingredients. Pulse on and off until the berries are mashed, then puree until you have a smooth ice. Serve at once or store in the freezer until ready to serve. If you store in the freezer until it freezes solid, allow to soften in the refrigerator for 30 minutes before serving. The sherbet will keep several weeks in the freezer.

PER PORTION:

Calories	119	Protein	2 G
Fat	.94 G	Carbohydrate	23 G
Sodium	22 MG	Cholesterol	2 MG

STRAWBERRIES WITH CASSIS, BALSAMIC VINEGAR, AND MINT

MAKES 4 SERVINGS

This is an ingenious Italian dessert. The surprising splash of balsamic vinegar, which has a slightly sweet, rich flavor, both contrasts with the strawberries and brings out their sweetness.

1 pound (1½ pints) strawberries
2 tablespoons *crème de cassis*
1 tablespoon balsamic vinegar
6 large mint leaves, cut into slivers

Rinse the strawberries, hull, and cut large berries in half.
Toss the strawberries with the *crème de cassis* and refrigerate, covered, for 1 hour or more.
Just before serving, toss with the balsamic vinegar and the mint.

PER PORTION:

Calories	65	Protein	1 G
Fat	.43 G	Carbohydrate	11 G
Sodium	2 MG	Cholesterol	0

STRAWBERRIES AND ORANGES WITH COINTREAU AND MINT

MAKES 6 SERVINGS

The colors here are gorgeous, like the red and orange tulips that come into Mediterranean markets in the springtime, about the same time that strawberries begin to appear. I like to use the blood oranges that come from North Africa and Israel, as well as navel oranges, for this salad. The blood oranges are tart and dark red, the navels sweet and bright orange.

1 pound ripe strawberries, hulled and quartered or halved
1 tablespoon mild-flavored honey (such as clover or acacia)
  juice of 2 oranges
4 navel oranges *or* 2 blood oranges and 3 navels, peeled, white pith removed, cut into wedges
2 tablespoons Cointreau
3 tablespoons chopped fresh mint

Toss the strawberries with the honey and orange juice. Cover and refrigerate for at least 1 hour.

Toss together the strawberries, oranges, Cointreau, and mint. Refrigerate until ready to serve. The dessert will hold for a few hours.

PER PORTION:

Calories	102	Protein	2 G
Fat	.39 G	Carbohydrate	23 G
Sodium	2 MG	Cholesterol	0

STRAWBERRIES WITH FRESH MINT AND ORANGE JUICE CRÈME ANGLAISE

MAKES 6 SERVINGS

Every time I serve this dessert guests are astonished and pleased by the simple, delicious combination. All of the ingredients blend together perfectly: the strawberries, the rich-tasting but light *crème Anglaise* made with orange juice instead of milk, and the fresh mint.

> 3 pints (2¼ pounds) strawberries, washed and hulled
>   juice of 1 lemon
> 2 tablespoons slivered fresh mint leaves
> 1 recipe Orange Juice *Crème Anglaise* (page 360),
>   chilled

Cut large strawberries in half, but leave the smaller ones whole. Toss with the lemon juice, cover, and chill or leave at room temperature.

Just before serving, toss the strawberries with the fresh mint.

To serve, spoon strawberries and mint, and a little juice that has gathered in the bottom of the bowl, into individual bowls, then top with the *crème Anglaise*.

PER PORTION:

Calories	128	Protein	3 G
Fat	3 G	Carbohydrate	24 G
Sodium	6 MG	Cholesterol	120 MG

ORANGE JUICE CRÈME ANGLAISE

MAKES 6 SERVINGS

This is a very light, tangy *crème Anglaise* made with orange juice instead of milk or cream. It's terrific with fruit, and nobody will ever guess how low-calorie it is.

      3 medium or large egg yolks
      2 tablespoons mild-flavored honey (such as clover or
            acacia)
  1 ½ cups fresh orange juice, strained
      ½ teaspoon vanilla extract

Beat together the egg yolks and the honey until thick and lemony. Meanwhile, heat the orange juice in a heavy-bottomed saucepan to just below simmering.

Slowly beat the hot orange juice into the egg/honey mixture. Return to the saucepan and heat very carefully over medium-low heat, stirring constantly with a wooden spoon until the mixture thickens. Be careful not to let it come to a boil, or the egg yolks will scramble.

When the *crème Anglaise* coats the front and back of a spoon like cream, remove from the heat and continue to stir for a couple of minutes. Stir in the vanilla, strain, and allow to cool. Chill if serving cold.

Note: This can be made a day ahead of serving and held in the refrigerator.

PER PORTION:

Calories	78	Protein	2 G
Fat	3 G	Carbohydrate	12 G
Sodium	5 MG	Cholesterol	120 MG

MELON

CANTALOUPE WITH PUREED APRICOTS

MAKES 6 SERVINGS

I have already written about this dish elsewhere, but I can't leave it out of a Mediterranean cookbook. The melons used in Provence, which is where I was introduced to this dish, would be small, round *Cavaillon* melons. Their flesh is the same color as, maybe a little lighter than, cantaloupe, and their flavor is similar, though usually sweeter. But cantaloupe works very well here. The pureed apricots have an intense flavor that goes very well with the subtler melon.

 1 pound ripe fresh (about 8) apricots, pitted and
      quartered
 2 tablespoons fresh lemon juice
 1 tablespoon mild-flavored honey (such as clover or
      acacia)
 ¼ teaspoon almond extract
   juice of 1 orange
 3 small ripe cantaloupes, cut in half crosswise, seeds
      removed
 4 to 6 fresh mint leaves, cut into thin slivers

Puree the apricots with the lemon juice, honey, almond extract, and orange juice in a food processor or blender. Fill the melons with the puree. Garnish with slivers of fresh mint leaves and serve, or chill and serve, garnishing at the last moment. The puree will hold for a day in the refrigerator.

PER PORTION:

Calories	123	Protein	3 G
Fat	.86 G	Carbohydrate	29 G
Sodium	19 MG	Cholesterol	0

WATERMELON, WHITE PEACHES, AND MINT

MAKES 6 SERVINGS

I'm always surprising people with this dessert. Watermelon suddenly becomes elegant when it's tossed with white peaches and mint.

> 4 cups ripe, juicy watermelon, cut into chunks or balls
> 3 or 4 white peaches (to taste), peeled or unpeeled, sliced
> 2 tablespoons slivered fresh mint leaves

Toss together the watermelon, peaches, and mint and refrigerate until ready to serve. The dessert can be made several hours ahead of serving.

PER PORTION:

Calories	67	Protein	1 G
Fat	1 G	Carbohydrate	16 G
Sodium	2 MG	Cholesterol	0

MELON BALLS WITH FRESH MINT

MAKES 4 SERVINGS

Mint brings out the flavor of fruit and adds an unexpected lift. You can mix different kinds of melon here or use just one kind.

> 1 large or 2 small ripe cantaloupe, honeydew, or Crenshaw melons, or a mixture of melons
> 2 tablespoons slivered fresh mint leaves

Scoop out the melon with a melon baller and toss with the mint. Chill until ready to serve, up to several hours.

PER PORTION:

Calories	59	Protein	1 G
Fat	.46 G	Carbohydrate	14 G
Sodium	15 MG	Cholesterol	0

OTHER FRUIT AND BAKED DESSERTS

BAKED APPLE COMPOTE

MAKES 6 SERVINGS

This spicy apple compote is a beautiful, warming fall or winter dessert. It makes a delicious breakfast dish as well.

- 2 pounds (6 to 8) apples
- 3 tablespoons fresh lemon juice
- 2 tablespoons mild-flavored honey (such as clover or acacia)
- ¼ cup unsweetened apple juice
- 1 stick cinnamon
- ½ teaspoon ground allspice
- ¼ to ½ teaspoon freshly grated nutmeg (to taste)
- ½ teaspoon vanilla extract
- 2 tablespoons dried currants
- ½ cup plain low-fat yogurt for topping (optional)

Preheat the oven to 350 degrees. Lightly butter a 2-quart baking dish.

Peel, core, and slice the apples. Toss with the lemon juice in the prepared baking dish. Add the remaining ingredients except yogurt and toss together. Bake in the preheated oven for 45 minutes to 1 hour. Serve warm or at room temperature, topped with plain low-fat yogurt. The compote will keep several days in the refrigerator.

PER PORTION:

Calories	113	Protein	0
Fat	.47 G	Carbohydrate	30 G
Sodium	1 MG	Cholesterol	0

APPLE AND RHUBARB TART

MAKES 8 TO 10 SERVINGS

After experimenting with several recipes, I finally came up with a dessert crust with a light, crisp texture and hardly any butter. It's a variation on the *Provençal* pizza crust on page 210, with the addition of a little honey, and with butter substituted for olive oil. The resulting tart is light and heavenly.

FOR THE CRUST:

1 cup whole-wheat pastry flour or unbleached white flour
¼ teaspoon salt
½ teaspoon baking powder
2 tablespoons softened unsalted butter, plus 1 ½
    teaspoons for the pan
1 tablespoon mild-flavored honey (such as clover or acacia)
¼ to ⅓ cup water (as needed)

FOR THE TOPPING:

1 pound rhubarb, sliced
  juice of 2 lemons
1 tablespoon mild-flavored honey
3 large tart apples, 1 peeled and chopped, the other 2
    peeled, quartered, and very thinly sliced
2 tablespoons water
2 teaspoons raw brown sugar
  freshly grated nutmeg

PREPARE THE CRUST:

Mix together the flour, salt, and baking powder. Cut in the butter, either in a food processor or by rubbing the flour briskly between the palms of your hands. Add the honey, mixing it into the flour/butter mixture in a food processor or with a wooden spoon. Then add the water, a little at a time, and mix in until the dough comes together in a ball. It should be neither sticky nor dry. Gently gather the dough into a ball, wrap in plastic, and set aside while you prepare the remaining ingredients. The dough can be prepared a day or two ahead of time, wrapped in plastic, and refrigerated until you are ready to roll it out.

PREPARE THE TOPPING:

Combine the sliced rhubarb, the juice of 1 of the lemons, the honey, the peeled and chopped apple, and the water in a saucepan. Bring to a simmer and cook, stirring often, for about 20 minutes or until the mixture is thick.

Toss the remaining apples with the juice of the remaining lemon.

Preheat the oven to 475 degrees. Butter a 12- or 15-inch pizza pan. Roll out the dough to an ⅛-inch thickness or thinner, dusting the surface of the dough, the work surface, and the rolling pin as you go along to prevent sticking. Line the pizza pan with the dough and pinch an attractive lip around the edge.

Spread the rhubarb over the dough in an even layer. Arrange the sliced apples over the rhubarb. Sprinkle with sugar and nutmeg.

Bake in the preheated oven for 20 minutes or until the dough is crisp and brown. Remove from the oven and serve warm or at room temperature. This dessert will keep for a day, but the crust will become soggy under the fruit.

PER PORTION:

Calories	121	Protein	1 G
Fat	3 G	Carbohydrate	23 G
Sodium	78 MG	Cholesterol	8 MG

HONEY VANILLA FLAN

MAKES 6 SERVINGS

This is a very light flan made with skimmed milk. It will keep for several days in the refrigerator. The flan is baked in a *bain-marie* to assure that it cooks evenly and doesn't burn.

2 cups skimmed milk
4 medium or large egg yolks plus 1 whole egg
2½ tablespoons mild-flavored honey (such as clover or acacia)
1½ teaspoons vanilla extract

Preheat the oven to 325 degrees.

Heat the milk until hot but not boiling. Bring a kettle of water to a boil for the *bain-marie*.

Beat the egg yolks and whole egg in a bowl with the honey and vanilla. Slowly whisk in the milk and combine well.

Pour through a sieve into a pitcher and pour into 6 individual pudding or *gratin* dishes or a low-sided baking dish. Place in a baking pan and fill the pan with boiling water halfway up the sides of the pudding dishes. Lay a sheet of aluminum foil over the top and place in the oven.

Bake 40 minutes or until just set on the edges but still a little liquidy in the middle. Remove from the heat. Allow to cool, cover, and chill, or serve warm or at room temperature. The flan will keep 3 or 4 days in the refrigerator.

GINGER HONEY FLAN

Reduce honey to 2 tablespoons. Add ½ teaspoon ground ginger and beat into the eggs before adding the milk.

PER PORTION:

Calories	108	Protein	5 G
Fat	4 G	Carbohydrate	12 G
Sodium	58 MG	Cholesterol	202 MG

HAZELNUT BISCOTTI

MAKES 50 TO 60 COOKIES

This dough becomes very stiff when you are incorporating the nuts, but with persistence you can work them all in. The cookies should be made a few days before you wish to serve them. They will keep in a well-sealed container for weeks.

    4   ounces shelled hazelnuts
    ¼   teaspoon almond extract
    2¾ cups whole-wheat pastry flour or unbleached white
            flour
    ¼   teaspoon salt
    ½   teaspoon baking soda
    2   eggs
    ⅓   cup mild-flavored honey (such as clover or acacia)
    1   egg white

Preheat the oven to 375 degrees. Place the hazelnuts on a baking sheet and roast for about 15 minutes, until lightly golden and toasty-smelling. Remove from the heat. Roll the hazelnuts between your hand and the baking sheet to remove the bitter skins. Discard skins and put the baking sheet aside. Chop medium-fine and set aside.

In a mixer or a large bowl, blend together the eggs, honey, and almond extract. Mix in 2⅓ cups flour, the salt, and the baking soda. When all the ingredients are mixed together, place the remaining flour on a work surface, remove the dough from the bowl and knead for 10 to 15 minutes, dusting the kneading surface when necessary. The dough will be stiff. (The ingredients can also be mixed together like pasta; place 2⅓ cups of flour in a mound on a board and make a well in the center. Break in the eggs, add salt, baking soda, and the honey. Beat together with a fork, then mix in the flour, little by little. Gather into a ball and knead as above.)

Now incorporate the chopped nuts into the dough. This will seem difficult at first because the dough is so stiff. The easiest way to do this is to press the dough out flat, add a handful of hazelnuts, fold and knead a few minutes, then press out again and continue with this procedure until all the nuts have been added. You will get a good workout.

Divide the dough in half and shape into 2 long logs, about 2 inches in diameter. Flour the reserved baking sheet and place the *biscotti* on it, not too close to one another. Beat the egg white until foamy and brush it over the logs. Bake in the 375-degree oven for 20 minutes, until golden brown and shiny. Remove from the oven and turn down the heat to 275 degrees.

Cut the logs into thin slices, about ¼ to ½ inch thick, at a 45-degree angle (use a bread knife or a sharp chef's knife). Place the cookies on the baking sheet (or 2 baking sheets) and bake again for about 40 minutes in the 275-degree oven, until dry and hard. Remove from the heat and cool. Keep in a covered container. These last a long time.

PER COOKIE:

Calories	40	Protein	1 G
Fat	1 G	Carbohydrate	6 G
Sodium	19 MG	Cholesterol	9 MG

ORANGES WITH MINT

MAKES 4 SERVINGS

This is simple, light, and refreshing, especially after a spicy meal.

    4 large navel oranges
    2 tablespoons chopped fresh mint
    1 tablespoon Grand Marnier (optional)

Peel the oranges by holding a small knife against the skin at an angle and rotating the orange against the knife so that the skin comes off in a spiral and the white pith comes off with it. Hold the oranges above a bowl as you do this so that you can catch the juice. Remove the sections by cutting them out from between the membranes, again holding the oranges right over the bowl. Toss with the mint and the Grand Marnier if desired and chill until ready to serve, up to several hours.

PER PORTION:

Calories	81	Protein	2 G
Fat	.15 G	Carbohydrate	20 G
Sodium	2 MG	Cholesterol	0

PEAR GINGER FLAN

MAKES 6 SERVINGS

This is much like the honey vanilla flan on page 365, with the luscious addition of pears that have been marinated in a mixture of *eau-de-vie*, lemon juice, and honey.

FOR THE PEARS:
    1 tablespoon mild-flavored honey (such as clover or
        acacia)
      juice of ½ large lemon
    3 tablespoons *eau-de-vie* (Poire William or kirsch)
 1½ pounds firm ripe pears, peeled, cored, and sliced

FOR THE FLAN:

    1 ½ cups milk

    4 egg yolks plus 1 whole egg

    2 tablespoons mild-flavored honey (such as clover or
        acacia)

    1 ½ teaspoons vanilla extract

    ½ teaspoon ground ginger

    6 tablespoons liquid from the pears
      butter for the baking dishes

PREPARE THE PEARS:

Combine the honey, lemon juice, and *eau-de-vie* and mix well. Toss with the pears and let marinate for 1 hour, tossing from time to time.

PREPARE THE FLAN:

Preheat the oven to 325 degrees. Warm the milk and bring a kettle of water to a boil.

Beat together the egg yolks, whole egg, honey, vanilla, and ginger. Pour off the liquid from the pears and measure out 6 tablespoons. Beat into the egg mixture. Slowly pour in the warm milk (make sure the milk isn't too hot, or the mixture will curdle because of the lemon juice) and mix well. Strain through a sieve.

Divide the sliced pears among 6 to 8 lightly buttered pudding dishes or small *gratin* dishes. Pour the milk mixture over the pears and place the dishes in a baking dish. Pour the boiling water into the baking dish so that it comes halfway up the sides of the pudding dishes. Place in the oven and bake 40 minutes or until set. The flan will keep a couple of days in the refrigerator.

PER PORTION:

Calories	200	Protein	5 G
Fat	7 G	Carbohydrate	30 G
Sodium	48 MG	Cholesterol	236 MG

CHERRY CLAFOUTI

MAKES 6 TO 8 SERVINGS

A *clafouti* is a sort of cross between a flan and a fruit-filled pancake. June is cherry season in Provence, and this is one of many desserts we make with them.

    1   tablespoon butter for the baking dish
    1   pound black cherries
1 ¼   cups milk
    4   tablespoons mild-flavored honey (such as clover or
            acacia)
    3   eggs
    1   tablespoon vanilla extract
        pinch salt
 ½   cup sifted unbleached white flour

Preheat the oven to 350 degrees. Butter a 12-inch tart pan or a 2-quart baking dish.

Pit the cherries, if you wish, above a bowl (in France they usually leave in the pits, but you might not want to deal with them when you eat the dessert). Place the pitted cherries in a separate bowl and strain off any juices from the pits; retain the juice.

In a blender or an electric mixer, blend together the milk, honey, juice from pitting the cherries, the eggs, vanilla, and salt. Add the flour and continue to blend together for 1 minute, until completely smooth.

Pour into the bowl with the cherries, mix together well, and turn into the buttered baking dish. Bake 45 minutes to 1 hour, until puffed and browned and a knife comes out clean when inserted in the center. Remove from the heat. Serve hot or warm, but not cold. The *clafouti* will fall a bit upon cooling. Leftovers can be served the next day.

PER PORTION:

Calories	166	Protein	5 G
Fat	5 G	Carbohydrate	25 G
Sodium	76 MG	Cholesterol	112 MG

CHAPTER NINE

MENUS FOR ENTERTAINING AND FAMILY DINING

The menus in this chapter are divided into two sections: menus for entertaining and simpler menus for everyday dining. The menus in the first section are slightly more elaborate than those in the second part; they contain one or two more courses.

The menus for everyday family dining are meant only as suggestions. I often make a meal of a salad alone or of two or three of the salads and starters in Chapter Two. When we have pasta or soup, usually the only accompaniments are salad, bread, and fruit for dessert. We tend to eat late at our house—sometimes I don't even think about dinner before seven—so we want to keep it light and simple.

Accompany all of these menus with the bread of your choice from Chapter One.

ENTERTAINING—
SPRING AND SUMMER MENUS

RATATOUILLE (PAGE 66)
GRILLED RED MULLET WITH LIGHT
TOMATO SAUCE (PAGE 276)
GRATED POTATO TORTE WITH ONIONS (PAGE 318)
SIMPLE GREEN SALAD
CHERRY CLAFOUTI (PAGE 370)

ITALIAN HORS D'OEUVRE PLATE:
CROSTINI WITH SWEET RED PEPPERS (PAGE 53)
GRILLED SARDINES WITH LEMON (PAGE 65)
BROILED ZUCCHINI WITH LEMON, BASIL,
AND HOT PEPPER (PAGE 62)
SPRINGTIME MINESTRONE WITH BASIL (PAGE 128)
STRAWBERRIES WITH CASSIS, BALSAMIC
VINEGAR, AND MINT (PAGE 357)

CACIK (PAGE 102)
PILAKI (PAGE 104)
MIDDLE EASTERN SHRIMP WITH CUMIN (PAGE 296)
BASMATI RICE
BAKED TOMATOES (PAGE 327 OR 328)
STRAWBERRIES AND ORANGES WITH
COINTREAU AND MINT (PAGE 358)

GAZPACHO ANDALUZ (PAGE 156)
FUSILLI WITH ARTICHOKES AND
PORCINI MUSHROOMS (PAGE 180)
SPICY ITALIAN-STYLE BROCCOLI (PAGE 316)
NECTARINE GRANITA (PAGE 346)

PASTA CON SARDE (PAGE 174)
BAKED TOMATOES (PAGE 327 OR 328)
MIXED GREEN SALAD
MELON BALLS WITH FRESH MINT (PAGE 362)

CARTA DI MUSICA WITH SALSA CRUDA (PAGE 56)
MARINATED EGGPLANT (PAGE 61)
RABBIT COOKED IN WINE, WITH CAPERS
AND TOMATOES (PAGE 308)
SPINACH FETTUCCINE (PAGE 185 or PAGE 187)
STRAWBERRY SHERBET (PAGE 354)

ZUCCHINI MARINATA (PAGE 64)
ROASTED SWEET RED PEPPERS (PAGE 69)
GRILLED SWORDFISH WITH CAPERS, LEMON,
AND GARLIC (PAGE 281)
BAKED POTATOES WITH FENNEL (PAGE 319)
PEACHES AND APRICOTS WITH CURRANTS (PAGE 352)

ARTICHOKES À LA BARIGOULE (PAGE 68)
PROVENÇAL CHICKEN AND GARLIC,
COOKED IN ROSÉ WINE (PAGE 302)
FRESH SPINACH PASTA (PAGE 172)
OR STEAMED NEW POTATOES
TOSSED GREEN SALAD
BAKED PEACH COMPOTE (PAGE 349)

PISSALADIÈRE (PAGE 2 1 2)
TUNA À LA MARSEILLAISE (PAGE 2 8 5)
STEAMED NEW POTATOES OR FRESH
SPINACH PASTA (PAGE 1 7 2)
TOSSED GREEN SALAD
CANTALOUPE WITH PUREED APRICOTS (PAGE 3 6 1)

CHILLED YOGURT/CUCUMBER SOUP (PAGE 1 5 7)
GRILLED MACKEREL WITH CUMIN (PAGE 2 7 8)
PROVENÇAL TOMATO AND PEPPER TIAN (PAGE 3 2 6)
RICE PILAF WITH CUMIN OR CURRY (PAGE 2 3 3)
PEACHES AND APRICOTS WITH CURRANTS (PAGE 3 5 2)

CROSTINI WITH SWEET RED PEPPERS (PAGE 5 3)
TUNA CARPACCIO (PAGE 2 8 7)
SICILIAN PIZZA (PAGE 2 0 6)
TOSSED GREEN SALAD
STRAWBERRY SOUP (PAGE 3 5 5)

WHITE BEAN SOUP WITH TOMATOES,
ZUCCHINI, AND BASIL (PAGE 1 3 1)
BAKED FISH EN PAPILLOTE WITH
VEGETABLE JULIENNE (PAGE 2 9 3)
RICE
TOSSED GREEN SALAD
STRAWBERRIES WITH CASSIS, BALSAMIC
VINEGAR, AND MINT (PAGE 3 5 7)

LATE SUMMER AND EARLY FALL MENUS

SPINACH AND YOGURT SALAD (PAGE 103)
SPICY GRILLED SEA BASS (PAGE 280)
CORN ON THE COB
BAKED TOMATOES (PAGE 327 OR PAGE 328)
WATERMELON, WHITE PEACHES, AND MINT (PAGE 362)

GREEK SALAD PLATE:
TZATZIKI (PAGE 85)
MELITZANNA SALATA (PAGE 86)
ELLENIKI SALATA (PAGE 86)
BAKED RED SNAPPER FROM SIMI (PAGE 290)
STEAMED NEW POTATOES
FRESH FIGS

COLD MEZZE BUFFET:
FISH SALAD WITH CILANTRO AND MINT (PAGE 89)
TABOULI I OR II (PAGES 90-91)
HUMMUS (PAGE 92)
PITA BREAD (PAGE 40)
CACIK (PAGE 102)
BABA GHANOUJ (PAGE 94)
EGYPTIAN TOMATO SALAD (PAGE 100)
LABNA WITH CRUDITÉS (PAGE 97)
PEACH SOUP (PAGE 350)

FUL MEDAMES WITH PITA BREAD (PAGE 245)
ZUCCHINI AJLOUKE (PAGE 108)
FISH COUSCOUS (PAGE 220)
TOSSED GREEN SALAD
NECTARINE GRANITA (PAGE 346)

CAPONATA (PAGE 5 8)
TOSSED GREEN SALAD
PROVENÇAL FISH SOUP (PAGE 1 6 2)
STRAWBERRY SHERBET (PAGE 3 5 4)

NORTH AFRICAN SALAD PLATE:
ZUCCHINI AJLOUKE (PAGE 1 0 8)
MOROCCAN ORANGE SALAD (PAGE 1 1 9)
MOROCCAN CARROT SALAD (PAGE 1 1 8)
SAVORY CHICKEN COUSCOUS (PAGE 2 2 2) OR
COUSCOUS WITH PUMPKIN AND FAVA BEANS (PAGE 2 1 7)
MELON BALLS WITH FRESH MINT (PAGE 3 6 2)

EGYPTIAN TOMATO SALAD (PAGE 1 0 0)
FATTET WITH EGGPLANT AND DRIED MUSHROOM (PAGE 2 6 4)
CHICK-PEAS WITH SPINACH (PAGE 2 5 7)
STEAMED GREEN VEGETABLE
NECTARINE GRANITA (PAGE 3 4 6)

CAPONATA (PAGE 5 8)
FOCCACIA WITH SWEET RED PEPPERS (PAGE 3 8)
SPAGHETTI WITH MUSSELS (PAGE 1 9 2)
TOSSED GREEN SALAD
BAKED PLUM COMPOTE (PAGE 3 5 2)

FALL AND WINTER MENUS

TUNISIAN BEET AND POTATO SALAD (PAGE 115)
CHICK-PEA FATTET (PAGE 267)
ZUCCHINI À LA PROVENÇALE (PAGE 332)
PEAR GINGER FLAN (PAGE 368)
BISCOTTI (PAGE 366)

CROSTINI OR BRUSCHETTE WITH PORCINI MUSHROOMS (PAGE 54)
PASTA E FAGIOLI (PAGE 184)
SWISS CHARD OR SPINACH WITH FENNEL AND HOT PEPPER
(PAGE 330)
TOSSED GREEN SALAD
ORANGES WITH MINT (PAGE 368)

A TAPA OF EGGPLANT AND PEPPERS (PAGE 82)
ARROZ À LA MARINERA (PAGE 236)
TOSSED GREEN SALAD
GINGER HONEY FLAN (PAGE 366)

MADAME TARDIEU'S WINTER TOMATO SOUP WITH VERMICELLI
(PAGE 146)
BAKED MONKFISH, HAKE, OR SWORDFISH WITH WILD MUSHROOMS
(PAGE 289)
FENNEL AND RED PEPPER SALAD (PAGE 77)
ORANGES WITH MINT (PAGE 368)

TOSSED GREEN SALAD
CHICKEN BREASTS EN PAPILLOTE (PAGE 303)
LEMON RISOTTO (PAGE 227)
ZUCCHINI MARINATA (PAGE 64)
PEAR GINGER FLAN (PAGE 368)

ITALIAN BEAN AND TUNA SALAD (PAGE 60)
BAKED POLENTA WITH TOMATO SAUCE AND MUSHROOMS
(PAGE 238)
SPICY ITALIAN-STYLE BROCCOLI (PAGE 316)
FRESH PEARS

AÏGO BOUÏDO (PAGE 141)
BAKED FISH WITH TOMATOES AND SWEET PEPPERS (PAGE 298)
FRESH SPINACH PASTA (PAGE 172) OR
STEAMED POTATOES
TOSSED GREEN SALAD
APPLE AND RHUBARB TART (PAGE 364)

BRUSCHETTE OR CROSTINI WITH TOMATO TOPPING (PAGE 56)
RISOTTO AI FUNGHI (PAGE 228)
STEAMED GREEN VEGETABLE
TOSSED GREEN SALAD
BAKED APPLE COMPOTE (PAGE 363)

FAMILY DINING—
SPRING AND SUMMER MENUS

SALADE NIÇOISE (PAGE 74)
EGGPLANT, TOMATO, AND BASIL PIZZA (PAGE 203)
STRAWBERRY SOUP (PAGE 355)

PUREE LEONTINE (PAGE 150)
ITALIAN MASHED POTATO PIE (PAGE 315)
ZUCCHINI À LA PROVENÇALE (PAGE 332)
FRESH FRUIT

MIDDLE EASTERN PASTA WITH LENTILS (PAGE 198)
QUICK BAKED TOMATOES À LA PROVENÇALE (PAGE 328)
SPINACH AND YOGURT SALAD (PAGE 103)
FRESH FRUIT

FATTET WITH CHICKEN (PAGE 265)
CÉLERI AU CUMIN (PAGE 336)
TOSSED GREEN SALAD
STRAWBERRY-YOGURT SHERBET (PAGE 356)

CHICKEN KEBABS (PAGE 301)
RICE PILAF WITH CUMIN OR CURRY (PAGE 233)
SALATA BALADI (PAGE 102)
FRESH FRUIT

LATE SUMMER/EARLY FALL MENUS

BRUSCHETTE OR CROSTINI WITH TOMATO TOPPING (PAGE 56)
PASTA WITH BROCCOLI, PALERMO-STYLE (PAGE 178)
TOSSED GREEN SALAD
BAKED PLUM COMPOTE (PAGE 352)

BLACK-EYED PEAS AND TOMATO SALAD (PAGE 98)
SPINACH OR SWISS CHARD SOUP WITH YOGURT (PAGE 153)
FRESH FIGS

BAKED TUNISIAN EGGAH (PAGE 338)
TOSSED GREEN SALAD
FRESH FRUIT

TUSCAN BEAN AND VEGETABLE SOUP (PAGE 125)
TOSSED GREEN SALAD
FRESH FIGS POACHED IN WINE (PAGE 344)

FALL AND WINTER MENUS

MEATLESS HARIRA (PAGE 1 3 0)
TOSSED GREEN SALAD
FRESH FRUIT

MOULES À LA MARINIÈRE (PAGE 2 7 4)
TOSSED GREEN SALAD
FRESH FRUIT

PUREED WHITE BEANS (PAGE 9 5)
CHRISTINE'S POTATO AND PARSLEY SOUP (PAGE 1 4 9)
TOSSED GREEN SALAD
FRESH FRUIT

CARROT AND POTATO AJLOUKE (PAGE 1 1 0)
HAMUD (PAGE 1 5 2)
TOSSED GREEN SALAD
HONEY VANILLA FLAN (PAGE 3 6 5)

STUFFED ZUCCHINI (PAGE 2 6 2)
SPICY LENTILS WITH PEPPERS AND TOMATOES (PAGE 2 5 1)
TOSSED GREEN SALAD
FRESH FRUIT

SIMPLE SPANISH FISH STEW (PAGE 2 7 2)
TOSSED GREEN SALAD
ROASTED SWEET RED PEPPERS (PAGE 6 9)
ORANGES WITH MINT (PAGE 3 6 8)

TZATZIKI (PAGE 85)
PUREED YELLOW SPLIT PEAS (PAGE 84)
AVGOLEMONO (PAGE 144)
FRESH FRUIT

TOMATOES STUFFED WITH TUNA (PAGE 63)
LENTILS AND BULGUR PILAF (PAGE 243)
STEAMED GREEN VEGETABLE
FRESH FRUIT

SEAFOOD RISOTTO (PAGE 231)
TOSSED GREEN SALAD
FRESH FRUIT

MENUS FOR ANY SEASON

SALADE NIÇOISE (PAGE 74)
GEORGETTE TARDIEU'S PROVENÇAL PIZZA (PAGE 210)
FRESH FRUIT

WARM CHICK-PEA SALAD (PAGE 72)
SPAGHETTI ALLA CARRETTIERA (PAGE 181)
STEAMED GREEN VEGETABLE
FRESH FRUIT

TORTILLA ESPAÑOLA (PAGE 79)
RATATOUILLE (PAGE 66)
TOSSED GREEN SALAD
ORANGES WITH MINT (PAGE 368)

GARLIC SOUP WITH POACHED EGGS, FROM SEVILLE (PAGE 143)
CROSTINI WITH TOPPING OF YOUR CHOICE (PAGE 53)
TOSSED GREEN SALAD
FRESH FRUIT

CHAPTER TEN

INGREDIENTS

Say "Mediterranean," and my mouth begins to water as the flavors of garlic and olive oil, olives, capers, ripe red tomatoes, anchovies, herbs, and spices come to my mind. Next I think of fish, rice and beans, pasta, and gorgeous fruits and vegetables. The items listed below by no means comprise an exhaustive list of the ingredients you'll find in this book, but the list covers the most important ones and the foods that might be new to you.

SEASONINGS, FLAVORINGS, AND CONDIMENTS

Anchovies: Anchovies are usually an acquired taste, largely because they are packed in salt before being canned, so they have a very salty, strong flavor. But if you rinse them well before using them, they'll taste considerably milder. Also, along with the salt you'll rinse off much of the oil they're packed in, reducing the calories. Anchovies are high in fat, due mostly to the oil they are packed in, but their flavor is so strong that two will suffice for a sauce, or cut up into bits for a salad, and although more anchovies would make a stronger-tasting dish, you won't miss them if you use fewer. They are essential to many of the delicious pasta and pizza dishes from Sicily (Chapter Four).

Capers: These round green buds of the caper plant, pickled in a vinegary brine, add a pungent flavor to several Mediterranean dishes. Keep them on hand for salads, fish, and tomato sauces. I suggest you rinse them before adding them to dishes, because the brine is very salty.

Currants: These tiny dried raisin-like fruits originally came from Corinth (thus the name). They add an intense sweet flavor to desserts and also come up in several southern Italian pasta and vegetable dishes, such as the *pasta con sarde* on page 174.

Dijon mustard: Easy to find in supermarkets, this strong French mustard is a must for a good vinaigrette.

Garlic: The essential Mediterranean ingredient, especially in the cuisines of southern Europe and the Middle East. There are two varieties, white-skinned and pink-skinned. The white-skinned bulbs have a stronger flavor; the pink-skinned variety is slightly sweeter and, I think, has a more refined flavor. Look for bulbs with large cloves; a head of garlic with large cloves usually contains about 13. "Giant" or "elephant" garlic has large bulbs containing huge cloves, sometimes only a few per head. They are milder than the normal-sized varieties, with a sweet, nutty taste. New or fresh garlic, harvested in the spring in France, Italy, and Spain, has green stems like onion stems and soft, thick skins. Once you get through the skins to the cloves, you will find this garlic to be a great delicacy—juicy, tender, and sweet. If you have trouble digesting garlic, it may help to cut the cloves in half and pull out the green stem that runs down the middle.

One large clove of garlic yields 1 to 1½ heaping teaspoons of chopped garlic. My recipes, though, call for the cloves, not measures; most people don't measure their garlic in the Mediterranean, and neither do I. Before buying garlic, press the outer cloves to make sure they are firm and solid. If they are not, the garlic is old and beginning to dry out and deteriorate. Buy braids of garlic only if you use a lot of it, as some of the heads will dry out before you get to them (although using this book, you could go through a braid pretty quickly). Garlic becomes quite mild when cooked or simmered slowly, so don't let recipes like the garlic soups in Chapter Three and chicken or rabbit with 40 cloves of garlic (page 305 and page 309) intimidate you.

Harissa: This is a fiery-hot paste made by pounding together red chili peppers, spices, and olive oil. It is used to season *couscous* and many North African dishes. A tiny dot of it is usually enough to season a serving of *couscous*. There is a recipe for *harissa* on page 106, but you can find it ready-made in stores that sell foods imported from North Africa.

Lemons and limes: These deserve to be listed as condiments because fresh lemon juice and fresh lime juice are so often used to season dishes, especially in the Middle East and North Africa, but also in European countries. I am often astounded to discover that the only dressing on an exquisite salad, say a Middle Eastern *tabouli* or a Tunisian vegetable salad, is lemon juice. When choosing lemons and limes, give them a squeeze to make sure they aren't all skin. If the skins are very gnarly and the lemons stiff, they will probably have very thick skins and relatively little juice. I buy large lemons that give a little (but not too much) when I squeeze, and medium-sized limes.

Olive oil: Olives have been cultivated in the Mediterranean for thousands of years. I love to look at Grecian urns and imagine the olive oil traveling between the islands more than 2,000 years ago. Although you won't find olives in many of these recipes due to their high calorie content, you will find olive oil, for Mediterranean cuisines wouldn't exist without it. The quantities in my recipes are small compared with the amounts in traditional Mediterranean recipes, but the flavor of the oil is just as important. Olive oil is so fragrant that a little goes a long way. And because one bottle is going to last you quite a while with the small quantities you'll be using here, I recommend that you buy the best extra-virgin or virgin olive oil you can find, imported from either Provence or Tuscany. The bottle should have the words "Extra Virgin" or "Virgin" (*Vierge Extra* or *Vierge* in French) on the label. Because I've lived in

France for seven years, my choice is *Provençal* oil. It has an olive-green color and a mild, fruity bouquet. Tuscan oil is a little darker, with a more robust flavor but the same flowery bouquet. The oils I *don't* like, the ones that taste industrial to me, have a strong, acrid flavor and overpower dishes rather than perfume them. It's worth going to a gourmet supermarket or specialty shop to find a reliable brand.

Orange zest: A strip of orange zest from an orange peel, with the bitter white part cut away, adds an alluring perfume to Mediterranean soups, especially fish soups, and is a common ingredient.

Orange flower water: Orange flower water, extracted from the blossoms of the bitter orange tree, is used to perfume many Moroccan and *Provençal* dishes. It has a sweet aroma and slightly bitter taste. You can find it in imported-food stores and in some pharmacies.

Pine nuts: Also known as *pignoli*, these are sweet-tasting small white nuts from a particular species of pinecones. They have a soft texture and are particularly fragrant when roasted. They are added to many Italian and Greek dishes, and even though they're high in calories, you can use very few and still achieve a very satisfying dish, so I haven't excluded them from this repertoire.

Tahini: A nut butter made from ground sesame seeds used in several Middle Eastern dishes, such as *hummus* (page 92). It's high in calories, but a little goes a long way, as the rich, nutty flavor is quite distinctive. You can find tahini in natural-foods stores and specialty shops. Make sure to buy tahini made from raw sesame seeds and not the roasted variety, which has a completely different flavor.

Tomato paste: I don't call for it very often, but it does come up from time to time in this book. It enhances dishes with a deep tomato flavor and nice red color. In Italy and France it's easy to find delicious, concentrated tomato paste, and if you can find imported brands (either from Italy or France), I recommend that you use them. You can now find tomato paste in tubes, which is much more practical than canned tomato paste, because you usually need only a tablespoon or two for a given recipe.

Red wine vinegar: Quality vinegar is as important an ingredient as quality olive oil. Buy an imported French red wine vinegar, such as Dessaux, or make your own. It's easy: take a half-empty bottle of decent red wine, cover it loosely, and wait until a cloud appears in the wine (you can also use vinegar in which a cloud has appeared). This is called a *mère*, or mother, and will generate more vinegar when you add wine to it. I have a ceramic *vinaigrier*, an urn into which I pour all of my leftover bottles of wine, which gives me a constant supply of good, strong homemade vinegar. You can also simply use a bottle. Taste the vinegar before you use it, as homemade vinegars are sometimes very strong, and you may need less than a given recipe calls for.

Balsamic vinegar: This is a thick, strong, slightly sweet aged vinegar imported from Italy. In Italy they call it a sauce rather than a vinegar, because it's reduced like a sauce. Use it more sparingly than regular red wine vinegar.

Dry white and red wine for cooking: Always have a bottle of both dry white wine and red wine on hand. I recommend, for the whites, a not too expensive Loire Valley wine, such as a Sauvignon or a Muscadet; for a red, a Côtes du Rhône or a Chianti.

HERBS

Many of these herbs grow wild throughout different parts of the Mediterranean. In Provence, Tuscany, and Greece you find bushes of rosemary and clumps of thyme and oregano everywhere you walk; the countryside is always fragrant. Fennel grew wild all over the small Yugoslavian island of Korĉula, where I once rented a house for a summer, and is so abundant in southern Italy that it comes up in many of the vegetable dishes from this area.

Each cuisine favors certain herbs: the southern European cuisines tend toward basil, oregano, fennel, thyme, and rosemary; the Middle Eastern and North African cuisines abound in parsley, mint, cilantro, and dill. Some of these herbs, like basil, chervil, cilantro, dill, parsley, and fennel, must be used fresh; their flavors fade away when they're dried. Others (indicated below) are as effective as seasonings in their dry state.

Basil: Known as "the royal herb" in France, basil is made to go with tomatoes. The herb is sweet and slightly pungent, sometimes a little peppery. Dried basil hardly resembles fresh and is usually not an acceptable substitute (the exceptions are certain soups and sauces). It's an easy herb to grow, a treat to have on hand. The ultimate Mediterranean basil preparation is *pesto* in Italy, *pistou* in Provence, a heady sauce made by pounding together basil, garlic, olive oil, and Parmesan. Although the sauce is too rich for this particular Mediterranean diet (too much olive oil and Parmesan per serving), many of the recipes here, like the springtime minestrone with fresh basil (page 128), will have the same basil punch.

Bay leaf: Bay laurel trees are common throughout the Mediterranean, and their fragrant leaves, used to flavor soups, stews, beans, and vegetables, are shiny, pliable, and dark green, unlike the faded dry leaves we get in our supermarkets. If you can find fresh leaves, buy them, but the dry ones still pack a lot of flavor and are an essential ingredient in many Mediterranean dishes.

Chervil: These pretty, delicate stems with their bright green, featherlike leaves have a distinctive sweet, slightly anisy flavor. Chervil looks a little bit like flat-leaf parsley, although it's a lighter color green and more fernlike. Whole stems of chervil are marvelous in salads and make a beautiful garnish.

Chives: These look like tiny stems of green onions and have a sweet, mild oniony taste. Add to salads, soups, and potato dishes.

Cilantro (fresh coriander): This herb, with its strong, pungent flavor, is a favorite in Middle Eastern and North African dishes. It tastes nothing like the seeds from which it grows (see "Spices," page 392). Those of you familiar with Mexican cuisines will be as fascinated as I was to see how popular it is in other parts of the world. Cilantro resembles flat-leaf parsley, although its color is lighter and its leaves more delicate.

Dill: Fresh dill is popular in the Middle East. Its refreshing-tasting feathery green leaves go beautifully with cucumbers, potatoes, and yogurt. Like basil, chervil, and cilantro, it loses its flavor when dried.

Fennel: Fennel is one of the earliest known herbs. It was discovered in ancient times that the anise-flavored herb aided in the digestion of oily fish; thus the herb was and still is used widely in fish cookery. One of the most typically *Provençal* ways of preparing fish is to grill it over dried fennel stalks, with a few stuffed into the cavity of the fish, and flame it at the end with Pernod, pastis, or anisette (i.e., an anise-flavored alcohol). Among the ancient Greeks fennel was reputed to make fat people lean. The Italians understand this stalky, feathery-leafed herb as well as the French and use it abundantly in their vegetable dishes. The leaves of wild fennel should be fresh, but you can use the dried stalks for a *bouquet garni* and in fish dishes.

Marjoram and Oregano: These herbs come from the same family and are common ingredients in Greek and Italian cuisines. Marjoram has a minty, somewhat thymelike flavor and is great in salads and soups. Oregano is more rustic than marjoram, with a slightly peppery fragrance, and is more widely used. A pizza wouldn't be a pizza without it. Both herbs are suitable for use in their dried state.

Mint: Mint is used widely in Middle Eastern and southern Italian cuisines. In the Middle East dried mint is a common ingredient, but I find it much less appealing than fresh. Use either peppermint or spearmint. It's an easy herb to grow; it requires lots of water but very little sunlight. I use the herb most often to season fruit desserts. The simple addition of a few leaves of fresh mint to a bowl of peaches, melon, or strawberries transforms a simple dessert into an unforgettable one.

Parsley (flat-leaf and curly-leaf): You will find parsley in abundance throughout this book, as it is probably the most widely used herb in the Mediterranean basin. An authentic Middle Eastern *tabouli* is like a garden of chopped parsley with a little cracked wheat, seasoned with lots of lemon juice. The flat-leaf variety, often referred to as *Italian parsley*, has a richer, more satisfying flavor than the curly-leaf herb. One of parsley's useful attributes is that, eaten raw, it works as an antidote to garlic breath.

Rosemary: Bushes of this strong-flavored herb cover the *Provençal* and Tuscan countryside. The spiky, resinous leaves impart a pungent, savory flavor to vegetable dishes, breads, fish, and soups. Dried rosemary has a less acrid taste than fresh, and I sometimes find it preferable. This is a matter of taste. The leaves of dried rosemary are harder and spikier than fresh rosemary and must be crumbled before adding to dishes.

Rosemary was considered a symbol of immortality by the Greeks and Romans and favored for its powers of rejuvenation by the court of Louis XIV. This makes sense, as its medicinal virtues are well documented. As an infusion it is a tonic and digestive, stimulating the liver function and circulation.

Sage: The gray-green, knobbly-textured leaves of this herb have a stunning earthy, slightly bitter flavor particularly appreciated by the Italians and French. It's commonly added to garlic soups in Provence and goes beautifully with beans, potatoes, and all manner of vegetables. Rubbed dried sage has a much stronger, more bitter flavor than fresh and cannot be substituted in recipes that call for fresh.

Tarragon: The long, elegant leaves of French tarragon have a luxurious, sweet flavor, somewhat resembling basil but tangier and slightly anisy. A few tablespoons of freshly chopped tarragon added to a soup or salad will transform an ordinary dish into a truly elegant one. Although I do use dried tarragon in salad dressings, it has only the sweetness but not the punch of its fresh counterpart. Be sure you have true French tarragon and not the useless Russian variety.

Thyme: Like rosemary, this herb is ubiquitous in southern Europe. Sprigs of thyme are essential to a *bouquet garni*, and the herb, either fresh or dried, is an important ingredient in many soups, sauces, and vegetable dishes. It has a strong, savory, slightly bitter flavor, and a little goes a long way.

SPICES

The use of spices is one of the most enticing aspects of Middle Eastern and North African cuisines. Middle Eastern and North African people have taken the most marvelous ingredients from the new and the ancient worlds (chili peppers from the New World, Indian spices from the ancient one, making their way across the spice routes) and developed their own distinctive, spicy dishes. North African cuisines especially combine fiery-hot chilis with pungent spices like caraway and coriander and sweet ones like cinnamon and allspice. Middle Eastern cuisines favor the earthy spices like cumin and coriander seeds and the sweet ones like allspice and cinnamon.

You'll get a much better flavor if you buy whole spices and grind them in a spice grinder.

Allspice: Whole allspice berries, slightly larger than peppercorns, are picked green and dried in the sun, whereupon they take on their rusty-brown color. Purchase allspice berries whole and grind them as you use them.

The name *allspice* derives from the flavor of this sweet spice, which is reminiscent of several other sweet spices, most notably cinnamon and cloves, with a hint of nutmeg. It's used commonly in Morocco and the Middle East.

Aniseed: Aniseed, native to Asia Minor, the Greek Islands, and Egypt, was used by the ancient Egyptians, Greeks, and Romans to sweeten and flavor. The seeds have a sweet licorice flavor and are the flavoring agent for the various licorice-flavored liqueurs and cordials popular all over the Mediterranean. Pastis, anisette, ouzo, and arak are all flavored with anise, as well as with fennel and star anise.

Caraway seed: These seeds have a distinctive flavor that I always associate with Jewish rye bread. Ground caraway is used in many North African dishes.

Cardamom seed: These small, black fragrant seeds come in white or green pods. The pods are easy to open to extract the seeds, and the spice should always be bought in this whole form (it keeps for years), because it will quickly lose its perfume once ground. Cardamom has a distinctive earthy-perfume flavor and aroma.

Cinnamon: A familiar spice with a sweet, pungent flavor. Used in Middle Eastern and North African cuisines to season savory dishes as well as sweet ones. Ceylon cinnamon is the most delicately flavored.

Coriander seed: These light brown round seeds, slightly larger than pepper-corns, have a completely different flavor from the fresh leaves of the plant. The flavor is mild and kind of musky-sweet, with a subtle hint of orange peel. It is widely used in Middle Eastern and North African cuisines, both whole and ground.

Cumin seed: Cumin seeds in their whole and ground state are an essential ingredient in Middle Eastern and North African cuisines. The spice has a very special, unmistakable nutty-earthy taste.

Fennel seed: The seeds of the fennel herb plant have a licorice flavor like anise, and the two can be used interchangeably. An essential ingredient in the mixture of *Provençal* herbs called *herbes de Provence,* fennel seeds are common in *Provençal,* Italian, and North African dishes.

Fenugreek seed: The seeds of fenugreek, an annual herb that is a member of the bean family, are native to the Middle East and India. The small, hard, vaguely triangular seeds have a very strong aroma and bitter taste. Recipes call for a very few, and they impart a distinctive curry flavor. They are known to be a digestive and for this reason are often cooked with legumes.

Dried ginger: Although fresh ginger is associated with Oriental cuisines, the pungent spice comes up a few times in powdered form in these Mediterranean recipes.

Mustard seed: These are the seeds that are ground to make dry mustard powder and all prepared mustards. They will come up in these pages in some of the marinated vegetable dishes. Mustard seeds are used in some dishes because they act as a preservative, one reason they are used widely in pickling.

Nutmeg: The inner part of the fruit of the nutmeg tree, this spice has a delicious sweet and pungent, nutty flavor. An ingredient in several Middle Eastern and North African dishes, it is used in Western cuisines to sweeten baked goods and sweets and to season soups, vegetables (especially spinach), cream sauces, and many pasta and cheese dishes. It should always be freshly grated, as it will quickly lose its zesty aroma in powdered form. The spice should be used with discretion; the flavor can easily overpower a dish.

Paprika: Also known as *Hungarian pepper* and *Spanish pepper,* this is the national spice of Hungary but has also found its way into many Spanish, Turkish, North African, and Middle Eastern dishes. Paprika is the dried powder of a mild, sweet, bright red pepper. It should have a mild, sweet flavor. It must be very fresh, or it will be bitter; if the color has gone from bright red to rust brown, it has deteriorated. Look for Hungarian paprika, which is the best (look for the word *Hungarian* or *Magyar* on the label). The next best is Spanish. Store it in the refrigerator in an airtight container.

Hot peppers: Hot peppers, both dried and fresh, occur again and again in these recipes. Fresh green chili peppers are common ingredients in many Egyptian salads. Dried red peppers, flaked, whole, and ground, liven up Italian, North African, and Middle Eastern dishes. When I went to the spice markets in Egypt, I bought several grades of hot pepper—some mild, some medium, and some like fire. The Italians use a hot pepper called *peperoncini*, which is often sold coarsely ground into flakes. It is quite hot and has a very rich flavor. Cayenne peppers are probably the easiest to find and can be used for most of the recipes here that call for dried red peppers. Store dried red peppers and pepper flakes in tightly sealed jars, either in a cool cabinet, away from the light, or in the refrigerator.

When recipes call for fresh hot peppers, use *serrano, jalapeño,* or other hot green peppers available at your market.

Saffron: This is the most luxurious and expensive of spices, and it comes up in special dishes in practically all Mediterranean cuisines, particularly rice and seafood dishes. It is made from the dried stigmata of the flowers of the saffron plant, a member of the crocus family. The reason it is so costly (it retails at $2,000 a pound!) is that it takes about 250,000 dried stigmata, painstakingly collected from about 75,000 flowers, to make a pound of saffron. It is usually sold by the 20th of an ounce or by the gram, in thread and powdered form. I buy the threads, as powdered saffron is often adulterated. In Paris I buy my saffron at the pharmacy, where it is used in some homeopathic preparations.

Saffron's magic lies in the gorgeous yellow hue it imparts to its dishes and its strong, sweet, vaguely sealike aroma. Fortunately, a little of this spice goes a long way. It takes only ¼ teaspoon to color and flavor a cup of rice. To achieve even coloring and flavoring, powder the saffron threads with your fingers or the back of a spoon in a small bowl and soak in a little hot water or milk for 15 minutes. Add this solution, with the threads, to whatever you are cooking.

Turmeric: Native to India, turmeric belongs to the ginger family and comes up occasionally in North African and Middle Eastern dishes. It imparts a lovely yellow color to dishes and has a woody, slightly bitter flavor.

VEGETABLES

Artichokes: The artichokes I associate with Mediterranean cuisines are small and tinged with purple. These are harder to find than the large globe artichokes we get in the States, but the globe artichokes are fine for these dishes. Two or three small artichokes are equivalent to one large globe artichoke.

Broccoli raab: This is like a cross between a turnip green and broccoli. The vegetable consists of long leafy stems with tiny broccoli flowers at the end, and the stems, leaves, flowers, and all are eaten. The flavor is closer to that of greens than broccoli. It's popular in southern Italy, and its popularity is growing in America.

Cucumbers: Use long European cucumbers whenever possible. They have much smaller seeds than the smaller thick-skinned variety and no bitter taste.

Eggplant: One of the most commonly used vegetables in all Mediterranean cuisines. Try to find the long, thin variety, sometimes called *Japanese eggplant.* They have a sweeter flavor than the large fat ones and cook more quickly.

Fava beans: Often referred to as *broad beans,* fava beans are also ubiquitous in the Mediterranean. A sign of spring, fresh favas come in thick green pods that are furry on the inside. The beans are large, flat, and green and should be peeled before being eaten (see recipes pages 334 and 335). Dried fava beans are also known as *giant white beans* and are as widely used as fresh favas.

Bulb fennel: Fennel is also gaining popularity in America. The crunchy, refreshing vegetable has the same anisy taste as herb fennel. It's quite versatile, both raw, in salads, and cooked, with fish, other vegetables, or by itself.

Kale: A dark leafy green with a slightly bitter taste, popular in the Middle East and southern Italy.

Leeks: These are the mildest member of the onion family and are used widely throughout the Mediterranean, in soups, stews, and by themselves. To clean the sand off leeks, cut off the stem end and cut the leeks in half lengthwise. Run under cold water, separating the layers with your fingers while you let the water wash the sand out, then soak in a bowl of cold water for 10 minutes and rinse again.

Fresh wild mushrooms: Wild mushrooms are now becoming easier to find in the United States. In Europe I most often use oyster mushrooms, *cèpes* (*porcini*), and *chanterelles*. In America *shiitake* are easiest to find. Wild mushrooms have a "meaty" texture, and each one has its own earthy, savory taste.

Dried porcini mushrooms or cèpes: Although Oriental mushrooms are easier to find than these, it's worth looking for them, because they add a marvelous rich, meaty flavor to dishes and their soaking water makes a nice stock. In several of the recipes in this book I've substituted dried *porcini* mushrooms for meat, with delicious results. You can find these in imported-food stores and gourmet shops.

Okra: I'd always thought of okra as a southern American vegetable until I went to Greece and Egypt, where I saw it in markets everywhere. Mediterranean okra dishes contain tomatoes, sometimes anchovies, and lots of garlic.

Red, green, and yellow onions: I use red onions and green onions (scallions) whenever raw onions are called for in a salad, because they have a sweeter, milder flavor than yellow onions. For the cooked dishes in this book I've used medium-sized yellow onions.

Sweet peppers (green, red, yellow): Peppers, roasted, raw, and cooked, come up almost as often as tomatoes in Mediterranean cuisines. I prefer the red peppers for roasting, the red and yellow peppers for salads and simple sautés, and the green peppers, which have the strongest flavor of the three, for soups, stews, and sauces.

Potatoes: For the recipes in this book I've used russet potatoes and new potatoes. The smaller and younger, the better.

Fresh pumpkin: Fresh pumpkin is very popular in France, Italy, and North Africa. Many dishes from the Basque region of France include pumpkin. It's a sweet, versatile vegetable. In Europe the pumpkins are large and thick, more irregular than round. If you can find small "sugar" pumpkins, use them for cooking. Otherwise jack-'o-lantern pumpkins will do fine.

Shallots: Tiny, elegant onionlike vegetables, their flavor is milder and more refined than that of onions. I often use them in combination with other vegetables, such as mushrooms.

Sorrel: Considered both a vegetable and an herb, sorrel is used widely in France in soups and purees. It grows wild in Provence, and I love to gather it and add it to pastas and salads. The dark green spinachlike leaves have a strong, acidic, slightly metallic flavor.

Spinach: Spinach is best in the spring, when it's so sweet and tender it tastes almost like it's been sweetened.

Swiss chard: Another leafy green, with thick, fibrous stalks and large, thick, dark green leaves. It comes up in dishes from all over the Mediterranean, often added to soups in the Middle East and North Africa, cooked with fish in Spain, and served on its own in Italy and France. Spinach may be substituted when Swiss chard is unavailable.

Tomatoes: Probably the most important vegetable in southern European cuisines. Where would Italy and Provence be without them? There is absolutely no similarity between a hard, pink, out-of-season tomato and a red, ripe, juicy one that smells like sunshine and the stalk from which it has just been picked and is so sweet and juicy you can eat it like fruit—in fact, botanically it *is* a fruit. Out of season, do not use commercially grown American tomatoes. You can now find decent tomatoes imported from Israel, North Africa, Mexico, and South America. But of course they are not as good as truly seasonal tomatoes. In all the cooked-tomato recipes, I recommend using imported Italian canned tomatoes (preferably from San Marzano) if you can't get good fresh ones.

Canned tomatoes: The best are Italian plum tomatoes, particularly the ones from San Marzano. The tomatoes have a riper, more intense flavor than American canned tomatoes, and they are less acidic.

Turnips: Turnips often come up in Mediterranean soups and *couscous*. They are best in the spring, when they're young and sweet. They should be small and hard, not large and fibrous.

Zucchini: Available year-round, but best when homegrown and in season. Look for small, firm zucchini. The larger they are, the more mealy the texture will be.

DAIRY PRODUCTS

Low-fat yogurt: One of the mainstays of Middle Eastern cuisines, it is a very important item in this repertoire, because it is often substituted for higher-fat oils and dairy products. Look for yogurt that is less than 1 percent fat. It's easy to thicken low-fat yogurt so that it seems like full-fat yogurt (see page 97).

Parmesan cheese and Parmesan rinds: Parmesan is the one cheese we can't do without, even in a low-fat cookbook. But because it has such a rich flavor, a little goes a long way. Buy the best: *Parmigiano Reggiano*, from Emilia Romagna, with its name stenciled all over the rind in little brown dots. Store in the refrigerator wrapped in a double thickness of aluminum foil, then sealed in a plastic container or a Ziploc bag. Always keep the rinds to use in soup broths. When you simmer the rinds in soup (then remove them), they give the soup a rich, cheesy flavor with almost no additional calories.

GRAINS AND LEGUMES

In many of the Mediterranean cuisines, notably those of the Middle East, grains and legumes provide people with the bulk of their protein. Every country has ingenious ways of transforming these elements into luscious, sustaining dishes. These are economical dishes, very low in fat and high in protein, fiber, vitamins, and minerals. With the exception of some of the imported items, like Italian Arborio rice and *basmati* rice, red lentils, and Egyptian brown beans, most of these beans and legumes can be found in regular supermarkets and natural-food stores. Keep them on hand in tightly covered jars in the pantry.

LEGUMES

Black-eyed peas: Black-eyed peas are popular in Egypt and other Middle Eastern countries. They have a rich, savory flavor and require no soaking. The Egyptians make a delicious black-eyed pea salad (page 98).

Borlotti or cranberry beans: These resemble pinto beans but are pinker. The Italians use them in *minestrones, pasta e fagiole* (page 184), and salads. The beans have a rich, sweet flavor.

Chick-peas: A mainstay in all Mediterranean cuisines, these have an unmistakable earthy fragrance and taste. Also called *garbanzos*.

Egyptian brown beans (ful): These are roundish, irregular-shaped brown beans that are a staple in Egypt, the equivalent of pinto beans in northern Mexico. *Ful* (page 245) is the Egyptian equivalent of refried beans and is eaten for breakfast in that country. They can be found in some imported-food stores.

Lentils (brown, red, and green): Another staple in many Mediterranean cuisines. The French like small green lentils from Le Puy and brown lentils; the Italians eat brown lentils. In Middle Eastern countries you see brown lentils and red ones. The red lentils have a much milder flavor than brown lentils, and their color goes from orange to yellow when they cook.

Giant white beans: These are dried fava beans, large flat white beans that have a marvelous, savory flavor. They are a favorite in Greece. They have thick skins that I usually remove after soaking.

White beans: These include great northern beans and navy beans, which have identical flavors, although the navy beans are smaller than great northerns. They have an elegant, savory taste and are marvelous for salads and soups.

Yellow split peas: Yellow split peas are popular in Greece. Their flavor is slightly like that of green split peas, though more subtle and with a more agreeable texture.

GRAINS

Barley: One of the most exciting displays from the tomb of King Tut, in the Cairo Museum, shows 4,000-year-old grains of barley buried with the king to nourish him in the afterlife. Barley was cultivated as far back as 6000 B.C. by the Egyptians and is still an important staple throughout the Middle East. The grain is very hearty, with a chewy texture and nutty taste. It's often added to soups and used for pilafs.

Bulgur: Bulgur is cracked wheat that has been parboiled and dried. A mainstay throughout the Middle East, it is most often used for pilafs and salads like *tabouli*. It has a light texture and nutty flavor. Bulgur comes in light, medium, and coarse textures. I prefer the medium and coarse for salads and grain dishes, and the light for adding to grain breads.

Couscous: This is the national grain in the North African countries of Morocco, Tunisia, and Algeria. *Couscous* is granules of cracked durum wheat. It has a tawny yellow color and a silken, light texture and can be very elegant. It's easy to find *couscous* that has been presoaked and dried, and I recommend using this, as it's so easy to work with. All you need to do is reconstitute the grains in water or stock and rub them between your fingers to prevent lumping. Working with unsoaked *couscous* demands more time and effort, as you must soak the grains and continually work them with your fingers to prevent them from lumping.

Rice (long-grained, basmati, brown, Arborio): Rice is another staple grain throughout the Mediterranean. It is cultivated extensively in Italy, France, Spain, and Turkey. There are several different kinds that will come up in recipes in this book. For *risotti,* use either the chewy, starchy round-grained Italian Arborio rice or French rice from the Camargue, which resembles Arborio rice, although it's slightly less chewy. For Spanish rice dishes I recommend Valencia rice, if you can get it, Italian Arborio, or long-grained Carolina rice. Valencia rice is rounder and chewier than Carolina rice. For Middle Eastern pilafs I recommend *basmati* rice, a light, small-grained rice imported from India that has a unique earthy fragrance.

Wheat berries: The whole grain from which flour is ground. Wheat has been a staple in the Middle East for almost as long as barley. Wheat berries are cooked in sweetened milk in Egypt and served in the morning as a delicious breakfast cereal called *belila* (page 244).

FISH

These are the fish that will come up in the recipes in Chapter Six. I have substituted fish you can find in America for many of the harder-to-find Mediterranean fish, and in the recipes I often give several options, especially in those calling for white-fleshed fish; often one kind may be substituted for another. Let the freshness of the day's catch help you decide which fish you use.

I recommend that you make an effort to find a good fishmonger, one who will tell you what the freshest catch of the day is. A fish store should not smell "fishy"; if it does, the fish isn't fresh. The fish should have firm, shiny flesh (touch it; it should spring back), and the eyes should be rounded and clear, not sunken. If possible, buy whole fish and have them filleted by the fishmonger. That's not possible in some cases (cod, for instance, is usually filleted right after it's caught, on the boat), but if you have an option, you'll be able to tell more about the fish if it's whole. Fish fillets should not be dry around the edges, but should be shiny and moist.

Sea bream, bream, or porgy: A large, firm white-fleshed fish, similar to red snapper, with a slightly stronger flavor. Considered a prize fish in the Mediterranean, bream lends itself to all methods of cooking. It is especially good grilled.

Cod: A versatile, white-fleshed fish with a very mild flavor and flaky texture. Cod often comes filleted or cut into steaks. *Ling cod* can be substituted for cod.

Conger: Conger eel, sold cut into steaks, is a very meaty-tasting fish with firm white flesh. It has lots of tricky little bones but a great flavor, and it's very economical.

Grouper: A delicious firm white-fleshed fish with a delicate flavor. Good grilled, baked, and in soups.

Red gurnard: A delicious firm white-fleshed fish, good in fish soups, baked, or poached.

Haddock: Haddock is a white-fleshed fish similar to and as versatile as cod.

Hake: Another white-fleshed fish with a flaky texture.

Halibut: A large flat fish. The steaks are good grilled, fried, and poached. The fish has a fine, firm texture.

Mackerel: An oily-fleshed fish with a rich, strong flavor. It's very good grilled. Popular in North Africa.

Monkfish: This is a very firm-fleshed fish, with a texture resembling that of lobster. It lends itself well to dishes that require long cooking.

Gray mullet: Although this is a Mediterranean fish, very popular in Tunisia (it's most often used for fish *couscous*), it has a cousin called the *striped mullet* that is available in America and can be substituted in recipes calling for gray mullet.

Red mullet: Although these small, delicate, somewhat bony red fish are also found mostly in the Mediterranean, where they are prized, they do sometimes make their way to America. They are terrific grilled. Their livers are often used as a base for a sauce.

Red snapper: Familiar to most American fish eaters, this is a firm white-fleshed fish, similar to bream or porgy but with a milder flavor. Very versatile.

Redfish or ocean perch: These are firm white-fleshed fish, somewhat like bream or snapper but with a more delicate texture. Very versatile.

Salmon: An oily-fleshed fish with a strong flavor and beautiful pink flesh. Very good grilled, poached, or baked.

Salmon trout: Small pink-fleshed trout that have a mild flavor and succulent texture resembling that of salmon. Delicious poached, baked, or grilled.

Sardines: Although fresh sardines are not easy to come by in the United States, I couldn't leave them out of this collection, so important are they in the Mediterranean. You can substitute other small, oily-fleshed fish for fresh sardines if you can't find them; for example, Atlantic silversides, shad, herring, or smelt. They are marvelous grilled.

Sea bass: An expensive, rich-tasting fish with delicate white flesh. Excellent grilled, poached, or baked. Very popular in Provence, where it is grilled over fennel stalks.

Sole: A delicate, flat white-fleshed fish that lends itself to all methods of cooking.

Swordfish: A very tasty fish with firm, meaty white flesh. It's especially good grilled.

Tilefish: A mild-tasting white-fleshed fish somewhat similar to cod.

Fresh tuna: Fresh tuna has marvelous, meaty red flesh that lends itself beautifully to grilling, baking, and broiling. It's also good raw. It is rich and meaty but will become very dry if overcooked.

Turbot: A prized fish with rich, firm white flesh.

Whiting: A delicate white-fleshed fish with a mild flavor and flaky texture. Whitings lend themselves to all methods of cooking.

SHELLFISH

Crayfish: In the Mediterranean, crayfish are spiny lobsters without the big claws of Atlantic lobsters. They are added to all manner of rice dishes and fish stews, as well as served on their own. Freshwater crayfish may be substituted in these recipes.

Mussels: Mussels are familiar to most people living on or near a coast. My favorite way to prepare them is *à la marinière,* simply steamed in white wine (page 274). But I also love them with pasta, rice, and *à l'italienne,* in a spicy tomato soup (page 166).

Shrimp and prawns: In Europe shrimp and prawns are two different animals, shrimp being very small, prawns being larger. In the United States the distinction between the different varieties of shrimp is made less often. In the Mediterranean you will find them in *risotto,* in another Middle Eastern rice dish, and grilled with lots of garlic.

PASTA

Bucatini: Long spaghettilike noodles that are hollow inside.

Fettuccine: Flat wide noodles.

Fusilli: Spiral-shaped pasta.

Linguine: Very narrow flat noodles.

Macaroni: Short, curved tubular pasta.

Orecchiette: Small "ear-shaped" pasta.

Penne: Straight, ridged tubular pasta.

Perciatelli: Long hollow noodles, thinner than *bucatini.*

Rigatoni: Short, fat tubular pasta.

Spaghetti: Long, thin round noodles.

Tagliatelle: Flat noodles, thinner than *fettuccine* and wider than *linguine.*

Vermicelli: Very thin, short round noodles.

FRUIT

Fruit, like vegetables, should be bought in season. If, however, you *have* to have a melon in winter, you can sometimes find them and other out-of-season fruits in gourmet grocery stores that sell imported foods. There you might be able to find melons, berries, and figs from Israel, North Africa, and Latin America, as well as blood oranges from Israel and Tunisia. Generally, though, follow the seasonal guidelines below.

Apricots: Mid- to late summer, early fall

Figs: Late summer, early to mid-fall

Melons: Late spring, summer, early fall

Oranges, Grapefruit: Year-round in the United States, but best in fall and winter

Peaches, white and yellow: Summer, early fall

Pears: Fall, winter, spring

Plums: Mid- to late summer, early to mid-fall

Strawberries: Spring, summer, fall

Tangerines: Late fall, winter

METRIC CONVERSION CHART

CONVERSIONS OF QUARTS TO LITERS

Quarts (qt)	Liters (L)
1 qt	1 L*
1½ qt	1½ L
2 qt	2 L
2½ qt	2½ L
3 qt	2¾ L
4 qt	3¾ L
5 qt	4¾ L
6 qt	5½ L
7 qt	6½ L
8 qt	7½ L
9 qt	8½ L
10 qt	9½ L

*Approximate. To convert quarts to liters, multiply number of quarts by 0.95.

CONVERSIONS OF OUNCES TO GRAMS

Ounces (oz)	Grams (g)
1 oz	30 g*
2 oz	60 g
3 oz	85 g
4 oz	115 g
5 oz	140 g
6 oz	180 g
7 oz	200 g
8 oz	225 g
9 oz	250 g
10 oz	285 g
11 oz	300 g
12 oz	340 g
13 oz	370 g
14 oz	400 g
15 oz	425 g
16 oz	450 g
20 oz	570 g
24 oz	680 g
28 oz	790 g
32 oz	900 g

*Approximate. To convert ounces to grams, multiply number of ounces by 28.35.

CONVERSIONS OF POUNDS
TO GRAMS AND KILOGRAMS

Pounds (lb)	Grams (g), kilograms (kg)
1 lb	450 g*
1¼ lb	565 g
1½ lb	675 g
1¾ lb	800 g
2 lb	900 g
2½ lb	1,125 g; 1¼ kg
3 lb	1,350 g
3½ lb	1,500 g; 1½ kg
4 lb	1,800 g
4½ lb	2 kg
5 lb	2¼ kg
5½ lb	2½ kg
6 lb	2¾ kg
6½ lb	3 kg
7 lb	3¼ kg
7½ lb	3½ kg
8 lb	3¾ kg
9 lb	4 kg
10 lb	4½ kg

*Approximate. To convert pounds into kilograms, multiply number of pounds by 453.6.

CONVERSIONS OF FAHRENHEIT
TO CELSIUS

Fahrenheit	Celsius
170°F	77°C
180°F	82°C
190°F	88°C
200°F	95°C
225°F	110°C
250°F	120°C
300°F	150°C
325°F	165°C
350°F	180°C
375°F	190°C
400°F	205°C
425°F	220°C
450°F	230°C
475°F	245°C
500°F	260°C
525°F	275°C
550°F	290°C

*Approximate. To convert Fahrenheit to Celsius, subtract 32, multiply by 5, then divide by 9.

CONVERSION OF INCHES TO CENTIMETERS

Inches (in)	Centimeters (cm)
1/16 in	1/4 cm*
1/8 in	1/2 cm
1/2 in	1 1/2 cm
3/4 in	2 cm
1 in	2 1/2 cm
1 1/2 in	4 cm
2 in	5 cm
2 1/2 in	6 1/2 cm
3 in	8 cm
3 1/2 in	9 cm
4 in	10 cm
4 1/2 in	11 1/2 cm
5 in	13 cm
5 1/2 in	14 cm
6 in	15 cm
6 1/2 in	16 1/2 cm
7 in	18 cm
7 1/2 in	19 cm
8 in	20 cm
8 1/2 in	21 1/2 cm
9 in	23 cm
9 1/2 in	24 cm
10 in	25 cm
11 in	28 cm
12 in	30 cm
13 in	33 cm
14 in	35 cm
15 in	38 cm
16 in	41 cm
17 in	43 cm
18 in	46 cm
19 in	48 cm
20 in	51 cm
21 in	53 cm
22 in	56 cm
23 in	58 cm
24 in	61 cm
25 in	63 1/2 cm
30 in	76 cm
35 in	89 cm
40 in	102 cm
45 in	114 cm
50 in	127 cm

*Approximate. To convert inches to centimeters, multiply number of inches by 2.54.

BIBLIOGRAPHY

Beck, Simone, and Child, Julia. *Mastering the Art of French Cooking.* New York: Alfred A. Knopf, 1961.

Bettoja, Jo, and Cornetto, Anna Maria. *Italian Cooking in the Grand Tradition.* New York: The Dial Press, 1982.

Bugialli, Giuliano. *The Fine Art of Italian Cooking.* New York: Times Books, 1977.

Casas, Penelope. *Tapas: The Little Dishes of Spain.* New York: Alfred A. Knopf, 1986.

Clayton, Bernard, Jr. *The Breads of France.* Indianapolis and New York: Bobbs-Merrill, 1978.

David, Elizabeth. *A Book of Mediterranean Food.* London: Penguin Books, 1955.

David, Elizabeth. *French Provincial Cooking.* London and New York: Penguin Books, 1960, 1969.

David, Elizabeth. *Summer Cooking.* London and New York: Penguin Books, 1965.

Davidson, Alan. *Mediterranean Seafood.* London and New York: Penguin Books, 1972, 1981.

Field, Carol. *The Italian Baker.* New York: Harper & Row, 1985.

Greene, Bert. *Greene on Greens.* New York: Workman Publishing, 1984.

Hazan, Marcella. *The Classic Italian Cookbook.* New York: Alfred A. Knopf, 1977.

Hazan, Marcella. *Marcella's Italian Kitchen.* New York: Alfred A. Knopf, 1986.

Hazan, Marcella. *The Second Classic Italian Cookbook*. New York: Alfred A. Knopf, 1978.

Howe, Robin. *The Mediterranean Diet*. London: Weidenfeld and Nicolson, 1985.

Johnston, Mireille. *The Cuisine of the Sun*. New York: Random House, 1976.

La Place, Viana, and Kleiman, Evan. *Cucina Fresca*. New York: Harper & Row, 1985.

Luard, Elisabeth. *The Old World Kitchen*. New York: Bantam Books, 1987.

Man, Rosamond. *The Complete Meze Table*. London: Ebury Press, 1986.

Middione, Carl. *The Food of Southern Italy*. New York: Morrow, 1987.

Olney, Richard. *Simple French Food*. New York: Atheneum, 1974.

Reboul, J. B. *La Cuisinière Provençale*. Marseille: Tacussel, Editeur.

Roden, Claudia. *A New Book of Middle Eastern Food*. New York and London: Viking-Penguin, 1985.

Scaravelli, Paola, and Cohen, Jon. *Cooking from an Italian Garden*. New York: Holt, Rinehart and Winston, 1984.

Scaravelli, Paola, and Cohen, Jon. *A Mediterranean Harvest*. New York: E. P. Dutton, 1986.

Scott, David. *Middle Eastern Vegetarian Cookery*. London: Rider and Company Ltd., 1981.

Shulman, Martha Rose. *Fast Vegetarian Feasts, The New Edition*. New York: Doubleday, 1986.

Shulman, Martha Rose. *Garlic Cookery*. New York: Thorsons, Inc., 1984.

Shulman, Martha Rose. *Herbs & Honey Cookery*. New York: Thorsons, Inc., 1984.

Shulman, Martha Rose. *Spicy Vegetarian Feasts*. New York: Thorsons, Inc., 1986.

Shulman, Martha Rose. *The Vegetarian Feast.* New York: Harper & Row, 1979, 1986.

Waters, Alice, Curtain, Patricia, and Labro, Martine. *Chez Panisse Pasta, Pizza, and Calzone.* New York: Random House, 1984.

Wells, Patricia. *The Food Lover's Guide to France.* New York: Workman Publishing, 1987.

Wolfert, Paula. *Couscous and Other Good Food from Morocco.* New York: Harper & Row, 1973.

Wolfert, Paula. *Mediterranean Cooking.* New York: Quadrangle/New York Times Books, 1977.

Zane, Eva. *Middle Eastern Cookery.* San Francisco: 101 Productions, 1974.

Zeitoun, Edmond. *250 Recettes Classiques de la Cuisine Tunisienne.* Paris: Jacques Grancher, Editeur, 1977.

INDEX

AG01Y